COMPARATIVE POLITICS

Comparative Politics is a series for students and teachers of political science that deals with contemporary issues in comparative government and politics. As Comparative European Politics it has produced a series of high quality books since its foundation in 1990, but now takes on a new form and new title for the millennium—Comparative Politics. As the process of globalization proceeds, and as Europe becomes ever more enmeshed in world trends and events, so it is necessary to broaden the scope of the series.
The General Editors are Alfio Mastropaulo,
Professor of Comparative Politics, University of Turin, and
Kenneth Newton, Professor of Comparative Politics,
University of Southampton. The series is published in association with the European Consortium for Political Research.

OTHER TITLES IN THIS SERIES

Coalition Governments in Western Europe
Edited by Wolfgang C. Müller and Kaare Strom

New as paperback
Parties without Partisans: Political Change in Advanced Industrial Democracies
Edited by Russell J. Dalton and Martin P. Wattenberg

Political Institutions: Democracy and Social Change
Josep M. Colomer

Mixed-Member Electoral Systems
Edited by Matthew Soberg Shugart and Martin P. Wattenberg

Divided Government in Comparative Perspective
Edited by Robert Elgie

Political Parties: Old Concepts and New Challenges
Edited by Richard Gunther, Joan J. Linz, and José Ramón Montero

Parliamentary Representatives in Europe 1848–2000: Legislative Recruitment and Careers in Eleven European Countries
Edited by Heinrich Best and Maurizio Cutta

Extreme Right Parties in Western Europe

PIERO IGNAZI

OXFORD
UNIVERSITY PRESS

OXFORD

UNIVERSITY PRESS

Great Clarendon Street, Oxford ox2 6DP

Oxford University Press is a department of the University of Oxford.
It furthers the University's objective of excellence in research, scholarship,
and education by publishing worldwide in

Oxford New York

Auckland Cape Town Dar es Salaam Hong Kong Karachi
Kuala Lumpur Madrid Melbourne Mexico City Nairobi
New Delhi Shanghai Taipei Toronto

With offices in

Argentina Austria Brazil Chile Czech Republic France Greece
Guatemala Hungary Italy Japan Poland Portugal Singapore
South Korea Switzerland Thailand Turkey Ukraine Vietnam

Oxford is a registered trade mark of Oxford University Press
in the UK and in certain other countries

Published in the United States
by Oxford University Press Inc., New York

© Piero Ignazi, 2003

The moral rights of the author have been asserted
Database right Oxford University Press (maker)

First Published 2003
First Published in Paperback 2006

British Library Cataloguing in Publication Data

Data available

Library of Congress Cataloging in Publication Data

Data available

Typeset by Newgen Imaging Systems (P) Ltd., Chennai, India
Printed in Great Britain
on acid-free paper by
Biddles Ltd., King's Lynn

ISBN 978–0–19–829325–5
ISBN 978–0–19–929159–5 (Pbk.)

Preface and Acknowledgements

This work had an early start. At the end of the eighties I had just published my book on the Italian neo-fascist party (*Il polo escluso. Profilo del Movimento Sociale Italiano* (1989)) and I found myself wondering about the development of right extremism in other European countries. After many discussions on the unforeseen successes of some extreme right-wing parties in Europe, my colleague and friend Colette Ysmal and I decided to call an ECPR workshop on the extreme right parties. After all, the almost complete lack of comparative analysis on the topic, with the remarkable exceptions of Christopher Husbands' and Klaus von Beyme's pioneering studies, was a gap that needed to be filled. At the 1990 ECPR Sessions of Workshops held in Bochum, a group of (then) young researchers discussed the various national cases and put forth hypotheses on the reasons for the development and endurance of the extreme right. On the basis of that fertile discussion I elaborated a framework of analysis (*The silent counterrevolution. Hypotheses on the rise of extreme right-wing parties in Europe* (1992)) that was published in a special issue of the European Journal of Political Research. The issue was devoted to the extreme right and collected some of the papers presented in Bochum. That article received some attention. Those reactions induced me to continue on the same track. After some years of intensive data gathering and collection of material on the various national cases, confronting myself with the extreme paucity of sources and with the barrier of the different national idioms, I published a comparative book in Italian (*L'estrema destra in Europa* (1994)). The interest in the scientific milieu has since exploded. Dozens of books and hundreds of papers have been published in the last decade or so.

The present study thus goes beyond a simple revision, enlargement, and update of my previous work. Developments in factual events and in academic analyses have forced me to an almost complete rewriting. On the other hand, most of the hypotheses developed in the 1992 article have resisted—and have been even corroborated by—the following numerous tests put forward by scholars either dealing with single national cases or with cross-national comparison. Other hypotheses have been successfully challenged (see e.g., the very recent, brilliant empirical test by Amir Abedi (2002)).

My work did not have the ambition of generating an original data set. But the availability of so many secondary country-specific or comparative analyses provided enough material: first to deal with the country by country analysis, and second to restate my general framework of interpretation.

This book could have never been conceived without the assistance and generosity expressed by many colleagues all over Europe for many years. At different points in time all the following have provided particularly useful materials and/or insights:

Jørgen Goul Andersen, Uwe Backes, Luciano Bardi, Tor Bjørklund, Xavier Casals, Pascal Delwit, Roger Eatwell, Meindert Fennema, Adriana Goldstaub, Roger Griffin, Bob Harmel, Christopher Husbands, Gilles Ivaldi, Pertti Hynynen, Rosario Jabardo, Jocelyn Evans, Dietmar Loch, Martin Lubbers, Paul Lucardie, Richard Luther, Xavier Mabille, Peter Mair, Renato Mannheimer, Cas Mudde, Nonna Mayer, Peter Merkl, Michael Minkenberg, Wolfang Müller, Pascal Perrineau, José Luis Rodriguez, Ben Soetendorp, Marc Swingedouw, Richard Stöss, Marco Tarchi, Jorg Ueltzhöffer, Jack Veugelers.

A particular mention goes to Colette Ysmal, whose intellectual stimulus was continuous and enlightening.

Without the intercession of the friends who provided me with translations from German (Irene Teiner, Alberto Tettamanti, and, above all, Paola Pecchioli) and Dutch/Flemish (Barbara Consolini), I would have never got access to so many sources.

The revision of the English text has been carried on by Peter Riley.

Finally, a particular thanks to Laura Lanzillo, who assisted me with invaluable commitment and competence in the editorial work.

This book is dedicated to my companion and spouse, Rita.

Introduction to the Paperback Edition

The first edition of the present book raised many comments and some criticisms. Some of the latter were quite acute (e.g. the culpable absence of the Swiss case, rightly pointed out by Hans-Georg Betz); some, however, missed the point. These remarks stimulated me to take the opportunity to make myself clearer on a series of topics in this paperback edition. One concerns extremism and anti-system, misunderstanding which vitiates proper comprehension of my interpretation of the phenomenon; another is the chain of causality in the Erp rise and the importance both of cultural ideological factors and of the interplay between mainstream right parties and extreme right parties. Moreover, the wealth of publications in the last few years has offered a splendid opportunity for a *tour d'horizon* of recent developments in the field.

The overwhelming majority of studies concentrate on empirical analysis of the extreme right *voters* alone. Unfortunately, many of these studies are somewhat repetitive and anchored to old-fashioned interpretations, and quite often, beneath the statistical elegance, a methodological weakness emerges since, in order to bypass the fatal dearth of cases, data from different surveys are pooled together irrespective of the time lag.

Whereas many studies exploit the availability of cross-national survey research on the mass public, other topics remain in the dark: The study of party members, middle-level elites and leadership groups themselves as well as of party internal structure is still quite neglected. Likewise, the internal debate and the cultural ideological production, apart from the electoral manifesto, are neither studied with the intensity they merit nor framed in a rigorous comparative approach.

The real issue, however, which will inevitably attract our attention for some time to come, is the fate of this 'party family': will it survive in the same shape as it appeared more than twenty years ago? or will it adapt to the (democratic) environment, thus playing a larger role in the political and party systems? Apparently, many components of the family have somewhat accommodated to the system and have been legitimated; consequently, in many cases, this affected the political discourse along their authoritarian or neopopulist lines. Others are still kept in isolation especially in France and Germany and maintain their anti-system profile quite high. This addendum has tried, *inter alia*, to provide some cues on the future development of this party family which lies in between adaptation and expansion on the one hand and defence of identity and isolation on the other.

My appreciation goes to all the colleagues who provided materials and useful comments and to Ralph Nisbet for his revision of this new part.

Piero Ignazi
Bologna, February 2006

Contents

List of Tables

Introduction

Until the 1980s the term extreme right was synonymous with that of neo-fascism. The reason was simple. The only relevant party which declared itself as representing the 'extreme right' up to then—the Italian Movimento Sociale Italiano (MSI) (Italian Social Movement—openly exhibited a direct lineage with pre-war fascism. At the same time, the other components of the neo-fascist political family all over Europe were very weak. The fate of neo-fascist parties was not reinvigorated by the passage from proto-fascist authoritarianism to democracy in Spain, Portugal, and Greece in mid-1970s. On the contrary, in these countries neo-fascism found such a limited audience as to be relegated to the status of the marginal fringe. The exclusion from mainstream politics and the limited, and even declining, electoral and organizational strength offered a gloomy perspective for the extreme right neo-fascist parties.

Everything changed in the 1980s. New parties emerged, older ones radically innovated themselves, and both gained unprecedented consent. The number of Western European extreme right parties which had entered the national or European parliament had passed from 6 at the beginning of the 1980s to 10 by the end of 1980s, then arriving at 15 in the mid-1990s. Their share of votes more than doubled by rising from 4.75 per cent in the decade 1980–9 to 9.73 per cent in 1990–9. In the 1980s, the extreme right made its breakthrough in six more countries: France, above all, gave real impetus to this political family with the Front National's resounding and sustained performances, capturing over 10 per cent of the popular vote; Austria, with the right-extremist turn of Haider's FPÖ; Belgium, with an (uneven) development in both linguistic parts (FN and Vlaams Blok); Germany, with the coming of the 'third wave' of right-extremism, which became a constant pain for the political system after the 1989 European election, even if it never broke into the Bundestag; the Netherlands, with a series of appearances and exits by the CD; Switzerland, whose right-extremism proliferated into various parties. The initial, albeit very limited, success of neo-fascist parties—in Spain with the Fuerza Nueva leader's Blas Piñar's election in 1979, and in Greece with the entry into national parliament by the EP in 1977 and into the European parliament by the EPEN in 1984—was not to be confirmed later on and the extreme right almost disappeared. The same is true for a new entry of right-extremism in the early 1990s, namely the NyD in Sweden, which vanished after a flamboyant appearance in 1991. Finally, only Finland, Great Britain, Ireland, and Portugal never elected a representative of an extreme right party in a nationwide election.

The extreme right has so far consolidated its presence all over Western Europe. The reason for this breakthrough, as discussed in the book, is multifaceted: from the emergence of new unaccounted issues to the creeping crisis of representation; from the emergence of proto-charismatic figures in the extreme right, well knit with the growing personalization of politics, to the increasing political and societal alienation and the dissatisfaction for traditional features of the political system and for politics as such.

But a further, highly salient, factor refers to the different 'nature' of the contemporary right-extremist parties. The extreme right parties of the 1980s, in fact, are no longer neo-fascist parties. On the other hand, they are perceived as right-extremist because they unquestionably occupy the right-most position of the political spectrum. However, as these new extreme right parties do not share any commitment to neo-fascism they are a different *type* of extreme right. Basically, these parties are anti-system as they undermine the (democratic) system's legitimacy through their discourse and actions. They are fiercely opposed to the idea of parliamentary representation and partisan conflicts, and hence they argue for corporatist or, mainly, direct and personalistic mechanisms of representation; they are against the idea of pluralism because it endangers (the ideal of) societal harmony; they are against the universal idea of equality as rights should be allotted on the basis of ascriptive elements (race, language, ethnicity); and finally they are somewhat authoritarian because they conceive supra-individual and collective authority (State, nation, community) as more important than the individual one. All these holistic and monistic elements put these parties in conflict with the basic principles of contemporary liberal democracy.

This new type of parties, instead of reviving the 'palingenetic myth' of fascism, provides an answer to those demands and needs generated by post-industrial society which traditional parties have failed to address. These demands and needs converge in the defence of the natural community, at national or sub-national levels, from alien and polluting presence—hence racism and xenophobia—and respond to the identity crisis produced by atomization at the societal level, by globalization at the economic level, and by supra-nationalism at the political level. Moreover, the claim for more law and order, the search for a 'charismatic' leader, the need for harmony and security, and the uneasiness over the representative mechanisms and procedures, express a desire for an authoritative guide in a society where self-achievement and individualism have disrupted the protective network of traditional social bonds. And, finally, the return of rigid moral standards is a definite counterpart of post-materialist libertarianism. The newcomers in the extreme right family therefore share a precise set of properties quite different and innovating regarding the previous (neo-fascist) tradition. This novel group of extreme right parties is the unexpected outcome of post-materialism; hence their label of post-material extreme right.

This book has three aims. The first one is an exploration of the extreme right in order to assess its ideological meaning(s) and its political/partisan expressions. Beginning with a discussion of the meaning and validity of the Left–Right terminology, this part deals with the various significance and nuances of the term 'right', discussing the appropriateness of the competing terms of 'radical', 'new', 'populist', and 'extreme' right, and suggests a classification grid of the parties pertaining to this political family. The second aim is to carry out an in-depth analysis of the evolution of the post-war extreme right for each country in Western Europe. In this part the analysis highlights the lineage with pre-war fascist regimes or movements, the different partisan expressions in the post-war period, with particular emphasis to the ideological profile, the party's relationship with the other actors in the party system, the socio-demographic and attitudinal profile of the voter, and finally the conditions which had favoured or inhibited their development. The final part, which constitutes our third aim, discusses in detail the present trend of the Western European extreme right and delineates a conceptual framework for interpreting the reason for the success and failure of the various parties.

1

Meanings and Varieties of the Right

Much ink has been used on the assessment of the heuristic futility, the conceptual vagueness, and the political ambiguity of the terms Left and Right. The frustration with this distinction is not new. Already by 1842, 50 years after the introduction in the political lexicon of the Left–Right dichotomy, the *Dictionaire du politique* stated that 'these ancient divisions have lost a lot of their value' (quoted in Crapez 1998: 44). Throughout the nineteenth and twentieth centuries the same impatience has repeatedly come to the fore. The criticism of the validity of Left–Right stems from a series of arguments such as the growing complexity of society and the simple dichotomy's inability to grasp the contemporary reality, the multidimensionality of political conflicts following the de-freezing of traditional political cleavages, the crisis of socialism and the collapse of communism, the end of ideology, the end of modernity, and, finally, 'the end of history'.

When and how did these two terms enter the political domain? Left and Right accessed the political discourse in the first stages of the French revolution and more precisely when the *Assemblée Constituante* had to decide whether to allow the right of veto by the King on the Assembly Acts. On 29 August 1789, in order to count the delegates' votes, the Assembly members were asked by the chairman to move to his right if they wanted to grant the veto power to the King or to his left if they were opposed to it. While this vote 'by separation' was far from novel, it represented a turning point because the split into two parts acquired an unprecedented political meaning. This spatial differentiation was immediately recognized by the pamphletists of the time as a political distinction between traditionalists and conservatives (right) and modernisers and renovators (left). Since their very first appearance in political language, the two terms were credited with 'meanings' which have endured, with minor modifications. Actually, the dichotomy did not take a firm hold in revolutionary France, as it waned during the Thermidor period because of the drive towards unity that pervaded the post-revolutionaries: '(the) Revolution created those categories . . . while, at the same time, acting for their elimination' (Gauchet 1994: 17).

After this 'false start', Left and Right returned with a definite assessment in the Restoration period (Gauchet 1994: 18ff). Since 1818 a series of *Tableaux, Plans,* and *Statistiques* has illustrated the spatial distribution of the MP in Parliament (Gauclef 1994: 21–2). The location attributed to the deputies went from the 'extreme Right' to the 'extreme Left', passing through various intermediate nuances. However, the full recognition of the political salience of the two terms did not clarify their 'meaning'; and the tumultuous politics of mid-nineteenth century France did not help to settle the question. In fact, as we have seen, the various *'Dictionaires du politique'* of the time already questioned the validity of the dichotomy. Notwithstanding these dilemmas, the two terms then spread throughout Europe, albeit at different times and with different emphasis on one of the terms (usually the Left). In all countries, except Great Britain, where the Left and Right terminology remained somewhat below the surface (see Butler and Stoke 1969), outweighed by the traditional Whig–Tory dichotomy, the conflicts in Parliament came to be represented (and self-represented by the protagonists) in spatial terms. Even when Left and Right were later supplemented by the term Centre, this new entry did not diminish the relevance of the two poles; on the contrary, its presence is only justified because it stands in between the two poles: it cannot exist outside the dichotomy (Gauchet 1994: 65; Bobbio 1999: 6–7).

Left and Right gained strength and pervasiveness in relation to the growing relevance of the class cleavage. The workers/owners opposition, upon which the political conflict hinged in Western societies for more than a century, has been universally translated into the Left–Right polarity, where the Right represents the interests of the owners and the bourgeoise and the Left the interests of the workers and the proletariat. This 'sociological' interpretation of Left and Right, despite the reduction of the multiform content of the spatial terms, has gained universal recognition. Moreover, on the basis of this sociological anchorage, the Left was credited with the meaning of social change toward a greater egalitarianism, and the Right with the maintenance of the traditional socio-economic capitalist order. The centrality of the class cleavage, which had moulded the party systems all over Europe since the age of the first wave of democratization (Bartolini 2000), would be replaced, according to Ronald Inglehart's (1977) famous thesis, by another basic conflict: between materialist (the defence of socio-economic achievements and law and order enforcement) and post-materialist values (the drive to participate more in the decision-making process and to enjoy more freedom). According to Inglehart, the 'new dimension is distinct from the traditional Left–Right dimension based on ownership and control of the means of production and distribution of income. Its existence is working to transform the meaning of Left and Right and the social bases of these two respective poles' (Inglehart 1990: 289). Taking for granted the mounting centrality of the materialist/post-materialist cleavage, on the basis of such value change and of the blurring of the class conflict, a new political space has been highlighted (Offe 1985). On one side, the 'Old politics' (the defence of interests and values interwoven with the traditional cleavages) and, on the other, the 'New politics' (non-material issues such as quality of life, the role of women, minority rights, unconventional styles of life, protection of the environment, political and social participation, social equality).

Actually, this new interpretation of the political space *does not replace* the Left–Right divide: it simply introduces different elements for the identification of the two terms, and it detaches the reference to the Left and Right from its traditional social interpreters. Left and Right no longer trace the antinomy between working class and middle class: with the 'silent revolution' and the affirmation of the new materialist/post-materialist cleavage, sectors of the 'traditional' middle class and working class located themselves on the same side facing the 'new' middle class. Therefore, 'variations and change in the content of preference formation are also associated with variations in the organizational forms of interest articulation' (Kitschelt 1995*a*: 124); as a consequence, the European electorate is swept away by a 'joint transformation of economic and non-economic political preferences and interests' (Kitschelt 1995*a*: 129).

In summary, the changing paradigm of the political space enriches the Left-Right divide rather than marginalizing it. The comparative empirical analyses done throughout Europe demonstrate that the traditional Left–Right orientations *'will remain constant or increase, while the correlations for materialists/post-materialists values will increase'* (Knutsen 1995: 76). Thus, the old cleavages (in particular class and religion) continue to hold and are flanked—not substituted—by new value orientations; and both old and new cleavages contribute to shape the individual location on the political spectrum: 'the Left–Right dimension remains a most significant if not dominant cleavage in Western democracies' (Kim and Fording 2000: 76). In conclusion, *there is no empirical support for the theory of the irrelevance of the spatial dichotomy* (Knutsen 1995: 86).

In spite of all that, many (mainly) Left-wing politicians and analysts reiterate that the breaking up of the traditional social alignments has implied the collapse of the Left and Right distinction. From Stephen Lukes' provocative essay *'What is Left?'* (Lukes 1992) to Anthony Giddens' *'Beyond Left and Right'* (Giddens 1994), the cultural mood on the Left side ranged from lament to advocacy of the overcoming of the dichotomy. Anthony Giddens, in particular, has highlighted how the collapse of communism, the crisis of social-democracy, globalization, social reflexivity, and the post-paucity society have disentangled the notion of Left and Right. Generative politics, dialogic democracy, and politics of life provide for the overcoming of the old spatial terminology. However, if even Giddens himself asserts that the dichotomy will survive 'in the context of party politics' (Giddens 1994: 251), we can conclude, solidly supported by empirical analyses, that Left and Right have not vanished.

THE 'ANTHROPOLOGICAL' BASIS OF THE DICHOTOMY

The solidity of the dichotomy has also been traced from an 'organic–anthropological' argument: the dichotomy is a kind of 'primary spatial perception'

(Laponce 1981) necessary to classify (and to align with) the physical space, and, accordingly, to define, through a symbolic use of these terms, a world-view (Galeotti 1984).

The term Right displays both an amazing stability over time and large diffusion in the Indo-European languages; on the contrary, the term Left is highly unstable and differentiated. This diverging linguistic fate underlines the positive connotation given to the Right, on one side, and the uneasiness felt when dealing with something negative and obscure such as the Left, on the other (Laponce 1981: 38ss).

Right is associated to positive adjectives such as honest, reliable, straight, even lively, to the juridical right and to political rights; while the term Left is linked with malicious, dangerous, unaccountable, untrustworthy, incapable, and even deathful. This differentiation has been attributed, in a seminal study by Robert Hertz, to the human organic asymmetry—the universal prevalence of the right hand—that mirrors and reproduces both a reality and an ideal (Hertz 1994 [1928]: 140). Surveying the dualism between the right and the left part of the body, and especially the hands, in primitive cultures, Hertz (see also Durkheim and Mauss 1951 [1901–02]) highlighted that the Left–Right antinomy determined social organization and religious cults. From the Polynesian Maori to the native Americans, the right hand indicates life, strength, courage, virility, and the opposite stands for the left hand. The right hand is used to invoke the divinity, to bury the dead, to sign a pact. This lateralization has then been later confirmed by further anthropological research (for an overview see Laponce 1981: ch. 2).

The same connotation is found in Western culture since ancient Greece, with the exception of republican and early-imperial Rome. It is the Christian iconography which definitively assigns a positive value to the right: one crosses oneself with the right; Christ sits to the right of the Father; God's right hand in the Universal judgement points to Heaven for the blessed, while the left sends the damned to Hell. The same is true for the popular use in proverbs and superstitions in daily life and social relationships (shaking the right hand, swearing with the right hand, offering the right side to women, sitting on the right side in the place of honour, and so on).

This 'horizontal' distinction is accompanied by the 'vertical' division between up and down, the other fundamental analytical scheme used by all the cultures. The references of the mundane and divine power—God, Heaven, and the King—are up, while the Devil, Hell, and the People are down (Galeotti 1984: 261). Thus, high and right represent the *locis* of the sacred, the mighty, and the righteous, while low and left that of the profane, the powerless, and the devilish.

In the French Revolution the *axis mundi* (Dumont 1991), that is, the verticality around which the symbolic representation of power has always been organized (Escobar 1995), rotates upwards to coincide with the horizontality of the Right–Left scheme. This rotation implies, by itself, a particular configuration of meaning of the horizontal terms. In fact, since the 1789 *Assemblée Constituante*, the Left has come to be identified with the expression of the 'lower part'—the Third State—and, *at the same time*, of the struggle against 'the highest parts'—the King, the nobility, the privilege of birth, and, later, the divinity and the Church. Therefore, low and left coincides in opposition to the compound of high and right. The passage 'from the hierarchical verticality to the egalitarian horizontality' implied a movement from hierarchy to equality (Dumont 1991: 551). The horizontal dimension of the Left–Right opposition will be immediately recognised as the crucial political distinction, and it will spread in European political culture. We can conclude then that the spatial unidimensionality founded upon the Left–Right antinomy clearly identifies, at the moment of its foundation, a basic opposition: equality against privilege. This archetypal interpretation of the Left–Right conflict—the 1848 *Dictonaire du politique* stated that on the left side were the 'defenders of the principle of liberty', while those seated on the right were declared 'defenders of the principle of power' (quoted by Sartori 1976: 324)—is still considered valid. Norberto Bobbio (1999), in particular, in his work on the subject, firmly advocates the persistence of a precise meaning to the dichotomy hinged on the equality/inequality divide (see *infra*).

To sum up, the 'impressive absorptive power' of the Left–Right semantics (Knutsen 1995: 86) is at the basis of its present validity and universal diffusion. At the mass level, political conflicts are still interpreted adopting the spatial metaphor, and this interpretative scheme displays a capacity to 'travel across countries' (Huber 1989: 603), assuming its role of 'political Esperanto' (Laponce 1981: 56). If this is true, are the terms Left and Right just labels of empty boxes filled in by everyone according to their personal value-set, or is there a shared and stable meaning, an enduring while underlying pattern of signification?

THE 'INSTRUMENTAL' INTERPRETATION OF LEFT AND RIGHT AND ITS MASS LEVEL CONSISTENCY

The instrumental interpretation sees Left and Right as blank labels which citizens compile according to their own preferences, with a varying degree of consistency between philosophical or theoretical attributes of the dichotomy and their own personal set of values. Giovanni Sartori has clearly stated that while '[h]istorically, Left and Right entered politics heavily loaded with cultural and religious meaning . . . . [These] labels are easily 'unloaded' and 'reloaded'—for their lack of any semantic substratum' (Sartori 1982: 255–256; see also 1976: 335). There is no specific or pre-assessed meaning of the dichotomy: the interaction between political thinkers, party elite, and mass public will provide it with the *real meaning*. What counts most is the 'recognition' of the dichotomy and its adoption by the citizenry in order to understand and to interpret the political world. According to the most recent literature (Listhaug, Macdonald, and Rabinowith 1990; Klingemann 1995; Huber and Inglehart 1995; Knutsen 1995, 1998; Kim and

Fording 2000) *the Left–Right dimension is highly familiar to the European electorate as a political 'schema'* (Kulinski, Luskin, and Bolland 1991; Lodge *et al.* 1991) which provides a map to orient the voters in the complexity and even the abtrusity of the political realm. Well above 85 per cent of the European electorate recognize the Left–Right dimension (Klingemann 1995: 192), and even when people disdain to attribute meaning, or allow heuristic power, to the dichotomy, they nevertheless use it as a lamp in the dark to distinguish the political issues, parties, policies, and leaders.

According to this 'instrumental' interpretation of the dichotomy, Left and Right are just tools that are employed to reduce political complexity. Irrespective of the subjective meaning attributed to Left and Right, the dichotomy 'works' because it provides a sort of 'political Esperanto' to the citizenry (Sartori 1976: 334, 342). The structuring power of Left and Right 'derives from their being indefinitely open terms, always susceptible to enrichment or renewal on the semantic level' (Gauchet 1994: 41). Left and Right are 'flexible' terms which gather a 'synthesis of attitudes' (Sartori 1982: 256) which change across time and country, along with the particular Zeitgeist and national political cultures. As Fuchs and Klingemann (1989: 207) write, 'the meaning of the Left–Right schemas as defined by the crucial conflicts of the specific social system. The basic structures of conflict manifest themselves in a variety of ways. They refer, for example, to specific conflicts between socio-structural bases (e.g. labour versus capital, clerical versus secular), to the ideological interpretation of these conflicts, and to their expression in organizations and political parties. *From this reservoir, individuals select their specific understanding of the Left–Right schema'.*

Therefore, Left and Right do not 'hold' eternal and unchanging meanings, but they vary 'in relationship to a determined historical situation and to its problems. In other terms, they are dependent on the issues and the *enjeux* of the time' (Rémond 1982: 32). Classic cases of this shift concern liberalism—which was Leftist and revolutionary in the early-mid nineteenth century, and then shifted rightward with the rise of socialist and libertarian ideologies—and nationalism, from the romantic period of self-determination of the people to the late nineteenth and early twentieth century's aggressive militarist attitude.

If this interpretation is true, a further question arises: what is the degree of consistency between the citizens' notion of Left and Right and party location in the political space? The comparison between 'the Left–Right positions of the party programmes and the mean orientations of survey respondents expressing support for each party' demonstrates 'the congruence of parties and their supporters' (Klingemann 1995: 195–6). The expert evaluation of the leftness and rightness of each policy in the parties' manifestos—while a debatable method of analysis (Budge 1999)—leads to an unequivocal conclusion: *Left and Right are not only recognised by the citizens but they are also filled with meaning which comes to be consistent with the 'intellectual' interpretation of the dichotomy.* And, in fact, Left–Right self-location proves to be the best predictor of the vote (van Deth and Guers 1989; Thomassen and Schmitt 1999: 198; van der Brug and van der Eijk 1999).

Why did these spatial terms resist the tests of time? Basically, because the political world is complex and orientation is difficult without clear and simple coordinates. The labels of Right and Left simplify the options offered by the political market, and the more the party system is complex, the more this is helpful. While in a two-party system the voter choice is simple (and this is why Bulter and Stoke (1969) argued for the irrelevance of the Left–Right dichotomy in Great Britain), in multiparty systems 'the information costs and indeterminacy multiply exponentially, and some drastic simplification becomes a sheer necessity' (Sartori 1976: 341). Therefore, the mass public tries to compress the various dimensions of the conflict (religious, linguistic, territorial, class-based) to reduce them to a unidimensional manageability (Fuchs and Klingemann 1989: 233). This simplifying attitude of the mass public signifies the passage from ideological 'sophistication'—belonging to those who have solid cultural tools which allow them to elaborate on a coherent world-view—to ideological 'identification' (Knight 1985), that is, an affective attitude, defined by a few essential elements which provide for a political 'identity' (Sani and Sartori 1983). In brief, the Right–Left schema has the basic function of giving sense to, and orientation in, a (complex) political world. According to René Rémond (1982: 30) 'the Right and Left distinction corresponds to the spirit's need to spatially represent the differences of opinions and to organize them according to some cardinal point.'

THE 'ESSENTIALIST' INTERPRETATION

The interpretation of the (relative) variability of the meaning of Left and Right across time and context is challenged by the view of a constant presence, over time, of certain features of the dichotomy. As already mentioned, Norberto Bobbio leads the essentialist theoreticians. He considers the 'different attitude that men assume in front of the ideal of equality' as the constant element of distinction between Left (egalitarian) and Right (inegalitarian). On the left side, people put the common traits amongst men first, while on the right side the differences come first. 'On one side one finds those who maintain that men are more equal than unequal, on the other those who think that men are more unequal than equal' (Bobbio 1999: 60). This distinction of ideals could be typically represented by Rousseau, on one side, and by Nietzsche, on the other (Bobbio 1999: 60). For the latter, in fact, equality is 'a nice mental device which, once more, like a second and subtler atheism, hides the hostility of the plebes towards what is sovereign and privileged' (quoted in Bobbio 1999: 61). According to Bobbio, this is the long-lasting element which across the centuries and the countries still characterizes the dichotomy.

Even more straightforward in the individualization of constant features in the Left–Right antinomy is the Italian philosopher Dino Cofrancesco (1986: 65): 'Right and Left refer to fundamental, enduring attitudes, to specific modes of relations to the social reality, to intentionalities transformed in instincts'; they 'are state of mind, . . . they correspond to natural tendencies of man' (Cofrancesco 1986: 72). More precisely, 'Right and Left correspond substantially to how human, and, above all, power relationships are perceived' (Cofrancesco 1986: 66). Therefore, 'the right is biased to see the positive side of the social bond; the left the negative and degenerative side. One sees authority as the father, the other as the boss; one sees the associative links as protection, support, safe haven; the other as (the risk) of exploitation of the many by the few' (Cofrancesco 1986: 66). Then, 'where the roots are highly emphasized, the social ties are perceived as correspondents to the natural order of things, there the Right is; where, on the contrary, the effort to limit, to check, to bargain over ties and social obligations—the power of man over man—is stronger, there the Left is' (Cofrancesco 1986: 67). In conclusion, according to Cofrancesco, for the Right the affiliation, the sense of belonging, the loyalty to 'being' instead of 'becoming', the sentiment of participation within a community and/or a vast and complex organism are fundamental.

René Dumont follows along the same track, although with a nostalgic flavour for the pre-modern, solidly tied, traditional society. Dumont argues in favour of an essential contradiction between Left and Right, articulated upon the universal/particular and freedom/equality antinomies. The predominance of individualism is the essential feature of this modernity; and as the Left was the advocate of modernity, it is the natural reference for individualism, while the Right points to the traditional 'communitarian' bonds. The holistic world-view imbues the Right. In this political pole, tradition, hierarchy, and belonging find their locus; from there they continue their struggle against a triumphal individualist (and, by consequence, leftward) society (Dumont 1993).

Somewhat similar is Jean Laponce's (1981: 118–19) conceptual scheme of four 'stable' oppositions articulated on the political, religious, economic, and temporal conflicts where egalitarianism, free thinking, lower classes, and discontinuity are on the left side and hierarchy, religion, high classes, and continuity are on the right.

Further hints came from the French pioneer of electoral studies, André Siegfried, who underlined in his work on electoral behaviour in West France (Siegfried 1913: 519) that the 'right-wing coalition leans, directly or indirectly, upon the Church or the Castle' both in cultural (hierarchy, tradition, religiosity) and in social (the religious institutions and the local nobility) terms. Following this seminal intuition a series of scholars, from Gougel to Duverger, effectively illustrated the Left–Right divide with reference to the party of movement and the party of the established order (for on overview see Sirenelli and Vigne 1992).

In the Anglo-American context, the dominant issue that shapes political attitudes and electoral behaviour along the dichotomy appears to be the economic one.

The seminal analysis of Anthony Downs (1957) reduced the Left–Right continuum to the State intervention–laissez-faire dichotomy. Further empirical analyses have supported this model. In post-war Europe, the overview of the party's electoral manifestos show the existence of 'a clear and unambiguous Left–Right dimension, loading highly and positively on the traditional interventionist emphases of the planning controlled economy . . . and loading highly and negatively on the classic conservative emphases on free enterprise' (Bartolini and Mair 1990: 6). Similarly, 'the meaning of "Left and Right" . . . refers to classic economic policy conflicts—government regulation . . . as opposed to free enterprise, individual freedom, incentives and economic orthodoxy' (Budge *et al.* 1987: 394–5). More recent comparative analyses have downsized the role of the economy, highlighting the relevance of the 'cultural' issues (to paraphrase Siegfried). The post-materialist agenda, and the reaction to it, have introduced 'non-material' issues into the electorate's value configuration and in its attribution of meaning to Left and Right (Flanagan 1987; Minkenberg and Inglehart 1989), so that Right is associated with authoritarian anti-libertarian issues.

In conclusion, the Right can be identified as that ideal space in which one finds various and even contradictory combinations of the principle of authority, the importance given to collective entities—the nation, the State, the Church— (although for *some* right-wing tendencies the importance given to the individual is also emphasized), the reference made to tradition and roots, the ideal of order, of harmony, and of hierarchy, the transposition on the socio-political context of the natural and social inequalities, the need for affiliation, and the nostalgic search for a natural community.

THE 'STYLES OF THOUGHT' OF THE RIGHT

Inside the political space of the Right, different 'ideological complexes' (Freedan 1996) or 'styles of thought' (Eatwell 1989) cohabit. Roger Eatwell (1989: 63) has suggested five 'styles of thought': the reactionary Right, the moderate Right, the radical Right, the extreme Right, and the new Right. A more established classification (Rémond 1982), moulded upon French history, distinguishes a legitimistic and traditionalist Right, pointing to reinstating the principles of the *ancien régime* after the 1789 revolutionary storm; a proto-liberal *orléaniste* Right, incubator of the political rights and the free market; and a bonapartist, authoritarian, and plebiscitarian Right legitimized by the popular will but disrespectful of freedom and of the limitations of power. These three ideal-types are inferred by the French experience, but they are applicable to the whole European context and, according to Rémond himself, they are still present today under the form of traditionalism, liberalism, and neo-fascist authoritarianism (see Sternhell 1987: 54–5). While Eatwell's classification is more in tune with the recent evolution of the Right, nevertheless we will follow the Rémond classification in assessing its present cultural–ideological landscape.

The doctrine of the counter-revolution represented by Maistre, Bonald, the first Lamennais, Donoso Cortes, and Haller expresses a neat radical opposition to the heritage of the French Revolution. This doctrine 'is connoted by a strong monistic, static and organicist approach: the only conceivable perfect order is naturally centred on God, who is, nevertheless, infinitely distant from men . . . so that the world appears abandoned to the iron laws of the nature' (Galli 1981: 11). Man is inevitably and inescapably corrupt: therefore he must be ruled in order to stop him from damaging himself and others. This rule proceeds directly from the unchangeable will of God and of nature. Legitimate power is of divine origin: only this kind of power might preserve some order on earth and prevent the downfall of society. Power is unique, indivisible, and hierarchically organized, and it transcends every possible human intervention. A 'good society' is naturally harmonious; it does not conceive conflicts because of the unity of intents provided by the authority which is legitimate because of the divine right. A 'good society' is therefore organic and hierarchical: everyone is assigned to a precise role defined by tradition (see Marino 1978; Holmes 1993). Liberal individualism fuelled by the eighteenth-century philosophers constitutes the prototype of the error: 'To fight for God and the King on the theoretical level is nothing more than a struggle for the interpretation of the world, for a world-view' (Geingembre 1989: 81).

Traditionalist thought, because of its focus on the past and its deep contempt for the seeds of the bourgeois society, never became a relevant and vital component of the Right. At the turn of the nineteenth century, Charles Maurras and other thinkers, fuelled by the 'ideology of decadence' (Sternhell 1994), the sentiment of a collapse of the liberal (and rotten) bourgeois society, argued for a revitalization of the traditionalist ideology. However, as the society of the time was considerably distant from that of the restoration period, having become a mass and industrialized society, the return to motionless organic societies and the pre-Revolutionary '*doucer de vivre*' was inconceivable. Therefore, Maurras' proposal pointed toward changing the legitimizing principles of traditional authority; in the rapidly developing industrial mass society, the monarchy could no longer be legitimized by the divinity; the people—while inspired by the Church—should be the ultimate source of legitimization. The throne and the altar could come back to impose their authority thanks only to popular consent. This is the modernization thrust highlighted by the leader of the Action Française (French Action). The theoretical effort by Maurras represents the ultimate effort to reinvigorate traditionalism.

Further attempts purported in the mid-twentieth century by two mainstream intellectuals, René Guenon and Julius Evola (Ferraresi 1988, 1995), followed a rather different logic. The latter, in particular (Evola 1969 [1934], 1951, 1973 [1961]), argued that the modern world had entered a phase of decadence since medieval times; and, as this long-term crisis was unconquerable, there was nothing left to do but testify to its own irreconcilable extraneousness with an exemplary life (and behaviour). The only ethically and politically plausible role is that of the 'political soldier': a hero who stands up over a ruined world. In other terms, the modern world, with its popular mass predominance, should be rejected *in toto*: the only way out is an individualist revolt. Evola's quixotic while fascinating vision reframed the hostility to modernity of traditionalist thought, providing novel and original ideas. Even if Evola acquired the role of *maître à penser* for the most radical fringes of the extreme Right, thanks to his esoteric, pessimistic, and 'alienated' thinking, his contribution did not result in an expansion of traditionalism, which remained confined to very tiny chapels.

Orléanisme, on the other hand, is a larger and unbounded category that includes both liberal and conservative visions. This ambivalence enfeebles the heuristic utility of this category because of the divide separating liberalism and conservatism. However, while the coincidence of liberalism with the Right is far from universal (in time and space), conservatism is, without any question, part of the Right. This ideology contains, in turn, two main traditions: the British one and the German one.

British conservatism, evolved through the 'reflections' of Edmund Burke, is connoted, essentially by: the pessimistic consideration of human nature (the inevitability of the 'fall'); the organic conception of society; natural inequality through status and property; and the respect for authority and tradition (Freedan 1996: 331). The idealisation and even sacredness of traditions emphasised by the conservatives does not imply that they are fixed or inflexible. Conservative ideology's concern for the status quo (see Huntington 1957) is not in necessary contradiction with change induced by market concerns. This is certainly true if such change is understood within a 'natural' framework, in the Adam Smith and Edmund Burke tradition, and not as a radical departure from the cultural, political, and economic setting of society. If change is 'natural' (Oakeshott 1967: 172) and 'sure-footed and respectful of the past' (Rossiter 1955: 12) conservatism could accept the new 'neo-conservative' tenets of freedom, individualism, and entrepreneurship which all find their locus in the market (Scruton 1980; Norton and Aughey 1981; Willetts 1992; Gamble 1988). In fact, 'the market needs conservatism': that is, whilst conservative scepticism on human nature can allow total freedom in the economic sphere, it cannot give up controlling man in other human activities.

Hence the emphasis on family and natural community bonds, on moral control, on the 'necessity' of hierarchical societal organization: 'law, religion, and the need for authority, all of which provide tempered control over people' (Freedan 1996: 412). These features depicting the post-1980s neo-conservatism pertain to a right-wing democratic ideology. In the Anglo-American context, the barrier between tough neo-conservatism and anti-democratic thinking has been—and still is—solid and precise. On the other hand, as it will be discussed *infra*, in continental Europe the role of neo-conservatism (and of neo-conservative policies) has—unconsciously—played a different role, providing a sort of legitimation to more extreme standings, precisely nurtured by the neo-conservative agenda (Minkenberg 1998*a*).

While British conservatism still laments the lack of authoritative thinking since Burke (see Freedan 1996: 318ss), German conservatism can rely upon the solid analysis of Karl Mannheim. Writing in the first decades of the twentieth century, Mannheim (1989 [1925]) traces the origin of conservatism from the process of class, interest, and value differentiation that marks the separation from the ancient feudal order and the entry into bourgeois society. This early nineteenth century conservatism attempts to recover norms and values that the modernization fostered by the French revolution was at risk of destroying (Tettamanti 1989). The German conservative world-view is therefore backward looking, pragmatic, anti-egalitarian, and against market capitalist property rights. Such 'counter-revolutionary conservatism' is practically identified with the fate of the nobility: the collapse of the latter implies the disappearance of the former. Precisely in order to contest this backward vision, German intellectuals of the 1920s developed the movement of the *Konservative Revolution*, hinging on anti-liberalism and anti-parlamentarism on one side and a sort of 'new nationalism' on the other. The ideological Babel of the *Konservative Revolution* was such that it has been provocatively suggested 'to expunge it from the list of the political ideas of the twentieth century' (Breuer 1995: 150).

While English conservatism is a midwife, however suspicious and prudent, of modernity, German conservatism is a radical opposer of it but, at the same time, it did attempt renewal by its dialectical standing towards political innovations.

The cultural–ideological tradition of the Right, beside reactionary traditionalism and conservatism, includes the new phenomenon par excellence of the twentieth century, that is to say, fascism. Comprising fascism within the Right is not so obvious. Some fringes of historical fascism and neo-fascism claim an affiliation to the Left rather than to the Right. The anti-capitalist, socializing, revolutionary, and modernizing drive of fascism has been sustained by Italian neo-fascist intellectuals such as Erra, Accame, and Rauti to the point that even prominent leaders of the post-war Italian neo-fascist party denied any relationship with the 'Right', because of its identification with conservatism (Ignazi 1993, 1998*a*).

The same is true for those interpreters of historical fascism, which in the early 1920s and later on in 1943–5 advocated what Renzo De Felice (1969, 1975) defined as the fascism-movement. This leading historian of Italian fascism distinguished fascism into two different streams, the fascism-movement (anti-bourgeois, anti-capitalist, revolutionary, and secular) and the fascism-regime (pro-capital, clerical, and conservative). While the fascism-movement has always been a minor tendency within fascism, both in Italy and in the other fascist movements and regimes, it left permanent and relevant signs in the fascist ideology.

In fact some scholars have emphasized the role of leftist influence in moulding the fascist world-view. Zeev Sternhell, in particular, has suggested disentangling fascism from the right-wing milieu because it constitutes an attempt at overcoming the decadent bourgeois society through a 'synthesis of organic nationalism and anti-Marxist socialism' (Sternhell 1987: 56): fascism merges streams of the socialist and anarco-syndacalist ideology, on one side, and legitimist and nationalist on the other. For Sternhell, fascism represents an ethical and political revolutionary break-up against individualism and materialism, against the inheritance of the Enlightenment and of the French revolution, against liberalism and equality, while it advocates an organic community embodied by the state. This break-up was mainly fostered by former Left socialists or anarco-syndicalists, who joined and nurtured the fascist synthesis (Sternhell 1976*a,b*, 1989). However, Sternhell, despite the provocative title of his more successful work—*Ni droite, ni gauche* (1987)—finally locates fascism on one side of the political spectrum by defining it as a 'revolutionary Right', 'a popular, also proletarian Right but violently anti-Marxist, that secretes a tribal organic nationalism, a nationalism of the Soil and the Dead, of the Soil and of the Blood' (Sternhell 1987: 55). In brief, fascism doesn't escape from the Right–Left schema: its ideology makes an attempt at 'building a Right-wing *Weltanschauung*, applying cultural material often borrowed from the Left adversaries' (Cofrancesco 1986: 76). Then again, fascism is 'Right', but of a new type because it constitutes a Right-wing answer to the industrial and mass society. In contrast to the conservatism which emerged as a mentality a century earlier, before the era of the masses, fascism is the by-product of that era (Mosse 1975) and it provided the Right-wing (radical) solution to modernity. The elaboration of a new vision of the world, of a new society not founded upon the modification of the socioeconomic setting (even if corporatism attempted to), while based upon an ethic and spiritual revolt against liberal democracy, makes fascism a revolutionary movement. However, 'its ultra-nationalism, anti-egalitarianism, hostility to internationalistic socialism, collusion with traditional Right-wing or conservative forces and constant appeal to primordial "spiritual" values, all point to the conclusion that fascism belongs to the extended family of Rightist ideologies' (Griffin 1993: 49). One can thus agree that: '*fascism is a genus of modern, revolutionary "mass" politics which, . . . draws its internal cohesion and driving force from a core myth that a period of perceived national decadence is giving way to one of rebirth and renewal in a post-liberal order* (Griffin 1998: 14); or differently, 'a form of thought which preaches the need for social rebirth in order to forge a *holistic-national radical Third Way* (Eatwell 1996*b*: 313, 1997: 14).

In conclusion, 'generic fascism' (Eatwell 1992*a*) is a Right-wing ideology built on different and even contrasting materials. The 'fascist synthesis' attempted, in fact, to merge the pessimistic vision of human nature with a vitalist thrust, confidence in and service of Christianity with a creeping paganism, private property defence with welfarism, the commitment to science with anti-rationalism and voluntarism (Eatwell 1992*a*: 189). However diverging the *original* pieces of fascism's ideological puzzle were, nevertheless, an intellectually solidly world-view was provided.

More specifically, we conclude this section by considering the ideas of 'the' ideologue—if any exists—of fascism, the prominent Italian philosopher, Giovanni Gentile. Starting from the Hegelian approach, Gentile identified the ultimate source of legitimacy in the State. Fascism had the historical goal of overcoming the 'traumatic' cleavage between the citizen and the State introduced by liberalism and bourgeois society. Modern society has displaced man by disrupting his social communitarian bonds through individualism, mechanization, and materialism; moreover, modernity has separated him from the state through the individual divisive mechanism of representation (Sasso 1998). Writing for Mussolini's entry on *Fascismo* in the authoritative *Enciclopedia Italiana* (1932), Gentile stated that 'Liberalism denied the State in the name of the individual, fascism reasserts the right of the State as expressing the real essence of the individual'. The only and real freedom is within the state: the individual could find real freedom only when he feels 'beating in his heart the superior interest of the community and the sovereign will of the State' (Gentile 1925: 52). In his famous words, 'the highest level of freedom coincides with the highest level of the State's power'.

In the process of the fascist ideology's formation, many different inputs merged, but once the regime was established, the theoretical construction of the 'ethical State', implemented through the contributions of the jurists Alfredo Rocco and Carlo Costamagna and of the corporatist Ugo Spirito, became the official ideology (Zunino 1985; E. Gentile 1995, 1996). The path followed by Italian fascism is not so different from the other national variants and regimes, including Nazism.

At the end of this short journey around the ideological traditions of the Right, fascism and conservatism stand as key references, while traditionalism is dramatically less important. But these two political traditions are totally different, without any shared elements. The overlap between fascism and conservatism is widely sustained by the Marxist–third-internationalist historiography—fascism as the armed wing of the bourgeoisie—on the basis, beyond common anti-socialism, of the cooperative relationships among fascists and conservative groups in the first post-war period in the process of the conquest of power by the fascists (Blinkhorn 1990). Also, the recall to traditions, to a great and heroic past (the Romanity for fascism, the Aryan mythology for Nazism) (Visser 1992) could constitute, at first sight, a point of contact (Griffin 1993: 49). However, with regard to the latter aspect, there are great differences: while for the conservatives the recall to the past involves a codification and an assessment of stable and solid anchorage, for the fascists it constitutes just a platform on which to build the new order. Even more, Payne (1980, 1995) suggests that fascism is essentially anti-conservative. In particular, he points to the cleavage with the 'conservative authoritarian Right' concerning social policy, the uneasiness with mass politics, the turnover of the elite, the break-up with formal rules and traditional institutions (rather than an authoritarian evolution by the conservatives), the thrust for innovations, vitalistic activism, and warfare. The inter-war fascist movements are different from the conservative movements not only because they were more extreme in every sense (Payne 1995: 25) and 'shriller in their nationalism, more plebeian in their social composition, and in their style, less respectful of tradition and of the official and traditional hierarchies, more violent in their behaviour and especially in their anti-Leftism' (Blickhorn 1990: 6), but because, in ideological terms, they belong to another *genus*. After all, a 'political ideology whose mythical essence is, in the varied versions, a palingenetic form of ultra-nationalistic populism' (Griffin 1993: 26) cannot cohabit with an ideology such as the conservative one that has its own gravitational axe in the respect of the existing order and in aversion to change. The vitalistic dynamism and the exaltation of the youth against the old, decadent, corrupt democratic–bourgeois system—a set of feelings that Pierre Drieu la Rochelle masterfully described in his novel *Gilles*—aim at a complete turnover, a new world, even a new man.

To sum up, very different traditions exist inside the Right: the conservative one that emphasizes order and tradition but somewhat accepts modernity, the counter-revolutionary one that rejects modernity and aims at recasting society according to nature, and the fascist one that expresses uneasiness towards civilization and points out utopian solutions to reconstruct a community (or at least a sense of it), in which spiritual rather than material interests are valued.

CONCLUSION

We might conclude this chapter by establishing three major points. The first one states the present validity and salience of the Left–Right dichotomy. Notwithstanding a widely diffused criticism in the intellectual discourse—with the landmark exception of Bobbio's analysis—the distinction still holds true for almost the totality of European electorates. Whatever interpretation one assigns to this persistence—either the constant element pertaining to the terms of Right and Left and their intrinsic nature (the essentialist interpretation), or the flexibility of the terms' meaning, variously portrayed by the mass public and by the intellectuals (the instrumental interpretation), or the anthropological–organic interpretation—the spatial metaphor still holds. Therefore, it could be adopted as a (valid) tool of analysis.

Having validated the hypothesis of the usefulness of the Left–Right dichotomy, the following passage has involved the search for a (or the) meaning(s) of the term 'Right'. At mass public level the 'images' of the Right have multiple facets. Either self-interpreted or suggested by expert analysis, the core of the Right's meaning is not boundless. French history provides highly suggestive interpretations: from the 'defence of power' of the hierarchy, in the revolutionary period, to the linkage with 'the Church and the Castle' and with the 'order' throughout the nineteenth century and beyond. Later, the economic divide, centred on private/public ownership or state intervention/free market, has provided the distinctive element. More recently, the materialist (Inglehart) and authoritarian (Flanagan) attitudes' and values' priority seem to design the political space of the Right in the New Politics paradigm.

In the realm of political ideologies, on the other hand, different styles of thought of the Right have appeared, according to René Rémond: the legitimist, *orléaniste*, and authoritarian-bonapartist Right. The *orléaniste* tradition, both in its conservative and its liberal lineage, covers the Right side of the political space up to the antidemocratic border. Beyond that line begins the realm of the extreme Right. This latter space is occupied by the remaining two traditions, with a quite divergent relevance. The legitimist–traditionalist heritage of the counter-revolutionaries, while revitalized by some thinkers, amongst whom Julius Evola acquired the role of *maître à penser*, plays nowadays a marginal role both in the intellectual domain and in organized political activity. On the other hand, Rémond's authoritarian bonapartistic tendency should be more appropriately translated into 'fascism'. The most recent line of research on fascist ideology has emphasized the element of 'synthesis' among different inspirations. However, fascism is not beyond Right and Left: it brought together a patchwork of different stimuli, but it established itself by self-assigning the role of the Right—as stated by Mussolini (1932) in his famous authoritative definition. Fascism is Right.

However, fascism is an early twentieth century ideology. In the age of post-industrialism and post modernity, fascism no longer fulfils the role of the 'mythical' reference, even at the extreme Right. The crisis of ideology has also hit the Right. As will be shown, fascist ideology has been playing a minor role since the 1980s in shaping the attitudes and moulding the world-view of the extreme Right. A different, less ideologically loaded value set has emerged which has offered a novel setting in the extreme Right area.

2

From Ideologies to Parties

FASCISM AND EXTREME RIGHT

The 'topological' analysis of the political ideologies and traditions, quickly highlighted in the previous chapter, indicated that three main cultural references pertain to the right: *orléanism*, legitimistic counter-revolutionarism, and mass authoritarianism, later epitomized in fascism. These three traditions, including their various sub-headings, have provided the right with intellectual–cultural meaning.

The present study deals with a particular facet of the right—the *'extreme right'*. The ideologies historians and political philosophers have attributed to this term are those of 'counter-revolutionarism' and 'fascism'. The property of 'rightness' of such traditions has already been discussed in the previous chapter, and even the troublesome case of fascism has been assessed: the 'fascist synthesis' was the by-product of right-wing *and* left-wing references (especially anarcho-syndacalist) but the ideological 'solidification' provided by the major fascist theoreticians— Giovanni Gentile on the Italian side and Carl Schmitt on the German side (while the latter was not so organic to the regime as the former)—and the fascist political culture itself denied any legacy from any previous ideology. The 'fascist synthesis', after the 'movement period' (1919–24) in Italy and the Otto Strasser influence in Germany, was skewed towards the right, while advocating the novelty, even the revolutionism, of that right. The present leading scholar on fascism, Emilio Gentile, has described with great skill the peculiarity of the fascist ideology in contrast with the other ideologies: fascism expressed 'a clear and brutal opposition to freedom, equality, happiness and peace as life ideals; . . . it exalted irrationality, the drive of power by the selected minorities, the obedience of the masses, and the sacrifice of the individual to the community, conceived as the state and the nation . . . . The fascists never intended to defend freedom and rationality; . . . fascism never promised emancipation and liberation; sacrifice, austerity, contempt for hedonism and happiness, discipline and unconditioned loyalty' were the necessary and enforced virtues for the power of the state and the nation (Gentile 1996: 8–9). These irrational, mythical, mass-based, *and* individualist-voluntaristic elements were the widely appealing propellants of the fascist ideology.

On the other hand, the counter-revolutionary tradition, while reframed by Julius Evola in the mid-twentieth century, remained circumscribed within a very small circle. Evola fascinated generations of radical right-wingers, but his esoteric and 'impolitic' thinking remained backstage in politics and was never adopted as a political agenda by any party (with the exception of the later British National Front). Rather, his writings were taken to be a type of gospel by those radical groups that engaged in a violent confrontation with the system, mainly in 1970s Italy.

These two intellectual traditions define the ideological space of the extreme right. Issues, attitudes, and world-views of the post-war extreme right are closely connected with those traditions, *or rather, they were for a long time, until the 1980s.*

For more than three decades, apart from the minuscule Evolian radical fringe, the post-war extreme right did not offer anything different from fascism's nostalgia, compliance, and reminiscence. This mould was fostered by the domination over the European extreme right family up until the 1980s by the Italian neo-fascist Movimento Sociale Italiano (MSI) (Italian Social Movement). The MSI exercised such an overwhelming influence thanks to its electoral and organizational strength (see Ignazi 1998*a,b*; Tarchi 1997) that the tiny, marginalized, and usually short-lived European extreme right parties could not match. The only partial exception was the German NPD in the very brief time span of the mid-late 1960s. In that period the NPD achieved representation in the *Land* parliaments, but failed to enter the Bundestag. This failure, together with its weak partisan institutionalization, contributed to its rapid collapse, leaving the MSI alone in a dominant position again. Therefore, *the ideological intellectual elaboration provided by the Italian neo fascist milieu and by some other (mainly German) groups, accounts for the 'master' extreme right ideology up to the 1980s.* This does not discard the relevance of the national variants such as, for example, British white suprematism, or the Vichy legacy and François Duprat's original 'national-revolutionary' strategy in France, or the revitalization of the *Konservative Revolution* and the reframing of the national question in Germany, or the ethnic racialism in Flanders. But the mobilizing capacity of the MSI among the intellectuals—beyond any assessment on the quality of their contributions—and the range of activities for implementing the party ideology, was incomparable vis-à-vis the other European partners (for an account see Chiarini 1995, 1999; Tarchi 1997; Ignazi 1998*a*).

It could be concluded that the ideological corpus of the post-war European extreme right was provided *until the 1980s* by the re-interpretation of historic fascism, mainly fostered by the Italian neo-fascist partisan and non-partisan milieu. In short, the common features of the neo-fascist political culture, directly derived from its historical legacy, point to a strong authoritarian state led by a charismatic-like figure, a hierarchical and rigid society, the subordination of the masses to the nation's and/or State's designs, the irrelevance of the individual's will and freedom, the inconceivability of rights beyond the needs of the State, the aversion to any social conflict whatsoever, the overcoming of the workers/owners cleavage in the name of a corporatist societal organization and political representation. The most striking difference between historic and post-war fascism lies in the de-emphasis of the mythical and mobilizing elements, such as the idea of rebirth, palyngenesis, and new order. Fascism's defeat at the hands of liberal-democracy (and communism) and its survival in liberal-democratic societies have fostered, beyond the endurance of an opposition of principle, more bargaining-oriented and rational attitudes. In the MSI propaganda, for example, one can find nostalgia for the past (fascist) regime rather than vitalistic *élan* against the present (democratic) regime (Chiarini 1999). Moreover, there has been an amazing lack of theorizing within the post-war extreme right. Even the notable exceptions of Adriano Romualdi, Pino Rauti, and Enzo Erra in Italy, of François Duprat in France and of the late Oswald Mosley in Great Britain, did not modify the core elements of the fascist 'ideological morphology' (to adopt Michael Freeden's (1996) terminology).

THE NEW CULTURAL SETTING

A turning point occurred in the 1980s. In that period a new set of ideas entered the political cultural discourse of the right fostered by neo-conservatism and— more marginally—the *Nouvelle Droite* (ND). These two new *courants ideologiques* influenced the extreme right, while they are not part of it (even if the latter is not so unambiguously distinct as the former). Fascism and its variants no longer remained the unique cultural sources.

As far as the *Nouvelle Droite* is concerned, it could be assessed as a tiny but vivid and over-ambitious group of intellectuals, originating in France and Italy (with a very close inter-relationship between the two), and then in Belgium, Germany, and Austria. It basically aimed at distancing itself from the original neo-fascist milieu, arguing for a new 'thinking' of the right (Tassani 1986; Taguieff 1983). This movement found its intellectual laboratory in the Groupment de Recherches et d'Etudes pour la Civilisation Européenne (GRECE) (Research and Study Group for the European Civilisation) circle and the related journal '*Nouvelle Ecole*', which were both founded by the French philosopher Alain de Benoist in 1968. The *Nouvelle Droite* gained a sudden audience in the late 1970s when Alain de Benoist became editor of the '*Figaro magazine*', a conservative magazine with a very large readership. For a couple of years the ideas elaborated by the GRECE circle found ample circulation and propagated beyond France, first and foremost in Italy, then in other countries.

De Benoist pointed out the ND's distinctiveness from the other ideologies very clearly by highlighting a series of unacceptable 'deviations': 'the nationalistic deviation with all its prejudices, its xenophobia . . . ; the all-economic deviation with its abstract liberalism, its implicit egalitarianism and its social injustices; the totalitarian deviation with its nostalgia, its authoritarian phantoms, its myth of the providential leader; the traditionalist deviation with its reactionary dreams, its metaphysical references, its innate passatism' (de Benoist 1983: 19–20). Synthetically, the *Nouvelle Droite* is characterized by the refusal of liberalism for its supposed reduction of every relationship to commodity; the hostility to the Westernization of the world, and the American political–cultural hegemony that entail the levelling of every difference and the annihilation of the 'natural communities'; the search for different means of participation rather than the liberal democratic ones; the aim at overcoming the traditional cleavages crystallized in the left–right divide; the rejection of egalitarianism, which is the inevitable by-product of the conjugation of liberal individualism and mass society. Regarding the last point, the hostility to the ongoing egalitarian drive in Western societies implies, for the ND, a *positive* evaluation of the differences rather than their stigmatization; and, in fact, the ND declared itself—at the cost of some internal bickering—to be against racism in any form, disguised or not.

More recently, the focus of the reflection of the *Nouvelle Droite* was directed upon 'anti-utilitarianism', that is, the opposition to a mercantilist conception of the social relationships which is considered the inevitable outcome of the triumph of liberalism. The anti-utilitarism polemic led de Benoist to question also the acceptability of modernity. In fact, de Benoist (1992: 45–7) stated that 'the traditional societies have their drawbacks. Modernity has others that are even worse. Modernity has replaced some visible, ascertainable constraints with abstract alienation and structural constraints. It pretended to make man independent; on the other hand it has isolated him, leaving him more vulnerable, more extraneous to his fellow man than ever . . . . It has replaced the oligarchy of money to the ascriptive inequalities'. This anti-modern perspective leads to a 'non-liberal' interpretation of representation, where 'the identity between the general will and the law, the identity of views among governors and governed' stems naturally from the bottom of organic communities, and provides for the 'true essence' of democracy. To sum up, while excluding any form of coercion and authoritarianism, the ND calls for an organic society, harmonic and non-conflicting, in which the individual dissent from the general will is not foreseen (otherwise liberal individualism, with all its damage, should find room). The anti-liberal standing of ND is unambiguous: de Benoist clearly maintained: 'I don't believe that political liberalism is the ideology or the system that better guarantees authentic individual liberties' (de Benoist 1992: 46).

A variant of the French–Italian original mould of the *Nouvelle Droite* has been provided by the German speaking area. In Germany, the debate on the national question—the *Historikerstreit*—emerged in the mid-1980s, and gave the opportunity to a group of right-wing anti-liberal intellectuals to create a cultural network, which had been limited up until then to a few journals such as *Criticón*, founded in 1970 by Caspar von Schrenck-Notzing. This network adopted many themes of the French–Italian *Nouvelle Droite,* conjugated with a particular concern over the German national question, and found its outspoken interpreters in the journal *Junge Freiheit* (founded in 1990) and in the leading writer Botho Strauss.

The same concern over the national identity and the recasting of the natural local community threatened by the 'American political–cultural dominance' characterizes also the Austrian and Belgian ND circles.

The ND, despite its minuscule dimension and its very limited direct impact on the political discourse in the various countries, has nevertheless produced a series of interpretations and intellectual tools that, *beyond the intentions of the Nouvelle Droite itself*, have been reframed and adopted by the extreme right parties. In particular, the argument for the 'right to difference' against the massification of contemporary society has been taken up as the cornerstone for the 'new racism' propagated by the extreme right. The exclusionary politics advocated by these parties is indebted to the ND theorizing (Taguieff 1994). And the same goes for the development of a *völkisch* (people's community) framing of the national question, especially in the germanophone area nurtured *also* by the ND's exaltation of the natural, homogeneous community.

The second, more powerful while *totally unconscious*, source of intellectual mould for the extreme right has been provided by neo-conservatism. A landmark change in the Western societies' cultural mood was provided by the reformulation of (mainly) American and British conservatism in the 1980s (Steinfels 1979; Bell 1980; Girvin 1988; O'Sullivan 1989; Devigne 1993). This parallel evolution took place in the late seventies, moving on from the dissatisfaction towards the socioeconomic Keynesian compromise, the (consequent) ample State intervention over the economic and social spheres, the excessive power conferred on trade unions and militant minorities, the cost of the welfare state especially in terms of high levels of taxation, and the loss of traditional values. The desire to counteract the trend of Great Britain's economic, social, and moral decline stimulated intellectual circles, ranging from the Salisbury Group to the Centre for Policy Studies and the Institute of Economic Affairs, to reframe the conservative agenda by rejecting the 'old conservative' paternalism, love for quiescence, harmony, and unity, and emphasizing instead individual self-reliance and self-confidence. These shifts in value priorities inevitabily produced some theoretical imbalances. The introduction of the market as a central tenet in the neo-conservative agenda is in line with the 'extra-human volition' of traditional conservatism: it refers to an entity which is beyond the human will; however, it introduces an economic and trans-national reference instead of the previous national (British), traditional, and natural order. The 'good society' forecasted by neo-conservatism is no longer encroached in the British tradition. The individualism connected with the novel emphasis on the market is justified by the fact that, if the economy has to be revitalized, market forces should be freed; by consequence individual incentives acquire a high priority. This contradicts the basic tenets of the old conservative pre-eminence of society and natural order over entrepreneuriality, but it does not go further with its ultimate libertarian implications. The neo-conservatives, in fact, insert this new individualism within the 'package' of social order, hierarchy, and submission to authority.

The American counterpart, centred at first around the Hoover Institute and the Heritage Foundation, differs from the British revision of conservatism on two main points: the role of the USA in the international arena and the reaction to the post-materialist agenda. American neo-conservatism is much more stimulated than the British one by its reaction to the intellectual hegemony of the New Deal tradition reinforced by the counter-cultural generation of the 1960s. The lack of a solid welfare system and the relative degree of State intervention in the economy were supplanted in the their role of anti-leftist mobilizing agents by the diffusion of a left–libertarian agenda. The moral traditional values, national pride, and tradition, have high priority in the American neo-conservative thought. On the same path, the small community is juxtaposed with the national/central state because it provides an organic solidarity instead of the atomized citizenship offered by the national institutions. The community, moreover, guarantees the preservation of the differences against massification and the universalist trend. The intrinsic rejection of multiculturalism in this thinking, and the repudiation of the individual will and choice on issues of public morality, may lead, in 'its unsophisticated form, . . . to a type of populism, concrete and irrational' (Freedan 1996: 405). The opening up of market forces affects the conception of social justice (Devigne 1993: 118), with the difference that British neo-conservatism emphasizes 'rule-governed morality' implemented by State-enforced obligations, while the American one relies upon a bottom-developed substantive morality to protect individual freedom. The moral recasting in contrast to post-material issues, the broadening of the authority and autonomy of the central State to counter an exceedingly participatory society, the expansion of the market role in society, individualism, and entreprenerialism to reverse the collectivist and welfarist trend, and the undesirability of a multicultural society as opposed to a communitarian homogeneous society, are the main characteristics of the neo-conservative cultural wave which acquired cultural hegemony in the 1980s—first in the Anglo-American domain, then, later on, all over Europe.

Basically, neo-conservatism differs from the old conservatism due to its popular and mass appeal, a meritocratic rather than elitist principle, preference for market and individualism instead of organicism, its radical standings rather than *juste milieu* patterning, and its (difficult) encounter with liberalism while sharply opposing post-material libertarianism (Girvin 1988; Eatwell 1989). These ideas, purported by solid cultural milieu and somewhat enforced by the Reagan and Thatcher governments, gained widespread circulation, moving the European 'moderate' parties' manifestos more to the right (Klingemann 1995) in order to attract a more conservative-oriented electorate. In the domain of ideas, neo-conservatism brought novel issues to the fore, such as moral traditionalism against the 'new politics' post-material issues, State enforcement, the recasting of national pride, communitarianism (sometimes veiled as organicism), and the uneasiness with a multicultural society, which will find *a much more radical* framing by the new political actors developed on the right of the conservative parties since the 1980s.

In conclusion, neo-conservatism and, to a very minor extent, the *Nouvelle Droite* represented the innovative character of right-wing thinking throughout Western countries. These two intellectual movements, but especially neo-conservatism, had nothing in common with the extreme right ideology represented up to then by fascism. However, since the 1980s, right-wing political entrepreneurs were able to both exploit favourable 'opportunity structures' and frame their discourse within a new *koiné*, which blended some of the right-extremist traditional references with the interpretation of society fostered by the new right thinking. The 'right to difference', for example, was adopted to argue the exclusionary anti-immigrant politics in a non-biological form; the national question was reframed to provide consistency with the nationalistic themes and the out-group hostility; traditional moral issues were reinforced to urge more general anti-civil-rights standings; state enforcement was strengthened to invoke tough law and order provisions (including the death penalty); and, finally, laissez-faire pro-market entrepreneurialism, and individualism were exploited, even if their advocacy was limited to the very beginning of the extreme right parties' rise.

The 1980s' ideological turn fertilized the soil for the potential growth of even more radical parties than the traditional conservative ones. The mechanics of such development and the reciprocal inter-relationships will be discussed in the final chapter.

THE EXTREME RIGHT PARTIES: DEFINITIONS AND BOUNDARIES

After having discussed what the ideological legacies and sources of the extreme right are, it is time to look at the effective components of the extreme right itself. More precisely, *the focus is directed upon the parties*, those (somewhat stable) organizations that regularly compete for elections in Western Europe. The small circles, the loosely organized groups, the skinhead movement, the 'Szene', and similar groups are not taken into account in this analysis.

The first point deals with the methodology for identifying the parties pertaining to the extreme right 'family'.

Until the beginning of the nineties, the extreme right parties never attracted particular attention. With the notable exception of Christopher Husbands' (1981) pioneering overview, the first comparative account was edited by Klaus von Beyme in 1988. In the introductory essay of the volume, von Beyme lamented the difficulty in assessing a common ground for these parties. In fact, the classification by party families had not devoted much attention to the extreme right by labelling it either as neo-fascist or treating it as a sort of residual category. Even a very accurate classification by party family, fostered by Daniel Seiler (1980, 1985, 1986), had not provided sufficiently clear insights.

Much of the attention was devoted to the identification of the *individual's 'extreme rightist' attitudes* impinging on the seminal Adorno *et al. The authoritarian personality* (Adorno *et al.* 1950). German and Anglo-Saxon literature has been particularly concentrated on this individual-level perspective. The numerous studies assessing 'extreme right potential', since the famous research by the German research institute SINUS in 1980 and the repeated attempts at refining and validating the Adorno *et al.* 'F-scale', have produced a reliable inventory of attitudinal traits related to the right-extremism which all ranged around the classical elements of dogmatism, rigidity, exclusionism, authoritarianism, nationalism, anti-permissivism, xenophobia, racism, intolerance, and so on. But all this referred to an *individual-level* analysis.

If one takes the party as the unit of analysis, the classification by party family follows a different path from the voters' attitudes. In this vein, two major approaches exist: one based on structural societal cleavages along Rokkan's framework, adopted and variously refined especially by Seiler; the other based on the ideological criterion along the pioneering Duverger's suggestion (see Mair and Mudde 1998).

Following the latter approach, internal sources (manifestos, platforms, internal press, leaders' speeches, and writings) provide the material to build on the party's identity. On this basis some authors have pinpointed the basic traits of a 'right-extremist' party, so that all the parties which share those traits could belong to the extreme right family. There are several examples: Backes and Jesse (1993: 474) highlighted 'the antidemocratic dispositions and attempts that are traditionally positioned at the extreme 'right' of the left–right continuum'; Backes (2001) further elaborated on the aspects of extremism and rightwardness, both impinged on the refusal of the moral principle of equality of man; Betz (1994: 413) underlined the 'rejection of socio-cultural and socio-political systems . . . and of individual and social equality'; Fennema (1997: 483–6) pinpointed ethnic nationalism, anti-materialism, anti-parliamentary, and conspiracy theory; and, finally, Kitschelt (1995*b*: 4–5, 25), somewhat influenced by the structural tradition, identified the 'new radical right' parties on the basis of their location on three dimensions: citizenship (cosmopolitan versus particularistic), collective decision modes (libertarian versus authoritarian), and allocation of resources (redistributive versus market-liberal). These few examples—amongst the copious literature—all have in common the attempt to discover the ideological core of right-extremism. Actually, Mudde (1996) counted 58 different features of right extremism out of 28 authors and Druwe and Mantino (1996) counted 42 out of 11 German studies. According to Mudde, five features are common to almost all the authors surveyed: nationalism, racism, xenophobia, anti-democracy, and a strong state (see also Mudde 2000).

As will be discussed *infra*, our core features of right extremism do not diverge that much. On the other hand, what singles out our analysis is the methodology: rather than listing the 'basic traits', we will first control whether the party's ideology refers either to one of the established right-extremist traditions of thought (ideology in a strong meaning) or presents an anti-system discourse (ideology in a weak meaning).

Before suggesting our classificatory grid, we would argue the reasons for the usage of the term 'extreme right' rather than one of its rival terms circulating in the literature on the subject: radical right, new right, populist right.

'Radical right' has an ambiguous connotation due to its original American use and its peculiar meaning in the German context. On the one hand, this term was introduced in the pioneering study by Daniel Bell in *The Radical Right* (1963) (a revision of the 1955 book *The New American Right*) and fostered by Lipset and Raab's *The Politics of Unreason* and Richard Hofstedter's *The Paranoid Style in American Politics*. Two main difficulties arise from these studies. First, radical right refers to both the Birch Society and McCarthyism, which are associations and movements rather than parties, and have been later convincingly labelled 'extreme conservative' instead of extreme right (Kolckey 1983: 35ff). Despite the fact that they are characterized by a strict moral traditionalism and an obsessive anticommunism, they could not be considered anti-system (Himmelstein 1990: 73ff). Secondly, the radical right is identified through individuals' personality traits rather than through a set of political values. Since radical right refers to a unique context (late 1940s–early 1950s America), to psychological traits, and to non-partisan organizations which are not unambiguously 'anti-system', this definition is too ideographic and too loose to account for right-wing political organizations in contemporary Europe.

On the other hand, radical right has been used to designate those movements and groups which found their ideological mould in the counter-revolutionary anti-modern tradition of thought (from Joseph de Maistre down to Julius Evola) and which boasted and even (tried to) adopt violent means, right up to terrorist actions (Ferraresi 1995). Following this approach, the radical right would tap a very limited sector of contemporary right wing extremism.

Therefore, none of the two original approaches of the term radical right could be fruitfully applied to the analysis of extreme right parties.

The preference for *extreme* rather than *radical* stems also from the thorough discussion in the German literature on the subject. The study of *rechtsradikalismus* since the seminal work by Scheuch and Klingemann (1967) has been refined on the basis of the assessment of loyalty to the constitutional order. The analyses worked on by the Office for the Protection of the Constitution since the early 1970s have defined the *radikalismus* as a radical critique on the constitutional order without any anti-democratic meaning or intention, while the *extremismus* defines an anti-democratic, anti-liberal, and anti-constitutional approach (Ueltzhöffer 1992; Backes and Jesse 1993; Minkenberg 1998a; Backes 2001). Actually, with the exception of the German studies, the employment of this term has been rather blind up to the point that it has been considered interchangeable with 'extreme right' (Weinberg 1993: 4), and even the most ambitious single-author work (Kitschelt 1995b) on the theme does not argue for the preference accorded to this term.

The use of 'New Right' has raised even more confusion. New Right indicates a cultural movement sustained by some think-tanks and publishing enterprises which originated from and operate within the conservative political space. The French version of the term, *Nouvelle Droite*, is even more specific (see *supra*) as it connotes a tiny group of intellectuals attempting to revise and readdress a right-wing cultural map. The *Nouvelle Droite* is similar to the New Right because of its reference to the cultural domain, but it does not share anything in terms of values or world-view. To summarize in a sentence, the former is anti-liberal and anti-statist, the latter anti-statist but pro-liberal. The term New Right is therefore misleading as it pertains to a cultural domain and does not convey extremist anti-system ideas.

A term which has found a wide audience in the most recent literature is 'populism'. Hans-Georg Betz (1993, 1994) introduced it, defining the 'radical right-wing populist' parties beyond their radicalism and rightism, due to their 'unscrupulous use and instrumentalization of diffuse public sentiments of anxiety and disenchantment, and their appeal to the common man and his allegedly superior common sense' (Betz 1994: 4). More recently, Betz and Immerfall (1998a: 3) have argued that 'pragmatic radicalism and populist appeal better tap the nature of contemporary right rather than the nature of right-wing extremism'. In the same vein, by 'New Populism' Paul Taggart (1993, 1995, 1996) identifies parties that are 'ideologically . . . on the right, anti-system in orientation, and claim[ing] to be speaking for the "mainstream" of society; organisationally . . . characterised by strongly centralised structures with charismatic and personalised leadership . . . ; and electorally . . . are disproportionately male, employed in the private sector, young and coming from a wide range of political orientation' (Taggart 1993: 8; also 1995: 36). The emphasis here is on the party organization and the political style (see also Ivaldi 1998b on this aspect), two analytical elements that differ from the ideological features alone. Analogously, Pfahl-Traughber utilizes the category of populism in order to define those 'modernizing right-wing parties' which appeal to resentments, prejudices, and traditional values and offer simplistic and unrealistic solutions to the socio-political problems (1993, 1994: 17–20). Finally, Herbert Kitschelt identifies a subcategory of the 'new radical right' in those 'populist anti-statist appeals [which] are primarily directed against "big government" and the "political class" ' (1995b: 21). On the other hand, the French scholars introduced the term 'national-populism', from the pioneering analysis by Pierre-André Taguieff (1984, 1986a, 1997) up to the most recent contributions of Pascal Perrineau (1997), Michel Winock (1997), and Pierre Milza (1992, 1994), by combining the nationalistic element together with the classical populist features.

However, populism is a multifaceted phenomenon according to the meaning attributed to its ultimate source of legitimacy, that is to say, the people (Mény and Surel 2000). Where 'the people' is interpreted sociologically—the people-class—the locus is in the lower, powerless part of society; where it is interpreted on a cultural basis—the people-nation—the basis is in the ethno-culturally homogeneous *volkisch* community; but where it is interpreted as the ultimate and legitimate source of representation and decision-making process—the people-sovereign—the locus is the citizenry at large (Mény and Surel (2000): 180ff). Populism sprung up for a lament for the poor functioning of democracy not for its negation. In fact, only the first two interpretations of populism might be referred to the anti-system and right-extremist position, while the third is fully consistent with democracy.

In conclusion it could be said that populism runs counter to an excessive level of denotation for its adoption in the analysis of the radical/extremist right: the properties suggested by the above mentioned studies for characterizing this kind of party—the leadership style, the organizational structure, the electoral profile—do not tap the cases under scrutiny. No specific organizational feature character-izes the extreme right parties: the old militia type suggested by Duverger (1951) for the fascist parties no longer holds; no leadership style pertains exclusively to the extreme right parties because 'personalization' and appeal to the people is spreading within all parties (von Beyme 1996), even if the extreme right parties bring this feature to the highest point with a mix of *Führerprinzip* and charismatic appeal; no specific electorate profile connotes the extreme right parties (while a recent trend towards its proletarization is underway). Moreover, populism is a more general concept. As Mény and Surel (2000) have brilliantly pinpointed, populism does not entail, a priori, anti-democratic standings: it is strictly related to democ-racy, it is the other side of the same coin, and it should therefore be disentangled from its right-wing location. For all of these reasons—inapplicability of the orga-nizational style and sociological characteristics, and the combination of pro-system and anti-system types—the preference will lead to the term extreme right (in the same vein see Hainsworth 2000: 6–7).

While the terms 'radicalism', 'populism', and 'new right' present various pit-falls, on the other hand the term 'extreme' offers a series of advantages. First, it recalls the notion of extremeness in a political and ideological *space*: extreme right denotes those *issues* and *organizations* that are close to one extreme of the political spectrum. Secondly, the extremeness is related to 'anti-system' value-sets.

If we adopt this approach, it follows that the extreme right parties' family is ascer-tained through a double screening on its *location* in the political spectrum and on its *ideology*. The first screening treats the left–right continuum as an approximate rule of thumb for differentiating the extreme right from the 'conservatives' *latu senso*. It assesses the 'right extremeness' of a party: it controls whether the party is located close to the extreme right of the political spectrum or, at least, *more rightward than any other party*. The second one has higher priority because the 'nature' of the party is provided by its *identity* (Harmel and Janda 1994), and, in turn, its identity is given by either a combination of sophisticated theorizing and recall of thinkers and cultural traditions at a high level of ideological construction, or by a set of less structured myths, symbols, beliefs, attitudes, issues, and policies. All these aspects, at their respective level of cultural sophistication, identify the party's ideology.

CRITERIA OF CLASSIFICATION

Following this two-step approach we are nevertheless confronted with some difficulties. The first step postulates that the extreme right parties are located at the right extremity of the spatial continuum. But, having stated this, two questions arise. How far to the right should they stay? And: is there a precise position marking the border between extreme and moderate right? The answer to both questions is that there is no fixed, clear-cut mark-point on the continuum. As each party position is given by the interaction with the other parties, it varies from party-system to party-system. Moreover, not all the parties that are spatially located to the right end of the continuum belong to the political family of the extreme right. Some right-most parties like the *Nea Demokratia* in Greece, the *Moderatarna* in Sweden (up to the 1990s), the *Partido Popular* in Spain, and the *Fine Gael* in Ireland (Knutsen 1998) have nothing to share with fascism or right extremism. The position on the continuum alone is thus insufficient to build up a party family. It represents only the *first* criterion of classification, a sort of preliminary screening.

It is necessary then to pass to the second criterion, the party's ideology. We have to verify first if the party makes reference to one of the intellectual traditions of thought of the extreme right, that is to say fascism or, much more unlikely, counter-revolutionary traditionalism. The legacy of fascism can be ascertained by the more or less overt recall of myths, symbols, and slogans, as well as the explicit reference to fascist ideology (or part of it). Whereas a total overthrowing of the system, a search for a palyngenetic rebirth, a corporatist socio-economic and representative system, and a 'new order' beyond the old political and social systems, are forecasted, there the reference to fascist ideology is unambiguous. The manifest visible presence of these traits constitutes a valid indicator of belonging to the fascist ideology. But the absence of such manifest traits does not disqualify a party from its belonging: in fact, some extreme right parties might follow a strategy of minimizing and setting aside any overt reference to fascism to avoid an highly probable, immediate stigmatization by public opinion. These parties tend to adopt a strategy of 'esoteric and exoteric appeal' in relation to the different (internal or external) audiences (Eatwell 1992*a*: 174; see also Linz 1978: 34). By concluding, the parties are included in the category of the extreme right if they recall cornerstone elements of fascist ideology, by expressing regret for the glorious inter-war past, by exhibiting that symbolism and phraseology, and finally, by invoking a 'third way' beyond capitalism and communism.

If fascism's legacy were the only criterion, the extreme right would coincide with neo-fascism and appear even more limited than ever, because the neo-fascist party par excellence—the Italian MSI—has recently undergone a profound transformation leading to a probable exit from the extreme right itself; and the MSI exit is not counterbalanced by any other parties' emergence, so that this group comprises the Italian MS–FT, the British BNP, the German NPD, and the now moribund Dutch CP'86, while the Belgian Vlaamas Blok and the German DVU are on the fringes.

Instead, the largest part of the extreme right, the newly born or refounded parties such as the French FN, the German Republikaner, the Belgian FN, the Dutch CD, the Austrian FPÖ, the Swiss SD, FDU, and Autopartei, the Danish FRP and DFPd, the Norwegian FRPn, the Swedish 'flash' party, NyD—and, while included (see *infra*), the Italian North League—*deny any lineage with historic fascism*. Why do they therefore enter the political family of the extreme right? Because they manifest an ideology (in a weak sense of the word) that, while not structured and articulated as in the case of fascism, contains a series of values and attitudes radically opposed to those that the respective political systems are founded upon.

This point raises the question of the mode of opposition: when does an opposition become anti-system? A tentative solution to this problem could be suggested on the basis of some authoritative speculations. Otto Kirchheimer (1966: 237) identified two ideal-types of opposition: the opposition of principle, where 'goal displacement is incompatible with the constitutional requirements of a given system'; and the loyal opposition, which implies just a 'goal differentiation'. Giovanni Sartori (1976: 133), who introduced the concept of the anti-system party, depicted it as the one whose aim consists in undermining the legitimacy of the democratic regime, and which expresses 'a belief system that does not share the values of the political order within which it operates'. Juan Linz (1978: 32–33) advanced the notion of 'semi-loyal opposition' which is willing to 'encourage, tolerate, cover up, treat leniently, excuse or justify' whatever action, even violent ones, performed by extremist groups. More recently, Gordon Smith (1987: 63–64; see also Zariski 1986) proposed a typology which combines 'compatibility of aims and acceptability of behaviour' and underlined the existence of a 'grey zone of acceptability' according to different time and context; in other terms, what is rated 'incompatible with the system in one era may be accommodated in other'. Finally, Andreas Schleder (1996: 303) argued for a distinction between anti-system and anti-political-establishment opposition; the latter 'focuses its attacks not on incumbent governments, but on all parties, government and opposition alike'. While 'anti-establishment actors profess to accept the basic rules of the constitutional game', they may 'wrap their antidemocratic attacks in democratic clothes, fashionable and presentable' (Schleder 1996: 304). In other words, the disloyal opposition tries to 'mask' its inner drive. Following these insights (see Capoccia 2002), we can conclude that most of the present extreme right parties display *non-compatibility of aims and acceptability of behaviour*. The refusal of violence, the advocation of freedom (for the natives, at least), and the practice of democratic representative institutions represent the standard style of the extreme right; *but it is in contrast with their 'esoteric' discourse and real behaviour* (Betz and Immerfall 1998a: 3).

Summing up, extreme right parties should exhibit an 'opposition of principle', via a well-constructed ideology or a rather loose 'mentality', undermining the constitutional rules of the democratic system. Fascism, the extreme right ideology par excellence, is, by any standard, alien and extraneous to liberal democratic systems. However, where the reference to this ideology does not exist, the presence of anti-system political attitudes and beliefs should be investigated. Many rightmost *non-fascist* parties share common features which are clearly anti-system, summarized as anti-parliamentarianism, anti-pluralism, and anti-partyism (for an empirical test, see Gabriel 1996). More generally, their opposition is inspired by a repulsion of divisions and a search for harmony, an emphasis of natural community and a hostility towards foreigners, a faith in hierarchical structures and a distrust for democratic individual representation, a rejection of 'unnatural' egalitarianism and the primacy of the *ethnos*, a call for unbounded authority, and leadership and the recasting of a strong state. The presence of specific traits such as xenophobia, racism, and nationalism in most of the contemporary extreme right parties further specifies the general syndrome of anti-systemness, but these traits are not sufficient per se to identify the more complex 'ideology' of the extreme right parties.

As *supra* underlined, almost all extreme right parties do not openly advocate a non-democratic institutional setting; on the contrary, it is easy to find ritual homage to the democratic principles in their official statements and documents. Nevertheless they *undermine* system legitimacy. Although they do not share any nostalgia for the inter-war fascist experiences, and may even refuse any reference to fascism, they express anti-system values throughout their political discourse. Annvi Gardberg (1993: 32) aptly stated that the political culture of the extreme right can be interpreted as a 'subversive stream that is anti-egalitarian and anti-pluralist and that opposes the principle of democratic constitutional states'.

In short, on the basis of the spatial, ideological, attitudinal criteria, we can present a *typology where parties more on the right of the political spectrum are categorized according to the presence or absence of a fascist legacy and to the acceptance or refusal of the political system*. In order to be included in the extreme right party family, the most right-wing parties should either fulfil the ideological fascist criterion, *or* exhibit a delegitimizing patterning on the political system, through a set of issues, values, and attitudes (rather than a structured and coherent ideology). If a party fits the ideological criterion (and, *a fortiori*, the attitudinal-systemic one), we can think of it as belonging to the old, *traditional*, neo-fascist type. If a party is not linked to fascism but has an anti-system profile, we can think of it as belonging to the new, *post-industrial* type.

THE TWO TYPES OF EXTREME RIGHT PARTIES:
TRADITIONAL AND POST-INDUSTRIAL

To sum up, the class of extreme right parties is divided into two types, depending on whether or not they are linked to fascist ideology. The *traditional* extreme right parties are the guardians of nostalgia. They are the heirs of the conflicts derived by the development of the industrial society when, in the 1920s and 1930s, the divergent social groups clashed violently on the question of resource allocation. The fascist parties, like the communist ones, are by-products of the industrial revolution.

The context and the conditions of the birth of the extreme right parties of the 1980s are quite different. They display a system de-legitimizing discourse, but they do not reflect the mere revival of the conflicts of the inter-war period. On the contrary, these parties are defined as *post-industrial* because they are by-products of the conflicts of the post-industrial society, where material interests are no longer so central, and the bourgeoisie and working class are neither so neatly defined nor so radically antagonistic. The post-war economic and cultural transformations have blurred class identification and loosened traditional loyalties linked to precise social groups. The development of the service sector, the decline of the capability of labour relations to determine social relations, and the process of atomization and secularization, have all nurtured different cleavages and aggregations. Sectors of the traditional working class and of the scarcely educated middle-class now face the unionized working class and the new middle-class in a conflict that has values at its core, rather than material interests. The conflict over the distribution of resources leaves room for value allocation. In this passage, the post-industrial society takes form while bringing together the post-materialist values which emphasize the non-material issues of self-realization and identity.

The established parties tried to give an answer to such changes but, inevitably, new actors respond better than old ones to new challenges. In fact, in the 1980s, two kinds of parties emerged on the opposite sides of the political spectrum, the ecologist-libertarian of the left and the (new) extreme right parties: both are the offspring of the 'silent revolution' and of the post-industrial society. The extreme right-wing parties that developed lately, instead of reviving the 'palingenetic myth' of fascism, offered an answer to the demands and needs generated by post-industrialism and not satisfied by traditional parties. As will be discussed in the last chapter, some of these demands and needs converge in the defence of the natural community, at national or sub-national levels, from alien and polluting presences—hence racism and xenophobia—and respond to the identity crisis produced by atomization at the societal level, by globalization at the economic level, and by supra-nationalism at the political level (Baumann 1998; Beck 1998). On the other hand, the demand for more law and order, the search for a 'charismatic' leader, the need for harmony and security, and the uneasiness over representative mechanisms and procedures, express a desire for an authoritative guide in a society where self-achievement and individualism have disrupted the protective network of traditional social bonds. Finally, the return of rigid moral standards is a definite counterpart of post-materialist libertarianism. Not one of the new extreme right parties points to a corporatist architecture of society, or to a 'new order', but rather to a mixture, often dazzling and fallacious, of free enterprise and social protection (limited to the native), of modernizing inputs and traditional reminiscences. This second group of extreme right parties is the unexpected outcome of post-materialism; hence their label of 'post-material extreme right'.

3

Italy: The Faded Beacon and the Populist Surge

Fascism is an Italian by-product. While the intellectual incubation of fascism may be traced back to French *fin de siècle* anti-republican thinking (Sternhell 1976*b*, 1989), it found its utmost concrete, complete, and long-lasting realization in inter-war Italy from 1922 until 1943–5. Fascism in Italy was deeply embedded due to the large network of fascist associations (E. Gentile 1995) and the massive, consensual adhesion to the regime, especially in the mid-1930s (De Felice 1975, 1981). The fascist regime collapsed with the 1943–5 civil war. This was fought in the centre-north of Italy between those loyal to Mussolini's pro-Germany new regime—the Italian Social Republic (Repubblica Sociale Italiana), founded in the north of Italy after Mussolini's dismissal (and brief imprisonment) by the King on 25 July 1943—and the anti-fascists, along with a sizeable portion of the Army loyal to the Crown.

The ending of the regime through a civil war, unlike Germany and Austria, implied a very deep and emotionally loaded divide between the fascist and antifascist camps. It is not surprising that the fascist political presence in post-war Italy had long been regarded as 'illegitimate' because it was reputed as *contrary in itself* to the democratic, anti-fascist new regime (Chiarini 1995).

Nevertheless, from the very beginning of the Italian republic, the fascists were openly able to organize themselves with the foundation of the Movimento Sociale Italiano, (MSI) (Italian Social Movement). No other extreme right party ever succeeded in post-war Italy. The (L'uomo qualunque) Common Man Movement, a proto-poujadist protest movement established immediately after the war, lasted only two years (1946–8) (Setta 1975), and the monarchists, apart from the institutional cleavage and their extreme conservatism, never shifted to an anti-system policy (De Napoli 1980; Ventrone 1996). Only in the nineties has a completely new party, the (Lega Nord) Northern League, while totally extraneous to the fascist mould, been credited with anti-system and right-extremist credentials; however, as will be discussed later, the Lega *may* be disowned by this political family.

THE RECOVERY AND INSTITUTIONALIZATION OF A NEO-FASCIST PARTY (1946–60)

On 26 December 1946, only one and a half years after the fall of fascism and the end of the civil war, a group of self-declared fascist veterans set up a partisan organization, the Movimento Sociale Italiano (MSI) (Italian Social Movement). The new party was officially led by a group of young ex-fascists with a low profile: the first general secretary was a young official of the RSI (Repubblica Sociale Italiana) (Italian Social Republic), Giorgio Almirante. But behind them, old and more experienced leaders of the fascist regime, who lived in hiding because of the prosecutions, guided the party. The MSI's first '10 points' programme somewhat veiled its ideological-political mould, insisting on 'national conciliation' and pacification, economic recovery, and so on (Ignazi 1998*a*), but all the symbolic and cultural references were unquestionably linked to fascism. The party depicted itself as a 'veterans' fraternity' which gathered together the 'losers' of the civil war.

Since both ideology and political personnel characterized the MSI as a nostalgic neo-fascist party, this genetic imprint raised the problem of the party's legitimacy within the democratic *anti-fascist* regime (and, at the same time, of the anti-fascist regime's legitimacy for the MSI followers).

This inner contradiction was solved immediately when the party opted for legal conduct and participated in the elections; moreover, it organized itself along the mass-party model (Ignazi 1998*a,b*), abandoning any temptation of militia-style organization. The MSI contested election for the first time in October 1947 for Rome's city council. The far from negligible result (4.0% of the votes) enabled the MSI to present itself as the key reference for the nostalgic milieu which was courted by various more radical groups. While the party increasingly exhibited a legalistic attitude, the variegated world of right-extremism was still able to attract some of the MSI's rank-and-file, purporting spectacular and/or violent-terrorist activities. The party leadership, however, distanced itself from the extra-legal right-wing groups, exhibiting loyalty to the democratic rules, because it realized that this was the only way a neo-fascist party could survive in an 'anti-fascist' regime.

The MSI contested the first parliamentary elections held in 1948. The electoral results (2.2%) which enabled the party to get six seats, demonstrated the existence of a deep north–south cleavage: 69.6 per cent of the MSI votes were cast in the regions south of Rome and all the MPs came from southern constituencies. This skewed geographical distribution of votes had a direct impact on the party's politics. In fact, the party itself was divided into two diverging factions that followed the geographical divide. The 'northern' faction, more militant and radical, claimed to be the heir of the socialistic and antibourgeois 'republican' fascism of the 1943–5 period, while the southern faction had more in common with the clerical, conservative, authoritarian, bourgeois fascist tendency. This differentiation recalls Renzo De Felice's (1969) famous distinction between the 'fascist-movement' (revolutionary, anti-bourgeois, anti-capitalist, non-conformist, utopian, etc.) and the 'fascist-regime' (authoritarian, clerical, corporatist, traditionalist, etc.). Such an ideological cleavage compares favourably with the geographical one, as the northern fascists reflected the fascist-movement tendency, whereas the southerners represented the fascist-regime.

The MSI leadership initially identified itself with the 'movement' tendency, and was fiercely opposed to opening up the party to the 'notables' coming from the southern regions. However, the distribution of votes in the 1948 elections had showed that the MSI had its electoral reservoir in the south. As a consequence, the young radical leadership led by Almirante were not able to control the party for very long. In January 1950, Almirante was forced to resign. He was replaced by Alfredo De Marsanich, a former member of government in the fascist regime and leader of the moderate faction.

Whereas the radical faction expressed hardline opposition to the democratic system, the moderate faction was inclined to exploit any circumstance whatsoever in order to be accepted as a 'normal' political partner by the conservative parties. Instead of stressing the anti-system profile of the party, the new leadership attempted *to fit in with the system*. MSI policy shifted from the 'opposition of principle' to basically the support for the ruling Democrazia Cristiana (DC) (Christian Democracy). De Marsanich's leadership emphasized the MSI's role as a *national force* for the defence of the Christian, Western world against Communism and, consequently, promoted an electoral alliance with the monarchist party. He called for the acceptance of NATO—which the MSI had opposed in parliament a few years earlier—and an alliance (aborted at the eleventh hour) with the DC for the 1952 Rome municipal election.

This pro-NATO, moderate, clerical stance was amply rewarded by the electorate, as demonstrated by the result (11.8%) obtained by the MSI-Monarchist alliance in the local elections throughout the south in 1952. In a few years the MSI had moved from a semi-legal and marginal position to a sizeable force (at least in the south of Italy), governing, together with the monarchists and other minor conservative groups, important cities such as Naples, Bari, and Catania. Correspondingly, the party organization boomed—notwithstanding a quite selective and controlled recruitment process—attracting tens of thousands of members and installing branches all over the country, above all in the centre-south (exact figures are lacking, but see Tarchi 1997: 38). The party could thus consolidate its organization whose basic traits—large, complex, centralized, and closed—remained basically the same until the party's transformation in the mid-1990s (Ignazi 1998*b*: 160ss).

The sudden growth of the party provoked a twofold, radically diverging reaction from the DC-led government: on the one hand, it tried to outlaw the MSI as a fascist party; on the other hand, it offered cooperation and alliances at a local level, as in the case of the, then unsuccessful, common anti-Communist list for the 1952 Rome municipal election. This ambivalent behaviour vis-à-vis the MSI became a standard rule for the DC, which alternated the carrot and the stick in order to keep control of its right-wing competitor. However, having failed to outlaw the MSI before the 1952 local election, the DC abandoned any hardline approach and adopted an accommodating policy throughout the fifties.

The MSI's moderate politics did not go unchallenged inside the party. Despite the electoral successes (in the 1953 general election the party scored 5.8 per cent, almost tripling its votes and quadrupling its seats), the radical faction remained very militant and tried repeatedly to overthrow the majority until the 1956 Congress, where it lost by seven votes and quit the party, creating the Ordine Nuovo (New Order) group. The moderate faction under the new general secretary, Arturo Michelini, former vice-secretary of Rome's Fascist party in the 1930s, ruled uncontested after the 1956 showdown.

Until 1960, the party achieved unprecedented political success, even reaching the threshold of government. At first, *together* with monarchists and liberals, the MSI supported, without entering the cabinet, two DC minority governments in 1957 and in 1959. Then, *alone* it backed a DC minority government in 1960. The political impact of the latter agreement was enormous: for the first time in the post-war democratic regime, a government had received a vote of confidence thanks *exclusively* to neo-fascist support. The MSI was on the verge of finally being accepted as a legitimate governing partner by (and of) the Christian Democracy.

Michelini's strategy of accommodation thus seemed totally successful. The Sixth National Congress planned for July 1960 in Genoa was intended to celebrate the accomplishment of his '*inserimento*' (insertion) strategy. However, the growing role of the MSI had created deep concern among the leftist parties. In Genoa, on the eve of the MSI congress, a militant anti-fascist reaction broke out and then spread to other Italian cities over the next fortnight. The wave of protest, culminating in violent clashes with the police and the death of some leftist demonstrators, led to the government's banning the congress from taking place. A few days later the government itself resigned. As a result of both events, the MSI was again relegated to the sidelines. Its zenith had been reached and the decline had begun.

ISOLATION, RENEWAL, AND RADICALIZATION (1960–83)

Michelini's strategic defeat had two main effects. On the one hand, it enfeebled the party organization and revitalized the inner factionalism. On the other, it marginalized the party and fostered the development of new extreme right groups which aimed at contrasting the 'subtle and undermining communist strategy of world domination' with a novel relationship involving (sectors of) the Army. These radical groups contested the 'wet' MSI policy and claimed a hardline confrontation with the left, employing whatever means necessary.

The party crisis reached its peak in 1968, when its share of the popular vote plummeted to 4.5 per cent in the general election and the 1968 student movement devastated its youth organization (one of the party's backbones). The ideological and strategic immobility was ended by Michelini's death in 1969. The new leader, the 'radical' Giorgio Almirante, promoted organizational, strategic, and ideological innovations (Ignazi 1998*a*: 140ff).

At the organizational level, the party was reformed through a higher centralization of the decision-making process, a stricter control over (but at the same time a higher support for) local party cadres, and a restructured youth organization. In addition to the organizational engineering that the MSI developed from then on, a power concentration in the leadership occured at both the local and the national level. Accordingly, the party leader became increasingly free from any control by the national executive bodies.

The party strategy aimed at abandoning the neo-fascist ghetto by setting up a novel party structure, the 'Destra Nazionale' (National Right), which could attract conservative political groups and independent opinion leaders thanks to a softening of the neo-fascist nostalgia. In the early 1970s this strategy progressed, enabling the MSI to attract new forces: the Monarchist party merged with the MSI, and some DC and PLI (Italian Liberal Party) politicians, as well as some of the Army's high-ranking officers, entered the party. This opening and accommodating strategy, however, included a contradictory element, namely an appeal for a tough confrontation in the streets with the 'Reds' in order to mobilize the party and recapture the extreme right movements (in fact, Ordine Nuovo and its leader, Pino Rauti, rejoined the MSI). This attempt at merging a respectable, 'clean', and updated image with a militant and tough one, in order to increase the party's coalition potential, and to defend the 'silent majority' disturbed by the social unrest of that period, finally proved an impossible task.

The third major change, closely related to the preceding one, regarded ideological renewal. Almirante repeatedly asserted his acceptance of the democratic system, but a real debate on key points such as fascism and democracy never took off *within* the party. The declaration of democratic faith remained superficial and was consistent with the persistence of the fascist identity and militant attitudes. The ideological renewal was more to do with the external image (less black shirts and Roman salutes) than the principles.

In conclusion, Almirante's plans pointed to the MSI's recapture of dominance over the extreme right and to the conquest of the DC's more moderate constituency. Up to the mid-1970s, this strategy largely succeeded. The MSI gained its highest electoral score (8.7% in 1972) and was at its strongest from the organizational perspective However, the party's strategy was endangered by two factors: firstly, the inherent contradiction of the 'Destra Nazionale' project—a superficial ideological revision plus an inability to control the violent radical right groups and even some fringes of the party's own youth organization; secondly, the DC's counter-initiatives to stop the MSI's rise—political isolation and denunciation of party responsibility in the various violent actions of that period. Threatened by insufficient ideological renovation and by its violent militantism, the Movimento Sociale lost the support of a large share of the moderate electorate, and it fell back to 6.1 per cent (-2.6%) in the 1976 parliamentary elections (Table 3.1).

This defeat opened the way to a reconsideration of Almirante's leadership and policies. A new party faction, led by the MSI speaker in the Chamber of Deputies, called for an enforcement of the 'Destra Nazionale' strategy and the development of a better relationship with the DC. This faction failed to dismiss Almirante and thus left the party on the eve of the Ninth National Congress (1977), founding the

TABLE 3.1. *Votes for MSI/AN, Lega Nord, and MS/FT in parliamentary and European elections*

	MSI/AN	Lega Nord	MS/FT
1948	2.0		
1953	5.8		
1958	4.8		
1963	5.1		
1968	4.5		
1972	8.7		
1976	6.1		
1979	5.3		
1979E	5.4		
1983	6.8		
1984E	6.5		
1987	5.9		
1989E	5.5	1.8	
1992	5.4	8.6	
1994	13.5	8.4	
1994E	12.5	6.6	
1996	15.7	10.1	0.9
1999E	10.3	4.5	1.6

Source: Official sources.

ephemeral (Democrazia Nazionale) National Democracy party, which disappeared three years later after its fiasco in the 1979 parliamentary elections (0.6%).

The internal crisis led to an abandonment of the 'Destra Nazionale' strategy. This shift left room for a novel cultural-ideological frame of references produced by the faction led by the former Ordine Nuovo leader, Pino Rauti. Such approach focused on a renewed critique of the liberal and Marxist ideologies, both incapable of responding to the 'needs' of the youth and of the less privileged strata. Capitalist dominance on Western societies had dispossessed people of a real, authentic, communitarian life, enhancing standardization, consumerism, and alienation. Accordingly, the analytical framework, largely derived from the French *Nouvelle Droite*, had an impressive impact on younger generations. In the late 1970s, an unprecedented number of students and young people joined the MSI, fuelling such a new world-view. The Hobbit camps, for example, were youth summer camps organized at the turn of the decade, and thanks to their open, casual, and even self-ironic discussions, had nothing in common with the gloomy and militaristic atmosphere of previous similar initiatives. Above all, these young activists expressed a clear desire to stop the bloody confrontation with the 'Reds' and to get out of the neo-fascist ghetto (Tassani 1986; Zucchinali 1986). *They expressed the need to take part in Italian society.*

In fact, in that period, the MSI was highly isolated, even more so than after 1960, mainly because of its (more or less conscious) complicity with street violence and even terrorist groups (Ferraresi 1984, 1995). Therefore, Almirante's leadership, stimulated by Rauti's faction, moved to initiate changes. A new less militant attitude towards street confrontations gained ground; a new electoral constituency was posited—young and southern protesters rather than the northern middle class; and a new political strategy was deployed by substituting the anti-Communist appeal with a call for an anti-system anti-DC opposition. The MSI's main concern was no longer the Communist danger but all parties' 'partocracy' which was responsible for Italy's agony. The party self-defined as the collector of the 'protest'. In this context it expressed a clear denunciation of violence. For the first time the MSI unambiguously placed itself against the extreme right radical fringes which remained completely isolated. Even if this process took some time, it allowed the MSI to present itself to the public without the alarming face of hardline, tough militantism.

However, these changes did not imply the abandonment of MSI's traditional ideological identity: the party glued the new image of a peaceful 'protest party' to its traditional neo-fascist references. Loyalty to political and economic corporatism, to authoritarian and nationalistic attitudes, went untouched. Fascist nostalgia maintained its role of manifest ideology.

THE MSI'S OPENING TO MODERNITY AND THE FIRST STEP TOWARDS THE PARTY'S LEGITIMATION (1983–93)

The new MSI non-violent attitude was coupled with the same feeling in the ultra-left movements, so that ideological and political tension rapidly collapsed (Della Porta and Rossi 1986). At the same time, the 'question of fascism' underwent reconsideration. On the basis of a new wave of studies promoted by the leading historian Renzo de Felice, fascism was no longer interpreted without the ideological anti-fascist prejudice. This cooler approach, widely debated in the mass media, and well beyond the narrow circle of intellectuals, developed neither indulgence nor nostalgia; it merely produced the end of a black and white perception of 1920s and 1930s Italy.

Thanks to the de-radicalization of political conflict and the 'historicization' of fascism, the MSI became less stigmatized than in the past. A few examples of the political life of the early to mid-1980s demonstrate such a shift in the political mood: in 1983 the Socialist Prime Minister, Bettino Craxi, declared, during the parliamentary confidence debate on his government, that he would have treated all parliamentary groups in the same vein without any discrimination; MSI leaders were invited for the first time to public meetings together with other anti-fascist party leaders; and Almirante was admitted to the PCI headquarters in June 1984 to honour the body of its party secretary, Enrico Berlinguer.

Quite amazingly, this favourable condition, from which the party had profited in the 1983 elections obtaining 6.8 per cent (+1.5%), produced serious problems for the MSI itself. In fact, the MSI had not been the *agent* of its integration into the system: such a process had been initiated autonomously by external forces, above all the Socialist party. Moreover, the MSI had not elaborated any coherent strategy for this new political phase. Almirante kept the anti-system and neo-fascist traits of the party intact. Instead of abandoning part of its cultural and ideological identity and accepting the democratic system, the party leadership maintained its advocacy of an alternative corporatist regime.

Very few within the party pushed for a clear renewal and *none* dared to suggest a clear rejection of fascism: even the most courageous 'renovators' wanted to preserve the ideological roots. Therefore, in the mid-1980s the MSI continued to oscillate between verbal radicalism and the desire to be overtly accommodated within the system. The unambiguous acceptance of the democratic system once more reopened the problem of party identity, an issue that was constantly set aside.

Even Almirante's resignation, due to poor health, at the Fifteenth National Congress (1987) and the new leadership of the 35-year-old Almirante dauphin, Gianfranco Fini, did not help to resolve the issue. The new secretary maintained the traditional line, stressing the fascist identity and proclaiming the party's radical opposition to the 'partocracy'.

Fini's politics were not successful, leaving the party in complete isolation and unable to profit from the new atmosphere of acceptance and legitimation. Moreover, Fini was too obviously controlled by the old guard to acquire the status of real party leader. After two years, part of the same old guard finally withdrew their support for Fini and forced the call for a new Congress (January 1990), where Fini was defeated by Almirante's historical opponent, Pino Rauti.

Rauti, one of the most prestigious leaders who had encountered various experiences and tendencies inside and outside the party, had played a crucial role in the MSI's internal debate since the mid-1970s. His faction, to which most of the young members belonged, provided elements for a new identity. This identity can be summed up in five crucial points: (1) an abandonment of the reference to the right: fascism is (and was) not a rightist conservative movement but a leftist revolutionary one; therefore, the MSI should look to the left of the political spectrum in trying to attract that electorate; (2) a rejection of the values of Western liberal civilization and of the Americanization of society—agnosticism, materialism, hedonism, egotism, and consumerism—in favour of an 'authentic' spiritual life; (3) a rejection of capitalism and 'money power'; (4) an opposition to NATO and the EEC (and whatever sounds Western) in favour of Third World stances; (5) an exaltation of the 'differences' against the 'false egalitarianism' and the homogeneity of a mass (democratic) society.

The result was a blending of the 'fascism-movement' tradition with some insights from the *Nouvelle Droite*. Rauti was to replace the MSI's traditional authoritarian, conservative, *petit bourgeois* political culture with a 'leftward', anti-capitalist, and anti-Western one—without contesting, incidentally, the loyalty to fascism. Actually, the most novel element introduced by Rauti, even before his appointment as secretary, namely the emphasis on, *and the right to*, 'distinctiveness', provided the ideological-cultural tool for the rejection of xenophobic or racist attitudes.

These rather eccentric positions did not (and could not) please the traditional MSI electorate. At the 1990 regional election the party got the lowest score ever: 3.9 per cent of the votes. Instead of leading a mass movement against the capitalist regime and the establishment, the party was increasingly isolated and verged on irrelevance. When Rauti was confronted by a further devastating defeat at the local election in Sicily, where the party dropped from 9.2 to 4.8 per cent, he was forced to resign. In July 1991, Fini, who had led the internal opposition, regained the secretaryship.

His policy consisted mainly of reintroducing the traditional party identity and reappraising the *inserimento* strategy by exploiting whatever chance might arise to definitely emerge from the ghetto. Apparently nothing had changed, neither in the political system nor in society, to enable more success for Fini's politics. On the eve of the 1992 election extreme concern over the electoral outcome was widespread. On the contrary, quite surprisingly, the MSI maintained its position, losing just 0.5 per cent: not an insignificant result compared with the heavy losses of the traditional parties, from the PCI-PDS to the DC. The political landscape in the northern regions was in fact devastated by the eruption of a new party, the Lega Nord (Northern League), which gained around 20 per cent of the votes in those regions. While the Lega Nord also campaigned on some of the MSI's traditional issues—security, fiscal protest, and partocracy—the MSI and the Northern League never shared the same electorate. The electoral analysis of the 1992 voters' switch demonstrates that the League profited mainly from the former governing parties (DC and PSI mainly) rather than from the MSI (Gasperoni 1995). And the charismatic Northern League leader, Umberto Bossi, repeatedly and unambiguously declared his anti-fascist sentiments.

Notwithstanding the recovery of its traditional electorate after the bewildering setback suffered during Rauti's secretaryship, the political perspective of the party became quite gloomy as the result of a new electoral law, which substituted proportional representation for plurality. As is well known, a minor party in a plurality system runs the risk of being devoid of parlamentary representation if it does not enter into a coalition. Actually, despite the fact that the ideological temperature had cooled down, the ideological distance (Sartori 1976) had remained very large: the party was still located at one extreme of the political spectrum. This situation appeared potentially very harmful to the party's survival. In order to find a way out of this cul-de-sac, the MSI promoted a new umbrella organization, 'Alleanza Nazionale' (National Alliance), so that under this new label it might collect some independents unlikely to join the party directly. When this project was launched in the summer of 1993, no one paid any attention because it did not offer anything new compared to the traditional issues of the party (presidentialism, plebiscitaranism, moral conservatism, etc.) and it was seen as one of the many attempts already experienced in the past—like Almirante's 'Destra Nazionale'—to aggregate a wider support.

In conclusion, when the MSI had almost achieved full legitimacy, its incapacity to promote an ideological renewal, along the same path experienced by the

PCI a few years earlier, pushed it into a corner once again. The majority principle could once and for all demonstrate completely, the party's irrelevance, and even question its survival.

THE ELECTORAL AND POLITICAL BREAKTHROUGH:
FROM MSI TO AN (1993–9)

The MSI's fate radically changed in December 1993 with the administrative elections of some major cities (Rome, Naples, Genoa, Venice, and others) held using the new two-ballot electoral system. When these elections were called, the activities of the magistrates against political corruption, the 'Clean Hands' investigations initiated the year before, had reached their peak. All of the governmental parties were hurt by the investigations and all of the party leaders had resigned: the DC and, even more so, the PSI were in total disarray. Consequently, the DC was not even able to present plausible candidates in the main cities where the electoral contest was to be held. On the contrary, the MSI put its best assets into the two most important cities: the party leader, Gianfranco Fini, stood in Rome, and Alessandra Mussolini, the Duce's granddaughter, in Naples. To widespread surprise, both MSI candidates beat the other moderate conservative candidates in the two cities and contested the second ballot against the leftist candidates, and, although losing, scored 46.9 and 44.4 per cent, respectively. Moreover, the party gained the mayorship in four provincial capitals and in another 19 medium-sized *comuni* (more than 15,000 inhabitants), all located in the centre-south.

This unaccountable and resounding success greatly increased the MSI's 'coalition potential'. However, on the eve of the national elections of March 1994 none of the traditional parties had yet expressed any interest. The DC, in particular, led by a leftist faction, was totally disinterested in any partnership with the MSI. What was needed was a new political actor, immune from the 'mould' which characterized the established parties, that is, *anti-fascism*. For all of them, cooperating with the neo-fascists was still a taboo.

The entry of Berlusconi's Forza Italia (Go Italy) provided that tool. First, the declaration in favour of Fini in his contest for the Rome mayorship, and, second, the offer of a coalition with the MSI in the south in the 1994 legislative elections, constituted a watershed compared to the traditional attitude of the political establishment regarding the MSI.

This unexpected overture was immediately exploited by Fini, who paid homage to the principles of democracy and capitalist economy and implemented the 'Alleanza Nazionale' umbrella organization, contesting the incoming election under that name and restyling the party symbol. This image lifting proved very successful: in the 1994 national elections the party scored an unprecedented 13.5 per cent (+8.1%) and elected 109 MPs (17.3%) in the Lower Chamber. Such an impressive breakthrough could be explained by two sets of factors.

The first set concerns the *long-term* changes in Italian society, in particular to the above-mentioned de-radicalisation of the political conflict and historicization of fascism. Therefore, the MSI was progressively perceived as a 'normal', less anti-system (notwithstanding its proclaimed loyalty to fascism) political actor. The second set of factors comprises five *short-term* elements: (1) the collapse of Christian Democracy; (2) the party's non-involvement in the investigations on political corruption; (3) the unexpected and relevant success in the local elections in December of 1993, mainly in Rome and Naples; (4) the legitimacy offered by Berlusconi's Forza Italia, when the MSI was accepted for the first time as a partner in a coalition; (5) the excellent performance of Gianfranco Fini in the media: cool, quiet, reasoning, accountable, quite the contrary of the aggressive 'fascist' stereotype.

The combination of these long-term and short-term factors, *rather than a new party message*, enabled the MSI to tear down the gates of the ghetto, electorally and politically. On one hand, the party collected votes from all of the old governing parties in the 1994 elections: 29.3 per cent of the *new voters* were previous DC voters, 16.8 per cent former PSI voters, and 13.2 per cent came from the other three minor governing parties (Segatti 1997: 227). On the other hand, as a consequence of the electoral success of the right-wing coalition—the Polo per le Libertà (Freedom Pole)—to which the MSI belonged, it entered the Berlusconi government in May 1994. For the first time in post-war Europe, an extreme right party had gained membership of a cabinet.

During the short-lived Berlusconi government (May–December 1994), the MSI tried to de-emphasize its ideological leaning in order to be fully legitimized. However, throughout 1994 party officials, and Fini himself, alternated between official declarations of acceptance of the 'democratic method' and the refusal to overtly disown their fascist mould. The difficulties in the latter goal derived from the refusal to take into consideration the elaboration of a critical assessment of fascism. It was not by chance that Fini offered a rosy interpretation of fascism, declaring that it was a good regime up until 1938 because 'in certain periods freedom is not an essential value' (*La Stampa*, 4 June 1994). Moreover, the party manifesto still paid homage to the fascist and anti-democratic political culture without enduring any criticism (Ignazi 1994, 1998a; Chiarini 1995; Griffin 1996; Tarchi 1997). In fact, when the MSI had launched the AN project, it rejected approaching a different ideological space. Fini clearly stated the party's fierce opposition to liberal democracy: 'Alleanza Nazionale does not imply a liberal democratic *regression*' (*Il Secolo d'Italia*, 29 July 1993).

THE AN: TRADITIONS AND RUPTURES—A COMPLEX IDEOLOGICAL CONSTELLATION

Given these premises, the Congress which celebrated the transformation of the MSI into the AN in January 1995 produced no more than a change of name.

TABLE 3.2. *Evaluation of fascism by the AN middle-level elites*

	1995	1998
It is still the best regime	7.1	3.0
Apart from some questionable decisions, it was a good regime	61.5	61.1
It was the inevitable answer to the communist threat	13.0	18.0
It was an authoritarian regime	18.2	17.7
It was a brutal dictatorship	0.2	0.3
N	(561)	(334)

Source: Baldini and Vignati (1996); Vignati (2001).

The long-awaited debate on the roots of the party was concentrated into a single, while highly relevant sentence, whereby the Congress recognized that anti-fascism was 'an historically necessary moment to regain the freedom that fascism had denied'. This important declaration was however tempered by the solid loyalty to the fascist tradition emerging from the participants of the 1995 Congress (Baldini and Vignati 1996). A series of questions highlighted the ideological profile of the party's middle-level elite. The theme concerning the evaluation of fascism reveals an astonishing attachment to it: an overwhelming majority (62%) agreed with the item which states that 'notwithstanding some questionable choices, fascism was a good regime'; and another 7 per cent considered fascism as 'the best regime ever conceived'. *Almost none* (0.2%) criticized it as a 'brutal dictatorship' and only 18 per cent conceded that it was 'an authoritarian regime'. The remaining 13 per cent avoided a condemnation of fascism stating that it was 'the inevitable answer to the communist threat' (see Table 3.2).

This amazingly positive evaluation of fascism is reinforced by the data on the preference for a list of political thinkers (from fascists to liberals). Of all the listed names, those who scored the highest were the representatives of the fascist and right radical tradition, starting from Gentile (91%), followed by Mussolini (82%) and Evola (71%).

Therefore one can state that the cultural ideological references of the new party were still embedded in the fascist and anti-democratic tradition. *However, whilst true, this is only part of the picture.*

A rather different profile from the traditional nostalgic and neo-fascist image in reality exists, and *it even emerged well before the process of transformation into the AN*. The data collected by two similar surveys carried out at the fifteenth (1987) and the sixteenth (1990) MSI Congresses on a set of items ranging from clericalism to nationalism, from racism to militarism and authoritarianism, demonstrated that the MSI middle-level elite exhibited attitudes quite divergent from the party's official politics and manifest ideology, and from other European extreme right-wing parties (Ignazi 1998a; Ignazi and Ysmal 1992). In fact, on issues related to civil rights—drug addiction, homosexuality, police questioning, death penalty, conscientious objection, gender relationships, and, to a certain extent, even immigrants'

TABLE 3.3. *Attitudes of the MSI and AN middle-level elites (1990 and 1995) (Percentage of those who agreed on the items)*

	1990	1995
Too much financial power in the hands of Jews*	47	47
Immigrants endanger national identity*	80	59
Immigrants cause criminality	14	35
Social security allowed to immigrants	33	65
Strikers in public sector should be sacked	46	25
Abortion is sometimes a necessary evil	29	46
Introduce death penalty	40	30
Drug addicts in gaol	47	56
Eliminate conscientious objection	42	41
Homosexual should not be employed in bars, restaurants, etc.	34	25

* Wordings are slightly different in the two surveys.

Source: Ignazi and Ysmal (1992); Baldini and Vignati (1996).

rights—the MSI cadres displayed a somewhat tolerant view. *Less than half of the 1990 survey respondents supported authoritarian positions* on the following issues: imprisoning drug addicts (47%), opposing conscientious objection (42%), introducing the death penalty (40%), arguing for tougher treatment in jail (36%), denying homosexuals the right to run public services such as coffee shops and restaurants (34%), allowing the police to 'freely' question criminals (28%), and assigning the ultimate decision in family matters to the male head of the household (24%). These data show a break in the stereotypical interpretation of extreme right cadres (see Table 3.3).

The crucial point, however, is that *these more open attitudes did not at all influence the party's political culture*. The MSI official ideology did not move from the standardized reminiscence of the fascist and anti-democratic tradition. The leadership has made no effort to abandon the traditional identity.

Paradoxically, where the party leadership has tried to modify some elements of the anti-democratic ideology, as in the case of xenophobia and racism, it has not been successful. The party's approach to this topic is rather peculiar. Immigrants should not be stigmatized per se because they are just the last link in the chain of exploitation: immigration is the result of capitalist domination over the Third World. Therefore, in order to stop immigration, a tough approach to immigrants is injurious and useless; instead, the North–South relationship should be modified. While this line of reasoning is also reminiscent of certain fascist justifications for the Italian colonial presence in Africa (Chiarini 1995), it remained abstract and removed from the middle-level elite's (and voters') feelings. In fact, in the 1990 survey, only two items concerning more aid to less-developed countries and the refusal to link immigration with increasing crime received majority consent by the party cadres. In other cases the attitudes are quite xenophobic: fear of the loss of national identity because of the immigrants' presence (80%); expulsion of illegal immigrants (62%); no social security provisions to immigrants (46%); belief in the existence of superior and inferior racies (approved by 46% and rejected by 40%); and anti-Semitism (sustained by 47% and refused by 19%) (see Table 3.3). Taking into account the limited appeal of anti-immigration sentiments in late 1980s–early 1990s Italian political discourse (Kitschelt 1995: 183ff; Perlmutter 1996; Bonifazi 1998), xenophobia was quite appealing to the MSI cadres.

Given this previous setting, the celebrated passage from the MSI to the AN should have revealed a cleavage, dampening the most authoritarian and xenophobic sentiments and heightening the most tolerant and modernizing ones.

In the 1995 Congress, which unequivocally condemned any form of racism and anti-Semitism (Ignazi 1998a: 447ff), the middle-level elite remained quite sceptical on those issues. Fear of foreigners as a danger to national identity was supported by 59, and 47 per cent wanted to reduce Jewish power in international finance. The crucial themes of immigration and xenophobia remain conflicting and unsettled: compared to 1990, out of four comparable items, two of them showed a tendency towards more openness while the other two showed an increase in tough positions (see Table 3.3).

The same contradiction emerges from other questions addressed by the 1995 survey. On themes like freedom of the press, the death penalty, and conscientious objection, the party delegates were more inclined towards a liberal stance rather than an authoritarian one. Meanwhile, the reverse was true on legalizing drugs, firing strikers in public services, and punishment for drug addicts; free choice on abortion split into two equal camps. Finally, a strong nationalist opinion still circulated where they approved the likelihood of military intervention without the consent of NATO allies (51%), where they considered the USA an 'imperialist' country (68%), and where they almost unanimously (90%) demanded sovereignty over former Italian territory (the regions of Istria and Dalmatia) in ex-Yugoslavia.

In conclusion, from 1987 onwards, the party cadres demonstrated a surprising openness to numerous salient 'civil rights' questions, typical of postmodern society. However, these stances were contradicted by both a leaning towards right extremist attitudes, especially on those themes which the leadership tried to modify (racism and anti-Semitism), and a solid loyalty to the original identity provided by fascism. *Some changes have taken place within the party's middle-level elite, but they have not made a breakthrough.* At the same time, identification with fascism is still at the core of their political culture. The point is that real change needs a trauma. Until 1997 the AN had run with the wings of fortune. Only after its first backlash, in late 1997, has the party fostered more radical innovations.

A Party Away from the Extreme Right Family?

The Alleanza Nazionale strengthened in the 1996 elections where it obtained 15.7 per cent (+2.2%), representing its best ever score. However, the party did not succeed in gaining leadership within the right-wing coalition, the Freedom Pole. While the opinion polls had credited the AN as the major force of the right, the electoral outcome still favoured Berlusconi's Forza Italia (20.1%). The AN was handicapped by its extreme location in the political spectrum (8.2 on 0–10 left–right scale (Montero and Gunther 1998)) and its feeble accountability as a truly non-nostalgic party (in a 1996 national opinion poll, 41.2 per cent of citizens against 38.4 per cent declared their conviction that the AN 'did not sever its ties with the past' (Ignazi 1996*b*)).

The problem of the party's location on the political spectrum became less relevant after the 1996 election. In fact, Rauti's radical splinter group, the Movimento Sociale-Fiamma Tricolore (Social Movement–Tricolour Flame) (MS–FT) created in the aftermath of the Alleanza Nazionale Congress, offered the AN the opportunity to detach itself from its most extreme location.

The second problem—its links with the past—remained more sensitive as demonstrated by its degree of change in the party personnel, the party organization, and the party ideology.

As far as change in the party personnel is concerned, both at the national level and at the local level the AN is run by experienced former MSI members. No newcomer has in fact acquired the status of national leader. Moreover, at the parliamentary level, more than 80 per cent of the MPs elected in 1994 were socialized within the party: *there were even fewer independents than those elected in 1972* (Verzichelli 1995). And in 1996 the AN was the party with the highest number of MPs with previous administrative experience and with previous 'high level' offices in the party organization (Verzichelli 1997: 336–7). The AN MPs scored the highest among all Italian parties' MPs on political professionalism (Verzichelli 1997: 240): a performance that testifies to continuity in elite recruitment. The limited turnover in the parliamentary groups (Verzichelli 1997: 316) and in the party executive bodies *until 1994* (Tarchi 1997; Ignazi 1998*a*) has been supplanted by an effective generational, if not political, turnover in the last few years. A new generation is nowadays in power: Fini's leadership group is composed of a core of 40–50-year-old *former MSI youth organization leaders*.

In terms of organizational structure, some changes are ascertainable. Beyond the dramatic increase in the number of party members (and beyond the reliability of these data)—from an average of 150,000 at the beginning of the 1990s, to 324,344 in 1994 and 467,539 in 1995 (Tarchi 1997: 40)—the party forecasted an abandonment of the traditional mass-party type of organization (local branches, bottom-top chain of election, elected local party leaders, collective bodies of decision making) in favour of a more flexible structure where the local members are organized in 'circles' (Tarchi 1997: 140ff). A more open and flexible party, however, goes hand-in-hand with a rather 'bonapartistic' decision-making process. According to the new statute, the party leader has full control of the party: he is no longer responsible to the national executive, only to the Congress; he has the right to appoint the national executive (even if the Central committee has the last word); he appoints almost half of the members of the Central committee; he directly nominates the regional secretaries; and he has the right to remove the federation (provincial) secretaries. The mass-party model on which the party was built has been replaced with a highly personalized, hyper-centralized party, moulded on the *Führerprinzip* (Ignazi 1998*b*).

Finally, if we consider ideology, as underlined *supra*, the reason for condemning the fascist regime has never been deeply discussed throughout the party: the formula adopted to bypass such a crucial question is that fascism collapsed in 1945 and history will pass judgement (MSI–DN 1994: 8–9; Tarchi 1997; Chiarini 2001). In this way no evaluation of the regime and of fascist ideology has been provided. Therefore, even if the party leaders declare their adhesion to the 'principles of freedom', an ambiguity regarding the ideological references remains. The absence of liberal-conservative thinkers in the cultural pantheon, underlined by the manifesto of the Alleanza Nazionale at the 1995 founding congress, reveals the extraneousness of the 'new' party to this ideology and its enduring immersion in the anti-democratic culture. Julius Evola, together with Gentile and Mussolini, are still the key references for all of the local party cadres and a large part of the national leaders.

This ambiguity started dissolving in 1998. Confronted with the electoral backlash of the local elections in late 1997, the party promoted an 'ideological conference', held in Verona in early 1998, to assess its new image and identity. Even before that conference, the party underwent a profound renovation of its political personnel. In a dramatic showdown, while acknowledging the role of the emerging factions, the party leader altered the internal balance of power (Ignazi 1998*c*) by nominating newcomers to the party's hierarchy.

More so than the (quite innovative) manifesto issued at the party conference, the series of declarations by Fini himself on very sensitive issues created a turning point. The most dramatic statement referred to the distancing from the Fascist RSI army's role in 1943–5: Fini declared that he would have not flanked it because it was 'on the wrong side' in the fight for democracy. This quite explicit statement hit at one of the party's more solid taboos. In addition, Fini maintained a very clear stand against any racist, xenophobic, or anti-Semitic positions, leaving the monopoly of these issues to Rauti's MS–FT and even Bossi's Northern League.

However, these official statements did not find adequate support in the party's middle-level elite. The survey carried out at the 1998 conference highlights the persistence of a widespread compliance vis-à-vis the fascist regime (Vignati 2001). *The large majority (61%) still agreed with the idea that fascism was overall a good regime* (see Table 3.2). Even the newcomers (those who joined the

TABLE 3.4. *Evaluation of fascism by the population*
(1996 and 2001) (national sample)

	1996	2001
Apart from some questionable decisions, it was a good regime	16.3	13.0
It was a brutal dictatorship	38.9	38.1
It was the inevitable answer to the communist threat	4.3	5.0
It was an authoritarian regime	26.3	22.4
It is still the best regime	2.4	1.7
Don't know	11.8	19.8
Total	100	100
No. of cases	(4,717)	(4,105)

Source: SOIP Institute.

party after 1994) shared this view by 55.1 per cent. The same ideological viscosity emerged in the rank ordering of the most reputed thinkers: once more Gentile, Mussolini, and Evola came first—while the gap with the liberal thinkers, especially Croce and Tocqueville, shrank. Moreover, on the groundbreaking statement by the party chairman on the RSI, the AN cadres were very dubious: *only one quarter agree with Fini*, rising to a third among the post-1994 members.

Summing up, *while on authoritarian issues the party cadres show an evolution towards conservative-democratic positions rather than right-extremist ones, they are quite prone to nostalgia and, to a certain extent, xenophobia.* The persistence of nostalgia, in particular, contrasts with the attitudes shared by the electorate at large. As Table 3.4 shows, the compliance with fascism is practically limited to AN voters. As a matter of fact, AN keeps silent, waiting for a 'natural' overcoming and oblivion of such a cumbersome heritage.

The party leadership has been moving quite rapidly along a path out of neo-fascism since the 1997 electoral setback. After having superficially modified the party image with the successful marketing-style operation of the MSI passage to the AN, the party leader, backed by the faction of the renovators gathered around the journal *Charta Minuta*, introduced groundbreaking innovations, partly accepted by the rank-and-file. This commitment was paralleled by the party's involvement in the Parliamentary Commission for Constitutional Reform in 1997/8. The party's participation in this process neatly contrasted with its exclusion from the drafting of the first Constitution in 1948. At that time the MSI was the only party to be excluded, and for a long time it denied the legitimacy of those rules. Fifty years later the AN is fully legitimate in the political arena.

Still on the threshold

The MSI was *the* reference for the European extreme right from the end of the war until the late eighties. Paradoxically, when the extreme right gained substantial popularity all over Europe, the MSI started to decline. Until very specific and exceptional conditions appeared, the party was losing ground primarily because of its solid neo-fascist lineage. The widespread feeling of mistrust towards political institutions and the party system, heightened by the Clean Hands investigations and by the collapse of the old parties, provided the opportunity structure for a new start. The MSI's extraneousness to political corruption enabled it to collect the moderate and protest constituencies that used to fuel the DC and the abstentions. Even before initiating an ideological revision, the party benefited from a devastating party system crisis. However, the exploitation of those conditions needed a party change. There were two alternatives: putting emphasis on the themes of the new successful European extreme right parties, or distancing itself from the extreme right family. While agonizingly deficient, and sometimes unconsciously so, the MSI choose the latter.

The party is now moving away not just from the neo-fascist tradition, but from right extremism *tout court*. The refusal to create a common Euro-parliamentary group with Jörg Haider's FPÖ in early 1999, the lack of any relationship with Le Pen's Front National and other extreme right parties, the recognition of its democratic accountability even from the more leftist parties, the official declarations on liberal democracy, and the refusal of racism, clearly show that the party is moving away from extremism.

Abundant empirical data on the party voters support this interpretation and may even date it further. The party voters *are clearly and by far the least ethnocentric, xenophobic and authoritarian of all the other European extreme right parties* Kitschelt 1995; Gabriel 1996; Abacus 1999; Ivaldi 2001). Even in the Italian political space its policy positions are not so distant from the Lega Nord and Forza Italia, except for its location on the left–right continuum where the AN is still located at the extreme. The AN voters are predominately male (55%) and young adults (50% below 40 years of age) (Mannheimer 1999), like many extreme right-wing parties, but their occupational status diverge from them since the occupations above the mean are the entrepreneurial and executive ones (+5 points), the self-employed (+4), and the white collars (+3) (Natale 1999: 563) (see Table 3.5). The tendency towards the proletarization of the party supporters expanding all over the European extreme right does not touch the AN. It is a further element of distinction.

For all these motives, both ideological and socio-demographic, *the AN is on the fringe of the contemporary extreme right, on the threshold of its exit.*

The AN detachment from the extreme right milieu might favour Rauti's MS–FT splinter group. This party scored unexpectedly well in the 1996 elections (0.9% nationally but 4.3% in the constituencies where it contested); and the 1.6 per cent (1 Euro-MP) polled at the 1999 European election demonstrates its persistence. The MS–FT recruits particularly in the inner cities and among marginal social groups, which is a different constituency to that of the AN. The MS–FT radical position on immigration, Europe, globalization, liberal economy,

TABLE 3.5. *Socio-demographic profile of AN and Northern League Voters (1999). Deviations from the population mean*

	AN	League
Man	+11	+13
Woman	−11	−13
18–30 years	+5	+8
30–45	−2	+2
45–60	−1	0
+60	−3	−11
Elementary (5 years)	−7	−8
Medium–Low (8 years)	−2	+18
Medium–High (13 years)	+7	−6
High (+13)	+2	−4
Entrepreneur/manager	+5	−2
Employee/teacher	+3	−5
Self-employed	+4	−4
Worker	−3	+15
Housewife	−9	+1
Student	+4	+3
Unemployed	−1	−2
Pensioner	−3	−6

Source: Natale (1999: 563).

and democracy, mixed with pro-welfare demands, qualifies it as the true interpreter of the extreme right family in Italy.

REGIONAL POPULISM: THE NORTHERN LEAGUE

Besides the traditional anti-system party represented by the MSI, in the last decade another party, the Lega Nord (Northern League), has been frequently classified as an extreme right party, especially by non-Italian scholars (Betz 1994,1998*a*). According to the classificatory criteria adopted—spatial position, ideology, and attitude toward the system—we will discus the plausibility of its inclusion in the extreme right family.

From the Leagues to the Northern League

The Lega Nord was officially founded in 1991, accomplishing a two-year federation process of various autonomist movements active since the 1970s in the northern regions of Italy. The Liga Veneta (Venetian League) was the first one to acquire a relevant political status. It made its breakthrough in the legislative elections of 1983, attaining 4.2 per cent in the region where it contested (Venetia) and electing one deputy and one senator. The result is even more striking when compared to the high viscosity of electoral behaviour in Italy at the time

(Corbetta *et al.* 1988). The Liga Veneta, which had been active since the mid-1970s (Diamanti 1993), aimed at defending and reviving the local Venetian cultural heritage: the dialect, traditions, and way of life. In the 1980s the party stressed its ethno-regionalist character, calling for greater administrative autonomy, including taxes, schools, and health systems, and for an exclusionist policy towards the non-allogenous Italian southern immigrants. Concentration on the ethnic element and advocacy of a Venetian 'nation' radicalized the Liga discourse to the point of endangering any further diffusion; in 1987 it scored 3.0 per cent, (-1.2%) losing any representation in Parliament.

As a counter-weight to the temporary decline of the Liga, in the 1987 national elections further autonomist-regionalist movements surfaced: the Lega Lombarda (Lombardy League) which collected 2.9 per cent of the votes in Lombardy and gained one deputy and one senator, and the two different lists in Piedmont, which collected a resounding 4.3 per cent in the region, but were not able to send a representative to Parliament due to their division.

These movements gained a following in the peripheral areas of the northern regions, rather than in the large cities, and more particularly in all the pre-alpine areas ranging from east to west. The offer of an ethnic identity, while highly problematic given the looseness of real distinctive elements, met the need for symbolic references in an area formerly moulded by the Church's presence and, at the time, affected by the rise of secularization. Not by chance, in the 1983 elections the Liga achieved better results in the communes where the decline of religious practice had been steeper (Diamanti 1993: 48). In this initial phase the leagues could be interpreted along the classic centre-periphery cleavage: the marginal and peripheral areas against the regional and national centres (Diamanti 1993: 50).

A new phase started with the unexpected outcome of the 1989 European elections. The various leagues merged together in a single list (Alleanza Nord—Northern Alliance) polling 1.8 per cent and one Euro deputy; but what made the difference was the performance of the Lombardy League, which got 8.1 per cent in the region, attaining fourth position in the regional party system (Biorcio 1997: 50). This result was no more than the first flake of a snowball. In the 1990 administrative elections all the various leagues collected positive scores: 6.1 per cent in Liguria, 5.9 per cent in Venetia, 5.1 per cent in Piedmont (plus 2.3% of another competing autonomist list), up to an amazing 18.9 per cent in Lombardy (21.4% if a small splinter group is added), thus occupying second place only to the Christian Democrats. All together, the various leagues scored almost 6.0 per cent at national level, a large share of which (4.8%) was due to the Lega Lombarda (Anderlini and Leonardi 1991: 266–9).

Under the leadership of Umberto Bossi, the Lega Lombarda set aside the ethnic-cultural discourse, reframing the territorial identity in economic terms. The scapegoats of the protest that Bossi pointed to were the lazy, parasitic, inefficient, welfare-scrounger southerners—concentrated in the public sector—contrasted with the hard-working, entrepreneurial Lombardy people. The State is a 'Molokh' which devours all the resources—produced by the laborious Lombardy people—and redistributes them, wasting them on everybody except the 'producers'. This discourse met a still then latent hostile feeling towards the Southerners which, from the early eighties onwards, affected between one third and one quarter of the Lombardy population (Biorcio 1991: 59). The Lega Lombarda drew a large part of its support from this ample reservoir, whose concerns had never been politicized before, despite the fact that the North/South divide has been an enduring question since Italy's unification.

After the 1990 electoral success, the Lega Lombarda gradually lessened its ethnic-regionalist references, with a consequent fall in xenophobic messages, in favour of a populist anti-politics approach. According to the Lombardy League, the responsibility of the draining of resources no longer lay in the hands of the southerners but, above all, in the corrupt and clientelistic party system. The Lega intended to defend the common man against the national political establishment, the parties, the politicians, and the central administration along with an effective Lega slogan: 'Against Rome' (Betz 1998*a*).

The redirection towards anti-politics discourse met mounting dissatisfaction vis-à-vis politics in the country. In 1990, 82 per cent of citizens estimated that politicians 'are not interested in what a person like me thinks' (Bardi and Pasquino 1995: 40); in 1992, more than 50 per cent considered that all parties were the same, against 25 per cent in 1985 (Mannheimer 1993*a*: 83); and the working of democracy (Morlino and Tarchi 1996) was rated very poor in that period. All that, plus the deployment of the Clean Hands investigation into political corruption that would break out after 1992, would breed anti-politics sentiments and thus the leagues' support.

The federation process of the various leagues into the Lega Nord (Northern League) by the beginning of the decade was fulfilled on the wings of this populist turn. The anti-politics discourse, conveyed with unusual rhetorical skills by the uncontested leader Umberto Bossi, who introduced very direct, outspoken, and even vulgar language, proved to be the winning formula in enlarging the party's audience.

The triumphal 1992 elections (17.3% in the region North of the river Po, which means 8.6% nationally (Biorcio 1997: 81)) set the League at the core of the political system: whatever party comes first in Lombardy and in Milan, the richest and most developed area of the country, by definition attains a central role. The Lega collected votes from all parties, especially from the major governing parties, the Christian Democrats and Socialists, and also from the Communists, while the contribution of neo-fascist voters was quite limited (Corbetta 1993: 241; Biorcio 1997: 65). It was 'a cross-cutting, undifferentiated vote distributed across the political spectrum' (Corbetta 1993: 248). Its electorate was mainly mobilized by anti-corruption sentiment and by the demand for regional autonomy from Rome (Biorcio 1997: 67–8). However, these two basic elements were also supplanted in the voters' minds by anti-alien (both Italian and foreigners) sentiments, although the party had downsized such issues at that time. The fruitful combination of anti-politics, anti-centralist, and (latently) anti-alien positions provided the Lega with success. Moreover, the continuous references made by the party leadership to a 'community' of Northern people, strengthened by common interests (much more so than values, as laboriousness was the only common trait), created a solid party constituency.

The positive cycle of the Lega reached its zenith in 1993 with the conquest of the mayorship of Milan. The new majority two-ballot electoral system led to a final confrontation between the left candidate and the Lega one: the latter won with a resounding 57.1 per cent. The Lega's massive breakthrough is linked to the development of the Clean Hands investigations on political corruption initiated in early 1992. The revealed dimension of the parties' bribery—particularly in Milan—shook public opinion and, at the same time, annihilated the governing parties by favouring an anti-party par excellence such as the Lega. This massive inflow of new voters pushed the Lega to enlarge and differentiate its discourse by de-emphasizing the 'protest' appeal, (attempting at) presenting itself as a national governing party. Moreover, consequent to its penetration in the urban milieu the Lega advocated a neo-liberal approach, against State intervention in the market. The demand of fiscal federalism flanked the traditional anti-tax issue: the resources produced by the North should be managed directly and autonomously by the northern regions.

The party's positive trend ended with the 1994 elections: the Lega found an unexpected competitor in the newly created Forza Italia party, which concentrated on the same issues but with a national scope and more moderate tones. The 'forced alliance' between the two parties in the 1994 elections proved very fruitful for the Lega in the short run as it managed to get more seats than before, but it stopped the party's growth. The Lega experienced a slight decline in the voters' percentage, both nationally (8.4%: −0.2%) and in the North (17.0%: −0.3%) (Biorcio 1997: 81). Moreover, the Lega's territorial distribution had altered. It lost the newly conquered urban electorate and retrenched north of the river Po, losing weight in regions such as Liguria and Emilia-Romagna.

The attempt to 'nationalize' the party by broadening its messages beyond the localist ones had failed. Forza Italia on one side and the Alleanza Nazionale on the other contained the Lega's political space. While there was no transfer of votes between the Lega and other right-wing parties (Segatti 1997: 225), Bossi's party had no more room. The risk of being squeezed and absorbed was highlighted by the first real setback following the 1994 European elections where, in the face of the triumph of Forza Italia, the Lega consistently lost (6.6%: −1.8%). Quite rapidly Bossi started distancing the party from the right-wing government coalition composed by Forza Italia, the Alleanza Nazionale, and the Lega itself, leading to its break-up by the end of the year. Bossi abandoned the former allies in the name of the 'popular soul' of the party against the monopolistic tycoon (Berlusconi) and the unchanged neo-fascists (AN). This popular/populist turn led the party to support a technical government sustained by the centre-left. This move did not imply a shift to the left, since Bossi declared that the Lega was 'at the centre and above': a further formula to avoid a precise location in the political spectrum and to move freely along it.

The break-up with the right and the difficult relationship with the centre-left pushed the Lega towards isolation. This occurence nevertheless gave the Lega the drive for a further strategic development. The party re-emphasized the localist issues with an unprecedented radicalization: *no longer federalism but independence.* The 'separatist' strategy was baptized in June 1995 after a surprisingly good performance in the regional elections, especially in the Venetian region (17.4%); in May 1996 the Lega founded the 'Parliament of the North', for the purpose of promoting its increasingly radical anti-centre politics. However, the separatist theme remained under the surface until the 1996 general elections. The Lega refused to make any agreement with the former right-wing allies and campaigned on its extraneousness to both centre-left and centre-right coalitions. The very positive electoral result, 10.1 per cent (20.5% in the north), and the shift in the voter distribution, along with the growing weight of the Venetia (the most radical component of the Lega), implied a further radicalization. The Lega moved along the secessionist strategy immediately after the elections, trying to force the government to provide for some provision in favour of the 'northern people' (Diamenti 1997*b*). Actually, while this strategy was pursued with a series of initiatives, it inevitably led up a blind alley. The Lega had activated a zero-sum conflict that could end up only with the final success of the party strategy, that is, the break-up of Italian unity, an almost impossible goal.

Following this path, in the late 1990s the Lega reformulated and radicalized most of its themes with a particular emphasis on the anti-immigration issue (now completely devoted to non-Italians). On the economic side, the party still defended the small enterprises and the self-employed against the fiscal burden, but introduced pro-welfare positions also. A referendum among the readers of the party press asking to choose between two ideal types of society—the 'Anglo-Saxon' one, multicultural, individualistic, and finance dominated, and the 'Continental' model founded on nationhood, sense of community, welfare provisions, and social concern—highlighted an overwhelming preference for the latter.

The juxtaposition between the people—including small entrepreneurs—and big business and the banks, between the ordinary man and 'Rome's' politicians, between the native people and the aliens, between the people's rights and international organizations, represents the classical repertoire of populist appeal. In this vein, Bossi joined the other extreme right parties in support of Serbia in the Kosovo war, in opposition to globalization, and in hostility towards European and international institutions.

This 'extremist' strategy left the Lega in total isolation and deprived it of any success whatsoever. The loss of the mayorship of Milan in 1997, the poor outcome in the 1998 administrative election, and the decline to 4.5 per cent in the 1999 European elections (below the 1990 result!) caused a series of splits and a never before experienced political marginality. The shift to the right, even beyond the Alleanza Nazionale on certain issues, and the demand for the North's independence deprived the party of any coalition potential. However, as the party is totally dominated by its leader (even the various splits occurred throughout 1999 did not affect him), Bossi could quite abruptly impose whatever new, totally different strategy to draw the party from marginality. And in fact, by the very end of 1999 it started approaching once again its former 1994 allies (Forza Italia and Alleanza Nazionale).

THE *LEGA'S* VOTER: A CENTRE EXTREMIST

In the early 1990s, after having attracted a predominately male, adult, low-educated, and self-employed electorate, the Lega acquired a profile similar to the average voter or, according to some (Mannheimer 1993*b*: 258), similar to the former Christian Democrats' voter. Afterwards the party mobilized two different social groups whose coexistence needs further explanation. These two groups are the small entrepreneurs—frequently so small as to shift into artisan-like activities—and the workers (Table 3.5).

An ecological analysis of the 1996 election demonstrates that 'the League succeeds in those areas with a high level of industrialization, a high number of workers, a high number of enterprises and, at the same time, with a low level of employees in the private and public tertiary sector' (Diamanti 1997*a*: 159). Where the rate of unemployment is the lowest and the number of occupied is the highest, the Lega is the strongest. This means that the party, by moving its epicentre towards Venetia, the region where the rate of industrial development and enterprise creation was the fastest and highest in the early to mid-1990s, attracted a constituency of small, sometimes family-centred, enterprises, where both owners and workers voted for the Lega. *The blue-collars have represented the largest group of party voters since 1996.* In 1998, 38.5 per cent of the blue collars and 31.3 per cent of the self-employed in the northern regions were willing to vote for the Lega (Biorcio 1999: 58). This profile does not represent an innovation, because in the 1996 elections the Lega returned to its pre-1992 constituencies, leaving behind the urban middle class it had conquered at its apogee in 1992–3. In 1996 the Lega retrenched in its former fiefs, that is to say in the less urbanized areas comprising the hills between the Po valley plain and the Alps. It became hegemonic in these swiftly developing areas of very small and diffuse enterprises. This was exactly the same area where the DC was the dominant party (Dimanti 1997*a*: 162).

This relatively young, male, and 'productive' constituency is quite different from the electorate of the other extreme right parties. Contrary to the latter, the Lega voters are not concentrated in either the main or inner cities, but are geographically quite peripheral (the Lega is below the mean in urban areas), *and they are not socially marginal: their level of income is among the highest in Italy*. Nevertheless, they share many of the attitudinal traits of the extreme right parties. More specifically, the Lega's voters display a high level of xenophobia, authoritarianism, and anti-system sentiments.

The xenophobic issue, having been de-emphasized in connection with the party entry into the institutions (1992–93), has recently been revitalized at the local and national level. The analyses of the party electorate in the early 1990s (Kitschelt 1995; Gabriel 1996) highlight the modest level of xenophobia vis-à-vis the other extreme right parties. But that phase had ended by 1996 and the Lega is now the only Italian party openly to address a xenophobic discourse. The opposition to multiculturalism and the practice of making foreigners the scapegoats are constant themes of party propaganda. The data show that the voters' attitudes are congruent with the party message: 58 per cent of the Lega voters interviewed between late 1996 and early 1998 exhibit a high level of 'popular xenophobia', an index which compiles attitudes towards a set of questions referring to the excessive number of immigrants and their responsibility for criminality, unemployment, and welfare costs. This percentage is 22.7 points above the mean and is by far the highest among all parties (the AN voters percentage is 'only' 7.8 points above) (Natale 1999: 77). Analogously, 77.4 per cent of Lega voters are rated 'ethnocentrist', 14 points above the mean and, again, by far the highest (Biorcio 1999: 76). As far as authoritarian attitudes are concerned, 66.5 per cent of Lega voters share a high level of authoritarianism, 12 points above the average, even if, in this case, the other right-wing parties (Alleanza Nazionale and Forza Italia) share the same score (Biorcio 1999: 76; Cova 1999: 298–9).

The diffusion of authoritarian attitudes, however, is rather inconsistent with party discourse. Bossi himself repeatedly declares his attachment to freedom and democracy, although with populist tones. And the party's ideological references—whilst very much at odds with theorizing and thinkers—come from the American federalist tradition plus some liberal/libertarian patchwork; no classical right-wing extremist reference is ever recalled and the anti-fascist leaning of the party has been repeatedly proclaimed without any ambiguity at all. This imbalance leads us to formulate the hypothesis that the localist and familist discourse, derived by the regionalist anchorage of the Lega, plus the promotion of xenophobic attitudes have 'inevitably' attracted a quota of authoritarian voters; xenophobia, familism, and ethnocentrism are part of a syndrome where liberal democracy, contrary to authoritarianism, has no room (independent of the party messages). Actually the recent radicalization of the Lega forces reconsideration of Kitschelt's statement that '(the) populism of the Lega is directed against the State and the establishment more than against libertarian politics'(Kitschelt 1995: 181), as the latter has become the new target of Lega dicourse.

Finally, regarding attitudes towards the system, the Lega voters display the highest distrust towards the parties (see also Biorcio 1999: 77–8; Cova 1999: 313), 14 points above the mean. Moreover they have the lowest trust in Parliament, only 30.2 per cent compared to a mean of 47.7 per cent (Biorcio 1999: 78), and the lowest confidence in the workings of democracy.

This outline depicts a party whose voters are quite close to the extreme right: ethnocentrist, anti-system, authoritarian. However, they diverge from them because of the peculiar origin of this set of attitudes. They do not derive from authoritarian anti-liberal thinking, but from the regionalist-autonomist origin of the party. The attempt at creating a (non-existent) northern identity by the Lega leadership implied the identification and demonization of an 'enemy'; in the absence of religious, ethnic, or linguistic specificity, not even in terms of cultural traditions, the party leadership introduced a populist discourse in order to mobilize the 'northern people' against the centre, 'Rome', the nation-state, the politicians, the parties, and finally the 'alien' people. In this attempt Bossi has activated the most profound veins of Italian anti-system political culture. In a country with a weak national identity such as Italy, the revitalization of the North/South cleavage, reinforced by the people/elite divide, has mobilized deeply rooted constituencies characterized by a latent anti-system profile.

The opposition to the system found a new vector in the Lega, different from the neo-fascists on one side and the communists on the other. And the fact that the Lega prospered mainly in former Catholic and DC bastions demonstrates that it activated the protest of those constituencies traditionally not at ease with the nation-state, because of the Church opposition to the process of unification. This enduring hostility towards the 'centre' was reactivated by a novel, 'modern' set of issues expressed by the more dynamic social groups: the frustration of the economic actors in front of a voracious and inefficient central administration, and towards political corruption, was skilfully represented by the Lega, which politicized the issue of 'local' interests. Following this path, the Lega implemented the anti-centralist and anti-statist discourse with familist and anti-alien themes. Under the uncontested leadership of Umberto Bossi, the Lega voiced the uneasiness of a large portion of an economically very dynamic area. The dissatisfaction against the 'inefficient' centre was fused with parochial and localist tendencies. The populist appeal to the 'virtue' of the northern people was consistent with the objective of providing it with an identity; and in this process every distinctive element was acceptable, to the point of recruiting authoritarian and xenophobic voters. Notwithstanding the mix of pro-market and welfare chauvinism, of federalism and independence, of libertarianism and xenophobia, of anti-fascism and authoritarian-ism, and, above all, of reference to the 'people' against the establishment, the party leader himself always provided the unitary and uncontested mastic.

On the other hand, this melting pot is at the root of the peculiar location of the Lega in the political space. All the surveys show that the Lega electorate is not at the extreme right but is mainly located in the centre-right. In 1992 the centre location appeared as the by-product of a dispersion of the party self-identifiers along the left–right continuum: there was no particular concentration on the central position and the centre-location was basically the outcome of the arithmetic mean (Mannheimer 1993a: 258–61). However, the party positioning

TABLE 3.6. *Self-location of potential Lega Nord voters*

Self-location	1991	1994	1996	1998
Left	6.7	3.3	6.0	5.5
Centre-left	11.2	7.5	16.1	9.6
Centre	14.1	13.8	28.7	29.4
Centre-right	22.5	32.6	18.2	21.5
Right	22.2	28.1	8.1	17.4
Not located	20.4	23.0	27.9	23.9

Source: Biorcio (1999: 73).

moved progressively and more consistently towards the centre (Biorcio 1999: 73): *since 1996 more than one quarter have located themselves in the centre position*, and according to the 1999 post-European election survey, 50.5 per cent placed themselves in the central position (Mannheimer 1999) (see Table 3.6).

This self-location, less extreme than the AN and even Forza Italia, dramatically confronts the hypothesis of the Lega belonging to the extreme right family. Beyond the anti-system and xenophobic attitudes, which depict the Lega as the rightmost party in Italy, the voters' location is totally inconsistent. This imbalance reinforces the previously underlined hypothesis of the absolute extraneousness of the party to the extreme right milieu and of its peculiar mould. In a way, the profile is similar to the Belgian Vlaams Blok, as both parties pleaded for the auto-nomy/independence of their region. However the two parties differ, not just in their respective spatial location, but also in their relative emphasis on the various issues. The basic theme of the Lega is opposition to State centralism (the north/south cleavage is very salient for its voters: 65.8% against a mean of 47.6% (Biorcio 1997: 143)) with its inefficiency, drain on resources, and corruption. The anti-immigration issue, while growing sharply and already largely adopted at the local level, has not yet become the key party issue.

In conclusion, the Lega could be defined as an anti-system but not extremist party—or an extremist party of the centre—which collects an ethnocentric, alien-ated, and authoritarian electorate well beyond its discourse. Therefore, the Lega is on the border of the extreme right family rather than one of its components. Had we adopted the 'national/populist' framework of analysis, the Lega would qualify as the populist party par excellence (Betz 1998*a*: 45).

4

Germany: The Spectre That Never Materialized

The twelve years of the Nazi regime (1933–45) constitutes the unavoidable, while not exclusive, reference for the post-war extreme right. Non-Nazi components of the extreme right have their roots in the beginning of the century's fusion of nationalist, authoritarian, and anti democratic sentiments. The 'national question (. . .) forms the core of right-wing extremist thought and behaviour in West Germany [so much so that] nationalism is practically a synonym for right-wing extremism' (Stöss 1991: 17). In Germany, contrary to the experience of many other European countries, nationalism has always had anti-democratic features. This is mainly due to the tormented history of the German nation, which for a long time was dispersed throughout various different states. The continuous search for a (territorial and cultural) identity fed the nationalist movements of the Imperial Reich (1871–1918) and of the Weimar Republic (1918–33). In the Weimar period, leveraging on military defeat and the 'iniquitous' peace treaty, two national-authoritarian tendencies developed: the first was the national-Germanic one, which gathered around the Deutsch Nationale Volkspartei (DNVP) (German National Popular Party). It advocated a strong state—in line with authoritarian Prussian conservatism—and a weak version of democracy, with parties and labour unions reduced to a marginal role. The second was the national-socialist one, which emphasized the constitution of a new, great, powerful Reich with totally new ideological references.

Paradoxically, the disastrous outcome of the Nazi regime has contributed to keeping the national question alive. The loss of a quarter of the territory of the Weimar Republic, the feeling of total defeat, the subjugation to the winning powers' authority, and the country's partition, fed feelings of retaliation and revenge. The problem of the reconstitution of the German 'community of people' (*Völkgemeinschaft*) was by small circles of nostalgic or extremist groups, but deeply moulded the German political culture at large. These turbulent historical events, including the wars, the changes of regime, and, above all, the instability of the national borders, led to overemphasizing safe and stable social structures such as the family, the bureaucracy, and the government. Such a process not only brought about a 'cult' of the State, the withdrawal from politics of the bourgeoisie, and formalism and legalism in politics, but also fostered the need to return to the *Völkgemeinschaft*. In German history, therefore, the authoritarian State and *völkish* (ethnic popular) nationalism are the two, inseparable, faces of the same coin (Minkenberg, 1998a: 108–13; see also 1994, 1997). The *völkish* conception of the

German nation is so deeply rooted that even the 1949 democratic constitution of Federal Germany makes a precise reference to the 'German cultural space'—the *Kulturnation*—even if it is somewhat antithetical to the universalistic values of liberal democracy. The contradiction is clear: the people, defined in ethnic-cultural terms, contrasts with the people conceived in democratic-universalistic terms. This inheritance affects more than the Nazi past in forging potentially extremist attitudes.

Inevitably, the German Federal Republic had to face a serious identity crisis. The post-1945 German political system exhibited weak legitimacy for a long time: in 1959, the famous research on the 'civic culture' (Almond and Verba 1963) revealed that only 7 per cent of Germans (in contrast to 46% of Englishmen) were proud of their own political institutions, while a higher percentage (compared to that of the other countries) was proud of their country's economic achievements and of their own national 'character'. In other words, in face of a modest consideration for the institutions of the representative democracy, a strong national self-esteem and a satisfaction for the country's economic development emerged. The link between the people and the political system was therefore highly dependent on economic performance. Although the Germans have since filled the gap in their trust in the institutions, reaching high levels of satisfaction for 'the working of democracy', the strictest relationship still concerns the working of the economy. As a matter of fact, in every period of growing economic crisis the degree of confidence in the system diminishes and the extremist tendencies develop. So the relationship between economic crisis and the extreme right in Germany must be framed in the particular context of the relationship between economic development and legitimacy of the system, where the latter is legitimate only as long as it produces wealth. When the system no longer carries out this function, loyalty to the regime wanes in those sectors of German society with weaker system identification.

For the purpose of discussion, the development of right-extremism could be divided, according to Zimmermann and Saalfeld (1993), into three phases—from the first years of the new republic up to 1952; the second half of the 1960s; and from the end of the 1980s until today.

THE FIRST PHASE: 1945–52

The first extreme right parties to rise were the Wirtschaftliche Aufbau-Vereinigung (WAV) (Association for Economic Reconstruction) in 1945, the Deutsche Konservative Partei–Deutsche Rechtspartei (DKP–DRP) (German Conservative Party–German Right Party) in 1946, and the Sammlung zur Tat/Europaische Volksbewegung Deutschlands (SzT/EVD) (Action Group/ European People's Movement of Germany) in 1949. The WAV represented 'the dissatisfaction of authoritarian bourgeois groups with the economic and political situation in occupied Germany and was opposed to the "liberation law" (the de-nazification) and the construction of the parliamentary/democratic structures' (Stöss 1991: 85). The DKP–DRP followed the authoritarian-conservative tradition of the Weimar Republic's nationalist forces. The SzT/EVD represented the first example of a party of the 'new nationalism'; this tendency argued for a 'Third Way' beyond capitalism and communism and, by concealing past nostalgia. pleaded for German unification in a united Europe outside the two blocks (Stöss 1991: 27–8). This last party, however, did not enjoy the same success of the other two and disappeared shortly afterwards.

The right extremist parties, before the formal establishment of the FRG, were born under the eyes of the allied occupation powers as the latter had the right to allow or veto the constitution of every new party. The consent given to the formation of three movements clearly inspired by right-extremism might be explained by the intention to bring to the surface, and therefore better monitor, well-rooted anti-democratic tendencies. These movements proved very attractive. In the first elections for the regional (*Land*) parliaments, the WAV got 7.4 per cent in Bavaria (1946) and the DKP attained 3.1 per cent in Schleswig-Holstein. Then, in the first elections for the federal parliament (Bundestag) in 1949, they collected, together with the independent candidates supported by these parties, more than 10 per cent of the votes. However their seats were limited to 18 because the independent candidates did not succeed in overcoming the threshold of representation (Stöss 1991: 88). If one considers that the turnout was only 78.5 per cent, and that a large proportion of the abstentions was due to the refugees and the purged, the potential extreme right electorate was still quite large.

In fact, when visas for party formation were abolished by the Allies, new extreme right parties emerged: the Sozialistische Reichspartei (SRP) (Socialist Reich party) and the Deutsche Gemeinshaft (DG) (German community) in 1949; the Block der Heitmatvertriebenen und Entrechteten (BHE) (Refugees and victims of injustice block) and the Deutsche Reichspartei (DRP) (German Reich party) in 1950. With the exception of the BHE, they were geographically concentrated: the SRP and the DRP to the north and the DG to the south. The SRP proved the more radical one: it proclaimed itself neo-Nazi to the point of acknowledging admiral Dönitz, Hitler's designated successor, as the only legitimate authority, and re-evaluated Nazism in terms of the national-revolutionary ideal and the unity of the German people's blood, under the guidance of an indisputable leader (Stöss 1991: 111; Zimmerman and Saalfeld 1993: 52–3). Although concentrated only in the Protestant north of the country, its successes—11 per cent in the *Land* elections of Lower Saxony and 7.7 per cent in the *Land* elections of Bremen—with such an openly Nazi programme pushed the Adenauer government to advocate Constitutional Court intervention to ban the party.

The outlawing of the SRP, decreed by the court at the beginning of 1952, did not benefit the other extreme right organizations. While the SRP electorate was dispersed, some of its cadres passed to the DRP, a party of old traditional nationalism, much more cautious in its official declarations in order to avoid the attentions of the Constitutional Court. Nevertheless, in the DRP program there was also room for the typical nostalgic request for the release of all the war criminals, re-establishment of the historical frontiers of Germany, and reconstitution of a new Reich founded upon 'authentic German culture', as manifested in the Third Reich (Zimmermann and Saalfeld 1993: 53).

Finally, the DG was a party of 'new nationalism', neutralist and anti-Western (Germany had to stand in opposion both to the West and to the East) and tied to the '*Konservative Revolution*' that judged Nazism of 'bad taste': too noisy, too vulgar, too ignorant, and too boorish (Stöss 1991: 116). The economic programme recalled the social policy of the Nazi party of the 1920s (nationalization of the key industries, the curtailment of the power of financial interests and 'petit bourgeois socialism'). In an attempt to enlarge its constituency beyond former veterans and war victims, it flirted with the refugees' party, the BHE, that, freshly constituted in 1950, achieved a resounding success (23.4%) in elections for the Schleswig-Holstein regional parliament. The BHE, while 'naturally' inclined to make alliances with extreme right parties (such as the joint list with the DG in the elections in Bavaria, in Lower Saxony, and in Baden-Württenberg), could not afford a radical anti-system opposition due to its role as defender of specific interests which needed government intervention. In fact, the BHE quite soon broke its pact with the DG, which subsequently rapidly declined. The refugees were much keener on the defence of their interests embodied by the BHE than on the politics of nationalistic opposition promoted by the DG and the other minor extreme right parties.

With the 1953 elections, the first phase of right extremism came to an end. With the exception of the Refugees' party, which obtained 5.9 per cent of the votes, all the other parties running in the elections separately polled little more than half a million votes. At last, the BHE was drawn into the government coalition, and the extreme right remained alive only in the DRP's bare threads. (see Table 4.1).

What are the causes of the extreme right's sudden rise, and subsequent rapid containment? The persistence in the population of an attitude of compliance and justification towards Nazism is the first element in explaining their rapid surge. The survey data on the early post-war period are revealing: in 1947, national-socialism was considered a good thing, but badly managed, by 55 per cent of the people, a percentage which climbed to 66 per cent in the early 1950s; in 1951, 25 per cent of the people favoured a one-party government and only 32 per cent attributed responsibility for the outbreak of WWII to Germany; in 1952, national-socialism was considered 'on the whole' positive by 44 per cent; in 1954, 15 per cent would have voted for a man like Hitler; and in 1955, Hitler was considered, beyond the 'mistake' of the war declaration, a great statesman by 48 per cent (Merkl 1992a: 334ff; Stöss 1991: 41ff).

This attachment to the past reflected a difficulty in overcoming the trauma of defeat (Maier 1988). The process of de-nazification activated by the Western powers proved ineffective in the short run. In fact, the Allies, having adopted the (debated) interpretation of the collective guilt of all the Germans, set up a gigantic attempt at identifying the responsibilities of the citizens—to punish and re-educate—that proved, inevitably, unmanageable. The de-nazification, so radical in its original project, produced minimal effects in the purges and the trials. In the first place, half of the 180,000 Germans immediately arrested for their active role in the NSDAP were not prosecuted. Besides which, 95 per cent of the 3,660,648 initiated cases, for one reason or another, were released from any charge. Moreover, around one-third of the trials were not carried out and only 175,152 were sentenced. These figures should be viewed with the (symbolic) figure of 6479 sentences by the German courts. Finally, in the territory under Soviet occupation 150,000 people were arrested, half of whom died in imprisonment, and the number of those purged was just over half a million, the majority of whom ran away to the West (Stöss 1991: 61). All in all, the process of de-nazification proved a 'farce' (Stöss 1991: 68) compared to the initial purposes of a 'whole-nation trial'. The idea of collective guilt was rejected in the short run by a wide stratum of the population; consequently, a portion of it expressed its grudge towards the winning powers and the German government, by supporting '*revanchiste*' and nostalgic extreme right organizations.

The incomplete and awkward process of de-nazification managed by the Western powers, the lack of an anti-fascist political class that could lead and legitimate the de-nazification, and, partly tied to these two elements, the persistence of Nazi nostalgia and compliance, explain, together with the existence of the particular constituency of the refugees, the success of the extreme right in the immediate post-war period. These favourable elements were however contrasted effectively by four factors: (1) the 1951 amnesty which withered up a source of frustration of the nostalgic constituency; (2) the '*divide et impera*' strategy by the governmental parties toward the extreme right; (3) the ability by Adenauer's governments to defuse the devastating potential of the refugees' protest; (4) the immediate successes of the economic reconstruction that strengthened the government and the political system itself.

THE SECOND PHASE (1966–9): THE NPD

The German extreme right entered a long tunnel after the 1953 elections. The BHE, which had been half way between the parties of the *bürgerblock* and the extreme right, was then absorbed by the CDU, while the only survivor of the extreme right, the DRP, went unnoticed until it loosened and transformed itself into the Nationaldemokratische Partei Deutschlands (NPD) (National-Democratic German party) in 1964. The NPD took up many classical themes of right extremism, such as the rehabilitation of the Nazi past, the recasting of a 'great' Germany, and the reference to hierarchical, authoritarian, and militaristic principles, but it also introduced some novel ones. First of all, it was the first party to bring the problem of immigrants to the forefront; secondly, it denounced the decline of traditional moral values in opposition to consumerism, to the Americanization of life styles, to the '68 generation's libertarian and revolutionary values; and thirdly, it opposed the '*Grosse Koalition*', the alliance between the SPD and the CDU in 1966–9. In substance, the NPD tried to provide a partially new right-wing answer to the problems of 1960s Germany.

Beyond the NPD political offer, the reasons for its success between 1966 and 1968, when it overcame the 5 per cent threshold in seven of the eight *Länder*, electing 61 *Land* MPs, lie in the socio-political changes of that period rather than in a sudden resumption of nationalistic and authoritarian nostalgia. Despite the fact that the conservative sectors were shocked by SPD participation with the CDU in government (the '*Grosse Koalition*'), what really counts was the reaction to the economic crisis, *the first since 1945*. Since confidence in the German political system was mainly guaranteed by its economic performance, the crisis determined a weakening in the system's legitimacy. The NPD reflected anxiety for personal destinies and loss of confidence in the system, both provoked by the economic emergency. The symbiosis between the reaction to the *Grosse Koalition* and the displacement in front of a deficit in the system performance launched the NPD to the best score for an extreme right party in a parliamentary election since then: 4.3 per cent. The NPD electorate mirrored the party's strategy to attract new electoral constituencies: the traditional supporters of the nationalistic and authoritarian position—mainly elderly, middle-class, occupied in agriculture, and resident in rural areas—were joined by a sizeable presence of non-unionized workers (Stöss 1991: 149; Kolinski 1992: 64).

Failure to accomplish the 5 per cent threshold (to gain access to parliament) in the 1969 elections provoked an immediate, dramatic inner crisis in the party with members' dispersion, increase in violent actions, internal splits, and the party leader Adolph Von Thadden's resignation. All these internal ruptures, plus the post-1969 CDU radicalization, confronting the extreme right on some of its traditional issues (Minkenberg 1998a: 290–2), led to the loss of all seats in the *Land* parliaments and a miserable 0.6 per cent (-3.8%) polled in the 1972 elections. Up to the end of the 1980s, the NPD did not manage to resurface with its own representatives in a single *Land* parliament.

The crisis in the NPD was, in a sense, counterbalanced by the development of much more radical, openly neo-Nazi groups and movements devoted to violent actions and even to terrorism. In the second half of the 1970s, neo-Nazi movements attained their apogee, not so much due to their ability to recruit, being

TABLE 4.1. *Vote for extreme parties in Germany in parliamentary and European elections*

	1949	1953	1957	1961	1965	1969	1972	1976	1980	1983	1984E	1987	1989E	1990	1994	1994E	1998	1999E
AUD					0.2			0.1										
DG			0.1	0.1														
DKP/DRP	1.8																	
DNS		0.3																
DRP		1.1	1.0	0.8														
DVU													1.6				1.2	
NPD					2.0	4.3	0.6	0.3	0.2	0.2	0.8	0.6		0.3		0.2	0.3	0.4
REP													7.1	2.1	1.9	3.9	1.8	1.7
UAP						0.1												
WAV	2.9																	

Source: Backes and Jesse (1993: 257–8); Stöss (1999: 149).

limited to few hundred activists, as to their aggressive militantism: in fact the number of violent actions increased exponentially reaching a peak of 2475 in 1982 (Stöss 1991: 166; Backes and Jesse 1993: 254). This intensification of militant activity did not involve a corresponding growth in right-wing organizations; even the most active group, the Aktionsfront Nationaler Sozialisten (ANS) (National-Socialist Action Front) led by the only relevant leader in the panorama of neo-Nazism, Manfred Kühnen, did not succeed in attaining sizeable dimensions (Stöss 1991: 181ff; Backes and Jesse 1993: 98–9).

THE THIRD PHASE (THE 1980s AND THE 1990s): NPD, DVU, AND REP

At the end of the 1980s an unexpected revitalization of the extreme right, centred on three poles (the revived NPD, the Deutsche Volksunion (DVU) (Union of the German people), and the Republikaner (Rep)) occurred.

The DVU was founded in the early 1970s, but for the entire decade it more closely resembled a fan club of the popular-nostalgic publications of its founder, Gehrard Frey, than a real party. In fact, with a small additional payment on the subscription to one of the magazines published by Frey, whose circulation was constantly over 100,000 copies (Backes and Moreau 1993: 45), one could also become a member of the party. At the end of the decade, the DVU had evolved into a sort of collector of various 'action groups', all addressed to specific and politically aligned themes concerning the limitation of immigration, the re-evaluation of war veterans, the protection of the *Volk* culture, and amnesty for war criminals. Affiliation to one of these groups involved automatic registration with the DVU. The party's indirect membership was slightly more than 10,000 until the late 1980s, when finally they boomed reaching a peak in 1993 (26,000 members), then reduced to 15,000 by 1995 and ranged around that figure thereafter (Backes and Moreau 1994: 59; Backes 1997: 139–40; Bundesminister des Inneren 2000).

The DVU was born as a classical party of old 'nationalism', nostalgic for the military virtues of the German people, strongly nationalistic, and fiercely against immigration and the right of asylum which undermine the purity of the German race. The DVU did not participate in any elections up to 1987 when it formally constituted a (still embryonic) party organization and set up the Liste-D standing in elections together with the NPD. Actually, the two parties agreed to alternate their presence in the elections in order to concentrate all the votes onto one single list. Liste-D marked an immediate success in the 1987 *Land* election in Bremen, attaining 3.4 per cent and obtaining one seat, the first one for an extreme right party since 1968. After unification, the DVU (which did not run in the 1990 Bundestag elections) reorganized and ran alone in elections, keeping to its track of revisionism, mild nostalgia, military virtues, nationalism, and xenophobia until the mid–late 1990s. In 1991 the DVU broke through, once more in Bremen, with 6.2 per cent (in some districts it reached 10 per cent of the votes and even 30 per cent in one of them (Roberts 1992: 336)). This result, in face of the post-unification extreme right crisis, demonstrates the persistence of an extreme right voter potential beyond the Republikaner and NPD fiasco of the 1990 elections, and the absence of any monopolistic hold by the Republikaner themselves. In fact, the DVU performed quite well in the 1992 *Land* election in Schleswig-Holstein, scoring 6.3 per cent and gaining six seats. However, once the *asylanten* question deflated, it lost hold. In the *Land* elections in Hamburg (1993) and Bremen (1995) it scored poorly (2.8% and 2.5%, respectively) (Jaschke 1999: 149). Only at the end of the decade, modifying its appeal from nationalism to social concern and welfare chauvinism, and concentrating its efforts on the Eastern *Länder* (Stöss 1999: 151), did the party get such unexpected outcomes as 12.9 per cent in the Saxony-Anhalt 1998 *Land* election and 5.1 per cent in the Brandenburg 1999 *Land* election.

The national election of 1998 provided the DVU with only 1.2 per cent of the votes, but it came out as the major force of right-extremism in former East Germany, with 2.8 per cent. The party's appeal to a marginal and frustrated constituency (especially in the Eastern *Länder*) focused on the recasting of a popular, ethnically homogeneous (*völkisch*) community, disintegrated by liberal individualism, capitalist economy, and the process of globalization. This strategy relies upon the idea that only an ascriptive element such as ethnicity could face and solve the disruptive force of individualization and globalization (Minkenberg 2000*a*). But such an appeal has still gone unheeded (Table 4.2)

The NPD resurged in the late 1980s, but remained organizationally very weak; it was credited with something like 6000 members after 1982, which slightly increased in the following years (Backes and Moreau 1994: 38–9; Backes 1997: 139–40; Bundesminister des Inneren 2000). Thanks to agreement with the DVU, in the eighties it contested some *Land* elections, collecting 2.1 per cent in

TABLE 4.2. *Vote for the extreme right in West and East* Länder *in national elections*

	West	East
1990		
NPD	0.3	0.3
REP	2.3	1.3
1994		
REP	2.0	1.3
1998		
DVU	0.8	2.8
NPD	0.1	0.7
REP	1.9	1.5

Source: Stöss (1999: 149).

Baden-Württemberg and 1.2 per cent in Schleswig-Holstein in 1988. The NPD did not benefit from having an image as the oldest party of the extreme right: the nostalgic appeal played a less and less important role in mobilizing potential extreme right voters; rather, the 'coherence' with fascist or Nazi ideology constituted a handicap. Moreover, the party was later confronted with a new, less nostalgic competitor, the Republikaner. The sudden success of the Rep in 1989 marginalized the NPD, fostering, as a consequence, a radical turn. The NPD became increasingly more militant, promoting direct (and also violent) actions rather than building up a solid partisan organization and a party electoral platform. The *Verfassungsschutzbericht* (Office for the Protection of the Constitution) has recently charged the party with pursuing a double strategy: traditional and mildly nostalgic in its official statements, while promoting and fostering militant neo-Nazi activities.

The NPD is now concentrating its efforts in the Eastern *Länder*, promoting nationalism (and also DDR-Nationalism) and xenophobia fused with a national-socialist social policy in order to capture the working-class voters by luring them from the PDS (Jaschke 1999: 147). The NPD's 'nationalist anti-capitalism' (Jaschke 1999: 148) politics did not pave the way for success. The party won just over 1 per cent of the votes in some Eastern *Länder* in the 1998 national elections, which represents a good score compared to the Western *Länder* but, on the whole, is hardly promising. The same goes for the small increase (+0.1%) in the 1999 European elections. At the end of 1990s the NPD is the weakest and most traditional radical party of the German extreme right. However, as it has concentrated its activity more on street-level initiatives rather than on the electoral and institutional arena, it demonstrates a certain capacity for mobilization (Minkenberg 2000*a*; Loch 2001).

The Republikaner (Rep) represented a new phenomenon in the political panorama of the extreme right. The Rep was founded in 1983 in Munich by two former MPs of the Bavarian Catholic party, the CSU, dissenting from the party's easy-going policies towards East Germany. In fact at that time, the powerful CSU Bavarian leader Franz-Joseph Strauss managed a very particular policy of appeasement and financial support towards the DDR (Franke 1996: 91), legitimizing in so doing its existence. On the contrary, the primary goal of the new party was the reunification of 'Germany as a whole'. The first party programme of 1983 can be defined as 'national-conservative' (Stöss 1991: 113), with a special emphasis on the unification of Germany within the process of European integration. The Republikaner did not originate within the traditional environment of the extreme right, but rather attempted to differentiate itself from that milieu (Backes 1990: 14). For example, the Rep, contrary to all other extreme right movements and parties, refused to use denominations such as Germany, nation, or people in their title.

This picture changed with the advent to the party leadership of Franz Schönhuber, an ex-journalist dismissed by Bavarian television for his compliance with Nazism. He was author of a successful book of memoirs, *Ich war dabei*

(*I was there*) (more than 200,000 copies sold), vindicating his and his generation's war service. Once installed, Schönhuber swung to the right and in 1985 promoted the 'Siegburg Manifesto', which advocated a strong State, both in the international arena—restoration of full political sovereignty and appropriate international role for Germany also through reunification—and in the domestic arena—enforcement of 'law and order', more severe punishments, and restrictive measures toward immigrants, defined as 'carriers of crime'. The preamble to the manifesto textually recites: 'Unemployment, government deficit, the sale of German national interests and immigration threaten our country. The past means defeat and guilt, the present is division and invasion of foreigners, the future will be the result of this present policy' (quoted in Jaschke 1993: 113). All these themes were to be developed (and sometimes radicalized) in the 1987 programme, the basic point of reference for the party's successful propaganda. They involve re-establishing the national identity, exaltation of the *völkisch* (ethnic-popular) nature of the German nation, moral and spiritual renewal, closing of the frontiers to foreigners and immigrant repatriation, denunciation of the inefficiency, ineptitude, and corruption of politicians (Betz 1990*a*: 21), and (in this case, contrary to the corporatist, 'third-way' references of the Siegburg Manifesto) exaltation of capitalism and free enterprise. In short, the party displayed an accentuation of 'authoritarian, anti-pluralist, neutralist, and anti-European' attitudes (Saalfeld 1993: 185).

On the basis of this political–ideological framework, the Rep, after some uninspiring electoral tests—the best result was 3.0 per cent in Bavaria in 1986—broke through with 7.5 per cent in the West Berlin *Land* parliament elections in 1989 and 7.1 per cent in the European election of the same year. The importance of these outcomes is twofold: first, for the first time since 1949 (or since 1953 if the BHE—the Refugees' party—is included) an extreme right party achieved representation in a nationwide election; secondly, no extreme party in Germany had ever imagined that such a high score at national level was possible.

In these elections the party was able to attract male, poorly educated, elderly (over 60 years of age) working-class voters. The proportion of male and low-educated people was around two thirds of Rep voters and the unskilled and (especially) skilled manual workers represented the core of the Rep electorate, outstripping the self-employed, who had traditionally over-supported the extreme right (Stöss 1993*a*: 57, 1993*b*; Falter 1994: 28ff). More specifically, it has been argued that the Rep was able to penetrate well beyond the small bourgeoisie reaching the young authoritarian workers having a hedonistic lifestyle with no organizational or traditional bonds with the labour movement (Jaschke 1993: 123–8). An in-depth survey of Berlin voters' attitudes after the Republikaner breakthrough demonstrated that the Rep electorate scored very highly on the various indexes of nationalism, authoritarianism, ethnocentrism, and welfare chauvinism. In the combined index of 'extremism potential', 42 per cent of Rep voters occupied the two highest positions on a five-point scale, compared to 7 per cent of the electorate at large (Stöss 1993*a*: 65).

The collapse of the Wall and Germany's unification, satisfying one of the key points of the Rep's policy, and correspondingly favouring Chancellor Kohl's CDU, endangered the Republikaner party which, in the first elections of the united Germany (December 1990), did not surpass 2.1 per cent. The grave concern about a full resumption of the extreme right in Germany, fuelled by the April–June 1989 electoral outcomes, was settled by the poor score of the Republikaner (and the NPD). However, since most of the reasons for the extreme right's rise in Germany did not disappear with reunification, the Rep, as well as the DVU and the NPD, soon regained a following. After the DVU entry into the Bremen parliament in 1991 scoring 6.2 per cent, the Republikaner in the following year became the third of Baden-Württemberg, with 10.9 per cent of the votes (and the DVU polled 6.3 per cent in Schleswig-Holstein). Actually, this was the last significant performance of the Republikaner. From then on, it failed to enter the Bundestag (and the European Parliament) in the 1994 '*Superwahljahr*', and hence faced a long and irrecoverable decline, with the landmark exception of the 1996 election, again in the *Land* of Baden-Württemberg, where it reached a surprising 9.1 per cent. Some of the favourable conditions for the extreme right, such as immigration and the national question, faded away; and the spreading of violent actions against the immigrants and the *asylanten*, the relative anti-extremist counter-mobilization (also at the legal-constitutional level), the party's internal divisions, and leadership's lack of personality, all weakened the Republikaner's chances. The 1998 general election (1.8%) and the 1999 European election (1.7%) confirmed the Rep's troubles, while it still remains the strongest party of the extreme right. The party members' recruitment followed the electoral trend. After the breakthrough in 1989 when the Rep recruited 25,000 members, the number of members declined (with the exception of the 1992–3 recovery), remaining around 15,000 members in the following years (Backes and Moreau 1994: 38–9; Backes 1997: 139–40; Bundesminister der Inner 2000).

The party programme had undergone a series of modifications after the Siegburg Manifesto. In 1990 the REP softened some issues and toned down its language, professing allegiance to the democratic system, fearing it would be censored by the Constitutional Court as an extremist and anti-democratic party. On the other hand, it did not alter its basic 'nationalistic' roots since, for example, the demand for a restoration of the 1937 borders of the Reich was couched in even more explicit terms. Such toning down did not allow the Rep to escape the Constitutional Court's decision to put the party 'under surveillance' from December 1992, on the same level as the other extreme right movements. As a consequence, in 1993 the Rep prepared an even more accommodating and moderate programme, and the party leader Schönhuber repeatedly declared himself hostile to and distant from extremism and violence. But the party's compliance with the past nourished a reckless and irresolvable contradiction. In August 1994, after having being classified 'unconstitutional' by several *Land* offices of the *Verfassungsschutz*, the provision was enforced by the federal Office for the Protection of the Constitution. Furthermore,

Schönhuber's latent appeasement raised a furious hostility within the party that forced him to resign, leaving the leadership to Rolf Schlierer in late 1995.

ASYLANTEN AND *POLITIKVERDROSSENHEIT*: ENOUGH FOR A REVIVAL BUT NOT FOR A BREAKTHROUGH

What are the causes of the extreme right's resilience in the late 1980s and early 1990s? And what are the factors that inhibited its further success?

Basically, the resurgence of the extreme right was linked to: (a) the persistence of a 'national question'—which comprises many different elements: the metabolization of the past, the 'westernization and individualization' of the German culture, the reunification and national sovereignty, the question of immigrants, asylum-seekers, and German resettlers; (b) the enduring presence of authoritarian, extremist, and nostalgic attitudes; (c) the disaffection with politics, the political system, and the parties.

The National Question

The third wave of right extremism had a period of 'incubation' in the 1980s, well before its breakthrough. In that decade, the cultural–ideological development of both remote and novel references, and the emergence of new partisan cleavages, established the conditions for the rise of the extreme right.

Since the 1970s 'German intellectuals have revived the distinctly German conservative idea of a strong State' (Minkenberg 1993: 11), introducing Germany to the Western mainstream of neo-conservatism (Grande 1988). Moreover, the neo-conservative milieu was supplanted by the emerging circles of the *Neue Rechte* (Minkenberg 1993, 1994; Pfahl-Traughber 1999)—especially the Junge Freiheit and the *Mut* and *Criticón* journals—which provided the ideological tools for an indirect criticism of liberal democracy by developing a new version of nationalism and racism. The neo-conservatism recast nationalism in its *völkisch* version, in opposition to the process of westernization/Americanization of Germany. This process was indebted not only to the moderate bourgeois elite but also (paradoxically) to the protest movements of 1968 that, introducing post-materialist values to the political agenda (civil rights, more participation, informal interpersonal behaviours, free sexual mores), aligned German youth culture to the Western mainstream. Actually, the German neo-conservatism endorsed by the CDU at the eve of its comeback to power, when it advocated a radical change (*die Wende*), was the national and traditional counterpart to the post-materialist and 'liberal' political agenda, fostered by the 'Westernization' itself of the German society.

In particular, as far as the national question is concerned, the 'constitutional patriotism of the Left was challenged by the traditions of the German *Kulturnation* and *völkish* nationalism' (Minkenberg 1994). The convervatives' 'emphasis on an ethnocultural idea of nationhood and the desire to normalise the past [in order] to regain "cultural hegemony" from the Left and define the terms of the debate [were in tune with] the intellectual *Neue Rechte* and some right wing circles' (Minkenberg 1999: 28). But when the CDU returned to power on the wings of neo-conservatism, it failed to translate the promised cultural and moral turn (*die Wende*) into concrete political action (Franke 1996). Accordingly, thanks to the emphasis on some favourite themes of the right, and above all on German identity, the development of a new type of party, largely unrelated to the neo-Nazi tradition but more 'national-populist', such as the Republikaner, became possible. In fact, the Rep not only gathered the electorate of those discontented with the CDU, but founded its own constituency. The Rep's success was therefore indebted (also) to an earlier politicization of German ethnocentrism 'by the major parties' elite, well before the rise of the new radical right: (. . .) a shift to the right preceded then coincided with the rise' of the extreme right (Minkenberg 1998*b*: 8). The CDU was not able to handle the issue of national identity, so central to the right-extremist world-view, beyond a certain point. Since a large number of people felt threatened by immigration and/or wanted to recover all elements of the German past, the Rep could benefit from a rich reservoir that the CDU could not attract, because Kohl's party could not move too far to the right of the political spectrum (Franke 1996: 90). The 1993 Basic Law amendment was the most the CDU could afford.

Nostalgia Antisemitism and Authoritarianism

The reframing of the national question on the basis of ethnic homogeneity and compliance with the past reflected the feelings of a large proportion of German public opinion. In 1986, when the *Historikerstreit* (the passionate debate over the German past) broke out, around one third of Germans were tired of debating Nazism (among those under 30 years of age the figure was 59%, and among those with the lowest level of education 73% (Betz 1990*a*: 10)). Moreover, the figure of Hitler continued to be substantially appraised in a positive way: at the end of the 1970s around one-third of Germans considered that, apart from the war, Hitler had been a great statesman (compared to 48% in 1955) and that the Third Reich, with the exception of the war and the persecution of the Jews, 'was not too bad' (Kolinski 1992: 75–7). This desire to remove the blame was thus diffused amongst the mass public rather than concentrated only in the (very limited) extreme right electorate. Such desire was exploited in the political arena with unprecedented efficiency by the Republikaner. The Rep radicalized the political discourse on nationalism, offering an euphemistic and even proud interpretation of German history.

The compliance with the past, associated with other nostalgic, nationalist, ethnocentric, and authoritarian attitudes, is at the core of the so-called 'syndrome' of right-extremism. This syndrome was originally constructed, on the basis of

23 items, by the research institute SINUS in 1980, and later adopted and/or reframed by other survey analyses. The SINUS study showed that 13 per cent of the adult population could be defined right-extremists, and 37 per cent more people shared authoritarian but not extremist characteristics (Ueltzhöffer 1984: 80–94; Bauer and Niedermayer 1990: 15–26). More particularly, among the questions that identified the extremists, it emerged that: 14 per cent desired a new *Führer*; 28 per cent thought the politicians of Bonn undersold Germany's interests; 28 per cent maintained that if the *Lagers* still existed, discipline and order would reign; and 39 per cent asked for more effort towards the purity of the environment and of the race (Ueltzhoffer 1984: 82ff).

Beyond nostalgia, right-extremism relies upon xenophobia and racism, especially under the aegis of anti-Semitism. Various sources demonstrate the persistence of an 'anti-Semitism without Jews', given the minimal presence of this community in Germany. The 1989 EMNID survey identified 14 per cent of people as anti-Semitic, plus 4 per cent as furiously anti–Semitic (Merkl 1994). Other sources suggest that 6 per cent were decidedly anti-Semitic, 10–15 per cent had some explicit prejudices, and 15–20 per cent displayed some anti-Semitic features without openly expressing them (Stöss 1991: 49). In a study of the Allensbach institute in 1992, anti-Semitic stereotypes and prejudices had increased in comparison to a similar investigation in 1987: 54 per cent (against 42% in 1987) judged the Jews astute, 28 per cent (against 15%) unaccountable, 23 per cent (against 15%) without scruples, 19 per cent (against 7%) ominous (Anti-Semitism World Report 1993: 26). In addition, exclusionist attitudes, referring to those people who do not want a Jewish friend or colleague, range between 12 and 22 per cent (Bergman and Erb 1991: 149). Considering the weight on the German civil conscience of the extermination of the Jews, the endurance of anti-Semitic attitudes is somewhat surprising. On the other hand, these attitudes are constantly fuelled by neo-Nazi propaganda on the *'Auschwitz luge'* and Holocaust denial.

As far as xenophobia is concerned, Germany has been the 'asylum land' par excellence in post-war Europe. Apart from the millions of refugees from former German territories and German communities in East-Central Europe in the immediate post-war years, from 1950 to 1988 3.3 million Germans from East Germany and 1.6 million refugees from other countries with the right to German citizenship entered Federal Germany. These huge inflows of people were later added to by foreign workers (*gasterbeiter*) in the years of economic boom. The problem of the *gasterbeiter* never assumed primary political importance. Only at the turn of the decade between the 1970s and the 1980s did some concern arise in the southern *Land* of Bavaria and Baden-Württemberg. A latently hostile atmosphere surrounded the *gasterbeiter*: in 1982, 55 per cent of Germans agreed with the hypothesis of repatriating the immigrants once they had lost their jobs and 49 per cent were hostile to their presence (Stöss 1991: 49–50). These preoccupations induced the federal government to introduce visa restrictions (Karapin 1999: 434–5).

However, between 1980 and 1990 the negative attitudes vis-à-vis foreign workers declined: for example, only 31 per cent agreed in sending them back when a job shortage arose (Bergman 1997: 30).

The immigration issue exploded in 1989, in connection with the fall of the Wall. First of all, some hundred thousand Germans moved from the DDR to the West and then, starting in 1990, a massive inflow of refugees (*asylanten*) and resettlers (people who claim German lineage) entered Germany. In 1991 the resettlers amounted to 222,000, while the asylum-seekers were some 256,000 (equal to two-thirds of all the refugees welcomed by the EEC). The inflow reached a ceiling of 438,000 in 1992 and, after a still very high number of arrivals in 1993 (328,000), it rapidly and substantially decreased to around 100,000 (Kurthen, Bergmann, and Erb 1997: 8) once the restrictions on asylum rights were introduced (Küchler 1996: 256).

Consequent to the massive inflow, there was a boost in the sensitivity toward this issue, as well as in the negative feelings towards the immigrants and in direct (and violent) actions against them (Merkl 1997). The number of people that 'did not accept foreigners' increased dramatically (especially in the Western *Länder*), but the xenophobic wave retreated after the 1993 provisions. However, anti-foreigner sentiments diminished only in the Western *Länder* where it had previously skyrocketed, while they continued to increase in former East Germany creating a wide gap (50% more) in the level of xenophobia between the two parts—which is even more evident in young people (Hoffmann-Lange 1996: 124ff). Parallel to rising xenophobia is the number of violent anti-foreigner acts. The right-extremist 'offences' went from 2031 in 1990 to a peak of 10,661 in 1993; even more the violent actions purported by right-extremists jumped from 178 in 1990 to 1495 in 1992, and 1322 in 1993 (Table 4.3) (Bundesminster der Inner 2000). Comparing the Western and Eastern *Länder*, the number of violent acts in the East have been, more or less, double those in the West (Kurthen, Bergmann, and Erb 1997: 8); since 1998 the balance of violence is even more skewed in favour of former DDR (Minkenberg 2000*b*: 321).

The massive wave of immigrants and the violent actions by right-extremist fringes (which even provoked some deaths from arson attacks on immigrant centres) brought the immigration issue to the fore. Concern mounted in public opinion, peaking in September 1992 when 61 per cent of the people rated the *asylanten* question the most important one (Lubbers and Scheepers 2001). Also media attention on that issue, and on the extreme right, followed the same trend, with a particular emphasis in the aftermath of the Rep success in Baden-Württemberg in September 1992 (Brosius and Esser 1996). The consensual agreement between the CDU–CSU and the SPD modifying the Basic Law on the right to resettlement and asylum at the end of 1992 (enforced in mid-1993) toned down the issue and dismantled the extreme right agenda. After this institutional arrangement, and the consequent drop in new arrivals, right-extremist violence provoked a pervasive counter-mobilization by anti-racist organizations, trade

TABLE 4.3. *Violent actions and incidents by the extreme right in Germany*

Year	Incidents	Violent actions
1990	2.031	178
1991	4.073	849
1992	7.702	1.495
1993	10.661	1.322
1994	7.952	784
1995	7.896	612
1996	8.730	624
1997	11.719	790
1998	11.049	708
1999	10.034	746

Source: Verfassungsschütz (2000).

unions, and a large network of associations, producing a re-stigmatization of extreme right positions and organizations on the public scene (Merkl 1997). This was true especially in the West, while in the East the weakness of the democratic infrastructure hindered an effective reaction.

Disaffection with the Political System and the Parties

The presence and persistence of an extreme right potential should have encountered an obstacle, in principle, in the full legitimacy of the institutions and the democratic system that the German electorate overwhelmingly acknowledges. In 1988, a German public opinion survey pointed out that, among the motives of pride over being German, the institutions and constitution came first place, while the economy—motor of the system's legitimacy in the first years of Federal Germany—received little consideration (Bürklin 1991: 23). Furthermore, satisfaction over the working of democracy reached very high levels: 73 per cent in 1989 and as much as 85 per cent in 1990, probably due to the euphoria of reunification (Merkl 1992a: 335). However, this positive picture, assessing the pervasiveness of 'constitutional patriotism', proved to be inadequate in endangering the persistence of the extreme right potential and the rise of extreme right parties. As underlined above, this happened because the diffused (although hidden) concerns on past and present features of the national question were politicized (and better represented) by the extreme right rather than by the CDU, in the opportunity structure of the 1989–92 cycle. Moreover, the high level of trust in the system faded in the years after reunification, weakening the defence against extreme right recovery.

Reunification, in the very short run, marginalized the extreme right parties since one of their more vociferous demands had been met. The 1990 elections had a disastrous outcome for the extreme right. On the other hand, reunification brought new concerns and demands to the fore. First, as already mentioned, the number of German resettlers and asylum-seekers from Central-Eastern Europe increased substantially in a few months. Second, the economic imbalance between the two former Germanies led to widespread sentiments of alienation and frustration in the Eastern part, and of uneasiness in the Western part. Third, mistrust over the traditional setting of the political system and the parties themselves, better known as *Politikverdrossenheit* (dissatisfaction with politics), arose because of the widespread feeling that the socio-economic difficulties of unification were mismanaged; this was coupled with outrage triggered by the emergence of political corruption scandals (Betz 1990*b*; Pfahl-Traughber 1993; Rattinger 1993; Scarrow, 1996).

As a result of these concerns, the very high level of satisfaction over the working of democracy in 1990 sharply declined in the following years, plummeting by some 25 per cent between 1990 and 1993, and then recovered remaining slightly above the 50 per cent threshold. The same pattern is true for the disappointment with the established parties: the level of discontent, fluctuating around 30/35 per cent until early 1992, jumped to more than 50 per cent in the following months, precisely at the moment of the right extremist surge (Noell-Neumann 1994: 44).

THE NEW CONSTITUENCY OF THE EXTREME RIGHT WING VOTER

The extreme right voters display *by far* the highest level of political disaffection, nostalgia for the past, xenophobia, ethnocentrism, and anti-Semitism among all other voters (Falter 1994: 149; Gabriel 1996: 345; Klein and Falter 1996: 292ff; Weil 1997: 125–7; Stöss and Niedermayer 1998). The abundant survey data on the three right-extremist parties' voters unquestionably state that these traits distinguish this electorate from the population at large. For example, the EMID survey on the eve of the 1994 general election found that 40 per cent of the right extremist voters located themselves on the highest level of a 0–10 scale of right-extremism (Falter 1994: 141). And the same goes for their attitudes towards foreigners, the Nazi past, and the workings of democracy. A similar survey run in 1998 revealed that 58 per cent in the West and 53 per cent in the East of the REP/DVU/NPD voters shared a right-extremist world-view (built upon the scale of authoritarianism, nationalism, ethnic xenophobia, socio-economic xenophobia, pro-Nazi sentiments, and anti-Semitism) (Stöss and Niedermayer 1998: 11) (Table 4.4).

Beyond those who share a well-knit right-extremist set of attitudes, there are even larger constituencies which express a 'protest-potential': 19 per cent mistrust parties and politics in general (*Politikverdrossenen Protestpotential*); 22 per cent are alienated by the system (but are not openly anti-democratic); and 26 per cent are totally dissatisfied with democratic institutions (Stöss and Niedermayer 1998: 25). These data should not lead us to conclude, however, that such a large reservoir of 'protest' voters could easily be mobilised by the extreme right parties. On the contrary, the largest proportion of these voters either abstains or votes for the major parties. *Only those adhesive to a right extremist world-view and located on the right extreme of the political spectrum are conducive to the extreme right vote.*

Up to the early nineties, the extreme right voter was male, old, undereducated, with medium–low to low income, blue-collar, and (somewhat less) self-employed (Stöss 1989; Falter 1994: 99, 105–6). The 1998 DVU performance in the Saxony-Anhalt election projected an image of an undereducated young, blue-collar, *and* jobless extreme right voter: the DVU reached 28 per cent among 18–24 year-olds and 32 per cent among young males, compared to the mean of 12.9 per cent (Jaschke 1999: 150). In the 1998 general election the young and the young male cohorts were over-represented, as 7 per cent and 10 per cent of them, respectively, voted for the extreme right (Stöss and Niedermayer 1998; Minkenberg 2000b). They constitute the 'new urban under-class' (Jaschke 1999: 146) most receptive to the extreme right messages. The more militant profile of certain components of the extreme right parties (especially the NPD) might be linked to this juvenile–underclass shift in the socio-demographic profile (Table 4.5).

In conclusion, the extreme right parties are mainly enforced by the development of a world-view which rotates around the traditional references of authoritarianism, racism, anti-Semitism, xenophobia, ethnocentric nationalism, and Nazi nostalgia, plus updated and country-specific elements such as system dissatisfaction and *Politikverdrossenheit.* These attitudinal factors, when added to *subjective* elements such as frustration, displacement, alienation, and status inconsistency, have a stronger explanatory power than the *structural* factors (economic crisis, unemployment). In other words, the *perceptions* of certain structural conditions are much more important than the conditions themselves in forging a world-view and, in particular, the extreme right world-view (Stöss 1999). Therefore, the feeling of loss of authority at every level, the nostalgia for an orderly world, the desire to reduce the complexity of the decision-making process, the need for simple models of explanation, the change in values, the fear of losing German identity

TABLE 4.4. *Attitudinal profile of the German extreme right voter (attitudinal scales)*

Scale	Germany	Western Länder	Eastern Länder
Authoritarianism	11	10	16
Nationalism	13	13	13
Ethnic xenophobia	15	14	20
Economic xenophobia	26	23	39
Pro-Nazism	6	6	5
Anti-semitism	6	5	5

Source: Adapted from Stöss and Niedermayer (1998).

TABLE 4.5. *Socio-demographic profile of German extreme right voters and deviation from the population mean*

	Extreme right	Deviation
Men	4.4	+1.1
Women	2.2	−1.1
18–24 years	7.3	+4.0
25–34	4.5	+1.2
35–44	3.6	+0.3
45–59	2.5	−0.8
+60	1.9	−1.4
Elementary	3.5	+0.2
Middle / technical	4.6	+1.3
High	2.1	−1.2
University	1.1	−2.2
Unemployed	6.7	+3.4
Blue-collar	6.7	+3.4
White-collar	2.4	−0.9
Civil servant	2.0	−1.3
Self-employed	2.7	−0.6
Catholic	2.5	−0.8
Protestant	2.8	−0.5
Other religion	3.3	=
Not religious	5.5	+2.2
Mean	3.3	

Source: Minkenberg (2000*b*: 329).

and of being the losers in the process of modernization, the threat of a multicultural world, and anti-establishment sentiment, are all attitudinal preconditions for the acceptance of the extreme right discourse.

The last wave of extreme right voters have different socio-demographic characteristics compared to the past (Table 4.5): they are younger, non-religious, blue-collar workers, and unemployed (with still some self-employed), concentrated in urban areas and in the East. The extreme right parties attempted to represent the demands of the lower class, who feel alienated and underrepresented by the major parties. The proletarization of the German extreme right has met the challenge of representing the 'modernization losers', that social constituency shocked by the disruption of the traditional social milieu (including the social-democratic one), by family break-ups, by consumerist lifestyles, by new rules in the job market, and, finally, by globalization (Betz 1998*b*; Jaschke 1999). The extreme right aims at those frightened by the 'risk society' (Beck 1998).

In recent years the territorial distribution of right-extremism changed; it found new bastions in the former DDR. In the 1998 elections, aside from the Western *Land* of Baden-Württemberg, the extreme right scored much better in the East than in the West.

East Germany's critical socio-economic conditions and its lack of a deeply rooted democratic culture (Fuchs 1999: 142–3) produced—far more than in the West—sentiments of alienation, frustration, and resentment, which found their preferred scapegoats in foreigners, the institutions, and the parties (in that order). Xenophobic attitudes and aggressive behaviour towards foreign people are many times higher in the former DDR than in the former RFD. Authoritarianism, ethnocentrism, and socio-economic xenophobia are 50 per cent higher (Stöss and Niedermayer 1998: 11). Moreover, the level of satisfaction is much lower in the former DDR (Fuchs 1999: 141) and the *Systemverdrossenheit* (the anti-system attitude) is double in the East compared to the West (Stöss 1999: 150).

In the past few years, the extreme right parties (especially the DVU) have concentrated their efforts on the former DDR in order to mobilize a supposedly more sensitive constituency. The outcome of the elections in Saxony-Anhalt in 1998, where the DVU scored an impressive 12.9 per cent, fuelled the prospect of a right-extremist breakthrough in the East. Actually, that result proved quite exceptional (the only replica being the 5.1 per cent in the 1999 election in Brandenburg). The modest results in the general election of 1998 and the European elections of 1999 substantiate this evaluation.

Apparently, the extreme right has failed—as Betz (1998*b*: 11–12) has recently stated—because of lack of legitimacy, linkage to the past, and inner structural weakness. However, the last general election demonstrates that *a potential for the extreme right still exists*. First of all, compared with the crushing defeat of the Republikaner in 1994 (the only extreme right party to run in that election), the extreme right in 1998, all together, scored 3.3 per cent—5.0 per cent in the East and 2.9 per cent in the West. Secondly, on the eve of the 1998 election, 'extreme right potential' still involved 13 per cent of the population (as in 1980), a percentage which represents the average of 12 per cent in the West and 17 per cent in the East (Stöss and Niedermayer 1998: 10). Accordingly, the Eastern *Länder* offer better conditions for the extreme right, whether because of uneasiness with the fundamentals of liberal democratic institutions and political culture, or the structural and attitudinal determinants of right-extremism.

To conclude, the third wave of right-extremism reflects the latent needs of a German society emerging from structural/economic and value modification. The breakthrough in Germany, as in other Western societies, of a 'new axis of conflict' representing a 'non-material' (cultural and moral) agenda, ranging from national identity to authoritarianism, from xenophobia to moral traditionalism, has provided a non-ephemeral base of consent for the extreme right. Moreover, reunification has provided further opportunities: it has produced economic stagnation (extremely pronounced in the East) which has fed hostility towards the government and the parties in general, and has relaunched—mainly because of immigration—the nationalist *völkish* interpretation of national identity. The lack of a large network of political associations in the East has liberated a violent mobilization by movements and groups and a (still latent) neo-Nazi revival. If the extreme right failed in the electoral arena it is still present (and aggressive) in street-level activity, especially in the East.

5

France: Prototype of the
New Extreme Right

The origins of the extreme right in France are both old and contemporary. Old because France is the first country where, according to Zeev Sternhell, the fascist ideology emerged with an 'articulated body of thought' (Zeev Sternhell 1980: 480). Contemporary, due to the fact that a relevant post-war extreme right party only emerged in France in the mid-1980s. Even in the inter-war period, the fascist-like movements were weak, short-lived, or politically marginal. In any case, the tradition of the extreme right is both culturally and politically rich and varie-gated (Sirenelli and Vigne 1992; Winock 1993). René Rémond, in his famous book *Les droites en France* (1982), traced the different cultural leanings of the right from the French revolution onwards. The three 'archetypes, ... similar to the Weberian ideal-types' (Rémond 1982: 39) identified by Rémond are the counter-revolutionary, the liberal (or Orleanist, from the royal house's reign during which it developed), and the Bonapartist-authoritarian (see Chapter 1).

As the present work is focused on the development of the *extreme* right, then only the counter-revolutionary and the Bonapartist traditions remain subjects for discussion.

Furthermore, the counter-revolutionary right is of limited importance. It was partially reactivated at the beginning of the twentieth century by Charles Maurras's *Action Français* (French Action), modernising the 'tradition' in order to suit it to the demands of the new mass society. Because the monarchy had lost the charisma and legitimacy of divine right, it needed a new mode of legitimation, which could only be provided by [the 'mystical body' of] the nation. Traces of this tradition can be found in the Vichy regime (1940–44), and more recently among some components of the *'Nouvelle Droite'* and the Front National.

On the other hand, the Bonapartist right, associating 'democracy and authority, [and] privileged reference with the people and personal power' (Rémond 1982: 41), is a central reference because, in its varied incarnations and tones, it constitutes the hardcore of the extreme right. It emerged during the epoch of industrial development and the related conflicts and mass politicization. Since then, it has resurfaced many times under different forms such as Boulangism, *fin de siècle* Nationalism, 1930s Leagues, IV Republic Gaullism, Poujadism, and finally National-populism.

Do all these multiform expressions of right extremism comprise of fascism? According to Rémond and almost all French historians, apart from Doriot's short-lived Parti Populaire Français (PPF) (French Popular Party) and Deat's Rassemblement Populaire National (RPN) (National French Rally), fascism never took hold nor attained a sizeable organizational dimension. The various Leagues that emerged in the 1930s had the choreographic symbolic elements of fascism, but not the spirit. They have been defined 'caesarist, authoritarian, plebiscitarian and nationalist' (Rémond 1982: 208) and while they opposed parliamentarism, they did not invoke a fascist regime; instead, they aimed at a 'parliamentary dictatorship' or a strong presidential regime. In sum, 'while it was conservative, the French right was not fascist' (Rémond 1982: 222).

On the contrary, Zeev Sternhell (1987, 1989) advanced the provocative hypothesis that fascism was culturally born in France *and was embodied in various parties*, even if it did not take hold. Many ideas that sprang up in *fin de siècle* France are at the core of fascist ideology: voluntarism in opposition to the levelling mechanization of industrial society; anti-intellectualism and anti-rationalism in the name of the cult of action, of energy, of the *élan vitale*; moral relativism as a base of the biological exaltation of the race and its 'mission'; refusal of bourgeois values and, at the same time, the attempt to regenerate the elite; organic interpretation of the world and society; hierarchal while solidaristic social fabric, devoid of all degenerative elements such as individualism, class antagonism, and alien presence. All these elements, which Sternhell has masterfully pinpointed in 1890s French society, compound the basic traits of the to-come fascist ideology.

FORERUNNERS AND REAL INTERPRETERS OF FRENCH FASCISM

Without participating in the ongoing debate on the 'French' origin of fascist political culture and its reification in political organizations (for an excellent review see Burrin 2000: 247–66; Milza 1987; Winock 1993), we will nevertheless map the various interpreters of anti-democratic and populist feelings in the first half of the twentieth century. Such supposed interpreters emerged in three successive waves. The first one is represented by the Action Française and its offspring, the second by the 1930s Leagues, and the third by two unequivocal fascist movements, the PPF and the RNP.

In the early years of the century the most influential group was the Action Française. Established in 1905, encompassing various associations linked to the magazine that Charles Maurras had founded at the end of the nineteenth century, the Action Française was characterized by Catholic integralism, by a nationalism that verged on xenophobia and anti Semitism, and by anti-parliamentarism and hate toward the Republic (to be demolished in favour of a 'national' monarchy). All this was fuelled by the cult of violence which, from the pages of the otherwise culturally sophisticated magazine, was brought to the streets by the young activists, militarily organized into the Camelots du Roi. However, the importance of the

Action Française did not concern its militant mobilization but its intellectually sharp destructive criticism of democratic principles. All in all, the Action Française represented the only movement having something in common with the counter-revolutionary tradition, even if it distanced itself from that tradition due to the advocacy of a 'popular-national' legitimization of the monarchy.

In the same period, the Cercles Proudhon, inspired by Georges Sorel, the revolutionary union activist author of '*Réflections sur la violence*', proposed to unify the revolution and the nation in order to unhinge the bourgeois order and its values. Like Maurras, honorary president of the Cercles Proudhon at their foundation in 1911, Sorel's first and foremost enemy was democracy, 'the greatest error of the century', that supplanted 'the blood's law with that of capitalism and of gold' (quoted in Sternhell 1980: 484). As in the case of Action Français, the influence of the Cercles was limited to the intellectual sphere.

In this first phase, a plausible precursor of fascism appeared in the form of Pierre Biétry's Federation des Jaunes de France (Federation of the Yellows of France), which was then transformed into the Parti Socialist National (National Socialist Party). Founded in 1903 upon a programme of 'national socialism', commending corporatist representation and solidarity in spite of the class struggle, it reached a large audience with thousands of members and succeeded in electing its leader to parliament, but soon disappeared with Biétry's death in 1912. While it has been considered 'a true forerunner of fascism' (Milza 1987: 84), its short life did not leave significant traces.

During the first post-war period, the extreme right underwent an organisational boom. On one side, non-political movements such as the Federation Nationale des Combattants (National Federation of Veterans) and the Union Nationale des Combattants (National Union of Veterans) recruited hundreds of thousands of members. On the other side, a number of more or less fascist-like and violent 'Leagues' were created. Among them, the most remarkable were the Jeunesses Patriotes (Patriotic Youth), the Croix-de-Feu (The Fire-Cross), and, for other reasons, the Faisceau, the Solidarité Française (French Solidarity), and the Francisme.

The Jeunesses Patriotes was founded in 1924 by the multi-millionaire Taittinger to oppose the revolutionary threat, provoked by the success of the left in the 1924 elections, in the name of a somewhat legitimist nationalism. The Croix-de-Feu was established in 1928 as a veterans' association decorated with the 'fire-cross'. Under the leadership of Colonel La Rocque it acquired a nationalist and anti-parliamentary political leaning (Soucy 1991). Nevertheless neither the Croix-de-Feu nor the Jeunesses Patriotes were as revolutionary as the movements to come: they were the armed guards of the bourgeois order, rather than the avant-garde of a 'new order'. In fact, the more pro-fascist tendency abandoned the Croix-de-Feu in 1935 due to incompatibility with its moderatism (symbolized by the dissociation of La Rocque from the street demonstrations of 6 February 1934) and became diffused within the PPF. Despite these defections, the Croix-de-Feu maintained a mass membership (apparently even one million in 1937 (Burrin 2000: 256)), although this was not translated into comparable parliamentary representation (3.5% in the parliamentary by-elections between 1936 and 1938, and 11% in those of 1939), even after its transformation into the Parti Social Français in 1936.

The Faisceau was the first movement founded in imitation of the Italian fascist party, the PNF. The Faisceau, heir to the Cercles Proudhon, whose activity had been brusquely interrupted by the death of Sorel and the outbreak of war, was propelled by a desire for action and mass involvement. The movement, founded by Maurras's former *bras-droite*, George Valois, developed a clear leaning towards fascism, as it was anti-bourgeois and anti-conservative, militarily organised, and keen to direct violent actions. But Valois's incendiary rhetoric and the appeal to the left for a common national, anti-capitalistic revolt soon isolated this movement from its financiers and from other extreme right groups, resulting in its dissolution (Sternhell 1976*b*).

The Solidarité Française and the Francisme were more clearly proto-fascist movements (Milza 1987), but they did not benefit from a mass appeal as in the case of the Croix-de-Feu. The Solidarité Française was created in 1933 by the parfumier François Coty following the success of his fascist-like magazine, *'L'Ami du Peuple.'* However, while the newspaper's circulation exceeded 200,000 copies, party members were ten times less and activists numbered a mere thousand. The Francisme was formed in 1933 under the initiative of a former leader of the Faisceau. It was recognized as the 'legitimate' representative of French fascism, thanks to an invitation to the Fascist International meeting in Montreux in 1935, but it never exceeded 10,000 members. Its struggle on all fronts, against the reaction, capitalism, and the Judaeo-Marxists calling for a national revolution, did not arouse great enthusiasm, partly due to its intellectual poverty.

The third 'generation' of right-extremists represented a break with the past. because the two movements at the end of the thirties, Jacques Doriot's Parti Populaire Français (PPF) and Marcel Déat's Rassemblement National Populaire (RNP), were not rooted in the right wing environment where the national question was *the* founding element (Sternhell 1980; Brunet 1983; Burrin 1986; Milza 1987). In these new parties the national problem was put to one side, while the proscenium was occupied by the social question and by the idea of a new corporatist social fabric. What is more, while the Leagues primarily addressed the ordinary man or the small bourgeois with populist appeals (with the exception of the Faisceau which mainly appealed to the workers), the PPF and the RNP found their initial support in the working class because the party leaders both came from leftist parties.

There were no multi-millionaires or rich industrialists behind the foundation of the PPF: instead, there was an intelligent and ambitious communist leader, mayor of one of the working class strongholds of the Parisian belt (Saint-Denis), former general secretary of the Communist Youth, MP, and candidate to the PCF secretariat, Jacques Doriot. Expelled in 1934 for his revisionist and corporatist ideas, he founded the new party in 1936 with large support from the working class and former communists: in the first National Executive, seven out of eight members came from leftist organizations and five of them were workers (Sternhell 1980).

The last fascist movement to be founded, Marcel Déat's Rassemblement National Populaire, was also the most radical. Déat was the leader of the left faction of the SFIO, a member of the *Front populaire* government, and author of the 1931 manifesto '*Perspectives Socialistes*' arguing for an anti-Marxist, national, authoritarian, and class-bargaining socialism. Marginalized within the SFIO, Déat and his group (called the 'neo-socialists') left the party and founded a movement of 'socialist purity' to carry out a moral revolution. The encompassing of the class conflict in a corporatist State did not mean abandoning the socialist roots to which the RNP continued to be faithful. Veneration for Jean Jaurès (the founding father of French socialism), celebration of the 1st of May, and opposition to the more reactionary features of the Vichy Regime, demonstrated its loyalty to its roots. On the other hand, the desire for 'regeneration' in face of 'decadence' (Sternhell 1994) resulted in its embracing the more palingenetic outcome identified in the German Reich as the only necessary way for a radical renewal.

On reflection, the inter-war movements are testimony to the existence of a strong *corpus* of anti-democratic values and attitudes, antithetical both to the liberal system and to Marxist ideology. The anti-parliamentary opposition had very wide appeal, recruiting hundreds of thousands of members, and often surpassed the leftist parties in their militancy. Nevertheless, their results at the polls were always modest, if not derisory. The Action Français, at its apogee in 1919, only elected about 30 deputies, who were then reduced to a few members in 1924; the PPF and the PSF together obtained less than 10 per cent of the vote in 1936 and only in 1939 did they get over 15 per cent. In essence, the intellectual elaboration and diffusion of ideas demonstrated by the large editorial success of the extreme right press, the mass mobilization and organization, were not matched by the parties' electoral fortunes. Therefore, they failed to take power.

This 'lack of fulfilment' cannot hide the great attraction that fascism exercised on the *intelligentsia* (Girardet 1955), attracting support both from the left and the Catholic world, especially during the Vichy regime, and granting solid cultural roots to future extreme right movements.

FROM THE VICHY REGIME TO THE EXTREME RIGHT
OF THE IV REPUBLIC

The Vichy regime represents a synthesis of the varied streams of the extreme right—Maurrassian, integralist, neo-socialist, fascist—that had never found full expression of their anxiety over spiritual and national renewal in the anti-democratic and anti-parliamentary movements of the 1930s. The Vichy regime was established in Central-Southern France after the May defeat in 1940 and was led by Marshal Pétain (Azema and Wieviorka 1999). The regime embraced the counter-revolutionary tradition, while updating and modifying it with various contributions: the 1930's 'non-conformists', the social Catholics looking for a third way, the fascists of Doriot and Déat. The ideology of Vichy, exemplified by the famous triad 'work, family, country', consisted: 'in the refusal of individualism and egalitarianism, in nationalism, in the search for a national unity above all the divisions, in the mistrust toward industrialism, in anti-intellectualism and in the rejection of cultural liberalism' (Azema 1993: 199). Under the influence of Maurras, Vichy's nationalism was imbued with xenophobia and racism: all the '*métèques*', the non-pure French—freemasons, communists, internationalists foreigners, and particularly Jews—had to be marginalized in order to preserve the purity and integrity of the nation. The Vichy regime was not just a puppet regime controlled by the Germans: it represented the long-awaited opportunity to bring about a national 'revolution' that would purify France from the political and moral disorder into which it had been thrown by parliamentarism. The dream of a morally superior alternative to decadent bourgeois democracy had finally been accomplished.

In conclusion, Vichy became a point of reference for the post-war extreme right because it embodied three deep-rooted tendencies: 'the obsession with the internal enemy; exclusionist ethnocentrism; and the conviction of the imperious necessity for a moral and intellectual recovery' (Azema 1993: 214). Whether Vichy was a fully 'fascist' regime is still an open question (Slama 1986).

Post-war right extremism initially had to face the problem of the legacy of Vichy and of a dramatic purging process (there were around 10,000 executions, including those without trial) (Rousso 1992). In the fifties, most of the extreme right activity was concerned with the veterans' recovery, which affected a large number of people—the courts examined around 300,000 dossiers producing some 100,000 sentences—but no relevant organization emerged. There was, on the other hand, intense editorial activity; some newspapers gained circulation and notoriety, as in the cases of the neo-vichiste *'Paroles Françaises'* and of the 'national opposition' weekly, *'Rivarol'*. The extreme right made their first public appearance by the participation of many *groupuscules* in the 1951 general election under the umbrella of the Union Nationale des Indépendants et des Republicains (UNIR) (National Union of Independents and Republicans) led by Pétain's defence lawyer, Jacques Isorni. This list succeeded in electing four deputies without creating particular concern. In fact, the UNIR deputies would shortly join other political groups. In the same period, the founder of *'Paroles Françaises'*; Charles Luca, unceasingly if unsuccessfully promoted a series of editorial and political activities all advocating an 'anti-democratic and anti-Marxist socialism, contrasting both with liberal capitalism and with socialism and in which the notion of class is replaced by that of nation and of race' (Algazy 1986: 144).

The most meaningful extreme right movement of the Fourth Republic was Jeune Nation (Young Nation) because it was the first organization to overtly declare itself neo-fascist and, at the same time, it broke with the *Pétainiste* tradition. Dealing instead with contemporary issues, above all decolonization and the Algerian question, Jeune Nation attracted a following amongst students rather than in the nostalgic milieu. It was dissolved by the authorities in 1958 for numerous violent actions, but in reality continued its activity under different guises. It could not, however, profit from the favourable opportunity structure provided by decolonization and the Algerian crisis to make a breakthrough. All extreme right groups were squeezed between the terrorism of the OAS (Organisation Armée Secret—Secret Armed Organization) and the prestige of General de Gaulle that held hegemony amongst the conservatives. Consequently they continued to play only a marginal role (Algazy 1986: 244).

At the end of the IV Republic, a new rightist (while not extremist) movement emerged, the Union de Défense des Commerçants et Artisans, (UDCA) (Union for the Defence of Shopkeepers and Artisans) (Hoffman *et al.* 1956; Hoffman 1976; Roux 1985). Created as an anti-tax movement in 1954 under the initiative of Pierre Poujade, a dealer from the French Provence region, it mounted an anti-establishment campaign whose populist tones were summarized in the slogan '*Sortez les sortants*' (kick out the incumbents). The Poujade movement enjoyed immediate success, mobilizing up to 100,000 sympathizers with public rallies and influencing government politics with a series of spectacular and provocative events. In the 1956 elections it got 11.6 per cent of the vote (almost all in the South-west of France) and elected 52 deputies, among whom was a young Jean-Marie Le Pen. However, faced by highly dramatic events—the collapse of the IV Republic—it almost entirely disappeared in the 1958 elections, when Poujade and Le Pen alone were re-elected. The UDCA's rejection of the modernization and rationalization of French society provided new room for the extreme right milieu. Nevertheless *Poujadism* could not be assimilated within neo-fascism because of its vagueness and scattered world-view (Roux 1985: 223; Milza 1987: 307). Rather, it was the expression of the common man's uneasiness when confronted with a process of 'unknown and destabilizing' modernization.

The transition from the IV to the V Republic brought about additional frustrations for the extreme right. The Gaullist regime removed a possibility for it to destabilize the system by exploiting the Algerian question—'the missed opportunity', lamented by the right-extremists for a long while (see Duprat 1972). Moreover, the dismantling of the OAS did not leave any room for a revolutionary outcome. Forced to abandon such wild dreams, the extreme right adopted the electoral approach, by launching the candidacy of Tixier-Vignancour (the defender of the French felon generals in Algeria) for the 1965 presidential elections. Despite great organizational effort and some original initiatives, such as the 'Tixier-Vignancour caravan', a propaganda tour along the most crowded tourist places (the *tour des plages*), they failed to get 5 per cent of the vote.

This failure plunged the extreme right into marginality again, from which it only emerged 20 years later.

In the years that followed, the Tixier-Vignancour support group, the Alliance Républicaine pour les Libertés et le Progrès (ARLP) (Republican Alliance for Freedom and Progress), found a *modus vivendi* with Gaullism, excluding the more radical tendencies. The latter were represented first by Occident (West), a militant group, active in the student revolt of May 1968 and devoted mainly to street fighting—because of which it was outlawed at the end of 1968—and later on by Ordre Nouveau (ON) (New Order), born from the ashes of Occident. ON became the major extreme right group in the 1970s. Well organized, with at least 5000 activists and prone to violent confrontations, ON was a popular and national revolutionary movement emphasizing anti-communism and anti-immigration. While declaring itself to be antagonistic to the system, it wanted to contest elections too. It therefore tried to reconstitute the remnants of the extreme right—anti-Gaullists, national-revolutionary, Maurrassians, integralists, *solidaristes*, etc.—finally reorganizing itself as a new organization called the Front National (FN) (National Front).

THE FRONT NATIONAL

The Beginning and the Dark Years

In April 1972, under the initiative of the Ordre Nouveau, the Front National was born. The two main tendencies of French post-war right-extremism, the '*nationalistes*', represented mainly by ON, and the right-wing anti-gaullist '*nationaux*', merged in one organization (Camus 1989: 17ff). The ex-Poujadist MP, Jean-Marie Le Pen, was called to its presidency. The designation of a man who, despite his long-time affiliation to the French extreme right milieu, had never been openly associated with neo-fascist chapels nor had faced any questions from the legal authorities (Milza 1987: 422), was a concession made by the ON hard-liners on the basis of a unitary strategy. The original themes of the FN—anti-communism, nationalism, immigration, a strong state, the defence of traditional values (Camus 1989: 20–1)—would characterize the party in the years to come. The only changes would concern international alignment—from support of NATO to anti-American nationalism and the economy—from social-national statism to ultra-liberalism and back again (Roy 1998).

In this initial phase, the same consensus on the programme was not shared on strategy. In the first FN congress (28/29 April 1973) the ON delegates, comprising around 50 per cent of the floor, called for the constitution of a neo-fascist 'national right' party similar to the Italian MSI (with which the ON leaders had a good relationship). Meanwhile, Le Pen opposed the neo-fascist leanings, exalting the national tradition of the French right and advocating the creation of a party operating within legality. This conflict was further complicated by the ON inner contradiction between its incendiary and anti-system revolutionist stance and the flirtatious attitude towards the classical right (Chiroux 1974: 213ss). In fact, Ordre Nouveau (or at least a large part of it), in contrast with its resounding declarations, attempted to make an agreement by providing the Gaullist and Giscardian right with logistic '*musclé*' support. In the end, thanks to Le Pen's leadership, the first FN programme was low profile and bargaining-oriented vis-à-vis the moderate right. Even the violent attacks against the Gaullists (defined as traitors of French Algeria) served the purpose of encouraging the most conservative sections of the classical right to accept the 'national forces' supposedly represented by the Front National. In brief, the FN declared its availability to sustain the classical right.

The electoral results of the 1973 parliamentary elections were far from encouraging. The candidates, approximately 100 in number (out of 475 constituencies), collected 106,527 votes (2.3% on the basis of the constituencies where the FN was present). This was a modest result not matched by the 5.2 per cent scored by Le Pen in a Parisian constituency. The negative response of the polls provoked ill-feeling in the ON group against the moderate Le Pen. But the ON was soon outlawed because of violent clashes against the extreme leftist movement, the Ligue Communiste (Communist League), in June 1973. Paradoxically, the ON's break-up weakened Le Pen's leadership. The ON militants, instead of hiding inside the party, created another organisation, Faire Front (Making Front), where they all congregated, and, after few months (September 1973), merged with the FN, thus conquering two-thirds of the party's national executive and isolating Le Pen. However, the party chairman, thanks also to the decision of the court to give him the right to use the FN's name, succeeded in resisting the former ON members' assault on his leadership, forcing them to abandon the FN. The splintered group founded the Parti des Forces Nouvelles (PNF) (New Forces Party) which would confront the Front National up until the 1980s. The hyper-fragmentation of the extreme right continued.

The exit of Ordre Nouveau left room for the other components that would make up the 'ideological *fourre-tout*' of the FN: the national-revolutionary, the catholic-traditionalist, the counter-revolutionary, the neo-liberal, the '*solidariste*' (Camus 1989). All these different tendencies coexisted within the party thanks to the powerful cement constituted by the uncontested leadership of Jean-Marie Le Pen (Birenbaum 1992; Ivaldi 1998*a*), who would play upon the different tendencies depending on the situation. In the 1970s two tendencies gained more importance within the party: Francois Duprat's national-revolutionary and Pierre Stirbois's *solidariste*.

François Duprat was one of the very few intellectuals of that milieu, and the editor of many magazines (*Cahiers Européennes* in particular). He was the author of an interesting history of the extreme right and follower of Julius Evola and the national-socialism Strasserian tendency. Under his influence, new, or newly formulated, themes gained more ground: the defence of the French identity from extraneous 'bodies' that threaten its purity; the racialist approach to immigration; the organic and corporatist view of the State and reference to the 'third way'; the anti-parliamentarism and the tougher attitude toward the 'wet right' of the Gaullists and the Giscardians as part of a radical opposition to the system (Duprat 1972; Camus 1989).

The violent death of Duprat (killed in 1978 by a car bomb) deprived the national revolutionary tendency of its foremost leader. Some of his themes were kept alive by the *solidaristes*, led by Jean Pierre Stirbois, who had entered the party in late 1977 on the basis of a strong anti-NATO, anti-Western sentiment, a mistrust towards neo-liberalism, and a racist and anti-Semitic outlook. While both the national-revolutionary and the *solidariste* tendencies were playing an important role at that time, Le Pen imposed a relevant ideological turn throughout the manifesto *Droite et Démocratie economique* (Right and Economic Democracy) and the electoral programme for the 1978 parliamentary elections, officially declared by the fifth party Congress. Corporatism was replaced by neo-liberalism, Catholic traditionalism found an unprecedented emphasis through anti-abortion mobilization and support for archbishop Lefevre's religious integralism, anti-Americanism left room for pro-Westernism (the identification of the West with Christian civilisation provided the logical linkage), and the racist connotation was disguised under the formula of 'the right to the difference' (Taguieff 1985*a*, 1988).

Those positions would be strengthened in the following years thanks to the influx of some members of the 'Horloge club', a think-tank connected to the more famous *Nouvelle Droite* group GRECE, gathering many members of the moderate right disappointed by its compliance with socialist policies. The Horloge Club called for a 'national liberalism' and a retrenchment of the State and a reconsideration of the 'difference' among men underlying both the inequality among individuals and ethnic groups and the superiority of the West (Taguieff 1985*a*, 1988, 1994). This intellectual elaboration became the pivot of FN discourse on immigrants: ethnic-cultural differences are unavoidable, and must not be eliminated; however, they create tensions in society—not only by reducing the sense of national identity, but also by contributing to delinquency and unemployment—that are resolvable only with the expulsion of aliens (Taguieff 1984, 1986*a,b*). While most of the Horloge club members integrated with the FN and contributed to elaborating many of the party's issues, the uncontested *Nouvelle Droite* intellectual leader, Alain de Benoist, and the GRECE maintained a very cold attitude—when not hostile—towards the Front National (Rollat 1985: 146). However, beyond any personal involvement, the *Nouvelle Droite* gave a cultural dignity to a set of issues which the FN oversimplified and politicized, thus contributing to a better reception for the FN itself amongst the larger public.

The Rise

At the beginning of Mitterrand's presidency (1981) the extreme right was totally marginal. Despite organizational efforts (the creation of the youth organization

Front National de la Jeunesse, of the weekly '*Le National*', and of an embryonic peripheral structure) and ideological renovation, the FN never achieved any visible presence. All the elections ended in failure:

- The 156 candidates running in the parliamentary elections of 1978 obtained less votes than in 1973 (0.4% against 1.3%);
- In the European election of 1979 a common list between the FN and the PNF, attempting to overcome the 5 per cent threshold, was withdrawn at the eleventh hour. However, the day before the deadline for presentation, a PNF-only list, with Tixier-Vignancour at its head, was presented (with a disastrous outcome for the PNF: 1.3%);
- In the presidential election of 1981 Le Pen did not even succeed in obtaining the necessary signatures to be a candidate—because they had been increased from 100 to 500;
- And finally, in the parliamentary elections of 1981, immediately after the presidential ones, the FN hit rock bottom with 0.18 per cent.

Despite this gloomy setting, the FN suddenly enjoyed a series of fortunate results that brought it the amazing score of 11.2 per cent of the votes in the European elections of 1984. How was it possible that the FN passed from the most absolute marginality to success in only three years? A chain of oddly favourable events occurred: it began with the cantonal elections of 1982 where the FN scored more than 10 per cent in five cantons and more than 5 per cent in another five; it continued with the municipal elections of March 1983, where the party polled 11.3 per cent in the twentieth *arrondissement* of Paris and 9.6 per cent in the first electoral district of Marseilles; and it culminated with the by-election in Dreux (held again due to an irregularity), the native town of the FN's secretary, Jean Pierre Stirbois. On that occasion the FN, which had collected a resounding 16.7 per cent in the first ballot, thanks to fierce competition between the moderate right (RPR and UDF) and the left, was accredited for the first time as an acceptable partner by the moderate right, creating internal conflicts amongst the latter. The agreement proved successful as the RPR–UDF–FN list got 55 per cent in the second ballot. The elections of Dreux, which received extensive coverage because of the unusual alliance and the intense debate surrounding it, brought the FN to the attention of the wider public and raised the problem of alliances on the right, a problem that would hang over the moderate right like the sword of Damocles in the years to come.

The sound of the results of Dreux was amplified, in rapid succession, by FN successes in the municipal elections of Aulnay and in the parliamentary by-election in the Morbihan, Le Pen's native land, where the FN leader himself stood as candidate. In the first case the party got 9.3 per cent and in the second 12.0 per cent (even surpassing the PCF by a fraction). The invitation for Le Pen to appear on a popular TV talk show inaugurated the leader of the FN as a national political figure. It was not by chance that the Front National and Le Pen

TABLE 5.1. *Vote for the FN in parliamentary, presidential,*
regional, and European elections (valid votes)

Year	Election	Votes (%)
1973	Parliamentary (first ballot)	0.4
1974	Presidential (first ballot)	0.8
1978	Parliamentary (first ballot)	1.3
1981	Parliamentary (first ballot)	0.18
1984	European	11.08
1986	Parliamentary	9.80
1986	Regional	9.60
1988	Presidential (first ballot)	14.61
1988	Parliamentary (first ballot)	9.73
1989	European	11.80
1992	Regional	13.85
1993	Parliamentary (first ballot)	12.68
1994	European	10.61
1995	Presidential (first ballot)	15.27
1997	Parliamentary (first ballot)	15.23
1998	Regional	15.27
1999	European	5.74
		(3.30*)

* MNR.
Source: Official sources.

subsequently began to be monitored by the public broadcasting survey of political presence (*Service d'orientation des programmes audiovisuelles*) and by the opinion poll institutes. The Le Pen TV appearances presented the mass public with a political leader possessing great oratorical skills, and an outsider politician who did not hesitate to speak out on taboo issues and openly departed from conventional wisdom on a number of themes. His communicative skills were immediately recognized by a survey carried out after the transmission: the voting intentions for the FN doubled from 3.5 to 7 per cent (Sofres 1985: 200). This survey, however, like many others to come, underestimated the effective electoral dimension of the FN. In the 1984 European elections the list headed by Le Pen, in which many outsiders—notables and former RPR and UDF officials such as Olivier d'Ormesson and Michel de Camerat—were inserted (29 out of 81), collected, in fact, 11.1 per cent of the votes. Such a success gave the FN an unprecedented profile and respectability: *no 'new' party had attained such a score in a nationwide election since the establishment of the V Republic* (Table 5.1).

The Reasons of the Rise

What had provoked this sudden and resounding rebound for the Front National after a decade of 'obscurity and sarcasm', as Le Pen put it in the aftermath of the European elections? The explanation could be divided into two sets of electoral-institutional and socio-political factors (Ignazi 1989). Among the first set is the sequence and type of election and the electoral system. The FN first ran at local level, then at national level; moreover, the first nationwide elections were the European elections which are 'second-order elections' where people are more keen to differentiate their vote compared to the most important elections (parliamentary and presidential). Furthermore, the electoral system that was adopted for the European elections—contrary to the other elections—was the proportional system, which lowers the threshold of access and eliminates any considerations of a 'useful vote' making the entry of a new party into the system easier.

These electoral–institutional factors are but one side of the coin. The second set of socio-political factors provides the missing element. They concern increasing polarization, the introduction to the political agenda of new themes, the crisis of representation by the traditional parties, and growing anti-establishment sentiments.

The victory of the left in 1981 provoked a move to the right by the conservative parties, at the same time favouring the circulation of a 'national-liberal' discourse, derived from the combination of the 'values of xenophobic nationalism and of radical economic liberalism with an overt anti-social leaning' (Taguieff 1985*b*: 87). In this period the RPR and the UDF progressively shifted 'towards an extremely conservative, not to say reactionary, view of French society and of the values it should defend' (Ysmal 1984). In terms of spatial location, *the RPR and the UDF middle-level elites moved from 18 per cent of self-declaring centre-right and right in 1978 to 72 per cent in 1984* (Brechon *et al.* 1986: 131).

The FN succeeded in politicizing issues such as immigration (and its supposed effects: delinquency, increasing costs in welfare assistance, unemployment) and insecurity, both considered to be of utmost importance by a limited but very concerned proportion of the population. While these issues had never been a high priority in the mind of the general public, the dissatisfaction vis-à-vis personal safety and the presence of immigrants had been growing for sometime, accelerating in the early 1980s (Sofres 1985; Ignazi 1989). These themes, never dealt with by the traditional parties, were introduced into the political debate with force by the FN, which succeeded in becoming the key reference for 'law and order' and anti-immigrant demands.

Finally, the FN profited from a general mistrust toward party politics, the democratic institutions, and the international status of France. The spreading of a general sentiment of *malaise* and the growing alienation of citizens from the political system in the period between 1983 and 1985 (Ignazi 1989: 74–6) meant an increasing proportion of French people were predisposed to voting against the establishment. The FN became the most obvious emissary of their dissatisfaction. To recap: (a) the proportional system and the fortunate succession of local, partial, and second-order ('*sans enjeu*') elections; (b) the radicalization of the political conflict and the polarization of the party system, thanks to a move to the right of the Gaullists and Giscardians; (c) the break through of new crucial themes like immigration and insecurity and their politicization by the FN; and (d) the crisis of political representation that had widened the gap between the citizen and politics, are all factors that contributed to the emergence of an anti-establishment, anti-system party on the right of the political spectrum such as the Front National.

Consolidation

The FN success in the European elections, due to low electoral turnout and its irrelevance in the national political system, needed to be confirmed in the major elections. The 1985 cantonal elections offered a double opportunity for the FN: to demonstrate that its success was not the outcome of a sudden and short-lived protest (as in the case of Poujadism) and to increase its presence locally, having its own representatives elected throughout the country. But the development of the party had overridden its organizational structure to the point where the party had to appeal to the readership of its internal press to supply it with candidates for the forthcoming cantonal elections. Actually, the call for candidates was successful. *The FN succeeded in presenting candidates in 1521 cantons out of 2044, compared to 65 three years before.* Also the party turnout was positive: 8.8 per cent. Moreover, thanks to the threat of maintaining all 114 candidates eligible to run in the second ballot, Le Pen came to an unofficial agreement with the moderate right to drop over half of them so as not to harm UDF and RPR candidates. Even if the remaining 50 FN candidates did not receive any support from the right, *as only one got elected*, the deal was politically rewarding for the Front because it was 'taken into consideration' by the established right.

The FN continued with the 'politics of opening' experimented with in the cantonal elections, offering candidatures to independent notables and former UDF and RPR officials at the 1986 parliamentary elections. The 35 deputies (corresponding to 9.8% of the votes) that the FN sent to parliament, *thanks to the proportional system introduced on that occasion*, were quite heterogeneous. This created some embarrassment in maintaining a unified party in parliament. In fact, when the politics of accommodation towards the right was replaced with hard opposition towards Jacques Chirac's RPR-UDF government, charged with accepting '*cohabitation*' with the socialist President of the Republic François Mitterrand, some deputies left the FN parliamentary group. Since then the FN endorsed its role as the sole opposition to the '*socialo-communistes*' and, above all, to the political regime and the 'gang of four' (i.e., the four main parties: UDF, RPR, PS, PCF), fully performing the '*tribunicienne*' function (Lavau 1969) of being the receptacle for dissatisfaction.

Actually, the moderate-bourgeois vote that had shifted from the moderate right to the FN in 1984, mainly protesting against the left inclinations of the UDF–RPR list led by Simone Veil (who had introduced many 'feminist' reforms when she was in the right-wing government), had returned to its natural outlet by 1986. But the FN had gained ground in the popular milieu affected by the 'urban crisis' and immigration. The Paris area, Lyon, the Mediterranean departments, and the

Alsace region became FN bastions. In line with its electoral success, the party developed a sizeable party organization. From a few thousand members at the beginning of the decade, the party declared a membership of around 65,000, even if a more reliable figure indicates 15,000 members (Ysmal 1989). Whatever the real figure was, the party since then had been building up an authentic party organization (Birenbaum 1992; Ivaldi 1998*a*).

The strategy of the 'protest party', emphasizing anti-establishment issues alongside the immigration–security refrain, allowed Le Pen to reach 14.6 per cent in the first ballot of the 1988 presidential elections. This resounding performance acquires more weight when one considers that *in 124 constituencies out of 555 Le Pen outran the two candidates of the right (Chirac and Barre)*. In particular, in some of the above-mentioned areas the score of the FN leader surpassed 20 per cent of the votes. Le Pen succeeded in merging 'the self-employed and the owners with the blue-collars, and the old *Poujadism* with the workers' protest' (Perrineau 1997: 53).

Due to this achievement the '*Lepeniste*' electorate had become essential for the right. In the parliamentary elections called a month later (with the traditional double-ballot majority system), the moderate right, rejecting its previous exclusionist attitude towards the FN, signed an agreement with it. In the region of Marseilles, where the FN was particularly strong, the party withdrew its own candidates in eight constituencies to the advantage of the candidates of the right, and the right reciprocated in favour of the Front in the other eight. This agreement, *the first one openly declared since Dreux*, apparently represented a political victory for the FN: it was finally accepted, *apertis verbis*, by the right and it had achieved an implicit legitimacy as a potential partner of government, something Le Pen had been seeking since the first 1973 electoral programme. However, while in the first ballot the FN and the moderate right together had a majority in six out of the eight constituencies where the Front National candidates stood, in the second ballot only one FN candidate (Yann Piat) got elected. Moderate voters refused to sustain a *Lepeniste* candidate.

In conclusion, the 1988 elections highlighted Le Pen's attraction to a larger and diversified constituency of voters in the presidential contest and the party's appeal in the parliamentary contest too (9.7%), even presenting a list without 'notables', but mainly composed by 'simple and obscure militants'. And, above all, the elections stressed the possibility of a stable agreement with the established right—even if the moderate electorate proved unlikely to support FN candidates.

The party profited from the 'disillusioned of the right', namely those voters who were dissatisfied by Chirac's policies both in the domestic arena—modernization and liberalization—and in the international arena—support for the EEC and the inability to regain France's prestige in the world. Moreover, the issues which characterized the FN did not seem at all transient. On one side, the established political leaders adopted unheard of expressions on the immigration issue running behind Le Pen. On the other, even the uproar—and the consequent loss of support—provoked by some outrageous statements by Le Pen (Mayer and Perrineau 1993), such as a sinister pun on the name of the minister Durafour—*Dura/four-crématoire* (Dura/oven-crematory)—and the definition of the extermination of the Jews as 'a question of detail', did not harm it. The (rather limited) criticism which was aroused within the FN (an MP quit the party) gave Le Pen the opportunity to reinforce his own control by restructuring the party organization (Ivaldi 1998*a*: 50). In the 1989 municipal elections the FN achieved a nationwide presence. It stood in 143 cities out of 219 with populations over 30,000, in 214 out of 390 with populations between 20,000 and 30,000, and in 306 out of around 900 with populations between 20,000 and 9000 (Birenbaum 1992: 169). The electoral outcome was inferior to the parliamentary and presidential elections (even if in the cities above 20,000 inhabitants it collected 10.1% of the votes). However it allowed the FN to establish itself locally: the number of elected councillors had risen from 211 in 1983 to 1336 in 1989. Moreover, the FN managed to get all these representatives elected contesting alone, against everybody else, without any agreement with the right. The strategy of confrontation found support in Stirbois' widow's success in the Dreux parliamentary by-election where she was elected with 61.3 per cent, in opposition to the RPR candidate.

The Strategy for the Conquest of Power

The 8th party congress held in Nice in 1990 represented an important event. For the first time an FN Congress was composed of locally elected delegates, surrounded by a very large number of activists (around 1600 people attended), that mirrored a complex nationwide organization. At its head 'reigned' Jean-Marie Le Pen, the uncontested charismatic leader, whose right to set out the party political agenda was recognized by everybody.

The congress launched a new, much more ambitious strategy, that is, the conquest of power. Le Pen believed that between the FN and the left there was only a void: only the Front National was an effective counterbalance to socialist power. The traditional right was squeezed in between due to its ineffectiveness. The socialist/frontist challenge was the only salient political conflict because it hinged upon different conceptions of 'national identity' which, according to Le Pen, confronted two opposite camps: in one the supporters of a cosmopolitan and multiracial society, without identity and subdued towards foreigners (the socialists and their allies); in the other, the defenders of Christianity, of the West, and of the French identity (the Front National). The confrontation with the PS would be fulfilled by the Front alone because the moderate right parties too belonged to the present 'corrupt and unaccountable' system, which was dramatically divorced from the demands of the people and the nation. The FN, without abandoning any of its traditional themes, definitively embodied the anti-establishment (and anti-system) protest to enlarge its electoral constituency and raise a decisive challenge to the PS.

This ambitious strategy found consent in the electorate. Neither the anti-racist mobilization after the desecration of the Jewish cemetery of Carpentras (1990), nor the isolation due to support for Saddam Hussein in the Gulf war (a position that re-launched the creeping anti-Atlanticism of the FN, for a long time silent) arrested the march of the Front National. On the contrary, in late 1991 the percentage of those who agreed with the ideas of Le Pen *doubled in comparison to the year before, jumping to 32 per cent.* Even more significant is the fact that 50 per cent of RPR and 38 per cent of UDF sympathizers approved of the positions of the FN president. More so than in the past, the electorate supported Le Pen's policy, both on his classical themes—immigration (38%), security (31%), and traditional values (30%)—and on the more recent issues, such as his anti-establishment positioning (24%) (Mayer and Perrineau 1993).

The latter element provided the FN with the basis for its continuing growth. French society was affected by a feeling of malaise. The level of party identification, of confidence in the institutions—trust in the parliament fell from 56 per cent in 1981 to 48 per cent in 1990 (Listhaug and Wiberg 1995: 305)—and of the workings of democracy had been declining for years (Sofres 1990: 161–70). Moreover, there had been a constant decrease in the number of people who viewed politics as 'an honourable activity' (from 65% in 1985 to 49% in 1991), who considered politicians as 'honest' (from 38% in 1987 to 29% in 1991) and 'sensitive to citizens' problems' (from 45% in 1983 to 29% in 1991) (Duhamel and Jaffré 1993: 234). This deepening crisis of representation (Cayrol 1994: 126–9) favoured FN's consolidation.

The electoral results throughout the 1990s were proof of the party's increasing capacity for attracting voters. In the 1992 regional (13.9%) and cantonal (12.4%) elections, the Front National definitely set itself up as a *national* political force: it fielded candidates in almost all the *cantons* (1868 out of 1945) and it spread beyond its bastions, so much so that in only 29 departments out of 96 did it fall below 10 per cent (compared to 66 in 1988) (Brechon 1993: 53). Despite the 'republican quarantine' adopted by the moderate right, rejecting any agreement with the Front, the FN boasted 33 mayors, 239 regional councillors, and 1,666 town councillors (Mayer 1993: 331). Its territorial penetration and consolidation had now been attained (Ysmal 1992: 201).

These results were confirmed by the 1993 parliamentary elections where the FN attained fourth position in the French party system, with 12.7 per cent of the votes, *surmounting the Communists and the Greens.* The party was able to benefit from a well-defined and stable electorate: the coefficients of correlation between the 1993 vote, on one side, and the 1988 parliamentary elections, the 1989 European elections, and the 1992 regional elections, on the other, were very high (respectively, 0.86, 0.87, 0.94) (Mayer and Rey 1993: 43). The voters now reiterated their own support for the FN, election after election (Meyer and Rey 1993: 47). Even more, the FN voters' loyalty was the highest amongst all the parties (Shain 2001).

Despite the strong hostility of two thirds of the electorate that would never vote for the FN or for its leader, and the dubious credibility of Le Pen as a statesman

(Mayer and Perrineau 1993: 78), the FN had conquered a solid electoral niche. As the 'Le Pen phenomenon' was fading away, it was replaced by the emergence of party loyalty: the *'national-frontisme'* gained more appeal, rather than just the figure of the leader himself.

Radicalization and Proletarization

The consolidation of the Front National was also linked to a policy change. In the wake of the 1993 general election the FN had abandoned the 1978 ultra-liberal programme and adopted a socially-minded agenda: *'The 300 measures for the renaissance of France'*. The traditional nationalistic, xenophobic, and authoritarian references were flanked by concern for unemployment, workers' problems, and welfare provisions (Taguieff 1996*b*: 359–66). The FN declared itself the defender of low-income people, who (they claimed) were more affected and more frightened by the double process of immigration and economic globalization.

The ninth party congress held in February 1994 officially stated the *proletarisation* of the FN's policy: the real national sentiment and interests threatened by the EU, international finance, and capitalism could only be represented by a 'popular and national' party such as the FN. The party therefore addressed the popular strata of the French electorate, betrayed and discharged by the traditional left and right parties, that is, the establishment. This ideological and strategic shift was in tune with the sociological profile of the FN electorate (see Table 5.2)—increasingly more working class, low educated, and low-income—and with a growing percentage of regular non-voters coming to the party. Moreover, this 'popular-populist' turn was also consistent with the new challenge that the FN had to face, that is to

TABLE 5.2. *Social stratification of the FN voter 1986–97*
(exit polls parliamentary elections)

	1986	1988	1993	1997
Men	53	61	50	60
Women	47	39	50	40
18–24 years	18	18	16	12
25–34	21	18	14	21
35–49	27	21	28	28
50–64	23	24	23	22
+ 65	11	19	19	17
Peasant	12	3	6	0
Trader/Self-employed	10	5	9	8
Liberal profession/high official	7	10	4	5
Employee	24	23	23	23
Worker	26	27	25	30
Pensioner/not active	21	32	33	34

Source: Perrineau (1997: 210).

say, a new grouping of the traditional right led by the ex-UDF Philippe de Villiers, which emphasized the same nationalistic issues with a more moderate style and discourse.

The outcome of the June 1994 European elections (10.6%) confirmed the party's breakthrough into the popular milieu: the FN attained more than 20 per cent in blue-collar areas (Perrineau 1997: 80). Moreover, in the 1995 presidential elections, in which Le Pen stood once more reaching 15.3 per cent of the votes, the popular strata was quite responsive to the party's anti-system rhetoric: *30 per cent of workers and 25 per cent of the unemployed voted for Le Pen* (Perrineau 1995: 83). This sociological profile, variously labelled as '*ouvriéro-lepénisme*' (Mayer 1999) or '*gaucho-lepénisme*' (Perrineau 1995), was quite different from that of the mid-1980s. In 1988, the party attracted voters across all social classes, gaining most from the workers and slightly less from the small entrepreneurs. In any event, it was 'everything but an underdog vote' (Mayer 1999: 81). While the 1988 vote was the by-product of 'relative frustration', originating in the gap between aspirations and reality, the 1995 vote was the expression of alienation and marginalization: in fact, *more than 50 per cent of Le Pen voters place themselves in the lowest two (out of ten) cases of a self-evaluating status scale* (Mayer 1999: 83–6).

After the 1995 presidential election success the FN accentuated its extremeness by declaring the 'right of insurrection' in the name of a 'system alternative'. The FN denied any value or legitimacy to the democratic system by defining it false, formal, anti-popular, anti-national, and so on. The populist reference became more and more pervasive in 1990s FN discourse. As it defines itself as the only plausible alternative, it builds up a sort of 'world apart' by creating a network of organizations and unions aiming at embedding the members and sympathizers (Ivaldi 1998a). This dynamic touched its zenith in the Tenth party Congress held in Strasbourg in early 1997. The party showed off its organizational strength with a grandiose setting and reinstated its national-popular (and populist) standing. On the other hand, a massive wave of counter-mobilization, with a very large anti-FN demonstration in the streets of Strasbourg and the widespread perception of Le Pen and the Front National as a 'danger to democracy', (shared by 75% of the French) were evidence of the party's isolation. Notwithstanding this ghettoization, the party attained its best score in a parliamentary election with 15.2 per cent of the votes in the parliamentary election called in May 1997. With the retreat of the other right parties, *the FN represented 30 per cent of the overall right vote*. The party had acquired a strategic role in the party system. It could determine the victory or the defeat of the moderate front.

However, the cleavage that separates the FN from the moderate right was so deep that the traditional right parties refused any relationship with the FN, even at the cost of losing the elections. In fact, in the absence of any agreement or even of any contact, the FN kept its candidates in the second ballot in all but one of the 133 constituencies (out of 445) where they had passed the first ballot. This was one of the primary reasons for the moderate right's defeat.

The 1997 election reinforced the party's encroachment into the popular strata. The working-class vote increased from 17 to 24 per cent. Furthermore, 58 per cent of FN voters had at least one member of his or her family in the working class (only the French communists have a higher percentage: 69%). And the likelihood of voting for the FN increased along with the number of working-class family members (Mayer 1999: 92–7).

The triumphal march of the FN was linked to the enduring state of malaise of the French society. The concern for the immigration/security twin question (Grunberg and Schweisguth 1997: 151ss), and mistrust of and alienation from the political system, continued to grow (Sofres 1998: 244–7; Mayer 1999: 138–9).

Triumph and Disintegration

The FN confirmed its *état de grâce* at the 1998 regional elections, where it ended up with 15.3 per cent of the vote. Well beyond the resounding score itself, the political impact on the moderate right was devastating. *The FN collected more regional councillors (275) than the UDF (265), and just a little less than the RPR (285).* After 15 years, the long march the Front National had finally pulled in the traditional parties of the *droite*. The FN was in a new position to offer co-operation in those regions where an all-right coalition would have assured a majority. The initiative, strongly advocated by the FN deputy-leader, Bruno Mégret, was initially successful in 5 regions out of 22, but the UDF and the RPR national headquarters reacted very sharply and forced the local parties to break the agreements. The *cordon sanitaire* tightened by the moderate right since 1988 was finally maintained, even if at the cost of inner conflicts and some splits.

Actually, when the FN seemed at the point of having accomplished a political breakthrough, it entered a disruptive dynamic. For a while, a latent conflict was passing under the surface of the Front National between the radical anti-system stance of Le Pen and the more bargaining attitude fostered by the deputy-leader Mégret. The latter contrasted with Le Pen both in party strategy and in many personal features—low profile, cultivated, bourgeois origin, uninspiring rhetoric, managerial style. Mégret argued that the FN had to make inroads into the traditional right, abandoning its confrontational attitude and following instead the path of AN in Italy. The conflict exploded with devastating impact in the autumn of 1998 and was even exacerbated by Le Pen, who could not tolerate any dissent. With a series of provocative actions aiming at marginalising Mégret, such as the defenestration of Mégret from the head of the FN list at the European election (Le Pen was not allowed to stand because of legal sanctions) in favour of Le Pen's wife—the FN president favoured a show-down. The result was a split in December 1998, with almost half of the local representatives and two-thirds of the cadres following Mégret in his newly established Mouvement National, later named Mouvement National Republicain, (MNR) (Republican National Movement) (Laurent and Perrineau 1999; Camus 2001).

The break-up substantially reduced the voters' appeal. In the 1999 European elections both parties suffered from the split: the FN got one third of the votes it had previously attained (5.7%) and the new MN reached 3.3 per cent. Together they totalled the worst electoral score of the extreme right since 1984; 53 per cent of former FN voters remained loyal to Le Pen, while only 17 per cent followed Mégret.

THE FN VOTE: MALE, ETHNOCENTRIC, AND AUTHORITARIAN

The FN no longer represents conservative and rural France but rather the urban, industrialized (and de-industrialized) areas. This vote has been defined as 'the echo of the urban anomie' (Perrineau 1988), that is to say the by-product of the de-structuring of the social relationship in large cities and especially in their *banlieu*. The loss of social bonds without the compensation of high consumerism created a sizeable number of displaced people. The frustration over such a poor quality of life needed a scapegoat; it was offered by the FN in the form of immigrants, delinquents, and the political–industrial–media establishment—corrupt, selfish, anti-national, and distant from (and uncaring of) the common people's needs. Put differently, the Front National founded its fortunes both on nationalist appeal, veined with authoritarianism, racism, and anti-Semitism, and on an anti-system/ anti-establishment appeal.

Immigration has always been at the core of the party propaganda and discourse, together with the issue of security, and the FN electorate appeared very sensitive to both. In 1997, faced with little more than 50 per cent of the French people agreeing that 'there were too many immigrants', 84 per cent of FN voters believed so (Mayer 1999: 52–3). Besides, the degree of antipathy towards other ethnic groups among the FN electorate is much higher than the population mean, especially regarding people from the Maghreb: *the gap between FN voters and the mean electorate is 45 percentage points* (Perrineau 1997: 152). Security and immigration issues are at the top of voter motivation for choosing the FN: in 1997, 65 per cent against 35 per cent in the electorate at large highlighted the role of personal safety in voting FN, while 67 per cent against 22 per cent underlined immigration (Perrineau 1997: 177–8).

Unquestionably, the frontist electorate was mobilized by the party's priority messages. Therefore, it should have been concentrated in those areas affected by a high level of immigration. This in fact is correct. The *départments* where the party score is at its highest are also those where immigration is very high. But the relationship is not so strict, because the coefficient of correlation is only 0.42 between number of immigrants per *départments* and votes for Le Pen at the 1995 presidential elections (Perrineau 1997: 146). Moreover, the relationship almost disappears at the municipal level: cities with more than 10,000 inhabitants had a higher correlation between number of immigrants and Le Pen votes ($r = 0.40$) as opposed to the popular *banlieus* ($r = 0.07$) where the foreign population is more concentrated (19.4% against 9.5% overall in France) (Rey 1996: 136–7; Perrineau 1997: 146). This suggests that the equation immigration + security = FN vote does not hold as such.

One explanation has been highlighted by the hypothesis of the '*effet halo*' (Perrineau 1993: 144). Since the FN is stronger in the towns and the neighbourhoods *without high immigration, but close to high immigration areas*, support for the Front National is the by-product of a 'non-experiential' xenophobia, that is to say of the perception of a near while unknown threat. This outcome may also be due to the fact that immigrants living in densely immigrant areas do not vote FN, causing a low party score in that area, and that potentially xenophobic native French move away to the suburbs (Martin 1996: 21–2). Analysing survey data, Nonna Mayer (1999: 262) demonstrated that the presence of foreigners becomes a 'political' issue only once a voter's ethnocentric world-view is developed. This means that *the ethnocentrist attitude is the real motive for voting FN, irrespective of the number of foreigners*. The personal world-view much more than the 'experiential racism' seems at the heart of the FN voters mobilization.

The second explanation is that other factors should be included in the 'FN vote equation', above all mistrust of, and alienation from, the parties, the political establishment, and politics in general, dissatisfaction over the working of democracy and its institutions, and the perception of waning national identity. The relationship between the mass public and politics has been under stress in France for quite some time (Boy and Mayer 1997). The number of citizens who agree that politicians do not care about ordinary people has been growing since the late 1970s, *totalling 80 per cent in 1997*. The same mistrust goes for the honesty of politicians and the notion of fair representation by a party or a political leader (expressed by only 31% of people) (Mayer 1999: 138–9). Moreover, as mentioned above, confidence in parliament and in the workings of democracy has decreased; and the same goes for the level of party identification and party membership (Knapp 1999). All these indicators show a mounting feeling of alienation from the political system, which has been affecting France since the 1980s. In the face of such malaise, the FN represented the natural collector of all these dissatisfactions.

The attitudinal profile of the Front National electorate reflects the party agenda and is quite distinct from the moderate right and the average electorate. The FN voters' attitudes diverge from the mean electorate mostly on the rejection of immigration (94% against 59%), the re-introduction of the death penalty (83% against 50%), pessimism vis-à-vis the future (81% against 66%), the ineffective working of democracy (77% against 59%), the dishonesty of politicians (58% against 33%), and confidence in the EU (38% against 61%) (Perrineau 1997: 116). The FN 'loyal' voters, in particular, display anti-politics and anti-establishment attitudes in a percentage *more than double* the population mean,

TABLE 5.3. *Attitudes of FN voters compared to the population mean*

	Mean	FN
Death penalty	50	83
Pro EU	61	38
Politicians corrupt	33	58
Too many immigrants	36	88
Working of democracy	59	77
Rejection of immigrants	59	94
Authoritarianism index	36	68
Xenophobia index	47	84

Source: Perrineau (1997: 116); Brechon and Cautres (1998: 244–5).

and the same ratio concerns the level of authoritarianism (68% against 36%) and xenophobia (84% against 47%) (Brechon and Cautres 1998: 244–5). According to a recent survey, FN voters are massively against economic liberalism (56%), in favour of social protection (76%), anti-EU (67%); 61 per cent of them do not trust politicians and 88 per cent denounce the poor functioning of poor democracy (Ysmal 2000; 158–60). Summing up, the FN electorate is extremist, authoritarian, xenophobic, ethnocentrist, nationalist, and anti-establishment (Mayer 1999: 148).

The same is true for the middle-level party elite. A 1990 survey at the Eighth FN congress revealed the presence of the same set of attitudes (Ignazi and Ysmal 1992). Hostility towards foreigners had unanimous consent as well as for all the authoritarian issues. There was no crack in such a rigid, closed, authoritarian world-view: the cult of discipline, familism, harsh punishments, anti-Semitism, xenophobia, hierarchy, and tradition were all overwhelmingly approved (Ignazi and Ysmal 1992: 110–17).

CONCLUSION

The FN is an extreme right party. It is perceived by the other parties and by its own voters and cadres as being on the right extreme of the right-left continuum (Mayer 1999: 349). The same is true for FN cadres: 18 per cent locate the party to the most extreme right position and 62 per cent as the nearest one (Ignazi and Ysmal 1992). Furthermore, the political curriculum of the FN leaders and of many of its cadres show a political socialization in the extreme right milieu.

The FN is also an extreme right party in terms of its world-view. While Rene Rémond defined the FN as an 'ideological *fourre-tout*' because of its various ideological leanings ranging from Duprat's national-revolutionary to Stirbois' *solidarisme*, from Le Gallou's ultra-liberalism to Roman Marie's Catholic integralism, the party displays a coherent right-extremist tendency. Its pillars stand in defence of the French national identity threatened by the continuous influx of foreigners—from the exterior (the Islamic 'invasion') as well as from the interior (Jews, freemasons, communists)—and by Americanization and globalization. The party is also committed to the restoration of traditional moral values (traditionalist and ritualist Catholicism, anti-feminism, rigid family sex roles, discipline, and hierarchy), of the nation's pride and power, of the common man's defence against the establishment and uncaring politicians. The differential racism, law and order enforcement, the anti-politics sentiment, the populist appeal, the welfarist and 'third way' economic approach all characterize the Front National's stances. These elements, without exception, have been introduced, modified, and emphasized in the last 20 years according to the relative importance of main internal tendencies: the Catholic *integristes* are characterized by their emphasis on traditional values, by their Maurassian interpretation of the extraneous bodies to the nation, and by their exaltation of the Christian West; the '*horlogiers*' articulate racism in a much more refined way—defending the 'differences'—and support economic liberalism; and the *solidaristes* are more corporatist and social-minded. These tendencies have been managed for some considerable time by a party leader who puts his decisive weight on one or the other, or provides a synthesis. The basic internal conflict has ranged around the national-revolutionary and *solidariste*, on one side, and the ultra-liberal, pro-American *horlogiers*, on the other. The latter faction lost its hold in the nineties with the anti-system radicalization fostered by Le Pen, but resurfaced in recent times (with different lines) leading to the December 1998 party split.

Since then the extreme right has taken a leap backward to its tradition of fragmentation and internal quarrels. The two parties pursue their diverging strategies, confrontational for the FN and bargaining oriented for the MNR, but none of these has accomplished any results. The '*cordon sanitaire*' enforced by the moderate right against the extreme right, even after the outstanding success of the FN in the 1998 regional elections, has been, *a fortiori*, maintained. Even if many of the favourable conditions for the develoment of the extreme right are still present, its political supply is endangered by its internal divisions.

6

Austria: Away From Liberalism

According to the historian Adam Wandrszuka (1954), Austrian society is divided historically into three ideologically diverse, equally hostile, watertight compartments called 'Lager'. Each Lager found political expression in the form of parties, trade unions, and a network of voluntary associations following socialist, Catholic, and national traditions. The national Lager (or 'third Lager') has never attained the same level of social distinctiveness and political homogeneity, nor has it coalesced into a single well-structured political party like the socialist ('red') and catholic ('black') Lager have, since the end of the nineteenth century. The national Lager has always been very fragmented: the plurality of parties and groups linked to this Lager can be essentially divided into two main streams. The first, inspired by a liberal constitutional tradition, is the minor stream. The second is the major one, inspired by nationalism, pan-Germanism, anti-clericalism, and anti-Hapsburg feelings. The peculiar trait of Austrian nationalist anti-clericalism was based on the assumption that the close link between the Hapsburg's dynasty and the Catholic Church had been an obstacle to the ultimate nationalist aim: unification with Germany (Luther 1988: 214).

The division by Lager is considered to have been the main cause of the collapse of the first Austrian republic. The conflict between the socialists and the Catholics (through their respective militias), plus the support provided by the national-socialist groups to the Catholics, led to parliamentary democracy being seriously restricted and to the formation of Dolfuss' clerical-corporatist regime, or 'Staendestaat', in 1934. These events paved the way for the ascendancy to power of the Nazis and for the long-awaited unification, or Anschluss, with Germany in 1938.

The victory of Austrian fascism, according to some historians (Wandruska 1954), has been attributed to political movements extraneous to the third Lager. This hypothesis, which considers national socialism as an external force, has had widespread acceptance and has been largely instrumental in forging the post-war Austrian political culture. Actually, it disregarded the presence of radical anti-democratic tendencies inside the national Lager itself. These tendencies, however, had to meet the similarly anti-democratic streams of the Catholic Lager in order to prevail. Thus, both Lager—national and Catholic—were responsible for the incubation of fascism. While Catholic conservatives sowed the seeds for the development of the Patriotic Front and the paramilitary organization Heimwehrens (rural, aristocratic, traditionalist, pro-fascist), the national Lager, through the DNSAP and later the NSDAP, gave life to the pro-Nazi tendency (urban, industrial, anti-Catholic) (Botz 1980: 194ss). These two components found a synthesis in the clerical-corporative authoritarian regime established by Dolfuss in 1934 (Botz 1980: 197; Pauley 1980: 233). Dolfuss' regime implied, however, a cooling of aspirations to recast the 'German nation' because his *Staendestaat* impinged on an Austrian-specific nationalism. It was only with the elimination of Dolfuss, murdered by Austrian Nazis after he, as Prime Minister, had outlawed them, and with the Nazi take-over in 1938, that the dream of a pan-German state was accomplished through the *Anschluss*. The union with Germany, the basic aim of the third *Lager*, was finally achieved, although not by the pan-German liberals but by the most anti-democratic forces.

The popular support for the Anschluss was overwhelming. And even more, the Nazi organization flourished better than in any other country, Germany included; recruitment to the Nazi party, and later on the *Wehrmacht*, the SS, and the Waffen SS, reached an unprecedented level (Botz 1980: 210–15). The identification of a large part of the population with the destiny of the Reich and the enthusiastic support for Hitler's policies especially towards the Jews, was reflected in harsh resistance until the end of the war. When Vienna capitulated, the level of Nazi membership was still impressive (Luther 1988: 220).

THE NOSTALGIC AND NEO-NAZI GROUPS

In the second Austrian republic, the extreme right had a double inheritance: one that was strictly Nazi and another that was nationalistic. Post-war right extremism assumed various forms, from the veterans' association that framed and voiced the views of ex-members of the NSDAP, to small extremist groups; from associations that were apparently apolitical but were actually closely associated with the past regime, such as sports, patriotic, and veterans' associations, to borderline organizations, which lay between extremism and conservatism, finally creating some fractions within the VdU and, later on, the FPÖ (Bailer Galanda *et al*. 1992). In addition to these, some truly neo-Nazi organizations were founded secretly, immediately after the war. Among the latter, the (Werwolfgruppe) Wolves, particularly strong in Stiria and High Austria, played a relevant role. Fundamentally a terrorist movement, this group was active until 1948, when it was finally dismantled (Bailer Galanda *et al*. 1992: 287).

Later in the 1950s, other 'nostalgic' groups were formed, hidden under a cover of stated apolitical goals. Among the various veterans and refugees' organizations, the Österreichischer Turnerbund (OTB) (Austrian Association of Gymnastics), a sporting organization founded in 1952, was in reality 'the most important organization of the Austrian extreme right' (Bailer Galanda *et al*. 1992: 292). In 1981, just before its break-up, it consisted of 75,000 affiliates, including 30,000 young people. Behind the screen of its statutory activities, the OTB kept alive nostalgic references to the past regime. Despite an attempt to present itself as a democratic association in order to benefit from public financing, it was classified in 1981 by the Commission for the Defence of the Constitution as 'pro-Nazi' because of its fascist 'style' and its 'tendency toward national-socialist ideology' (Bailer Galanda *et al.* 1992: 292–3). As a consequence, it was denied public funding and immediately dissolved.

Another important organization of the 1950s was the Ring Freiheitlicher Studenten (RFS) (Alliance of Liberal Students). Despite its name, the RFS leant towards the nationalist tradition and even to right radicalism. In fact, it has been the incubator of many leaders of the anti-liberal component of the FPÖ, including Jörg Haider, RFS federal secretary from 1970 to 1974, and of the extreme right, like Norber Burger, RFS founder, who was later to become a protagonist of right-extremism. The RFS attracted many members, recruiting between one-third and a quarter of all Austrian students until 1971. After a long decline, the RFS had completely disappeared by 1989 (Bailer Galanda *et al.* 1992: 288).

Finally, the only right extremist political movement which entered the electoral arena was the National Demokratische Partei (NDP) (National Democratic Party), founded in 1967 by Norbert Burger, and by former FPÖ members who were disappointed with the party's moderation (Mudde 1995*a*). In the 1960s and 1970s, Burger was the uncontested leader of Austrian right-extremism. At first, he devoted attention to the South Tyrol question, promoting a series of terrorist actions that gained him vast support amongst the Austrian and German far right. The most resounding event of his political career was nonetheless in the legal arena: Burger stood in the 1980 presidential elections, despite a continuous series of electoral disasters. On that occasion, due also to the presence of a rather liberal FPÖ candidate, Burger received 3.2 per cent of the votes, a result that took him out of his marginal position within the tiny extremist chapels. That success, however, put the NDP under the spotlight of the Commission for the Defence of the Constitution. The commission eventually outlawed the party in 1988. Burger rapidly repackaged himself by founding the Bürger-Rechts-Bewegung (BRB) (Citizens' Rights Movement), playing on the homology between 'citizen' (Bürger) and his name. However, growing competition within the far right on the one hand, and the fascination shown by the electorate and various extreme right cadres with Haider's FPÖ on the other, prevented its development. The same is true for the Ein hertz für Enlander (A Heart for the Native) party, also founded by Burger in 1988, which scored 1.2 per cent of the votes in the regional elections of Low Austria. Since it played upon xenophobic and racist appeals and neo-Nazi nostalgia, it was later excluded by rule of law from the 1990 general elections.

THE VDU: A HAVEN FOR THE NOSTALGICS

These extremist and pro-Nazi groups, with the exception of the student association RFS, made up only a very small proportion of the third (national) *Lager*.

In the post-war period, the third *Lager*'s inheritance was secured by the Verband der Unabhängigen (VdU) (League of Independents), a party created in 1949 to incorporate former NSDAP members purged by the de-nazification process (a huge number given the scale of the NSDAP), and to oppose the hegemonic duopoly of the socialist party (SPÖ) and the Catholic party (OVP). In order to be accepted by the post-war occupation powers, the VdU could not avoid paying formal homage to liberal constitutional principles, but the heart of its original programme consisted in the abolition of restrictions against the ex-Nazis and the scarcely veiled reformulation of pan-Germanism (Luther 1988: 217–20).

Its success was immediate: first, in the 1949 elections, it received 11.7 per cent, but with substantial variations among the regions due to open boycotting in the Soviet-controlled zone; secondly, in the 1951 presidential elections, the VdU candidate got 15.4 per cent of the vote. These initial performances show that the third *Lager* gained a conspicuous number of votes from 'de-nazified' people. In fact, thanks to the 1947 and 1949 amnesties, the number of those who acquired the right to vote between the 1949 and 1951 elections, almost half a million (Steger 1993: 5), corresponds to the number of votes gained by the VdU in 1951 compared to 1949. Above all, such results highlighted the existence of unresolved questions concerning the Nazi past and national identity.

The problem of the burden of the past had been countered in the immediate post-war period with a massive programme of democratic 'education' and with a purge of supporters of the past regime. However, both projects failed, either because of the size of the population involved (around a quarter of Austrians at the end of the war were still affiliated with the NSDAP and its paramilitary organizations (Luther 1988: 220)), and because of its imperviousness to liberal democratic ideology, traditionally extraneous to Austrian political culture. Moreover, the two major parties conducted a recruitment policy among ex-Nazis in order to integrate them into the system and to remove a potentially dangerous monopoly of this constituency's representation from the VdU. This strategy was particularly effective and the VdU, already divided between an anti-socialist and an anti-clerical faction, was somewhat deprived of its own electoral constituency. The final blow to the VdU came from the 1955 peace treaty that healed the painful national wound of the country's division and removed the VdU's main *raison d'être*.

The unresolved national question represented the second key feature of the third *Lager*'s politics (Riedlsperger 1991). The problem of Austria's national identity—as an autonomous entity or an appendix of a 'Great Germany'—periodically emerges in Austrian history. The *Anschluss*, the 1938 unification with Germany, for a brief period accomplished the nationalists' beloved aim of a single German nation. The return to the borders of the first republic in 1945 implied the abandonment of the idea of political unity as well as that of German cultural unity, the 'romantic concept of the *Kulturnation*' (Riedlsperger 1991: 54). At the same time, this 'return' brought about the need to create a founding myth of the new republic. This myth came from the misleading, and even deceptive, interpretation of the *Anschluss* as an act of aggression by Hitler's Germany.

Given these premises, the second republic was inevitably born with an incomplete identity. The weakness of the Austrian identity was revealed by a 1949 survey in which 49 per cent of the citizens did not consider themselves to be Austrian citizens: an impressive weakness of the 'institutional bond' (Katzestein 1977: 149). This 'original sin' was substantially overcome in the early 1960s when those who did not recognize an autonomous national Austrian identity plummeted to below 50 per cent: and finally, in 1990, 74 per cent of the people agreed that 'Austria is a nation' compared to 47 per cent in 1964 (Plasser, Ulram, and Grausgruber 1992: 22). Nevertheless, the problem of national identity continued to touch a sensitive nerve, as demonstrated by the case of the President of the Republic Kurt Waldheim in the late 1980s.

The national *Lager* appealed to the pan-German feeling and therefore drew support from those who rejected the Austrian nation. The VdU and, after its dissolution, the FPÖ reaffirmed the affiliation of Austria to the German *Kulturnation*. But even inside the FPÖ the 'anti-Austrian' faction rapidly decreased from the 1970s onwards, and in 1989 it constituted only 13 per cent of the party's supporters, while 64 per cent recognized Austria as a nation (Riedlsperger 1991: 63). It was not by chance that Haider moved from pan-Germanism to Austrian nationalism in the mid-1990s.

THE FPÖ: THE FAILED ATTEMPT AT LIBERALISM

The FPÖ entered the Austrian party system, replacing the defunct VdU in representing the third *Lager* and occupying the right-extremity of the political spectre. Up to the end of the 1970s, the FPÖ remained marginal because of its ties with the past. The largest section of its members comprised ex-Nazis, its leadership had declared and undeniable previous experience in the NSDAP (Luther 1988: 220–1), and nostalgic groups such as the AFP and the AULA had close contacts with the party (Bailer Galanda *et al.* 1992: 291). Some of its proposals also brought back the ghosts of Nazism, like the idea, formulated in the 1968 programme, of applying genetics in order to guarantee Austrian ethnic purity and integrity. The party represented the traditional 'third *Lager*': middle class (self-employed and white-collar), pan-German, anti-clerical, hyper-conservative, and nostalgic.

However, since the late-1960s the party had been relaxing its references to the past, affording a modernization of its programme emphasizing in particular free market and economic liberalism. The 'recognition' by the SPÖ's (Jewish) prime minister Bruno Kriesky in those years contributed to reducing the FPÖ's isolation in the political arena. In the mid-to-late seventies, an authentically liberal tendency (the 'young Turks' of the Attersee Circle), always on the fringe of the party, gained more influence to the point of determining a different political–ideological orientation. The new leader, Norbert Steger, who replaced Friedrich Peter in 1980, had the profile of a competent and upright person devoid of any relationship with the extreme right. Under his leadership the party moved along the same path of the German liberal party, gradually accepting the ideological features of authentic liberalism. This process was propelled by acceptance of the FPÖ into the Liberal International in 1979 and found its final confirmation in the 1985 Salzburg programme, considerably different from previous (and subsequent) party platforms. This ideological and programmatic revolution was completed by a more cooperative relationship with the Social democrats that set the conditions for the SPÖ–FPÖ government coalition in 1983–6. For the first time the FPÖ attained governmental responsibility in acquiring the respect and democratic legitimacy that it had previously been denied. In reality, this proved to be ephemeral and superficial.

The close cooperation with the SPÖ, and the lack of official support for Kurt Wahldheim's candidacy for the presidency of the republic (who anyway received the votes of one out of two FPÖ voters), weakened the party's hold on its traditional electorate and produced a split within the party. The dissent for the overly leftward party policy led to a change in the party's internal alignments. The milieu of the *Burschenshaften*, the nationalist student associations that had long-provided party cadres, and the nostalgic groups made a comeback. The new, more traditional, internal coalition, fuelled by the forecast of a dramatic electoral downturn, defeated the liberal leadership in the 1986 Congress and brought the young leader of the FPÖ in Carinthia, Jörg Haider, to power.

The incoming party elite seized the majority with a radically different programme in which the forgotten nationalistic, pan-German position returned with some force, and the politics of total opposition to consociational practices and to all the other parties was fostered (Riedlsperger 1992). The immediate consequence of Haider's victory was twofold: the collapse of the government coalition and the call for new elections by the socialists. Contrary to general expectations the FPÖ had a resounding success in the early general elections of 1986 (Table 6.1), with a doubling of the votes from 5.0 to 9.7 per cent. The exit from the government, instead of provoking an electoral decline, had reinforced the anti-system feelings of the traditional third *Lager* electorate that Haider revitalized with his populist rhetoric. In fact, both the 'protest voting' and the party candidates' profile, with Haider at the top, were at the core of the voters' motivations for choosing the FPÖ (Plasser, Ulram and Grausgruber 1987: 246–7).

The new party leadership's messages covered many themes, ranging from the bureaucratic-fiscal oppression of the State to the waste of the welfare system which favoured the idlers instead of the poor, from the dishonesty of politicians and the rapacity of the banks and financial power (said to be controlled by the Jews) to the defence of national integrity (Luther 1988: 245). All these themes were moulded and effectively articulated by the flamboyant personality of the

TABLE 6.1. *Votes for the FPÖ*
in parliamentary and
European elections

Year	Votes (%)
1949	11.7
1953	11.0
1956	6.5
1959	7.7
1962	7.1
1966	5.4
1970	5.5
1971	5.5
1975	5.4
1979	6.1
1983	5.0
1986	9.7
1990	16.6
1994	22.5
1995	21.9
1996E	27.6
1999E	23.4
1999	26.9

Note: 1949–56 votes for VdU.
Source: Luther (1998); official sources.

new leader. Throughout the years of his leadership Haider has presented a brilliant, cultivated, dynamic, youthful, smiling, outspoken, and informal image. His rhetoric (Schleder 1994) masterfully merges and alternates between modernizing, pro-market, and entrepreneurial accents and solidaristic, *Volkgemeinshaft* references; commitment to individual freedom and complaisance for the Austrian (Nazi) past; loyalty to constitutional rules and demand for radical change and a direct appeal to the people.

Since 1986 both the ascent of Haider and the rise of the FPÖ have been steady. The growing power of the leader within the party was directly in line with its improving electoral results in all regional and general elections; in particular, it gained a dramatic increase in support in the mid-to-late 1990s, bringing the party's share of votes closer to the other parties, even surpassing the ÖVP by a handful of votes in the 1999 general elections.

The first FPÖ electoral breakthrough occurred in Carinthia—Haider's fief—in 1989, when the party scored 29.0 per cent in the regional elections, gaining 13 percentage points compared to the previous elections. This victory gave the presidency of a region to an FPÖ member (Haider himself in this case) for the first time and, simultaneously, set the stage for the outcome of the 1990 general election. The FPÖ attained 16.6 per cent, polling its best result up to then. Its anti-establishment, law-and-order, anti-immigration campaign attracted votes from

TABLE 6.2. *Social composition of the FPÖ electorate*

	1986	1990	1994	1995	1999
Men	+2	+3	+6	+5	+5
Women	−3	−5	−5	−6	−6
18–29 years	+2	+1	+3	+7	+8
30–44	+1	−2	0	+2	+2
45–59	−4	−2	0	−3	−6
+60	−2	−1	0	−7	−4
Farmer	−5	−8	−7	−4	−17
Self-employed/professional	+5	+4	+8	+6	+6
Blue-collar	0	+4	+7	+12	+20
White-collar	+3	−1	0	0	−5
Civil servant	−2	−3	−8	−5	−7
Housewife	−2	−6	−5	−10	−2
Pensioner	−2	−1	+2	−8	−3
In school	−1	−9	−4	−7	−4
Elementary	−4	−3	−1	−4	+2
Technical	+1	+2	+4	+5	−2
High school/university	+1	−4	−3	−6	−10

Source: Fessel GfK (1999); Riedelsperger (1998).

everywhere: 16.2 per cent of the FPÖ electorate switched over from the SPÖ and 27.6 per cent from the OVP. And as never before, the working class was the largest occupational group within the party (25%), followed by the traditional backbone of the national-liberal *Lager*, the self-employed professionals (21%) (Riedlsperger 1992: 40–1) (Table 6.2). A trend which will continue in the years (Table 6.3).

Even though Haider went on committing various *faux pas*, the upward trend never faltered. The first and probably foremost 'incident' or verbal slip by Haider was over the Third Reich's labour policy, which he exalted in front of the Carinthia *Land* assembly while serving as its president in 1991. The reactions provoked by this statement forced him to resign. But all of this harmed neither the party's standing nor Haider's career. In the following local and regional elections in Vienna, the FPÖ more than doubled its votes: in the municipal election it jumped from 9.7 per cent to 22.5 per cent. The party managed to mount an aggressive campaign against the consociational and patronage-like style of government of the two major parties, against political and administrative corruption, against the waste of social provisions, and, above all, it was successful in targeting immigrants as the main reason for crime and unemployment. Since 40 per cent of Vienna's population perceived immigration to be the most important problem, the FPÖ's steady propaganda against foreigners and multiculturalism contributed highly to its success (Riedlsperger 1998: 36). While some white-collar voters may have defected because of these xenophobic statements, the working class massively supported the party: 26 per cent of blue-collar workers (and 35% of skilled workers) voted FPÖ (Reidlsperger 1998: 36). The FPÖ's breakthrough in 'red Vienna', where the SPÖ for the first time went below 50 per cent and the OVP

TABLE 6.3. *Social stratification of the FPÖ vote (1999)*

Man	62
Woman	38
18–29 years	27
30–44	34
45–59	22
60–69	8
+70	8
Self-employed/Professional	10
Farmer	1
Civil servant	7
White collar	26
Blue collar	27
Housewife	8
Pensioner	18
Elementary	16
Technical	55
High school/University	30

Source: Fessel GfK (1999).

was overcome by the FPÖ, represented a watershed in the party's history (Table 6.3). After that the party outgrew its minority status and has since competed on the same level as the other parties (Riedlsperger 1992: 39ff).

Accordingly the party has become more and more Haider's party. The leader has made in-depth modifications to the internal party structure in order to manoeuvre more freely and have more direct contact with the public. The radical reform of the party statutes proposed in 1992–5 highlights a completely different party. The party's executive body is filled with elected officials; the leader and his staff are no longer responsible to any party organs except for the national congress—which is also filled with ex-officio members, mostly chosen by the leadership itself (Luther 1997: 288ff). The party executive has been deprived of any relevance, again because of the public statements made extemporaneously by the leader without any previous debate. The strategy of faits accomplis has become the rule and, by consequence, the party executive has acquired an ancillary status. Beyond this centralization process, in political terms, Haider acted in a twofold way: by eliminating the left and right factions in order to secure absolute control and by quietly encouraging a massive turnover.

In the first instance he forced, more or less smoothly, the true Nazi and *Nouvelle Droite* groups, as well as genuine liberals, to leave the party. The tiny but embarrassing neo-Nazi component was surplus to the requirements of, and even counterproductive for, a potentially large party, as was the anti-Christian *Nouvelle Droite* represented by Andreas Mölzer (although he continued to back and inspire Haider) (Moreau 1998; Luverà 2000). Secondly, the increasingly uneasy pro-liberal faction, led by Heidi Schmidt, FPÖ candidate for the presidency in 1992, was effectively forced to quit the party in February 1993. She then went on to found the Liberals Forum. This party, intended to represent the 'authentic liberal' component of the FPÖ, scored 6 per cent (13 seats) in the 1994 elections, confirming the result in the following 1995 elections. It did not, however, meet the threshold for representation in 1999.

The second instrument for gaining full control was represented by the cadres' turnover through the appointment of newcomers and of independents to medium-to-high levels of the party's hierarchy, overruling the traditional inner *cursus honorum*. At the same time, the party apparatus was reduced to some 150 officials by 1990, and the party membership was kept at a very low level, maintaining the traditionally small dimension (in comparison to other Austrian parties) of the party organization: the 36,683 members in 1986 increased to just 44,541 in 1996 implying a decrease in the voters/members ratio from 7.8 to 4.2 (Luther 1997: 293). On the other hand, the FPÖ stimulated the creation of various flanking organizations, which proved quite successful, such as the (Seniorring) Senior Association which gathered more members (53,672) than the party itself (Moreau 1998: 63).

Using these tools, Haider accomplished a massive elite circulation within the FPÖ, which granted him absolute dominance. His charismatic personality and the creeping cult of personality greatly aided such an outcome.

THE '*HAIDER EFFEKT*' AND BEYOND

Why were the FPÖ able to break into the party system in the 1990s? According to Riedlsperger (1992: 19), the FPÖ exploited 'traditional' conservative feelings such as the concern for law and order and hostility toward foreigners, placing emphasis on traditional moral values and national identity. Actually, the FPÖ broke with the traditional Austrian setting by politicizing the 'new issues' of immigration and (to a lesser extent) crime, and by introducing more candidate-centred politics using Haider's populist rhetoric.

However, the party's propaganda and profile do not explain its growth unless the structural modifications of the Austrian system are taken into consideration. Such modifications comprise: (a) the collapse of all the *Lager* with the consequent higher mobility of the electorate; (b) the return to ideological radicalization; (c) disaffection with the consociational constraints and of the *Proporz* system; and (d) the growth of anti-partisan and anti-system feelings nurtured by waves of political scandals. In a sentence, the passage of Austria from the 'island of the blessed' to the 'political culture of uneasiness' (Plasser, Ulram, and Grausgruberg 1992) is at the heart of Haider's party's rise.

After the post-war 'polarised ideological rhetoric', Austria experienced a period of de-polarization between the late 1960s and the early 1980s, thanks to the consensus and bi-partisan attitudes of the main parties, as well as to the pro-liberal ideological turn of the FPÖ under Steger's leadership. Since then both the Greens' rise in popularity and Haider's takeover of the FPÖ have not only altered the political agenda but also challenged the traditional 'parameters of party competition (e.g. mutual veto, social partnership, and *Proporz*)' (Luther 1999: 130). Hence, the 'nature of the political discourse in the electoral and parliamentary arena . . . has again become much more polarised' (Luther 1999: 130). The growing spatial and ideological distance among the parties (Moreau 1998: 71) fertilized the soil for the development of a radicalized party such as the FPÖ.

Austria's division into three segmented and equally conflicting *Lager* was so pervasive that, first of all, no other European country had as many partisan members as a proportion of the population as Austria (Müller 1992); and, secondly, party members were used to living in 'socio-politically consonant social networks' (this was the case for 86 per cent of SPÖ and 78 per cent of OVP members in 1972 (Plasser, Ulram, and Grausgruber 1992: 23)). The decline of this segmentation in the form of the decline of party membership, party identifiers, voting loyalty, and ideological votes appeared to be complete by the early 1990s (Plasser, Ulram, and Grausgruber 1992: 24ff; Ulram 1997: 517; Müller, Plasser, and Ulram 1999: 204–6). As a consequence, the number of floating votes largely increased, especially from 1986 (the year of Haider's breakthrough) onwards: compared to 1979, they had more than doubled by 1986 and almost tripled by 1990. Differently put, their net volatility jumped from 1.3 in 1979 to 9.9 in 1986, reaching a peak in the 1994 elections with 15.5 (Luther 1999: 127). From the mid-1980s, the de-freezing of the Austrian system was offering a reasonable opportunity for new parties to break through.

The de-alignment of the Austrian electorate brought together disenchantment, distrust, and anger vis-à-vis the parties themselves, as well as the political class and the political system. Therefore, dissatisfaction over the malfunctioning of the system and *Proporz*, over the unaccountability of politicians, and over mismanagement by the parties had been growing since the late 1970s. The anti-party and anti-political sentiments moved up from a minimum of 6 percentage points to a maximum of 13 points, according to different indicators, between 1974 and 1996 (Müller, Plasser, and Ulram 1999: 208). Already in 1985, *before Haider's breakthrough*, 68 per cent of the people were 'angry about political parties' (Plasser, Ulram, and Grausgruber 1992: 27). From 1980 to 1990 confidence in the political institutions decreased by 14 percentage points (the second highest decrease of over 24 democracies surveyed) (Dalton 1999: 68). All these indicators converge in depicting a context of de-alignment from previous, old loyalties, *inducing change and protest* for mounting dissatisfaction towards the system and politics.

In the 1980s, protest against the consociationalism and *Proporz* and mistrust toward politicians merged with the resurgence of right-wing sentiments such as anti-Semitism, xenophobia, and historical revisionism. The Waldheim case and the anniversary of the *Anschluss* in 1988 revealed both widespread uneasiness in confronting the problem of the Nazi past and creeping anti-Semitism. The international criticism of Kurt Waldheim, who was charged with having concealed his (however limited) involvement in the deportation of Jews, aroused a sense of frustration for a past that would never end and for the renewed tutelage which the Austrian people still had to endure. Nonetheless, anti-Semitism still appeared to be present in many sectors of Austrian society. For example, the ÖVP leaders manifested, in line with their early-century tradition, latent anti-Semitic prejudices and extremely muted criticism of only Nazi persecution (Wodack 1990). Finally, incidents provoked by neo-Nazi groups became increasingly more numerous. It is therefore not surprising that, according to a survey conducted in the mid-1980s, only 20 per cent of people were considered to be devoid of anti-Semitism (Bailer Galanda *et al.* 1992: 295).

As far as the new issues of crime and immigration are concerned, the rapid and steep increase in the total number of foreigners after the collapse of the Berlin wall, from less than 300,000 in 1988 to more than 500,000 in 1991 (including asylum-seekers, from 8639 in 1986 to 27,306 in 1991, and foreign workers, from 150,000 in 1988 to 266,461 in 1991) (Gachter 1992: 62), raised a wave of xenophobic resentment. In a 1990 survey, 21 per cent of the population was classified as strongly xenophobic (Steger 1993: 11). And in the 1991 Vienna municipal election, the immigration issue was considered to be the top priority for 40 per cent of the people. The level of xenophobia in Austria scored the highest in all of Europe in 1990: 77 per cent of Austrians agreed with the statement that 'nationals should have priority in receiving jobs' whereas Italy was at 74 per cent, France at 63 per cent, Germany at 62 per cent, Norway at 57 per cent, and Denmark at 52 per cent (Kitschelt 1995: 187). In order to deal with this situation the government passed two bills in 1992 (the Asylum and Alien Acts and the Residence Act) (Mitten 1994) which were so restrictive that they provoked criticism from both Amnesty International and the UN Refugee Agency (Steger 1993: 4–5). Notwithstanding these governmental initiatives, the level of xenophobic sentiments remained constant.

In conclusion, the societal and political changes that occurred in the 1980s concerning the 'de-pillarization' of the Austrian system, the decline of the party's encroachment on society, and higher voter volatility, prepared the way for new political entrants. In addition, the decline of confidence in the system fuelled by the wave of scandals and corruption, the distrust toward the traditional elite, the rise of new issues such as immigration and crime, plus the resiliency of old themes such as the question of nationalism, modified the political agenda. The reframing of the FPÖ's image (Table 6.4) proved essential in presenting the party as a new anti-establishment political choice; and Haider's populist, sharp, and kaleidoscopic rhetoric fulfilled perfectly the function of the 'magic flute' in this context.

TABLE 6.4. *Voter motivation for the FPÖ*

	1990	1994	1999
Scandals/corruption	62	68	65
Immigration	39	49	47
Haider personality	42	39	40
Send a message/new broom	44	39	63

Source: Fessel GfK (1999).

THE FPÖ TOWARDS GOVERNMENT

The FPÖ continued to grow, reaching 22.5 per cent in the 1994 general elections, stabilizing at 21.9 per cent the following year, and reaching 26.9 per cent in the 1999 general elections. That constant rise was encroached upon in the long-term structural process of change (highlighted in the previous paragraph), in the saliency of new controversial issues, and in a persistently parochial civic culture. Notwithstanding the political defeats encountered by the FPÖ in the 1990s—failure of the one-million petition for the adoption of a more restrictive policy on immigration in 1992; the split and relative success of the FPÖ's liberal faction (Liberales Forum) in 1993; the unsuccessful opposition to the referendum on EU entrance in 1994; the uproar and stigmatization of Haider's pro-Waffen-SS declarations in 1995; and internal financial scandals in 1996 and 1998—the party was able to counterbalance these negative performances thanks to the above-mentioned, structural, positive conditions.

Moreover, since the turn of the 1990s the FPÖ has modified some of its traditional positions in order to attract and retain a larger electoral audience. One point concerns the national issue. This sensitive subject, central to party identity, was rapidly revised in connection with the collapse of the old international context following the fall of the Berlin wall. The linkage to the German *Kulturnation* and the mistrust of the Austrian nation, repeatedly defined by Haider as 'an ideological miscarriage', was discarded by introducing instead a novel nationalistic *Austrian* sentiment. The 1997 party programme clearly stated the central role of national identity and the necessity to defend it from foreign invasion. This U-turn, abruptly announced by Haider in an press interview in 1995, was coupled with strong opposition to the EU: the FPÖ opposed Austrian adhesion to the European Union in the 1994 referendum on the basis of the defence of national culture and way of life against globalization and multiculturalism. The German people's cultural community (*Volkgemeinschaft*) was raised as a counteracting factor against the disruptive effects of the excessive presence of foreigners and the standardizing implications of the supra-national process. The defence of small homogenous communities becomes a key reference for the party. In this domain it reinstated linkages with the nationalistic milieu, gathered around the '*Aula*' review and the former members of the *Burschenshaften*.

The second novel aspect was the replacement of the traditional anti-clerical standing of the third *Lager* in favour of pro-Catholic positions. The attempt to undermine the traditional, Catholic ÖVP constituency pushed the FPÖ to promote itself as the defender of family and traditional moral values, pledging support for the traditionalist bishop, Kurt Krenn, and nominating the Catholic Ewald Stadler as Haider's spokesperson.

Finally, the 1997 program, while exhibiting a hyper-Thatcherite neo-liberal approach, substituting, for example, the traditional references to 'free social market' with the term 'free fair market' (Riedlsperger 1998: 33) and demanding the elimination of 'welfare privileges', it covertly advocated generous social provisions for the indigenous population (a classical case of 'welfare chauvinism').

These relevant innovations in the traditional ideological and political references of the party were accompanied by the maintenance of a very strong critique vis-à-vis the 'political class' and the *Proporz* system, up to the point that it fostered a change of regime from the second to the 'third republic' (another potential element of ambiguity given the assonance to the 'Third Reich').

It is quite clear that the FPÖ of the nineties does not resemble the FPÖ of the early eighties, nor even the old, nostalgic, and isolated third *Lager* party.

First of all, the party has moved to the right. Although in 1976, in the aftermath of Steger's leadership, the FPÖ was less to the right than the OVP, it has moved rightwards since 1989 and public opinion has located it as leaning quite far to the right (Moreau 1998: 71). The same trend and location appear in other surveys. On a 0–10 left–right scale the party goes from 7.00 in 1975 to 8.27 in 1991 (Campbell 1992: 169). On the same scale, Huber and Inglehart (1995) locate the FPÖ even further to the right at 8.63.

Second, the party developed a populist style moulded on the party leader, which, in turn, pushed the party towards the *Führerprinzip*, devitalizing internal democracy and forcing out dissidents. The post-1986 FPÖ is above all shaped by the image of its own leader: young, dynamic, and endowed with great rhetorical and communicative ability. The personalization of FPÖ politics was—and is— one of the party's best assets. Haider is the party's locomotive (Riedlsperger 1992): his standing and propositions are secondary to his image, and even when his declarations appear outrageous to the conventional political discourse, they do not adversely affect the 'protest' anti-political FPÖ constituency. The *Haider-Effekt* propelled the party until the 1990–1 electoral cycle when the vote for the party was mainly motivated by the leader's presence; afterwards, the more direct anti-establishment and anti-Proporz issues gained more room in its electorate.

Thirdly, the party radicalized along neo-liberal and authoritarian lines maintaining skilled ambiguity and trivializing the country's Nazi past. On many occasions, Haider has expressed sympathetic sentiments toward the past. The most resounding attempt at fostering a Nazi reconsideration—his admiration for the Third Reich's labour policy—forced Haider to resign from the presidency of Carinthia, but he continued along the same lines, later praising Waffen-SS veterans as an 'example for the youth'. Even if the references to the Nazi regime are not always so explicit, Haider normally uses terminology taken from the Nazi repertoire such as, for instance, 'the final solution', using it in completely different contexts, for example: 'the final solution to the problem of agriculture.' The pro-Nazi and racist 'verbal slips' are to be framed within a larger context. As made clear, Haider's outrageous statements demonstrate that he 'is willing to challenge taboos and offend Austrian "partocracy" that is united in its condemnation of racism and anti-Semitism. In a subtle way, racist signals may here contribute to the Freedom Party's anti-establishment message which is clearly the most important driving force of its electoral success' (Kitschelt 1995b: 187). On the other hand, FPÖ voters have a completely different evaluation of national socialism than other voters: while only 4 per cent of an FPÖ sample interviewed in 1992 stated that Nazism had mostly negative aspects (and 64 per cent mostly positive ones), 84 per cent of Green voters, 61 per cent of OVP voters, and 55 per cent of SPÖ voters underlined national socialism as mainly negative (Plasser and Ulram 1992: 13).

Fourthly, the FPÖ emphasized anti-establishment and even anti-system issues, offering demagogic, populist, and anti-liberal solutions. The polemical statements match the party followers' sentiments very well. Actually, the voters' motives for choosing the FPÖ since the 1990s point first to the anti-political and anti-system issues, then to the party and party leader profile, and finally to immigration issues. The anti-partisan feelings came first in 1990 with 62 per cent, in 1994 with 68 per cent, and in 1999 with 65 per cent (see Table 6.4).

Also at the elite level the FPÖ demonstrates its extremism. The FPÖ parliamentary group, surveyed in the 1996–9 legislature, displays a rather extreme profile (Muller and Jenny 2000: 151): its MP's are the least liberal on sociocultural issues such as the personal use of marijuana and dealing with crime, and the most critical of the workings of Austrian democracy and the European Union.

Finally the FPÖ anti-immigration standings should be weighted according to the national context. In fact, contrary to what happens in other countries, the xenophobic attitudes of FPÖ voters are not so removed from those shared by the average electorate; and the FPÖ voters' level of xenophobia is not that much higher than that of the other European extreme right parties. The point is that Austrian society as a whole has quite a high level of anti-immigrant sentiment (Müller, Plasser, and Ulram 2000; Ivaldi 2001).

While xenophobia does not distinguish FPÖ voters significantly from the electorates of the other Austrian parties, where authoritharian and anti-system attitudes are concerned, FPÖ voters diverge quite dramatically from the others. First and foremost, as already underlined, on the evaluation of the past and of the Nazi regime. The same is true for representative democracy, political parties, and politics on the whole: the FPÖ voters' position on the scale of 'political distrust' is positive while all the other voters' position is negative. Similar contrasts emerge from a comparison on authoritarian issues and EU support (Ivaldi 2001: 59–62).

TABLE 6.5. *Proportion of blue-collars voting for the FPÖ and SPÖ*

	FPÖ	SPÖ
1986	10	57
1990	21	52
1994	29	47
1995	34	41
1999	47	35

Source: Fessel GfK (1999).

The transformation of the FPÖ into an anti-establishment, protest, 'extreme' right party has occurred along with a transformation of its sociological constituency (see Tables 6.2 and 6.3). While maintaining the overwhelming support of males and a strong appeal among the younger age groups, the party has lost white-collar support in favour of blue-collar. The proletarianization of the party is quite dramatic. While it collected only 4 per cent of the blue-collar vote in 1979, it has progressively increased the share of the workers' vote, up to 47 per cent in 1999 (Fessel-GfK Exit polls 1999). In the last election, the blue-collar vote represented almost half of the party's electorate and the share of workers which have chosen the FPÖ has surpassed that of the SPÖ (47% against 35%): at the end of the century, the FPÖ is Austria's workers' party (Table 6.5).

A PARTY OF THE EXTREME RIGHT FAMILY?

On what basis can a 'liberal' party, as the FPÖ name suggests, be included within the category of parties of the extreme right?

Beyond its own genetic (Nazi-nostalgic) characteristics, somewhat revitalized by the Haider leadership through a long series of 'incidents' and misunderstandings, there has been a constant de-legitimizing of representative democratic institutions through the cult of the leader and the myth of the popular will.

The disdain for liberal democratic procedures and the continuous appeal to the *Völk* are crucial indicators of populist leaning. Morover, distrust for the idea of equality of man expressed by overt xenophobia and differential racism, the populist rhetoric (the common man and the 'powerless' against the establishment and the 'powerful'), the appeal to natural community and ethnicity (the *Völkgemeinschaft*) against citizens' rights, all expressed by Haider's FPÖ, place the party much closer to right extremism rather than liberal-conservatism. And not by chance was the FPÖ expelled by the Liberal International in 1993. Put differently, following one of the most authoritative scholars on the topic, since the FPÖ undeniably articulates 'opposition of principle' and has a *de-legitimizing impact* on the regime, it clearly meets Sartori's general criterion of an 'anti-system party' (Luther 1998: 139).

On the other hand, the FPÖ's entry into government in coalition with the ÖVP in January 2000 has led the same author to de-emphasize the above-mentioned traits of the party. Richard Luther has in fact boldly stated in a recent paper that 'the Freedom party is not a neo-fascist, neo-nazi or a right wing extremist one' (Luther 2000: 439). Actually we agree that the FPÖ is neither neo-fascist nor neo-Nazi but not that it is not right-extremist. Given Haider's absolute domination over his party and the media attention he receives, his statements should be considered core elements of the party identity. By consequence, as the same Luther admits, 'Haider's pronouncements are at the basis of the FPÖ negative evaluation'(Luther 2000: 439–40). Therefore, even if intentional use (and abuse) by Haider himself of calembours and jokes might be interpreted as a tool to break the consociational pack, the point is that such a political style and discourse 'promotes an atmosphere of intolerance and xenophobia' contributing to the radicalizing and polarizing of Austrian politics. In conclusion, the FPÖ leader has been—intentionally or not—pursuing for a long time a strategy of system undermining, accomplishing in so doing the basic criterion of the FPÖ being classified as an anti-system right-wing party. Whether entry into government in coalition with the ÖVP will de-radicalize the party moving it away from right-extremism goes beyond the present analysis.

7

Belgium: Right Extremism and Ethnic Nationalism

Belgium is a linguistically divided country. In the north is Flanders, where the language is Dutch, and in the south Wallonia, where the language is French. The capital, Brussels, is located in the centre, the only mixed linguistic region, with a prevalence of French and of a specific Brussels dialect. The extreme right, more than any other political family, developed in different ways according to the two main linguistic areas of the country.

NATIONALISM AND FASCISM: INTER-WAR BACKGROUND AND POST-WAR SETTING

The historically pronounced subordination of Flanders within the Belgian State provided the basis for the development of a Flemish nationalism, antagonistic to the French-speaking hegemony. Dramatic evidence of the exacerbation of Flemish nationalistic sentiments was represented by the formation of a clandestine group inside the Army during WWI, the Frontbeweging (Movement of the Front). The most militant nationalists among them collaborated with the Germans to achieve national sovereignty. In the inter-war period the nationalistic Flemish movement (Schepens 1980: 501–16; Gijsels 1992: 15–38; Mudde and van Holsteyn 2000: 81–5), while affected by an endless series of break-ups and mergers, found a clear reference in the Vlaamsche Front or Frontpartij (Party of the Front). This party, however, did not receive sizeable electoral support and faded after its defeat in the 1932 general election. Two further movements gathered the militant sentiments. One, the Vlaams Nationaal Verbond (VNV) (Flemish National Union), was founded in 1933 and ran successfully in the 1936 and 1939 national elections, polling 7.1 and 8.3 per cent, respectively. During the German occupation it became a collaborationist force. The other was the Verdinaso (Verbond van Dietse Nationaal-Solidaristen) (Association of the National-Solidaristic Diets). Founded in 1931, it disdained electoral competition and inspired militant activity aligning itself closely to the fascist model. Beyond its nationalistic aims, it was corporatist, anti-democratic, anti-Semitic, anti-Communist, anti-Masonic; it had an organized paramilitary militia and was based on the *Führerprinzip*. Verdinaso's influence was limited and it never attracted more than 5000 members, but its leaning towards fascism highlights the path which nationalistic movements might have followed in the 1930s and actually did follow later, during the war, as in the case of the VNV.

Nationalism was the driving force for the proliferation of extreme right movements in the French-speaking area as well, although their true motive concerned Belgian nationalism *tout court*, rather than Wallonian independence. Between the two world wars, patriotic and nationalist leagues proliferated, in imitation of their French counterparts. The most authentic and dangerous interpreter of Belgian fascism was the predominantly French-speaking Rex movement, led by Leon Degrelle (Wallef 1980). Previously active inside the Catholic party, Degrelle left the party at the end of 1935 to establish his own movement of clerico-corporatist, nationalist, anti-Marxist, and anti-Semitic tendencies. The Rex's fairly successful outcome in the 1936 general elections, only six months after its constitution— 11.5 per cent of the vote with peaks of 25 per cent in some Walloon constituencies—caused concern due to its rapid expansion at the Catholic party's expense. But Degrelle's driving ambition on the one hand, and the mobilization of the left and, above all, the reaction of the Church on the other, led to a rapid confrontation which ended up with the Rexists being defeated in the 1937 Brussels constituency by-elections, where Degrelle, confident of his own popularity, ran for election personally. An unprecedented coalition of all the parties, including the communists, was set up. Furthermore, the unitary candidate challenging Degrelle was none other than the Catholic party's Prime Minister. This anti-fascist mobilization, in addition to the Church's direct intervention (two days before the vote, the Archbishop of Malines, Catholic primate of Belgium, publicly defined the Rex as 'a danger for the country and the Church'), pushed Degrelle to the brink, his modest 19 per cent of the vote being overwhelmed by the Catholic candidate's 76 per cent. The challenge put forward by Degrelle had failed. After that defeat the Rex movement continued to lose votes and finished up with only 4.4 per cent of the vote in the 1939 general election (Etienne 1968; Conway 1996).

The outbreak of WWII and the Nazi occupation gave new spirit to the Belgian extreme right. The reorganization of Degrelle's party under the Nazi occupation took place in parallel with Flemish collaboration, and a special SS body was even formed. The period of occupation left deep wounds in Belgian society. The 346,283 cases of collaboration judged by the courts and the 1247 capital sentences (fairly equal between Flemish and Walloon) carried out during the immediate post-war years show the magnitude of the phenomenon (Husbands 1992c: 130). Accordingly, up until the 1960s, 'political demonstrations of the extreme right . . . were extremely rare' (Verhoeyen 1962: 2). The extreme right only restructured itself after the 1960 decolonization process.

In Wallonia the extreme right developed along the following lines: 'a violent anti-Sovietism, anchored to the idea that the third world war has already begun'; the need to 'defend the white world threatened both internally and externally by the supporters of de-colonisation'; a refusal of the 'regime of the parties (in favour) of a strong government and of "*salut publique*"' (Verhoeyen 1962: 3–4). These are all themes whose rationale is founded in the decolonization 'trauma'.

However, no organized extreme right movement reached a significant position; the Parti National Belge (Belgian national party), for instance, picked up 0.1 per cent of the vote in the 1961 elections (Husbands 1992c: 130). The only sizeable movement, due to its having a certain amount of influence in the student milieu and to the personality of the leader, was Jean Thiriart's Jeune Europe (Young Europe). Thiriart can be described as the most relevant figure in the panoply of Belgian right-extremism at this time. His movement occupied a somewhat strange position, proclaiming itself 'Nazi-Maoist', anti-bourgeois, anti-Western, and in favour of the national revolution and the Third way, against capitalism and socialism (Brees 1992: 26). It was short lived and soon confined itself to the *groupuscolaire* circuit: one of its heirs was the tiny Parti Communitaire National-Europèenne (PCN) (National-European Community Party) (Gijsels *et al.* 1988: 84).

On the Flemish side, extreme right movements were assembled within the nationalistic framework and therefore did not need to wait for the 'opportunity structure' of decolonization (Gijsels 1992: 38–78). The first nationalistic organizations to be set up were the Vlaamse Concentratie (VC) (Flemish Aggregation), in 1949, and the Vlaamse Militanten Orde (VMO) (Order of Flemish Militants) in 1950. These organizations recruited Flemish war collaborators, most of them still devoid of their political rights, the so called 'Incivikien' (Mudde 1995b: 7). The basic aim of these groups was, in effect, 'national conciliation' and an end to the isolation of former collaborators, granting them social protection and recognition of their state service. After the transformation of the VC into the most respectable and moderate Volksunie (VU) (Popular Union), the VMO, which had since served as *service d'ordre*, thanks to the entry of the VMO leader into the Belgian senate in 1971, merged with the Volksunie. However, the more radical fringe of the VMO did not accept this appeasement, taking up the original stance of the organization. It introduced an even more radical program (the removal of the parliamentary democratic regime and destruction of the national state) whilst developing contacts with other European extreme right groups. In this political milieu, which combined nationalistic claims with proto-fascist acquaintances, in the mid-1970s the Were Di (Association of Dutch Working Groups—Protest Yourself) played an important role. The members of the Were Di movement later formed the ideological and militant backbone of many other groups: the Vlaams Blok (Flemish Block VlB), the Voorpost (Outpost), the Vlaams Nationale Partji (Flemish National Party VNP), and the Vlaamse Volkspartij (Flemish Popular Party VVP) (Gjisel: 1992).

THE IRRELEVANT BUT CONTINUED PRESENCE OF THE FRENCH SPEAKING EXTREME RIGHT

At the end of the 1970s, the landscape of the extreme right in Wallonia was modified by the development of a very aggressive neo-fascist youth movement— Front de la Jeunesse (FDJ) (Youth Front)—and by the emergence of several 'populist' formations. The most important Walloon 'populist' groups were the Union Democratique du Travail (Labour Democratic Union) (UDRT) and the Nols circles. They bordered on rather than belonged to the extreme right, but nevertheless flirted with it (Nols was the first to invite Jean-Marie Le Pen to Belgium). Above all, they paved the way for the introduction of those issues and attitudes that were to be revitalized and radicalized by the true extreme right parties in the 1980s. The UDRT (van Eesbeeck 1985) was a political movement, directly sponsored by the General Federation of Self-employed Workers promoting 'the abolition of fiscal punishment on jobs' (Delwit and De Waele 1997: 17). The distinctive defence of these interests is cloaked by more general, vigorous anti-partisan, and anti-statist political standings: the political class was described in the most derogatory terms and accused of being the cause of all ills. The UDRT was certainly close to the poujadistic tendency due to its violent disputes over the party system (or rather, the parties' power, i.e., the *particratie*) and the political class, on one side, and the defence of self-employed workers, on the other, but it cannot be assimilated within the group of the extreme right parties. In 1978, the UDRT, a few months after its formation, ran in the general election and, despite its modest 0.9 per cent, succeeded in electing a deputy (the party leader, Roger Hendrickx) thanks to a favourable result in the Brussels constituency (2.3%). In the following elections held in 1981, the UDRT tripled its vote (2.7%), with a peak of 6.9 per cent in Brussels, but this result was dramatically below its own expectations. The disappointment, apart from activating inner conflicts which resulted in some defections, brought about a strategic change: the UDRT moved quite abruptly from fiscal protest to anti-immigrant mobilization. Such change of direction, however, was not rewarded by the electorate, which abandoned the UDRT pushing it down to 1.1 per cent in the 1985 elections. Despite Hendrickx being elected again, this movement had ended its lifecycle by the mid-late 1980s (Delwit and De Waele 1999: 141–2).

The Nols 'phenomenon' represented a rather similar movement (Brees 1992; Brewaeys *et al.* 1992). Roger Nols was a former member of the Liberal party and Mayor of one of Brussels' neighbouring towns. He had attracted attention for his hardline anti-Flemish initiatives in the early 1980s, but then changed his target directing his polemical arrows against immigrants, particularly those from the Maghreb. Nols, in emphasizing this issue and presenting a list under the heading of NOLS, achieved overwhelming success in his own town's local election (51.5%). Furthermore, he got 90,000 preference votes in the Liberal party list, where he stood as an independent candidate in the 1984 European elections. Nols' march towards the extreme right, which he could have led without difficulty, was interrupted by a fatal move, the meeting with Le Pen, who was invited to Belgium by Nols himself. The anti-fascist mobilization against Le Pen on the evening they met led to urban revolt and forced Nols into a hasty retreat. The would-be encounter between Nols and the extreme right collapsed and Nols subsequently founded an ephemeral party—the Nols club—in order to maintain his own political survival: at election time he always ran as an independent, on the liberal lists. On the whole, Nols, thanks to his relative notoriety, played an import-ant role in raising the issue of immigration in Belgian politics and also in the spreading (maybe beyond his intention) of xenophobic and racist statements. All in all, the UDRT and the Nols circles fertilized the soil for the development of a true extreme right that manifested itself in the mid-late 1980s.

The two parties that represented this tendency were the Parti des Forces Nouvelles (PNF) (New Forces Party) and the Front National (FN) (National Front). The PNF appeared first. Founded in 1975, it originated from the quite radical and violent Front de la Jeunesse (Brewaeys *et al.* 1992: 6; Gijsels *et al.* 1988: 23ss) and could be classified as a neo-fascist party. In fact, beyond its initial contacts with the Italian MSI and a certain nostalgia for Rexism, it was characterized by the exaltation of the European nation in opposition to Americanism, contempt for parliamentary politics, propaganda of the revisionist thesis on the Holocaust, xenophobia, and a new corporatist order. The anti-immigrant discourse was underpinned by biological/genetic motives rather than the subtler argument of 'differential racism' of the French Front National, which the PNF nevertheless evoked, although for mere propaganda. The electoral outcomes of the PFN were modest, generally speaking: in the towns of the Brussels region, it achieved 2 per cent in 1982 and subsequently slightly deviated positively and negatively from that percentage, sporadically gathering some significant results such as 2 per cent in Liege, with peaks of 15 per cent in some districts (Husbands 1992*c*: 133). The birth of the Front National as a competitive force and the lack of an electoral breakthrough favoured a more moderate leaning at the beginning of 1989. Along this path, the party opened its ranks to a sizeable, but not neo-fascist, right-wing group based mainly in Liege. This new component, however close to the *Nouvelle Droite* thinkers, soon itself clashed with traditional PFN radical stances. The Brussels International Book Fair provided the occasion for an internal showdown. Since the Forces Nouvelles stand was full of revisionist and anti-Semitic publications, this led to widespread and violent reactions, with clashes between the police and the PNF activists who were trying to prevent the dismantling of their stand. This event, along with the very poor result in the Brussels regional election (1%), provoked a split by the Liege group, which set up the Agir movement. By 1991 the PFN dissolved, partly merging with the FN (Brewaeys, Dahaut, and Tolbiac 1992: 8–9).

Agir was founded jointly by Willy Freson, a former prominent member of the Front de la Jeunesse and then founder of '*Europe Nation*', by Robert Steuckers, the most reputed interpreter of the *Nouvelle Droite* in Belgium, and by Robert Destordeur, a former member of the PNF secretariat. This group, highly influ-enced by the *Nouvelle Droite* ideology, claiming to differentiate itself from the other extreme right groups because of a 'culturalist' approach to the immigration issue rather than crude racism, declared itself an 'opposition popular party', not an extreme right party (Brewaeys, Dahaut and Tolbaic 1992: 38). However, its relationship with other extreme right groups both in Wallonia (the FN) and in Flanders (the Vlaams Blok) seems to contradict this self-interpretation. Agir acted as a local group based essentially in Liege; it ran in the 1991 national election achieving 4.7 per cent in the Liege 'canton' and 3.4 per cent in the Liege 'arrondisment', finally electing Willy Freson to the Liege provincial council. After that, it underwent a crisis, due to personal quarrels, and then merged with the FN in 1997 (Abramowicz and Haelsterman 1998: 101).

The Front National was born later than the PFN, in 1985, under the initiative of Daniel Féret, an old *routier* of the extreme right, formerly a member of Jeune Europe and of the UDRT (Brees 1992; Rea 1997). From the outset, the FN attempted to highlight its differences from its closest competitor, the PNF. In response to a poisonous welcome article published in the PNF newspaper, and later in a letter to *Le Soir* newspaper, Ferret expressly denied any fascist or racist heritage (Brewaeys Dahaut, and Tolbiac 1992: 21; Brees 1992: 40). Actually, Ferret's aim was to have the party credited as being 'respectable', but he was unable to achieve this due to a large presence of former right extremists inside the party. The FN programme ranged in fact between neo-fascism, racism, and ultra-nationalism, on the one hand, and neo-liberalism, fiscal protest, and anti-establishment, on the other. One can find therefore in the party press and in the electoral manifestos either an exhalation of the virtue of the market or a concern for social provisions. However, the party was focussed not so much on socio-economic issues, rather on the recovery of the 'traditional values of the right: homeland, honour, courage and the pursuit of achievement', as stated in the founding charter of the party (Rea 1997: 200). It also stood for the protection of the Belgian nation against internal (Flemish) and external (immigrant) disruptive forces; but the latter concerned the FN much more than the possible break-up of the country. The nation's integrity was being undermined by foreigners who provoked insecurity, unemployment, fiscal burdens, and even the lack of care towards 'the fourth world' (the poor and elderly Belgians) (Brees 1992: 53ss). The party followed quite openly the path laid out by the French sister-party (even if Le Pen never paid attention to its Belgian homologue) by adopting the same slogans (The Belgian first!) and the same manifestos, as in the case of the anti-immigration programme.

The crisis of the PNF after 1989 brought a certain influx of hardline activists into the FN, but the only radical concession made to this group consisted of shifting from a pro-Atlantic attitude to opposition against the two blocks and 'American hegemony'; in point of fact, the FN opposed Belgian participation in the Gulf War and began to support the PLO's views against Israel.

The FN's first electoral results are comparable to the PNF ones, namely irrelevant. In the 1987 election the two parties fiercely competed against each other, endangering their respective, modest, electoral chances even more. The FN got 0.9 per cent in the Brussels region, the only constituency where it competed (equivalent to 0.1% nationally). The first positive signal came from the 1988 local election, when the FN succeeded in electing a city councillor in a municipality of the Brussels conglomeration. In the 1989 regional election of Brussels, the FN subsequently polled 3.9 per cent and elected two councillors out of 75. This positive electoral outcome was confirmed by the general and provincial elections of November 1991. They represented a real watershed for the Front National: after those elections the FN acquired a national relevance. In the provincial ballot the party reached 3.3 per cent in the Brussels region, electing two councillors, and 0.9 per cent in Wallonia. This result should be scrutinized further in light of the reduced number of constituencies contested and of the competition from Agir, which monopolized the Liege constituency, polling a significant 4.7 per cent (and electing one councillor). The greatest success, however, came with its entry into parliament: the 4.2 per cent of votes obtained in the Brussels region (equivalent to 1.05% nationwide) gave, for first time in the post-war period, a parliamentary seat to a representative of the French-speaking extreme right (Table 7.1).

This breakthrough did not, however, strengthen the organization of the party, which remained quite fluid and unstable. On the other hand, the electoral success caused an increasing political isolation. The established parties reacted to the FN's entry into the representative institutions by decreeing a firm ostracism against it. The sense of isolation thus experienced by the FN pushed the party towards more pronounced anti-system and anti-political attitudes. It stressed its radical opposition to all the other parties, which, in turn, increasingly treated it as a pariah party. The 1994 European election and the 1995 national elections seemed to endorse this radical strategy. The FN collected an unprecedented 175,732 votes (7.9% in the Walloon constituency, that is, 2.9% nationally) in the

TABLE 7.1. *Votes for Belgian extreme right parties in parliamentary and European elections*

	UDRT			VlB			FN		
	Nat.	Brux.	Wal.	Nat.	Flandres	Brux.	Nat.	Brux.	Wal.
1978	0.9	2.3	1.3	1.4	2.1	1.9			
1979E									
1981	2.7	6.9	3.9	1.1	1.8	0.9			
1984E				1.3	2.1				
1985	1.1	3.9	1.6	1.4	2.2	1.4			
1987				1.9	3.0		0.1	0.9	
1989E				4.1	6.6				
1991				6.6	10.3	6.6	1.0	4.2	1.7
1994E				7.8	12.6		2.9	—	7.9
1995				7.8	12.3	7.2	2.3	4.7	5.5
1999+				9.9	15.3	8.7	1.5	1.6	4.1
1999E				9.4	15.1		1.5		4.2

+ FBN (Front Nouveau de Belgique); Nat.: 0.4; Brux.: 0.9; Wal.: 0.8.

Source: Official data kindly provided by Pascal Delwit.

European election, electing one EMP. It almost equalled this performance by collecting 138,496 votes in the 1995 national election (4.7% in the Brussels region and 5.5% in Wallonia, equivalent to 2.3% nationally). This election provided the party with two members of parliament, and the local elections simultaneously held brought it 8 regional and 72 municipal councillors (Rea 1997; Swyngedouw 1998*b*: 59).

These remarkable results did not lead to a more relevant role. Organizational weaknesses and personal quarrels inhibited any development of the Front National. At the end of 1995, an internal split (two groups contended in the courts for copyright of the party name) produced a deep crisis with the consequent defection of almost all the elected officials to the other parties. In 1997, the apparently moribund FN surfaced again, combining its own remnants with those of Agir (Abramowicz and Haelsterman 1998: 101). Unexpectedly, the new FN still proved that it had a capacity to attract votes: it gathered 90,401 votes in the 1999 general elections (1.5% nationally: 1.6% in Brussels and 4.1% in Wallonia). electing one MP in the Senate and three regional councillors in the Brussels and Wallon regional parliaments (even more unexpectedly, other minor extreme right groups collected 1.5% in Wallonia and 1.7% in Brussels). While its political activity has gone unnoticed over the last few years, an extremist right-wing constituency, based mainly on xenophobic and anti-establishment appeal, persists. The malaise of Belgian society provides for a reservoir of right-extremism.

THE RADICALIZATION OF FLEMISH NATIONALISM: THE VLAAMS BLOK

In Flanders the extreme right experienced a different development, unrelated to the decolonization process. Up until the 1970s, as we have seen, the VMO represented the more extreme tendency of Flemish nationalism. The VMO was a militant, small-scale group, mostly devoted to violent actions without any electoral leaning, and operated up to the point of being outlawed; in fact in 1981, it was charged with being a paramilitary militia. The legal party that embodied extreme right tendencies in Flanders was the Vlaams Blok. This party was created in 1979 through the merger of factions of two movements, the VNP and the VVP, which had left the Volksunie because of protest against the acceptance of the Egmont pact which paved the way to a federal state. At first, Vlaams Blok did not differentiate itself so much from the other nationalist movements: its main political goal concerned the question of Flanders' independence, and every other problem was subordinate to this. The 1979 party manifesto, the 'Principles', which recalled the 1973 Were Di programme, was centred on ethnic (Flemish) nationalism and 'social solid-arism' (a mixture of fascist corporatism and Catholic solidarism) (Mudde 1995*b*: 16–17). In its first formulation, Vlaams Blok nationalism was quite peculiar as it was neither popular nor populist, but elitist, aristocratic, and addressed to a superior race (Gijsels 1988: 183–7). Subsequently, the VlB abandoned the formulation that fostered the creation of a Flemish state for a pure Flemish race, in favour of an ethnocentric approach without the claims of Flemish superiority. Finally, the 'Principles' still echoed the VMO recommendation in the demand for full amnesty for Nazi collaborators (Mudde 2000: 114).

Starting in the 1980s, partly due to the disappointment of the electoral results of 1978 and 1981 that brought only one deputy to parliament, and partly in imitation of the Dutch Centrumpartij and, mainly, of the French Front National, the Vlaams Blok adopted an anti-immigration theme. A new generation led by Filip Dewinter under the auspices of the uncontested party leader, Karen Dillen, marginalized the old guard nationalists (Spruyt 1997: 210ss). In the VI Congress of the VlB (1984) anti-immigration became the central issue. Flanders should be purged not only of French-speaking Belgians but, and above all, of third-world immigrants (Husbands 1992c: 137). The approach to this theme had references to biological racism. Already in 1956, the historical leader of the VlB, Karen Dillen, wrote that 'the essence of our people consists in the maintenance of our biological substance according to quality and quantity' (Gijsels 1992: 205). Later in a 1988 interview, he confirmed that 'a race can be superior to another one, and this justifies the application of different criteria of evaluation to the different races' (Gijsels 1992: 204).

The Vlaams Blok campaigned in the 1987 election under the slogan 'Eigen volk eerst!' (Our people first!), which recalled the French FN 'Les Français d'abord' (French people before), combining nationalism with xenophobia: the Flemish come before the Belgians and, *a fortiori*, third-world immigrants. In 1992, the party introduced a detailed program on immigration, the '70 Proposals', following once again those presented by the French FN a few months previously. Among these proposals were the severe control over foreigners' organizations, the prohibition of multiracial education in schools, the restriction of foreigners' rights of ownership, a special tax on non-EEC immigrants' jobs, limitations on social benefits to foreign workers, and forced repatriation after three months of unemployment (Gijsels 1992: 209).

While immigration still lies at the core of the VlB propaganda and programme, the Vlaams Blok is far from being a single-issue party (Mudde 1995b: 20): it displays a vast array of right extremist positions (Gardberg 1993: 69–73; Swyngedouw 1998a). It defends the traditional values against 'permissivism', gay rights, sexual liberation, and feminism (anti-abortionist mobilization is intense); it invokes a hardline policy against crime, demanding the introduction of the death penalty; it supported apartheid in South Africa; it favours a Europe of the people and of the nationalities; it demands amnesty and full rehabilitation for WWII collaborators; it fosters free market and neo-liberal positions, playing down (but not repudiating) the former 'solidaristic' ideal (the third way between capitalism and communism is kept alive (Gijsels 1992: 188)); finally, it has adopted an anti-political and anti-establishment discourse. Referring to the latter, the party rhetoric is addressed against various targets: against the Flemish nationalist party (Volksunie, above all) for betraying the Flemish people's interests; against all Belgian parties for being intrinsically anti-Flemish; and against all established parties for being gangs, cliques, and oligarchies. The anti-party sentiment expressed by the Vlaams Blok has been reinforced since the beginning of the nineties with slogans such as 'we are against the political Mafia', 'we are one against all', 'we say what you think', and so on. This set of ideals has acquired increasingly more room in the party rhetoric as the malaise and distrust in the mass public vis-à-vis the Belgian institutions and the workings of the democracy have grown. Moreover, the party leadership, first Dillen and then, since the late 1980s Dewinter, is well suited to the role of provoking and breaking the rules of the consociational system (Swyngedouw 1998*a*; Swyngedouw and Ivaldi 1999).

In short, the Vlaams Blok evolved from old Flemish nationalism veiled by fascist nostalgia and even racial superiority, to an articulated, anti-immigrant, anti-establishment, and anti-party discourse. The party has developed an 'ideology' centred on ethnical hierarchization and ethoncentrism (nowadays articulated along culturalist rather than genetic/biological arguments), as well as the ideal of an ordered, communitarian, non-conflictual, 'solidaristic', and hierarchical-based society where there is no room for individual rights (Mudde 1998: 142–79).

Up until 1987 the VlB electoral results were modest, never having reached 2 per cent, and with the election of only one deputy, the leader Karen Dillen. The traditional regionalist-autonomy party, Volksunie, seemed more capable of representing the nationalistic sentiments of the Flemish and of containing the more extremist Vlaams Blok. However, despite its reduced appeal in the general elections, the VlB had achieved fairly good results in local elections, above all in Antwerp where, already in 1982, it had obtained 5.2 per cent of the votes and had four councillors elected. The breakthrough occurred in the 1988 municipal elections when the VlB elected 23 councillors (in the ten cities where it ran) and gained 17.7 per cent of the vote in Antwerp. From that moment on, the VlB climbed the ladder of success. First, in the European election of 1989 it achieved 4.1 per cent (6.6% in Flanders), and then it made its national breakthrough in the 1991 general elections by polling 6.6 per cent nationally, that is to say 10.3 per cent in Flanders and 3.9 per cent in Brussels (obviously it did not present a list in Wallonia). Antwerp confirmed itself as the capital of Flemish extremism: with more than a quarter of the votes (24.5% for the Chamber and 29.0% for the provincial council) the VlB was the first party of that province. The triumphal march of the Vlaams Blok continued. It gained afterwards 7.8 per cent of the votes (12.6% in Flanders) and two MEPs in the 1994 European elections; consolidated its presence by electing more than 200 councillors in the 1994 municipal elections; obtained 475,677 votes in the 1995 general election (7.8% in Belgium and 12.3% in Flanders); and finally transcended half a million votes in the 1999

European and general elections (9.9% nationally and 15.3% in Flanders) which brought the party to fifth position nationally (Swyngedouw 2000).

ETHNOCENTRIC NATIONALISM VS THE 'BELGIAN STATE' AND ANTI-POLITICS SENTIMENTS VS CONSOCIATIONALISM

The socio-demographic characteristics of the VlB voter emerged quite distinctively since the party's breakthrough in 1991. Apparently, 'blue collar workers, the lower educated and those who have had technical and vocational training, young people between 18 and 25 years of age, non-Catholics, and voters who were living in the urban areas were more likely to vote for the Vlaams Blok' (Billiet and de Witte 1995: 185; see also Swyngedouw 1995: 788). With the exception of a younger age distribution, the Vlaams Blok voters are quite similar to the socialist ones and very different from those who vote for other conservative and nationalist parties (Billet and de Witte 1995: 185). These traits were substantially confirmed in the mid-late 1990s. The survey carried out at the 1995 general election shows that there was a higher probability of the youngest voters (18–25 years), the non-Catholic, the middle–low educated, and the blue-collar workers voting for the Vlaams Blok (Swyngedouw 1998b: 68–9). In particular, where the mean probability of voting for the Vlaams Blok is 11.3 per cent, it increases to 13.2 per cent for those who are low–medium educated, to 14.8 per cent for 18–35-year-olds, to 17.4 per cent for workers, to 18.6 per cent for non-religious people (whereas it is only 6% for practising Catholics) (Swyngedouw, Beerten, and Kampen 1999). This profile changed somewhat in the 1999 election. Among the VlB potential voters, which constitute 14.4 per cent of the sample surveyed, the non-religious (18.8%), the workers (18.4%), the men (18.1%), and the middle educated (17.5%) display the highest probability of voting for the Vlaams Blok (Swyngedouw, Beerten, and Kampen 1999). In comparison with previous elections, the differences within the various categories have been reduced: workers are still prominent but the gap between them and other social groups has narrowed, and the same is true for the age distribution (Table 7.2). On the other hand, Vlaams Blok voters have quite distinctive traits compared to the mean population: they are overwhelmingly male, low educated, more working class, and less Catholic (Swyngedouw, Beerten, and Kampen 1999: 31).

As far as political origin is concerned, the Vlaams Blok got votes, in the early eighties, mainly from former blank/invalid votes (Swyngedouw 1998b: 70). Later, the VlB stole votes from almost all the other parties with particular reference to the Volksunie and the socialist party and, in the 1999 elections, also from the liberals (Swyngedouw and Beerten 1999: 17). The VlB criss-crossed the political space, attracting voters whose previous alignments were quite far removed, as in case of the socialists and first-time voters. The lower class profile of the party

TABLE 7.2. *Probability of voting for the Vlaams Blok according to socio-demographic characteristics*

	1995	1999
Men	—	18.1
Women	—	10.9
Worker	17.4	18.4
Employee	9.4	14.6
Self-employed/professional	9.5	14.5
Not active	8.5	13.0
18–35 years	14.8	14.8
36–55	10.5	12.9
56+	8.1	15.7
Low education	13.2	7.0
Medium education	13.7	17.5
High education	7.8	10.7
Churchgoing Catholic	6.0	8.7
Not churchgoing Catholic	12.3	15.5
Freemason	10.4	14.1
Not religious	18.6	18.8
Mean	(11.3)	(14.4)

Source: Swingedouw *et al.* (1999).

electorate is testimony to its competitiveness with the traditional socialist constituency. In fact, in its breakthrough in Antwerp, the VlB profited from the collapse of the socialist—and also liberal—'subculture' (Swyngedouw 2000).

At first, one of the attitudinal determinants for voters in choosing the Vlaams Blok concerns the question of immigration. This issue has become a relevant one since the 1980s because the presence of foreigners has expanded to around one million (of which two-thirds are extra-EU), equivalent to 9 per cent of the population. Brussels is a highly cosmopolitan city given its status as EU 'capital' but there is also a large share of non-European residents, especially in the municipalities of the conglomeration Greater Brussels. The same goes for the other areas which were affected by inflows of immigrants, such as Liege and Antwerp. It is not by chance that all the French-speaking extreme right movements have achieved their foremost successes in the Brussels area and in Liege, while the VlB is dominant in Antwerp (Swyngedouw 1998c). Notwithstanding a growing concern on the immigration issue, the general public never indicated that they viewed it as the most relevant issue. But extreme right voters did. In 1995, VlB voters singled out the immigration issue by 32.9 per cent compared to 4.2 per cent of the average population (Swyngedouw, Beerten, and Billiet 1997: 12–13). This widespread concern over the presence of foreigners is coupled with strong feelings of rejection by Vlaams Blok supporters. The score on an anti-immigrant scale of VlB voters, ranging from 0 (lowest) to 10 (highest), is 7.09—by far the highest of all the other parties' voters. Even more striking is the 5.00 score on the 'white race superiority' scale (Swyngedouw, Beerten, and Billiet 1997: 189). Also, the Euro-barometer survey displays an overwhelming presence of xenophobic and racist attitudes among VlB voters that is incomparably higher than other Belgian voters (Gabriel 1996: 354). Apparently, a 'negative attitude toward immigrants is the most important factor in choosing the Vlaams Blok' (Billet and de Witte 1995: 192).

Despite evidence of the centrality of the immigration issue for the extreme right electorate, a statistical relationship has not been established between the concentration of foreigners and the vote of the extreme right. The ecological analyses on the distribution of the vote in Antwerp did not confirm a direct relationship between the presence of immigrants and the VlB vote. In the 1980s, the vote for the Vlaams Blok was above the mean in upper-class districts, where there are practically no immigrants, and around the mean in districts with a high density of immigrants. While subsequent elections have increased the likelihood of such a relationship, it remains true that 'the electoral support for the VlB is interwoven by a complex net of motives' (Husbands 1992*c*: 141). This conclusion implies that there are further reasons for the breakthrough of the extreme right. These are linked to the transformation of the political and party system and to the new cultural–attitudinal landscape emerging in recent years.

The first strand of explanation points to the collapse of the consociational properties of the State (Dewachter 1987: 304–5, 337ss). The cohesion of the consensual structures organized around the three major parties—liberals, Catholics, and socialists—came to an end in the 1980s (Deschouwer 1994, 2000; Delwit and DeWaele 1999). The collapse produced two main outcomes. Firstly, it liberated voters from previous alignments, fostering weaker partisan identification and higher electoral volatility. This process favoured the emergence of new cleavage lines—above all the linguistic one—and propelled the development of new parties like the regionalists, the right-extremists, and the ecologists.

Secondly, it affected the system of *'particratie'* (partocracy), which lost its solidity and efficiency, and induced a widening gap between the citizens and the political class (Dewachter 1987: 311). The dissatisfaction over the suffocating and ineffective consociational system with such a pervasive party presence, supplanted by the outburst of political–financial scandals accompanied by assassinations of leading members of the political establishment with the deep suspicion of widespread complicity (the gang of the Brabant, the Augusta scandal, the killing of a PS minister, the 'mysterious' suicide of other politicians) (de Winter 1996), all favoured the growth of sentiments of cynicism and alienation. Mistrust in democracy has been growing from 34 per cent in 1973 to more than 50 per cent in the mid-1980s, reaching its peak in the mid-late 1990s (Mughan 1992: 97; Delwit *et al.* 1999: 3).

The VlB has increasingly concentrated its propaganda on anti-political, anti-establishment appeals. The party programme speaks of 'false democratization and the poisoning of parliamentarism' and parliament is described as a mere 'talk shop' (Mudde 1998: 169). Not only the practice but even the theory of democratic representation is under attack (Swyngedouw and Ivaldi 1999: 13). These themes, which are conveyed with flamboyant rhetoric, are very attractive to VlB voters. Among those who are dissatisfied with the political system, 19.5 per cent were potential voters of the VlB in 1995 and 20.5 per cent in 1999, the highest quota of any other party's voters (Swyngedow, Beerten, and Kampen 1999: 9). More generally, from those who manifested anti-political attitudes (mistrust and lack of confidence in politicians and any political party), 27 per cent chose the VlB in 1995 (Swyngedouw, Beerten, and Billiet 1997: 31). The VlB party attracts by far the highest share of anti-political citizens compared to the other parties: for example, compared to a national mean of 5.7 per cent of 'anti-political voters', the VlB collects 13.7 per cent of this kind of voter (Swyngedouw, Beerten, and Billiet 1997: 22). This data is supported by the massive distrust vis-à-vis politicians: the VlB voters, much more so than any other parties' voters, rate politicians as more corrupt than ordinary people (Billiet, Beerten, and Swyngedouw 1996: 7). Politically alienated citizens find a reference in a party that voices their frustrations more vehemently and radically, with apocalyptic and anxiogenous messages: the Vlaams Blok.

Beyond the transformation of consociationalism and of the 'old' party system, the enduring and ever growing presence of the Vlaams Block is related to

TABLE 7.3. *Profile of the Vlaams Blok voter (exit polls, 1999 parliamentary elections)*

	Mean voter	VlB voter
Men	48.3	60.7
Women	51.7	39.3
18–35 years	32.0	32.9
36–55	36.0	32.1
56+	32.0	34.9
Elementary education	31.5	37.2
Medium education	25.5	30.9
High education	43.0	31.9
Worker	13.7	17.5
Employee	28.6	29.0
Self-employed/professional	14.3	14.4
Not active	43.4	39.1
Church going Catholic	22.8	13.8
Not Church going Catholic	48.1	51.8
Freemason	11.1	10.8
Not religious	18.0	23.6
Politically satisfied	38.2	12.2
Politically dissatisfied	61.8	87.8

Source: Swingedouw *et al.* (1999: 31).

an in-depth transformation of Belgian political culture. This is the second strand of explanation. Two new cleavages seem to have shaped the political space since the late 1980s (Swyngedouw 1995): one recalls Ronald Inglehart's materialism/post-materialism, and the other Ferdinand Tonnies' *Gemeinschaft/Gesellschaft*. The first contrasts quality of life, self-expression, and environmental protection against economic growth, job defence, and the free market. The second separates the attitudes that grant equal rights to everybody, including immigrants, and defends the value of the Belgian community from those attitudes that create a divide between immigrants and non-immigrants and/or Flemings and non-Flemings. This second cleavage, in particular, separates the support of a community based on citizens' rights (the Enlightenment and French Revolution heritage of *solidarité et fraternité*), that is to say on universal principles, from those which keep the borders of an ethnic community clear, and distinct from the 'out-groups'. This antagonism may be called 'openness and universalism' against 'closeness and particularism'. Given such an interpretation of the most recent developments in the Belgian political space, it is no surprise that the Vlaams Blok has gained momentum. Its xenophobic, Flemish nationalist, and security driven appeal accurately matches those voters who are close to the particularism side of the universal/particularistic cleavage (Table 7.3).

CONCLUSION: THE DIVERGING FORTUNES OF THE WALLOON AND FLEMISH EXTREME RIGHT

The present Belgian extreme right, both Walloon and Flemish, is characterized by xenophobia and racism, by the advocacy of a strong (Flemish or Belgian) state with a harsher penal code, 'law and order' enforcement, the restoration of traditional moral values and sex roles, and radical opposition to the political system and the established parties. Nevertheless, the Walloon and Flemish extreme right parties maintain different approaches to the national question: the VlB is rooted in a long and articulated tradition of nationalistic claims, while the FN proclaims a Belgian nationalism that is much weaker historically and emotionally. Ethnic nationalism is, in fact, central to the Vlaams Blok and constitutes its true identity (Mudde 1998: 179). The same is not true for the FN. This is one of the explanations for their different holds on the electorate.

Both parties refuse to be labelled 'fascist'. The FN repeatedly made attempts at differentiating itself from neo-fascist movements such as the PFN. It partially succeeded in doing so, but it never attained that long sought 'respectability' because of its extremist, racist, and anti-system standings. The VlB, on the other hand, recalling the notion of superior and chosen races, the establishment of a 'new order', the advocacy of a solidaristic and hierarchical model of society, and historical revisionism, moved closer to neo-fascism; but the lack of precise cultural and symbolic references to Flemish fascist traditions leaves it at the periphery. Irrespective of any further assessment of a fascist legacy, the Vlaams Blok could be labelled an extreme right, 'racist, separatist and authoritarian party' (Swyngedouw 1998*b*: 202); a party which rejects the idea of equal human rights, fosters an ethnic nationalism by excluding any kind of out-groups, laments 'moral decay' and the loss of traditional values, and which puts the political system itself under constant attack by delegitimizing the democratic institutions, especially the parties and the party system (see Mudde 2000).

To conclude, 'three decades of volatility, fractionalisation, dealignment and linguistic division' (Deschouwer 1991: 84) had offered a propitious opportunity structure for the development of a party which represents a constituency of ethno-centric, moral traditionalist, authoritarian, and politically alienated voters (Swyngedouw, Beerten, and Billiet 1997: 28; Swyngedouw 1999: 168ss).

8

Scandinavia: The Progress Parties Between Protest and Extremism

In Scandinavia the parties that occupy the right-most positions in the political space are the Fremskridtsparti (FRPd) (Progress Party in Denmark) whose central role from 1998 onwards was handed down to its offspring, the Dansk Folkeparti (DFP) (Danish People's Party) and its Norwegian counterpart (Fremskrittsparti—FRPn). These parties constitute essentially a subtype in the category of extreme right parties. Their inclusion is, and has been, a matter of debate and somewhat problematic. However, as will be shown, some of their features qualify for inclusion in this political family, although their anti-system profile is quite limited compared to that of their other European counterparts. The Swedish and Finnish extreme right, given their present minor role in their respective party systems, will be only briefly outlined at the end of the chapter.

DENMARK

The Fremskridtsparti (FRPd) (Progress Party) has been considered (although differing views have been expressed) as the party located furthest to the right in the Danish political spectrum since its emergance in 1973 (Bille 1989; Andersen and Bjørklund 2000: 207). This party, however, shares nothing with the fascist or Nazi traditions of the 1930s and 1940s. Fascism in Denmark originated with the Danmarks Nationalsocialistiske Arbejeder Parti (DNSAP) (National-Socialist Workers Party) founded in 1930 in imitation of the Italian fascists, but later moulded on the Nazi model (Poulsen 1987: 158). The DNSAP played a rather marginal role in the Danish system both during the democratic regime, when it did not manage to reach the 2 per cent threshold in the 1935 and 1939 elections, and during the German occupation, when it received no support from the occupiers, who preferred to keep the incumbent government in place. Finally, in the 1943 elections, the DNSAP gathered no more than 2.1 per cent of the vote. Moreover, the risible electoral performances were not counterbalanced by an extensive mobilization: at the end of the 1930s the DNSAP had 4000 members, which grew to a maximum of 19,100 in the spring of the 1943 (Poulsen and Djursaa 1980: 709). The political relevance of Danish fascism is decidedly modest. In the post-war period this tendency only becomes apparent in the form of very small groups, that sometimes enter the limelight due to their violent activities.

The First FRPd: Mogens Glistrup's Party

The FRPd was essentially born in January 1971 with a brief television interview given by fiscal lawyer, Mogens Glistrup, who made some highly provocative and controversial statements that created a national outcry. Glistrup briefly declared he would not pay a crown of tax to so iniquitous fiscal system as the Danish one, acclaiming tax evaders and comparing them to railway saboteurs during the Nazi occupation. Given the dominant Danish political culture, these affirmations were nothing short of blasphemy, as they struck at the base of the highly consensual welfare system. In 1972, after some meetings with the Conservative Party that proved unfruitful for his candidacy, Glistrup founded his own party. He drew up a basic programme focussing on the suffocating bureaucracy, unbearable fiscal burden, and excessive regulatory policies. Surprisingly, Glistrup's party immediately won favour with public opinion, so much so that a February 1973 survey polled it at 25 per cent (Andersen and Bjørklund 1990: 196). Even more surprisingly, the predicted attraction for a new phenomenon in the quite conventional arena of Danish politics was transformed into strong electoral support, with the FRPd achieving 15.9 per cent in the landmark 1973 election (see Borre 1974; Pedersen 1987, 1988). Since then, and contrary to widespread forecasts which predicted a short-lived existence (like the French Poujadist movement to which it has been constantly compared), the FRPd repeatedly confirmed its own standing and took root in the Danish party system. Its electoral outcome (Table 8.1) fluctuated: it remained above 10 per cent in the 1970s, and then

TABLE 8.1. *Vote for the FRPd and DFP in parliamentary and European elections*

Year	FRPd	DFP
1973	15.9	
1975	13.6	
1977	14.6	
1979	11.0	
1979E	5.8	
1981	8.9	
1984	3.6	
1984E	3.5	
1987	4.8	
1988	9.0	
1989E	5.3	
1990	6.4	
1994	6.4	
1994E	2.9	
1998	2.4	7.4
1999E	0.7	5.8

Source: Andersen and Bjørklund (2000).

declined to a low of 3.6 per cent in 1984; finally it recovered and remained within a range of 5–10 per cent until its very recent crisis and split, which brought about the Danish People's Party.

The Progress Party was born thanks to a series of peculiar and favourable conditions. First of all, the late 1960s and early 1970s were characterized by an unprecedented climate of alienation and mistrust vis-à-vis the political class and institutions (Pedersen 1987). This particular discontent was fuelled by contingent, short-term factors: the deep disappointment in the moderate conservative electorate over the policy implemented by the bourgeois coalition when it had finally returned to power in 1968 after a long social democratic hegemony; the retention by the bourgeois coalition of all the provisions introduced by the Social Democrats and the continuation of the same policies leading, for example, to a dramatic increase in income taxation (Andersen and Bjørklund 1999:5); and the widespread uneasiness over the great reformist wave between the end of the sixties and the beginning of the 1970s (Pedersen 1982: 265–70; Goosken 1993: 17–18). The resultant discontent was such that *Danish citizens displayed, in the early 1970s, the highest distrust for politicians among all Nordic and EEC countries* (Nielsen 1976: 148).

However, more enduring and long-term changes had come to the surface in that period. The foremost of them concerned the weakening of class identification and the consequent loosening of the bonds between electors and parties both in the socialist and the bourgeois camps. Overall party identification declined from 56 per cent in 1971 to 47 per cent in 1973 and electoral volatility jumped from 9.1 to an impressive 29.1 (Bille 1999: 358, 366). Glistrup's new party *entered the political arena precisely when the old, consolidated party loyalties, in both socialist and bourgeois camps, were collapsing.*

Estrangement due to the profound changes in the societal customs and in the institutions, irritation over the increase in fiscal provisions, dissatisfaction with the unaccountability and unreliability of the political class (especially on the bourgeois side), *all arose simultaneously.* These conditions provoked the 1973 electoral earthquake and favoured the breakthrough of an anti-tax and anti-establishment party such as the FRPd (Pedersen 1991). The Progress party clearly benefited from this general sentiment because its electorate revealed the highest level of mistrust towards the political class (16 and 12 points above the population mean in the two most salient items) and displayed a particularly favourable response to authoritarian suggestions (support for 'a strong man' displays a gap of 26 points between FRPd voters and the mean for the electorate) (Nielsen 1976: 149ff).

To sum up, the general feeling of mistrust and unaccountability in the mass public, the 'displacement' produced by an early introduction of (what will be called later) the 'New Politics' agenda (in particular regarding sexual mores), frustration over the maintaining of the social democratic status quo even by the bourgeois government in 1968–71, the crosscutting, new and highly sensitive cleavage on EEC entry, the rise of income taxation, and the weakening of class conflict and class related loyalties, all produced the conditions for unprecedented electoral volatility and party system fragmentation. In this situation a new anti-establishment party had a distinct opportunity to break into the system, given, *inter alia*, the 'lack of substantive policy alternatives among the established parties' (Kitschelt 1995*b*: 267).

From Glistrup to Kjaersgaard: Marginalization and Splits

In its earlier phase, the Progress Party refused to adopt traditional organizational settings and style. Glistrup deliberately hindered any organizational structuring, preferring instead a fluid and loose movement that could easily follow him in his inflammatory statements, accompanied by robust humour and by his fondness for paradoxes, apparently completely unheard of in Danish politics. At this juncture, the FRPd could certainly be defined as a charismatic party, in which the leader had absolute power and was even the subject of real veneration (Pedersen 1987: 40). But inevitable pressure came from local elected officials in favour of a less casual organizational structure, inducing the leadership to formalize party enrolment and to build up peripheral structures within an embryonic apparatus. Up until the early 1980s, party membership remained just above 10,000, but halfway through the decade fell to below 3000, later recovering somewhat to 6400 members in 1989 (Bille 1992). Glistrup remained the undisputed party leader and managed the party autocratically, flanked by a nominal executive committee. The national Congress, the formal authoritative decision-making body, was constituted only by a limited quota of elected delegates chosen by the local associations, because the parliamentary group and the national executive were free to invite anyone to participate. The most striking organizational feature, however, came from a statutory rule which provided Glistrup with lifetime membership of the national executive. These features highlight how much the FRPd deviated from the organizational standards of Danish parties.

Radical opposition to the essence and praxis of the Danish 'welfare state' (Bille 1989) characterized the first years of the FRPd. Nevertheless, when Glistrup was sentenced to two years in jail for tax fraud (which he actually served in prison from 1983 to 1985), the anti-system approach loosened. The person who replaced Glistrup at this point, Pia Kjaersgaard, gradually emerged as a true leader and moved the party towards a more moderate attitude and bargaining tactics (Andersen 1992: 195). Following this new approach, the FRPd came to sustain the bourgeois government, though it was barely tolerated. When its votes became essential, in 1987 and 1988, they were even expressly required and welcomed (Damgaard and Svensson 1989: 743); and in view of the approval of the 1989 state budget, the three economic ministers met with three FRPd MPs (Maor 1990: 213), thus in a sense legitimizing the party.

However, as soon as Glistrup was released, he fiercely opposed these co-operative and conciliatory approaches. The conflict between the founding father and the moderate faction led by Pia Kjaersgaard became irresolvable, to the point that Glistrup was forced to abandon the party in November 1990, a few weeks before that year's elections. Glistrup founded a new party, the Well-Being Party, which did not succeed in collecting enough signatures to run for election. Finally, he accepted a candidacy in the lists of the Common Course, a minor left-populist and anti-immigrant party that did not overcome the 2 per cent threshold to enter parliament (it obtained 1.8%).

Kjaersgaard's victory brought the party further de-radicalization, such that the Conservatives and Liberals started the 1994 electoral campaign standing together with the FRPd as a government alternative to the social Democrats. However some outragious statements against immigrants by FRPn representatives forced them to dissociate themselves (Andersen and Bjørklund 1999: 29). Beyond this setback, the new leadership showed itself neither capable of fully controlling the apparatus after the 1990 organizational changes (including the removal of Glistrup's life-position in the national executive) nor the party parliamentary group (Svasand 1998: 80–2). This naivety left the ultra-libertarian faction of 'Glistrupians' room for manoeuvre. The heirs of the former leader actually continued his politics of anti-statism and hyper-individualism—to set the individual free from any state-controlled constraints both in economic activity and in lifestyle (this is why some have labelled the FRPd in those years as a 'right-libertarian party' (see Harmel and Gibson 1995)). This 'libertarianism', however, coexisted, in the minds of the 'Glistrupians', with xenophobic and law and order attitudes.

After the 1994 general election this faction took control of the parliamentary group, provoking the dissidence and exit of Kjaersgaard and her faction. Together with three MPs and roughly one third of party members, Kjaersgaard founded the Dansk Folkeparti (DFP) (Danish People's Party) in 1995 (Andersen and Bjørklund 2000: 197). The new party did not actually evolve along the lines of de-radicalization previously fostered by Kjaersgaard. On the contrary, the DFP indulged in radical anti-immigrant and xenophobic statements and even introduced some veins of nationalism, raising arguments against the Maastricht treaty in the 1998 referendum (Andersen and Bjørklund 2000: 203).

The 1998 general election revealed the crisis for the FRPd remenants and the takeoff of the new Danish People's Party. The Progress Party collected 2.4 per cent (−4.0%) and the Danish People's Party 7.4 per cent (after having been credited with 14% in October 1997 surveys). This meant that the Danish extreme right was actually recovering, since it gained +3.4 per cent and +6 MPs. Finally, in the 1999 European elections the DFP scored 5.8 per cent, winning one seat, while the FRPd collapsed to 0.7 per cent. Considering the traditional presence of ad hoc anti-EU parties in the European elections, the DFP scored quite well: Kjaersgaard's party equalled the 1979 FRPd performance, bringing one MP to Strasbourg, and the extreme right collectively got its best ever score in this type of election.

Beyond Anti-Tax: Ideological and Policy Evolution

The FRPd entered the political arena in the seventies as a single-issue anti-tax party. At the same time, however, it conveyed its message emphasizing its extraneousness to the political and party system, to the 'old parties and the old system', and even to party democracy. The following passage, taken from one of the first issues of the party newspaper 'Fremskridt' (Progress), highlights the party world-view:

Parties belong to societies in which deep cleavages are present . . . Such a situation is not characteristic of modern Denmark . . . The parliament deals with thousands of single issues and opinions are combined by the voters in a multitude of ways. There is no reason to believe that very many voters agree with a single party on every score. When it comes to the main goal of governing Denmark, we do not find significant disagreement. Practical politics is about finding the most skilful to govern the country. The party system is in this respect a strong counteracting factor. (quoted in Pedersen 1987: 15)

This passage evinces some aspects of FRPd ideology, such as the obsolescence of class conflict and, accordingly, of the parties linked to it (both the Social Democrats and the bourgeois parties); the impatience over the 'complication' of politics and the call for hyper-simplistic solutions; and hostility towards the political party as such. Therefore, the FRPd's initial image as a single-issue party, pivoted on the fiscal issue, should be placed within a wider context characterized by an underlying extraneousness to the democratic-representative political process and its logic. It is not surprising that a few years later, the party diversified its political stock by including further issues along a more radical and anti-system path.

In fact, if we analyse the FRPd electoral manifestos *up to the 1990s*, the party is not at all 'single issue': three main themes emerge, dealing with the economy (taxation and welfare), immigration, and law and order.

In the FRPd electoral programmes, the greatest attention is devoted to economic themes (Gooskens 1993: 30ff). The FRPd was in favour of free initiative overcoming all hindrances of suffocating regulations. But this pro-market position cannot be compared to neo-liberalism, because the FRPd accompanied its criticisms of the social system and high taxation with the request of maintaining or even improving social provisions such as pensions for the elderly (Andersen 1992: 197). While the bourgeois parties also called for cuts in public expenditure on social services to stimulate the economy, the FRPd wanted to reconcile *laissez-faire* with welfare provisions. In fact, in its programmes, apart from emphasis on the neo-liberal agenda, one can find both the maintenance of some social services and opposition to an indiscriminate and over-generous welfare system. In short, welfare is all right, provided that it does not adversely affect the entrepreneur, and is efficiently managed, removing every benefit from those who do not deserve it—in the 1970s scroungers and the cunning; in the 1980s the immigrants. With reference to the last position, the FRPd has been rightly labelled a party of 'welfare chauvinism' (Andersen 1992), aimed at reserving national resources for Danish citizens only. This brilliant definition should however be somewhat qualified. The term 'chauvinism' is usually connected with nationalistic and xenophobic attitudes; do both elements depict the FRPd discourse?

As far as nationalism goes, the answer is negative. Glistrup acquired immediate national fame in his 118-second speech for his provocative proposal to abolish the army and to prepare a recorded message—'we surrender'—to be broadcast in case of hostile attack. Such a statement is far removed from a nationalistic world-view: it was simply impossible that it could ever have emanated from a German, Italian, or French right-wing leader.

As far as xenophobia is concerned, the FRPd displays an economic form of xenophobia, rather than a cultural or biological one. However, circumscribing the immigration issue within the economic sphere, whilst avoiding targeting the immigrants as enemies, sounds like an impossible operation. Charging foreigners with exploiting national resources for their own needs effectively stigmatizes their presence. In such circumstances, an 'out-group'—a group clearly labelled as different and extraneous in comparison to mainstream society—becomes a predictable object of irritation and hostility. This approach to the immigration issue has resulted in producing 'a more diffused antipathy toward the foreigners' (Andersen 1992: 201) in the FRPd voters compared to other voters. In fact, only Progress Party voters agree substantially with xenophobic statements (Andersen 1992: 200).

The immigration issue has been increasingly emphasized in the party propaganda, and more so than in the party manifestos. Since his release from prison in 1985, Glistrup in particular has exploited this topic extensively. In the electoral campaign of 1987 and 1988, the FRPd flanked its core theme—taxation—with the question centred on immigration which had suddenly become a major issue in public opinion (Togeby 1998: 1142) after a steep rise in the influx of immigrants and asylum-seekers (Arter 1992: 358). On the other hand, concern about this topic had been circulating within the party for a while. A member of the national executive, Riemann, had already made overt racist statements in 1979, to the point of being condemned to 14 days in prison. The more conciliatory post-Glistrup leadership tried to soften the most virulent xenophobic expressions, but even the leader herself did not refrain from racist Riemann-style statements such as that 'immigrants procreate like rabbits' (Andersen 1992: 199).

The third distinctive element of party propaganda concerns the application of tougher provisions and more severe rules against crime. The appeal of law and order gained more ground from the mid-late 1980s (Harmel and Svasand 1989; Goosken 1993: 77).

These three key topics taken in order—taxes, immigration, and law and order—were voiced more frequently than other issues by the FRPd during 1987 and 1988 and, with minor variations, the 1990 electoral campaign.

In the 1990s the ranking of these topics changed, leaving the taxation issue aside. Immigration (plus security) gained more and more ground in party statements, in accordance with a growing concern and salience in public opinion

(Togeby 1998: 1142). Since the late 1980s, Denmark had in fact been receiving an increasing number of foreigners. The new influx of asylum-seekers from the Balkans, in particular, caused the total number of immigrants to double from 1987 to 1997, reaching 3 per cent of the population (counting only those of non-Western origin). Even if the percentage of newcomers was quite modest by European standards, a number of violent episodes that occurred in 1997 brought the question of refugee repatriation to the fore (Andersen and Bjørklund forth.: 29–31). Consequently, the whole question of immigration became the first priority of public concern in the wake of the 1998 general election: for 25 per cent of the population 'immigration was the single most important issue, mentioned twice as often as taxes, unemployment, and other economic problems put together' (Andersen and Bjorklund: 5–6). Moreover, among the most important issues mentioned for voter choice in the 1998 election, people indicated refugee/immigrants and law and order in third and fourth place after the public health system and care for the elderly. On the other hand, such heightened anxiety did not foster any increase in ethnocentrism or racial intolerance in the mass public, quite the contrary (Togeby 1998: 1144).

While Danish society in general remains quite immune from intolerance, FRPd voters retain quite radical views on these issues, largely outdistancing the voters of the other parties. Even if the Kjaersgaard leadership had rejected the hardline anti-immigrant statements of the late Glistrup, the FRPd electorate proved very sensitive on this issue (Table 8.2). Already in 1990 FRPd voters agreed almost unanimously with the statement: 'immigration constitutes a serious threat to the Danish national character and refugees have to conform to the Danish culture and way of life' (Andersen 1992: 200). In 1994, the percentage of those who agreed that immigration was a threat to national identity minus those who disagreed was almost equal for the mean population, while FRPd supporters overwhelmingly rated immigration a threat (+74 points above the mean!) (Andersen and Bjørklund 2000: 212). In addition, 79 per cent of FRPd sympathizers, compared to a national average of 42 per cent, were in favour of cutting foreign aid. In short, FRPd voters have an incomparably higher level of xenophobia compared with non FRPd voters (Gabriel 1996: 354; Andersen and Bjørklund 2000).

The priority given to these issues distinguishes the Progress Party from the other bourgeois parties: and it is precisely this difference that makes the FRPd,

TABLE 8.2. *Attitudes of FRPd voters (1994)*

	FRPd	Mean
Immigrants are a threat	+74	−1
Cut aid to foreign countries	+79	+42
Trust in politicians	−58	+8

Source: Adapted from Andersen and Bjørklund (2002: 209, 212).

and now the People's Party, an extreme party in the Danish system. Already in the period 1973–91 a comparison of the platforms of the respective Danish parties on selected issues of individual freedom, scope of government, and income/personal taxation demonstrated that the FRPd was to the right of any other party (Harmel and Gibson 1995: 105). In the 1990s the Progress party appeared even more extreme than in the 1970s (Goosken 1993: 47–8; Gijlman and Oscarson 1996).

The FRPd's extreme stance and distance from the mainstream moderate parties are finally demonstrated by its location on the left–right continuum (Knutsen 1998: 78). In national election surveys, the party's own sympathizers locate the FRPd—on a 0 (left) to 10 (right) scale—at 7.3 in 1979, 7.0 in 1981 (in this case the Conservatives are located slightly further to the right), 7.4 in 1984, 8.4 in 1990 (Gilljam and Oscarsson 1996: 31), and 7.5 in 1994 (Andersen and Bjørklund 2000: 208). Other surveys, such as the Euro-barometer for example, offer a similar picture: on the 0–10 left–right scale the FRPd is at 6.2 in 1974, 6.8 in 1977–8, 7.2 in 1984–6, and 7.8 in 1988–9. This shift to the right occurred while the overall distribution of the Danish electorate on the left–right scale remained relatively stable (Kitschelt 1995: 136). The FRPd supporters 'on average consider themselves further to the right than the supporters of any other party' (Andersen and Bjørklund 2000: 207).

A Peculiar Anti-System Party

At the end of this analysis the question of the precise location of the Progress Party (and now of the People's Party) in the context of the extreme right needs to be discussed. While Glistrup and the more moderate leadership never made a frontal attack on democracy by invoking authoritarian solutions, they certainly undermined the system's legitimacy, not just by displaying contempt towards the parties and the politicians, but also by considering the parties as useless, backward, and even harmful. There is a substantial anti-partism circulating in the veins of the FRPd, clearly indicated by its irritation with parliamentary procedures—the above-mentioned 'confusion' which is typical of anti democratic culture of the beginning of the century. Dissatisfaction over the workings of the political system in the early 1990s is in fact highest among the Progress Party's voters (Gabriel 1996: 354), and their trust in politicians also is *50 points* below the national mean (Andersen and Bjørklund 2000: 209). Their alienation (or 'cynicism') is a symptom of an anti-establishment (or even anti-system) attitude.

Furthermore, the three aspects which mark the distinction between the FRPd and the other bordering bourgeois parties (taxes, immigration, and law and order) constitute the typical and winning agenda of the European extreme right. On the other hand, the recovery of traditional moral values and anti-Semitism are totally absent from party manifestos.

Glistrup's libertarian-individualist approach, nurtured by free-market idealism, has caused some scholars to label the FRPd a 'right-libertarian party' (Harmel and Gibson 1995). However, the growing importance of immigration and security issues in the eyes of the party's electorate forced Glistrup, and then also Kjaersgaard, to abandon the libertarian approach and appeal to more traditional extreme right-wing issues, so as not to displace the party constituency. While the official party positions may not be so extreme, 'voters tend to perceive [the FRPd] at somewhat higher (more right-wing) positions then where they actually stand' (van de Brug and van der Eijk 1999: 145).

Finally, the FRPd revealed its anti-system characteristics in the socio-economic sphere, although no corporatist solution was suggested. In fact, it supported both *laissez-faire* and the reduction of taxes while maintaining, at the same time, a high standard of social services. But this is nothing more than classic 'politics of over-promising' (Sartori 1976), namely, promising everything without any preoccupation of accountability. This unrealistic and illusory socio-economic policy clearly depicts, following Sartori's conceptualization, an anti-system syndrome.

However, the FRPd (and the DFP) combine the emphasis on economic liberalism—which characterizes the initial phases of post-industrial extreme right parties—with a particular concern for the lower class. It is not by chance that their electorate has a socio-demographic profile closer to the social-democratic as opposed to the conservative-liberal one. After 1979 the FRPd had a higher per-centage of workers in their electorate than in the average population, reaching its highest in 1994 (+16), when it even surpassed the Social Democrats in the over-representation of workers (Andersen and Bjørklund 2000: 217). The DFP also exhibited the same workers' over-representation in 1998 (Table 8.3).

Therefore, the Progress Party (and its offspring, the Danish People's Party) cannot be assimilated with the Danish bourgeois parties. On the other hand, the FRPd disdained any relationship with the other European extreme right parties—it

TABLE 8.3. *Proportion of workers among FRPd and social-democratic voters (deviations from the population mean)*

Year	FRPd	Social democrats
1973	−4	+26
1977	−1	+20
1979	+2	+15
1981	+6	+18
1984	+9	+20
1987	+4	+19
1988	+14	+16
1990	+15	+16
1994	+16	+13
1998*	+15	+9

* DFP +13.

Source: Andersen and Bjørklund (2000).

refused to join the Le Pen and Schönuber Euro-parliament group and did not even attend one of its meetings held in Denmark. However, it has been pointed out quite correctly that 'while the differences between the FRPd and Le Pen's Front National are as great as those that separate the Social Democrats from Communists, they derive their own strengths from a same source' (Andersen 1992: 203–4). We can conclude that 'Progress Party supporters are not extreme right supporters on traditional left–right issues, but they consider themselves to be far right because of their position on "new politics" ' (Andersen and Bjørklund 2000: 215): on these issues they are more xenophobic, more authoritarian, and less green than the supporters of any other party.

The extraneousness of the FRPd (as well as of the DFP) to every fascist over-ture estranges it from the category of traditional extreme right parties. However, its anti-partyism and political cynicism, its irresponsible opposition and politics of over-promising, its latent xenophobia and advocacy of more authoritarian and repressive norms, include it in the category of the post-industrialist extreme right.

The FRPd had represented a new, and not ephemeral, answer to the structural changes produced by the collapse of the Social Democratic model, of the welfare system and of its values. Due to the particular characteristics of the FRPd electorate— high level of blue collar representation (almost 50%), low level of education (the poorly educated are four times more numerous than those with a high level education), and mild hostility to the welfare system (only a fraction more than the other bourgeois parties)—it could rightly be defined as a new phenomenon, produced by new cleavages and structural modifications, hence far removed both from a revived neo-conservative or neo-fascist party.

NORWAY

In 1933 a group of admirers of Italian fascism founded the Nasjonal Samling (NS) (National Union) (Larsen 1980). In the initial phase this party had a nation-alistic image nourished by criticism of parliamentarism, and by anticommunist rhetoric in the name of national socialism. After this 'fascist-nationalist' phase the party shifted to the 'national-socialist' phase, marked by an adhesion to Nazism with the development of an anti-Semitic thematic. The appeal of the NS was very slight, however: its membership totalled a few thousand people and in the 1936 elections its electorate was below 1.8 per cent (although in some areas it scored more than 20% (Larsen 1980: 598)). Even with the German occupation the NS did not automatically acquire a primary role. It was only in 1943 that the leader of the NS, Vidkun Quisling, was called by the Nazis to lead a puppet government. Between 1940 and 1943, the NS increased its membership to around 50,000, recruiting many women (more than one-third of the total membership) and young people (one-third of members were under 25-year-old) who largely remained faithful until 1945 (Larsen 1980: 606). Norway has therefore known a mass fascist party and national-fascist regime, contrary to Denmark and Sweden, but despite this no nostalgic party has risen in the post-war period.

The FRPn: The Anti-Tax Protest and Beyond

It was only in the seventies that a new party leaning to the right of the Norwegian Conservative Party (Høyre) appeared. In April 1973, on the wave of the Danish Progress Party's success, a dog breeder, Anders Lange, presented a party curiously named 'Anders Lange's Party for a Strong Reduction of Taxes, Duties and Public Intervention' (Anders Langes Parts til sterk nedsettelse av skatter, avgifter og offntlige inngrep). Its programme was described by its name: so far it was a true twin-party of the FRPd. In 1973, in its first elections, Lange's Party succeeded in gaining 5 per cent of the vote and bringing four deputies into parliament, arousing the same surprise as had occurred in Denmark.

This success reflects some of the underground changes in Norwegian society that had already manifested themselves in the results of the referendum for joining the European Economic Community in 1972. On that occasion the voters, contrary to party indications, voted against entry into Europe. The Social Democratic party, in particular, the most convinced supporter of entry into the EEC, suffered the counterblow of the loss of loyalty of its own electorate (Berglund and Lindstrom 1979). This liberation of voters from consolidated allegiances made a proportion of the electorate susceptible to a change of vote, and thus free to turn towards new political offerings, such as the SF on the left and the bizarre, folklorist, and anti-political party of Anders Lange on the right (Urwin 1997: 45). In the same period, the people's lack of esteem for the Norwegian political class was at its highest and, for the first time, the tax problem was singled out as a priority issue by a remarkable proportion of voters (Andersen and Bjørklund 1990: 202). These conditions were favourable for the success of Lange's anti-taxes and anti-establishment party.

The sudden death of Lange in 1974 created a void in leadership and political direction, which marginalized the party, preventing it from gaining parliamentary representation in the 1977 elections. The inner conflicts were settled only with the nomination as secretary of Carl I. Hagen, who soon became its undisputed leader. In order to initiate this new phase, the party changed its name to Fremskrittsparti (FRPn), which means Progress Party, just like Glistrup's Danish Progress Party. This nominal homogeneity does not imply any unity of action between the two parties; rather, despite a good relationship, including on personal grounds, a certain cooling surfaced. On the one hand, Hagen played on the bandwagon effect of a successful 'brand name', while on the other, he wanted to present himself as a more responsible and less demagogic leader. The results partially supported this strategy, as the FRPn re-entered parliament in the 1981 elections. However, for about a decade, its electoral outcomes were rather modest, under 5 per cent.

It was only with the 1987 local elections that suddenly and unexpectedly the FRPn jumped to 12.3 per cent, placing it third. This outstanding result did not dissipate immediately, but it pushed the party even higher, and in the 1989 legislative elections the FRPn obtained 13.0 per cent of the vote.

The electoral success was accompanied by organizational expansion: from 10,000 members and 112 local branches in 1982 to 16,874 members and 256 local units in 1989 (Svasand 1992: 745). Actually, the party had been against the idea of building up a formal organization for a long time (Harmel and Svasand 1989) and, since the mid-1980s, few party supporters had considered becoming party members; in 1985, 75 per cent of FRPn voters did not want to become party members (Svasand, Strøm, and Rasch 1997: 109). At any rate, the party, while dominated by Hagen, evolved towards a quite 'normal' internal life, with precise rules and standardized procedures for the selection of office candidates and policy decision making.

The electoral pendulum shifted again and the FRPn lost half of its votes and seats, plummeting to 6.3 per cent in the 1993 elections. This negative outcome deepened tensions within the party to the point of provoking a split. Four out of ten MPs left the party and founded an ephemeral Free Democrats party (Fridemokratene) in 1994, advocating a more responsible and accommodating policy. Notwithstanding this split, the FRPn recovered rapidly and, by somewhat modifying its electoral agenda, emphasizing health care and the problems of elderly people, scored an impressive 15.3 per cent in the general election of 1997 (Table 8.4), attaining second position in the Norwegian party system.

The sources of the FRPn performances: *Oil Economy,* *Party System Change, and Immigration*

The conditions for the recent growth of the Progress Party are rooted in the changes which have taken place in Norwegian society since the 1970s. A turning point can be traced in the changes in the socio-economic and cultural sphere induced by the country's economic transformation following the discovery of oil in the North Sea. This new economic factor accelerated the structural changes

TABLE 8.4. *Vote for the FRPn in parliamentary elections*

Year	%
1973	5.0
1977	1.9
1981	4.5
1985	3.7
1989	13.0
1993	6.3
1997	15.3

Source: Andersen and Bjørklund (2000).

that had already been ongoing, implying, in particular, a decline in manual occupations (Urwin 1997: 46). The 'oil economy' provoked the shift from the productive to the financial economy, and affected both the prominence of the industrial sector and the central role of the working class: this loss of centrality, in turn, affected both the Labour Party and the unions in terms of their organizational strength and their embeddedness in the electorate. In fact, since the 1970s, there has been 'an erosion of the linkage between occupation and voting' (Urwin 1997: 46). Moreover, the sudden availability of financial resources, due to oil production, involved an 'explosion of indebtedness, speculation, and consumerism' (Lafferty 1989: 86). Greater individual wealth entailed far more consumerist lifestyles, involving the acquisition of status symbols, quite opposite to the traditional sobriety affirmed (especially) by Labour.

These socio-economic and cultural changes weakened Labour's hegemony and its radically-reformist, public-sector expansionist, and wage-increasing politics. At the same time it produced a conservative counter effect, with a new agenda focusing on the revitalizing of the free market, the dismantling of the welfare system, and the reduction of income related taxes. This shift was of great benefit first to the Høyre (Conservative Party), allowing it to access new social milieus, and, later, to the FRPn (Urwin 1997: 46). The Progress Party, in particular, presenting itself as the more coherent representative of the new right-ward mood, advocated more radical policies. The party system entered a phase of 'polarisation accompanied by fragmentation and disruption' (Urwin 1997: 43). This dynamic increased pressure on the centre and produced a push to the extremes. *The collapse of the old cleavage structure produced fragmentation and voiding of the centre, but the diffusion of a neo-conservative agenda in Norwegian political culture promoted the growth of the extreme right rather than the extreme left.*

The birth of the FRPn in 1973 was due to the 'structure of opportunity' which resulted from the 'acrimonious atmosphere' following the divisive EEC referendum in 1972, and from the growing 'perception of elite and bureaucratic authoritarianism and remoteness, a climate of frustration and alienation, and disruption of traditional party loyalties' (Urwin 1997: 43). The second leap forward of the FRPn in the late 1980s was related, beyond the deepening crisis of old party ties and encapsulation of the electorate (Sundberg 1999), and the centripetal strategy of the Høyre and the Labour Party (Miller and Listhaug 1990), to the politicization of the new issue of immigration.

The latter issue unexpectedly promoted the party's sudden leap forward in the late eighties. In the 1987 local elections the party polled 12.3 per cent, repeating its performance in the 1989 general elections with 13.0 per cent, almost four times the previous election score (3.7%). For the first time the immigration issue came to the political forefront, this being in 1987 (Bjørklund 1988), because of a steep increase in foreigners. Between 1986 and 1987, new arrivals doubled from 7500 to 13,000, bringing the total number of foreigners to 115,000, equivalent to 2.7 per cent of the population (Pettersen 1997: 265). A 1987 survey demonstrated that 'immigration policy topics are important to the electorate—and strikingly so for the supporters of the right and left wing parties' (Pettersen 1997: 272). The annoyance in certain sectors of public opinion was so widespread that King Olav, in the opening speech of the 1987 autumn parliamentary session, called upon the people to remember their duty in welcoming refugees and immigrants.

Beyond its salience in the eyes of the general public, the problem of foreigners clearly differentiated the FRPn from the other parties. FRPn supporters, compared to those of other parties, overwhelmingly charged immigrants as 'wordless and unproductive' (45% against a mean of 20% (Pettersen 1997: 175)) and refused to allow them any economic support unless they integrated into Norwegian society (82% against a mean of 40%; Andersen and Bjørklund 1990: 211).

Legislative restrictions on the entry of foreigners, approved in 1988, gradually lessened the potential explosiveness of this problem, but the FRPn connected the immigration issue with security and law and order issues, which became the party's new main theme in the late 1980s/early 1990s. The xenophobic sentiments of FRPn voters still greatly differentiated them from the voters of other parties. In 1993, while the average electorate was slightly against the statement that 'immigrants are a threat to national identity', FRP voters massively agreed with it—the same being true for a reduction in third world aid (Andersen and Bjørklund 2000: 212).

While this theme was the driving force for the party's success in the late eighties, notwithstanding the 1993 election backlash partly due to Hagen's support for Norway's EU membership, its dramatic success in 1997 demonstrated that the party could profit from other factors and maintain an enduring presence in the Norwegian party system.

The Rise of the FRPn in the 1990s and its Search for Respectability

The FRPn has been defined as a 'radically anti-Statist, pro-free market, populist, law and order and anti-immigrants party' (Lafferty 1989: 91) or as 'a combination of extreme liberal economy, anti-Statism and right populism' (Heidar 1989: 147). Actually, on the basis of its electoral programs up to the early nineties (Goosken 1993), the FRPn appears to be characterized by: (a) an economic neo-liberal vision in the vein of Thatcherism (cuts in social spending and income taxes), while at the same time maintaining elevated standards of social services, simply through more efficiency and less bureaucracy; (b) opposition to third world aid programs, and the demand for restriction on entry for immigrants and asylum-seekers and their forced repatriation (but here it faced the opposition of its own juvenile organization, the FPU, totally against any forms of restriction); (c) pro-EU entry, despite internal bickering (in fact, more than one third of its voters voted against the EU membership in the 1994 referendum) (Strøm and Svasand 1997: 338–9); (d) a strong hostility to feminist issues without, however, endorsing traditional ethics (since the party's youth advocated soft drug legalization); (e) a more severe penal code and greater social control.

The party programmes paint a picture of a welfare chauvinist, anti-Statist, anti-immigrant (while not particularly ethnocentric (Evans 2001)), somewhat authoritarian, and definitely 'irresponsible' party. Precisely because of recurring complaints in this last respect, the uncontested party leader Hagen 'managed to portray himself as a responsible politician' in various circumstances (Aardal and Valen 1997: 63). This new party image was supplemented by a novel set of proposals on the health care system and elderly people, appearing in the party agenda in the mid-1990s. By adapting the previous welfare chauvinist framework, the party promoted a campaign in favour of devoting more resources to 'nationals' through health and care of elderly people, rather than wasting it on foreigners. Health care and assistance for the elderly were extremely sensitive topics in the months preceding the 1997 elections and topped a list of the most important issues. It appeared that Progress Party voters regarded these matters as far more important than did other voters. While the two issues stood respectively at 33 and 30 per cent in the general electorate's rank of priorities, they were 50 and 42 per cent, respectively, in that of the FRPn voters, and Labour voters came second with 38 and 31 per cent, respectively. This meant that the party was well in tune with the general feelings of the electorate, to the point that a pre-electoral survey carried out in June 1997 polled the FRPn at 22 per cent—data which 'sent shock waves through the political establishment' (Aardal 1998: 370). However, the FRPn did not abandon its original themes: immigration and taxation still occupied third and fourth position in the party's voters' preferences (Aardal 1998: 378).

The 1987–9 party breakthrough was thus confirmed by the 1997 general election. Convincing reasons underpinning this trend can be proffered, over and above short-term factors. Specific changes in some general political trends had occurred in the mid-1980s with regard to volatility, party identification, and political trust, and these changes had become established. Volatility (calculated on the basis of survey data) increased by 10 points between the 1985 and 1989 elections (from 29% to 39%), reaching 44 per cent in 1993 and 1997. The higher electoral propensity to switch votes is confirmed by the decline of party identification: strong party identification decreased from 41 per cent in 1985 to 29 per cent in 1989 and remained there. Finally, trust in politics plummeted from 71 per cent in 1985 to 41 per cent in 1989 (Aardal and Valen 1997: 69–74). These data clearly demonstrate that the FRPn breakthrough coincided with an acute crisis of

TABLE 8.5. *Attitudes of FRPn voters (values are differences between agreement and disagreement)*

	FRPn	Mean
Immigrants are a threat (1993)	+49	−6
Cut aid to foreign countries (1993)	+68	+26
Trust in MPs (1995)	−16	+19

Source: Adapted from Andersen and Bjørklund (2000: 209, 212).

confidence in the system and a loosening of party–voter ties. Therefore, the FRPn provided the 'most discontented voters with an alternative' (Aardal and Valen 1997: 72). In fact, the most alienated citizens are, by far, FRPn voters (23 points above the mean in 1989 and 15 points above in 1993).

The protest-like image of the FRPn clearly implied a certain degree of isolation within the Norwegian party system and widespread feelings of distrust and contempt from the political-economic establishment. For example, the FRPn's offer to sustain the Conservative governments by its own decisive votes in 1987 and in 1988 was rejected. The party was never considered a potential coalition partner, and was treated as a 'pariah party' (Meadely 1990: 292). It had a marginal status, which the outspoken and brilliant party leader Hagen used as a rhetorical weapon against the 'others' and the 'establishment', highlighting the distance between the FRPn and the other parties and fuelling its populist anti-system appeal. Even when, in 1995, the party gained entry to local government in Oslo, together with the Høyre, the coalition rapidly broke up because of the immigration issue. The FRPn's xenophobic characterization *apparently* constituted an insurmountable watershed between it and the other parties. However, its resounding success in 1997 increased its 'acceptability' such that it 'suddenly became an acceptable partner and was invited into political negotiation' (Andersen and Bjørklund 1999: 28), although still not considered fully trustworthy (Table 8.6).

In conclusion, the FRPn is a party with an original stance: pro-liberal but supporting welfare, especially for the poorest; xenophobic and authoritarian but neither traditionalist nor too ethnocentric; anti-elitist and populist but captivated by libertarian issues. The party 'contradiction' on welfare provisions and its 'welfare chauvinism' might be linked to the proletarization of the party (Table 8.6). Since the 1980s the party attracted proportionally more workers than the national mean: in 1989, 48 per cent of the party's voters were workers (Listhaug 1997: 87) and later, in 1995, the FRPn's quota of workers outnumbered Labour's (Andersen and Bjørklund 2000: 217).

TABLE 8.6. *Proportion of workers among*
FRPn and social-democratic voters
(deviations from the mean)

Year	FRPn	Social democrats
1973	−5	+19
1977	0	+18
1981	+9	+20
1985	+3	+16
1989	+7	+13
1993	+3	+7
1995	+8	+6
1997	+5	+2

Source: Andersen and Bjørklund (2000).

In any event, the party is spatially located by its supporters at the extreme right of the political spectrum: in 1995 it stood at 6.75 on a 0-10 left–right scale (Andersen and Bjørklund 2000: 208), or even at 9.18 according to different sources (see Knutsen 1998: 80). However, when a policy evaluation is carried out, the picture is less clear. The FRPn, having always been the farthest to the right on individual free-dom, scope of government, and income taxes (Harmel and Gibson 1995: 106; see also Gijlman and Oscarson 1996), has, in recent years, been flanked by the Conservatives who were further to the right on the issue of equality (Andersen and Bjørklund 2000: 207).

The FRPn has been described as an 'anti-consensus' party, a party against the general consent on the rules of the game, while not an anti-system one (Heidar 1989: 147). However, its opposition to the basic values of Norwegian society, supplemented by its contempt for the political system and politics in general, and its propensity for authoritarian forms of social conflict management, including a xenophobic penchant, portray a party that undermines the system's legitimacy and is, in Sartori's terms, an 'anti-system' party. Once more, however, its anti-systemness deviates from that of other extreme right parties both for its different cultural–ideological lineage and for its present world-view: the FRPn, even more than its Danish sister party, is at the fringe of the extreme right political family.

SWEDEN

Fascism in Sweden 'has been a fragmented phenomenon, eclectic in the ideology, imitative in the style and marginal in the Sweden politics of the 1920s and 1930s . . . and without any inheritance' (Hagtvet 1980: 715). In the post-war years, apart from tiny pro-Nazi chapels, the extreme right surfaced only with the 1991 electoral earthquake (Sainsbury 1992). Here the power relationships were not only drastically altered among the traditional parties—with the Social Democrats attaining their worst result in 70 years and the Conservatives their best since 1932—but also the party landscape in Parliament changed. The Greens, having entered for the first time in the preceding legislature, exited and, more signifi-cantly, two brand new parties entered: the Christian democratic party and the Ny Demockrati (NyD) (New democracy) (Widefelt 1992).

The Ny Demokrati was founded due to the initiative of two whimsical characters: Bert Karlsson, a flamboyant entrepreneur with the persona of a self made man, and Ian Wachtmeister, an aristocrat, member of numerous boards of directors, author of two successfully satirical novels, and executive of a research institute closely linked to the SAF (the largest white collar labour union). Wachtmeister, who had already tried, without success, at the beginning of 1990 to convert his institute into a political party, finalized his project few months later thanks to a meeting with Karlsson.

Notwithstanding the fact the Ny Democrati was only founded in February 1991, it overcame the 4 per cent threshold of representation in the general election held the same year with a resounding 6.7 per cent. The party breakthrough is related to the convergence of some favourable conditions. On one side, Swedish society was under-going a profound structural change which was affecting the traditional relationship between the working class and the Social Democratic party (Arter 1999). With a 20-year delay in comparison to the Danish and Norwegian sister parties, the Swedish social-democrats had suffered the same consequences due to the reduction in size of the working class and their increasing well-being, to the unbearable costs of the welfare, and the need for more taxes. The quota of social-democratic voters strongly identifying with the party fell from 50 per cent in 1976 to 41 per cent in 1988 (Bergstrom 1991: 13). The crisis exploded at the turn of the decade when the social-democratic-led government introduced approximately the same, vituperated, fiscal program as the bourgeois government (Andersen and Bjørklund 2000: 196). Moreover, the mass public was bewildered by the sudden and abrupt decision of the political elite to open negotiations for entry into the European Union. All these changes that occurred more or less at the same time—and ranged from the crisis of the welfare system to higher levels of taxation, from loss of neutrality and entry into the EU to loosening of social cleavages and party ties—all raised potential voter volatility and, furthermore, provoked a wave of mistrust towards the parties and political institutions (Pierre and Widefeldt 1992: 525) together with feelings of disenchantment and powerlessness: those who considered themselves capable of influencing the political decision makers dropped from 28 per cent in 1973 to 14 per cent in 1988 (Bergstrom 1991: 22–3). Precisely, those elements which had created propitious conditions for the breakthrough into the system of the Progress parties in Denmark and Norway in the early 1970s, occurred in Sweden in the late 1980s.

The NyD programme was quite similar to the manifestos of the first Progress parties: anti-tax, anti-state bureaucracy, anti-party, and anti-establishment (Gooskens 1993; Widfeldt 2000). The inflamatory rhetoric of the duo against 'crocodile politicians' was in accordance with sensitive public opinion, and was its most effective weapon in winning parliamentary seats (Westlind 1996). Less emphasis was devoted by the NyD on harsh punishment toward criminals and anti-immigrant provisions. The latter topic, in particular, was soft-pedalled during the 1991 electoral campaign. After the NyD's entry into Parliament, in keeping with the rise in sensitivity on the topic in public opinion—which touched its zenith in 1992—the party asked for the reduction and/or reallocation of (sizeable) government aid to the third world, for a total ban on immigration, and for a national referendum on this issue. Apparently, its voters were in agreement with the party on this (Andersen and Bjørklund 2000: 211).

The politicization of the immigration issue in Sweden occurred precisely at the turn of the decade. Between 1980 and 1989, the number of immigrants almost doubled, passing from 34,400 to 58,900. Although Sweden was considered a traditional asylum country for all political refugees, with legislation amongst the most generous, the steep raise in new arrivals and the change in public mood urged the government to introduce a series of restrictions between late 1989 and early 1990 (Hammar 1991: 187, 193). These new regulations were also conceived to stop the sudden proliferation of racist and neo-Nazi groups. In fact, at the end of 1980, a series of xenophobic parties arose. The first to appear (1988) was the Sverigedemokraterna (SD) (Swedish Democrats), then joined by the Sjöbopartiet (Sjöbo party) which took the name of a small town where the citizens had refused to harbour immigrants after a local referendum, and by the Fremstegspartei (Progress party). All together these parties collected slightly more then 30,000 votes at the various parliamentary and local elections they contested, electing a handful of local councillors (Arter 1992: 368; Lööw 1995: 121).

Immigration however, as already underlined, was not the key factor in relation to NyD fortunes. The party's anti-establishment populist rhetoric worked as the means of attracting a large share of the disillusioned and alienated electorate. The distrust of politics among Ny Democrati voters was in fact *three times higher than in the mean electorate* (Goosken 1993: 18). The traditional, comparatively high, level of confidence in the workings of democracy and in political institutions had been suffering a decline for a decade at least. A constituency of dissatisfied and alienated citizens was already there waiting for a political supply, which the Ny Demokrati provided. Such a constituency, similar to that of the Danish and Norwegian Progress parties, was primarily composed of the working class (43%) (against 40% of the national average) and unemployed (13% against 6%).

Contrary to its Scandinavian sister parties, Ny Demokrati did not consolidate its success. Personal quarrels between the founding leaders, the heterogeneity of the parliamentary group, persistent amateurism in daily politics, the disdain for any form of party organization, and the right-ward turn of the conservative parties drastically reduced the party's chances of success. In 1994, the party scored 1.2 per cent—well below the 4 per cent hurdle—and in 1998 practically disappeared with 0.2 per cent. On the other hand, there has been a proliferation of more radical neo-Nazi and skin-head groups. But no right-extremist *party* exists at present in the national political arena. The Ny Demokrati represented a short-lived, post-industrial, extreme right party.

FINLAND

Contrary to other Scandinavian countries, fascism gained a stable foothold in inter-war Finland. Firstly, the Lapua movement at the turn of the 1930s 'constituted the most powerful single factor in Finnish politics' (Karvonen 1988: 10, quoted in Kalliala 1999: 64), as it was the driving force for the authoritarian transformation of the Finnish political regime. After its dissolution another fascist party was founded, the Isänmaallinen Kansanliike (IKL) (Patriotic People's Movement). These movements won mass support (Alapuro 1980: 678–9) though the IKL electoral performances were not particularly outstanding.

The Second World War brought about civil strife. As a consequence of that trauma, and of the 1944 Moscow and 1947 Paris peace treaties, all fascist organizations were banned in post-war Finland. Moreover, the 'special relationship' entered into with the Soviet Union kept a rigid ostracism to whatever looked right-wing (Kalliala 1999: 76ff).

Actually, in the first years after the war proto-fascist activities continued, in the form of conspiratorial actions and under veterans' umbrella organizations. However, no fascist movement, not even disguised, developed. Even the pro-Soviet Union policy fostered by president Kekkonen until the 1980s did not revive the nostalgic anti-Communist milieu, because of the large consensus it enjoyed. While any critical statement towards Kekkonen's politics was immediately targeted as 'fascist', no opposition parties can be labelled in this way. Neither the Finnish Rural Party (SMP) nor the Constitution Party of Finland (POP) had anything in common with neo-fascism. However, both parties went through a process of radicalization in the 1990s. The Finnish Rural Party followed a somewhat populist and xenophobic line, especially after its departure from government in 1990, although 'it took a more moderate stand' compared to the Progress parties in Norway and Denmark on the immigration and asylum-seekers question (Pekonen, Hynynen, and Kalliala 1999: 40). After its setback in the 1995 election (1.3%), the SMP transformed into a new party, the Perussuomolaiset (the True Finns), moving along the path of radicalization (Arter 1999: 45). The voters did not reward the new party, as it only got 0.7 per cent of the vote in the 1996 European elections and 1.0 per cent in the 1999 parliamentary election. Even the True Finns, however, cannot be associated with right-extremism.

The only two political parties (despite never having acquired the status of official political parties because they did not obtain the minimum requirement of 5000 signatures) which might be included in the extreme right family are the (Isänmaallinen Kansanlis-Liitto) Patriotic National Alliance (IKL) and the (Remonttiryhmä) Reform group. The IKL, founded in 1993, reveals its nostalgic inspiration by its name, which recalls the pre-war fascist IKL. The party revives the ideal of the Great Finland, promotes chauvinist and nationalistic sentiments, and adopts the standard xenophobic slogans of European right-extremism such as 'our people first!' (Arter 1999: 42–3). Due to its revival of fascist symbolism and rhetoric, it could be considered a 'traditional' extreme right party (Pekonen 1999). But it has not participated in any elections. The most recently born party, the Reform group, was founded in 1998 by a former social-democratic MP. It gained 1.1 per cent in the 1999 parliamentary elections—campaigning with a populist, xenophobic, and welfare chauvinist appeal (Pekonen 1999: 46–7).

Because of its very loose programme and a certain moderation in tone, its inclusion in the extreme right family is questionable.

In conclusion, while some favourable conditions for the rise of right-extremist parties are emerging (political dissatisfaction, electoral realignment, increasing concern for foreign inflows), the input from the Finnish radical right is still very weak (Pekonen 1999: 24–5).

9

The Netherlands: A Fleeting Extreme Right

The lack of success for anti-system parties in the Netherlands denounced by Hans Daalder (1966) more than 30 years ago still holds true. At the national level, the 'new' extreme right parties (CP/CP'86 and CD of the 1980s and 1990s)—as well as the 'very old' (anti-modern, counter-revolutionary) and 'old' (fascist/Nazi) Dutch extreme right (Voerman and Lucardie 1992: 36)—have rarely polled more than 1 per cent of the votes.

The weakness of anti-system movements manifested itself also in the inter-war years when some fascist groups emerged, but even the most important one, the Nationaal Socialistische Beweging (NSB) (National Socialist Movement), never succeeded in breaking through. The NSB was founded in 1931 by an ex-liberal, Anton Mussert, with a programme filled with authoritarian, anti-parliamentary, corporatist, and nationalistic appeals (Van der Wusten and Smit 1980: 527). Due to the combination of aggressive and radical phraseology and a bourgeois respectability, accorded to the party leadership on account of its social profile (Van der Wusten and Smit 1980: 539), the NSB obtained 7.9 per cent of the votes in the 1935 local elections. Encouraged by this electoral success, the NSB radicalized along national-socialist lines (Orlow 1999) and formed an armed militia; together with other minor extreme right groups, it even gathered some 50,000 members, but did not become any more influential. Its development was inhibited both by tough opposition from the left-wing parties and by the negative attitude of the conservative-religious government that dismantled its embryonic military structure and forced the party on to the defensive. In fact, in the general election of 1937 the NSB did not exceed 4 per cent of the votes (Van der Wusten 1987). Only with the German occupation did Mussert's party play an important role as a domestic partner of the Nazis.

This phase of Dutch political history left deep wounds, witnessed not only by the massive purges of collaborators, but also by the emotional waves still raised in the 1980s by questions such as the NSB collaborators' widows pensions and the liberation of the last war-crime prisoners (Husbands 1992a: 95–6). Immediately after the war those most responsible among the collaborators were sent before the courts, and numerous capital sentences (Mussert was one of those executed) were imposed. Around 100,000 citizens were found guilty of collaboration, but by 1950 they had almost all recovered their political rights (Van Donselaar 1991: 28). The constitution of para-fascist movements was forbidden by rule of law.

THE EARLY POST-WAR EXTREME RIGHT: NOSTALGIC, FLEETING, AND IRRELEVANT

In the 1950s, the extreme right resumed its activities in the form of aid associations for former Nazis, such as the Stichting Oud Politieke Delinquenten (SOPD) (Organization for Former Political Criminals) (Van Donselaar 1993: 89ff). The SOPD had clashes with the authorities as a result of demonstrations glorifying the past. Later, in 1953, under the initiative of SOPD leaders and an (in)famous former member of the Dutch Waffen-SS, Paul Van Teienen, the Nationaal Europese Social Beweging (NESB) (National European Social Movement) was born. Although this party presented a moderate program which formally respected democracy, the Supreme Court outlawed it in 1955 on account of its latent intentions—that is, the reconstitution of the NSB—and of its membership, composed almost exclusively of former Nazis (Van Donselaar 1993: 90–3). Despite the prohibition, marginal and covert activities continued under forms of veteran-relief associations (the HINAG) or political-partisans (the NOU) (van Donselaar 1991: 80ff).

The only anti-system party, although not extreme right (van Donselaar 1991: 125), to achieve limited success in the 1960s was the Borenpartij (BP) (the Farmers' Party) (Daalder 1966: 232; Voerman and Lucardie 1992: 37). The Borenpartij represented a curious mixture of authoritarianism and individualism, anti-tax protest, and anti-parliamentarism, somewhat reminiscent of French *Poujadism*. Above all, it backed agrarian interests threatened by modernization and the religious traditionalists. The BP reached the apex of its success in the mid-1960s. In 1963, it entered parliament with three seats. In a 1964 survey the BP leader Hendrick Koekoek (former member of the NOU) came second in popularity to the secretary of the Socialist Party (Daalder 1966: 234). In 1966, it obtained 6.7 per cent of the vote in provincial elections and 4.7 per cent (seven seats) in the 1967 general elections. The BP harboured many extreme right activists, some of whom also had a collaborationist past. This did not appear to create a problem either inside or outside the party, until the furore over the Hendrik Adams case. When his name appeared in the BP lists as a candidate for the 1966 Senate elections, it created an uproar due to him being tainted with heinous crimes during the Nazi occupation. At last, the leadership disowned him—although belatedly and painfully. Hendrik Adams' dismissal implied the exit of the more radical elements: around a quarter (45 out of 204) of the town councillors elected the previous year left the party (Van Donselaar 1991: 133). After that, the BP lost ground: it suffered another split in 1968, and then began to decline until its dissolution in 1981, despite having changed its name to Rechtse Volkspartij (RVP) (Rightist Popular party).

More in keeping with the tradition of right-wing extremism is the Nederlandse Volksunie (NVU) (Union of the Dutch people). This party, founded in 1971, aimed at unifying all the Flemish-speaking people in a Great Dutch State and at expelling any ethnically diverse persons. This ethnocentric nationalism acted as the background to an authoritarian, anti-parliament, and corporatist ideology. In the 1972 NSU programme, the Queen would name a Prime Minister unaccountable to parliament, which would be elected according to criteria of corporatist representation. In the social domain, workers' presence in the management of the enterprise was envisaged (Voerman and Lucardie 1992: 38). In short, the NVU appeared to be a party with an unambiguous neo-fascist inspiration. The party entered Dutch political life in 1974 with the Hague local elections. Its candidate, Joop Glimmerveen, campaigned on law and order, safety, and xenophobia. Despite the absence of party support, since the party wished 'to remain out of the institutions', he polled 1.8 per cent—scraping through the election by a handful of votes. Thanks to this success Glimmerveen was elected party chairman and, in-keeping with his stormy past (*inter alia*, a volunteer in the Korean war), he fostered a radicalization emphasizing racist and pro-Nazi positions, going as far as invoking and practising violence against immigrants (Husbands 1992*a*: 111). This extremist position did not reap rewards: the results in the electoral arena were very modest (0.4% in the 1977 elections) and, above all, it led to the exclusion of the party from the 1978 local elections by the court in Amsterdam (van Donsellar 1991: 95).

THE CD AND CP/CP86: ATTEMPT AND FAILURE AT INSTITUTIONALIZING THE EXTREME RIGHT

A further consequence of NVU radicalization was the split by a group of members who founded the Centrumpartij (CP) (Centre party) in 1980, which aimed at the 'preservation of Dutch culture' whilst distancing itself from the NVU's extremist nationalism. The CP's political pivot was the extra-European immigration around which all the problems rotated: unemployment, delinquency, environment, and cultural identity. The centrality of the immigrants question is related to the CP conception of society; as society is conceived as a natural 'organ', it can change only gradually and moderately: accordingly, whatever disturbs the 'natural' evolution of society should be eliminated. Therefore, the clandestine immigrants must be expelled, the legal ones should be forced to integrate, and third world aid used for encouraging their return home (Van Donselaar 1991: 172–214).

The CP electoral result in the 1981 general elections, where it ran against the NVU, was irrelevant (0.1%), but a year later the party attained 0.8 per cent, enough to admit one deputy to parliament, the party leader Hans Janmaat. The modest percentage at national level was reduced by the limited number of constituencies contested, and hid the results attained in the largest cities (particularly

TABLE 9.1. *Vote for the NVU, CP/CP'86, and CD in parliamentary and European elections*

Year	NVU	CP/CP'86	CD
1977	0.4		
1981	0.1	0.1	
1982		0.8	
1984E		2.5	
1986		0.4	0.1
1989E			0.8
1989			0.9
1994		0.4	2.5
1994E			1.0
1998			0.6
1999E			0.5

Source: Husbands (1992); official sources.

Rotterdam: 4.0%). The election of Janmaat provoked a wave of counter-mobilization from the left, but such reaction did not prevent the growth of the party. Instead, the CP reached its best ever result (2.5%) in the 1984 European elections, campaigning on a xenophobic Europe-wide program ('out with foreigners from Europe'). Despite the positive election results, the Janmaat leadership was judged too moderate by the radical faction, which took control of the party and expelled him in October 1984. In the eyes of the radical fringe Janmaat bore the sin of not coming from the right-extremist milieu (he had been close to the religious parties) and of being too accommodating in his parliamentary activity (Table 9.1).

Devoid of its most representative figure, the CP had to face the competition of a brand new party, the Centrumdemocraten (CD) (Democratic Centre), immediately joined by Janmaat himself, one month after his departure. The CP still succeeded in electing six local councillors in the most important cities in the 1986 local elections, but gained a very poor score (0.4%) at the general election later that year (May 1986). Tormented by a financial crisis and by further quarrels and splits, the CP shut down in the summer of 1986 and resurrected one week later under the name of Centrumpartij'86 (CP'86). The renamed party also modified its world-views in the short run: moving along racist lines and proto-Nazi ideas of 'a neither capitalist nor socialist National Revolution', portraying itself as 'an avant-garde of a New European Order' (Voerman and Lucardie 1992: 42) confronting America and Russia, and advocating a complete upheaval of the system. The CP'86 ideological profile deviated quite substantially from the former party—and from the CD—because of a drift towards ethnic nationalism, national revolution, and an international (anti-Western) and socio-economic (corporatist) 'third way' (Mudde 1998).

Although prey to serious organizational difficulties (so much so that it was not in a condition to contest the 1989 parliamentary and European elections and had to work hard to find candidates for the 1990 local elections), the CP'86 succeeded in maintaining a certain hold over the electorate. Four town councillors were elected, including the ex-leader of the NVU youth movement, Stewart Mordaunt, a fervent admirer of Hitler (Voerman e Lucardie 1992: 43).

Janmaat's new party, the CD, differentiated itself from the CP'86 by occupying a more moderate position. Nevertheless, impatience with parliamentary proced-ures and advocating unaccountable government and plebiscitarian democracy meant the CD was now a part of the anti-democratic milieu, as the following declaration by Janmaat in 1986 highlights: 'endless [parliamentary] debates indicate one of the weak spots of democracy. For it seems to me impossible to reach solutions when ideas are opposed to each other. These oppositions are rein-forced by ideas and values of the multicultural society which do not increase but undermine the strength of our political system' (quoted in Voerman e Lucardie 1992.: 44).

At the heart of the CD's politics, and in continuity with the former CP, was the problem of immigration, dramatically described as foreign 'occupation' and 'domination' (Voerman e Lucardie 1992: 44–5). On this theme, synthesized in the slogan 'the Dutch first', the CD succeeded in obtaining a seat in parliament (again Janmaat) with 0.9 per cent of the votes in the 1989 election. In the 1990 local elections (Table 9.2), the CD broke through—electing twelve councillors and in the four largest cities (Amsterdam, The Hague, Rotterdam, Utrecht) oscillating between 5 and 7 per cent of the vote. Considering that immigrants also vote in local elections (since 1986) and supposing that very few had chosen the CD or the CP'86, the size of the vote of the extreme right in cities with high concentrations of foreigners, such as the four largest ones, assumed notable proportions (Husbands 1992b). The success—substantially confirmed at the provincial elec-tions of 1991 (1.0%)—provoked an uproar from anti-fascist and anti-racist organ-izations, and steadfast ostracism inside the elective assemblies (e.g. the

TABLE 9.2. *Vote for the CD and CP/CP'86 at the*
1990 and 1994 communal elections in
three main cities

	1990	1994
Amsterdam		
CD	4.4	7.9
CP/CP'86	2.4	1.8
Rotterdam		
CD	3.8	10.2
CP/CP'86	3.3	3.5
The Hague		
CD	4.3	9.2
CP/CP'86	2.1	2.7

Source: Husbands (1992); Mudde and Van Holsteyn (1994).

systematic exclusion from committees and limitation to the minimum of services normally provided by the institutions to parties and representatives) (Husbands 1992*a*: 113).

There were solid grounds for concern over the rise of the extreme right. The monthly public opinion poll (NIPO) on voters' intentions demonstrated a constant and steady growth of the CD from the aftermath of the 1991 provincial election. While the party scored less than 1 per cent until late 1991, it had already doubled by mid-1992, then reached 4 per cent in early 1993 and 5 per cent by the end of the year (Mudde and van Holstein 1994: 129).

The 1994 March local elections (Table 9.2) launched the party: the strategy of selective candidatures (only 43 cities out of more than 600) assured the election of representatives in almost all the municipalities where candidates contested, with a total of 77 seats. The CP'86 also profited from right-wing fervour, collecting 8 seats out of the 18 municipalities contested (Mudde and van Holstein 1994: 129). In the largest cities, the two extreme right parties together (including a local right-wing party in Utrecht, the Nederlands Blok (the Dutch Blok), with 2.1%) exceeded 10 per cent of the vote with a peak of 13.7 per cent in Rotterdam where the extreme right became the second party after the socialists. Taking into account only the cities contested by the CD and/or the CP'86 (50 out of 600), their share of the vote reached 7.4 per cent (Mudde and van Holstein 2000: 148). As far as the balance of power between the CD and the CP'86 is concerned, CD voters were three to four times the number of CP'86 voters.

The expectations for the coming May national elections were inevitably high, but scandals, and a certain demonization by the media, toned down the actual outcome. The CD polled 2.5 per cent, winning three seats (a substantial increase nevertheless), while the CP'86 did not obtain a single seat with its modest 0.4 per cent. Even worse, the subsequent June European election dashed the hopes of the right-wing extremists even more, reducing the CD to 1.0 per cent, with the consequent loss of its seat (while the CP86 did not even run). Both parties entered a phase of decline. Most of their members and local representatives quit (Mudde and van Holstein 1994; Lucardie 1998).

The wave of local and general elections in 1998 determined the final collapse of the Dutch extreme right. New electoral rules making the presentation of a list more difficult (30 voters' signatures collected in front of local officials instead of ten voters' signatures collected in whatever way) shrunk the CD presence to only 22 cities. In the municipal run, *only two* of the 77 local CD councillors elected in 1994 were re-elected (none by the CP'86), while the party scored 0.8 per cent nationally. And finally, all three MPs lost in the 1998 general election due to a drop to 0.6 per cent.

After failure in the 1998 electoral wave, the CD seemed on the edge of dissolution, but it managed to survive and ran in the 1999 European election, proving its definitive marginalization with a result of 0.6 per cent. The CP'86 (renamed NVP/CP'86 in late 1995, also to avoid legal proceedings) managed to survive, notwithstanding the endless internal rivalries among the various cliques. At last, having been under pressure by numerous courts for racial hatred, it was finally banned and dissolved by rule of law in November 1998 (Mudde and van Holstein 2000: 149). Restless and asphyxiating anti-fascist and anti-racist mobilization, legal and judiciary intervention, institutional ostracism, personal quarrels, and poor leadership were all among the most direct causes which contributed to the collapse of both parties.

CD AND CP/CP'86 IDEOLOGICAL PROFILE

Analysis of the electoral programs of the two parties (see Mudde 1998) reveals substantial similarities, as the CD followed the earlier CP mould while modifying some issues and toning down others. The CP'86 undertook a process of radicalization, taking up fascist mythologies ('the third way') and advocating a nebulous 'national-revolution' and fascist-like corporatist ideology.

While nationalism is common to both, they can be differentiated in some nuances of the concept. CD nationalism invoked an internal homogeneity (the common features of the Dutch people are to be strengthened) while the CP'86 called upon an external exclusiveness (elimination of any foreign presence) (Van Holstein and Mudde 1992: 20). CD nationalism, summarized in the famous slogan 'The Netherlands for the Dutch first!', is not based on ethnic criteria. The CD is basically 'a state (or civic) rather than an ethnic nationalist party' (Mudde 1998: 199). After 1994 the party slid somewhat towards more ethnocentric arguments but did not abandon its peculiar 'State nationalism'. Within this framework, European integration was of increasing concern to the CD, which perceived the EU and all international organizations as potential threats to national identity.

The CP/CP'86 presents a different face of nationalism, namely the ethnic one: 'Country and ethnic community should be one' appears in a 1989 party document (Mudde 1998: 229). Therefore, external exclusiveness is at the heart of CP'86 ideology. This core element, accompanied by the standard extreme right concerns on traditional ethical values, strong state, xenophobia, and by revolutionary and nostalgic references (from Nazi symbolism to 'third wayism' and national revolution), plus a novel ecological concern, makes the CP'86 a 'national revolutionary party', much more radical than the CD.

As for racism, neither the CP'86 nor the CD used biologic/genetic arguments. They do not speak of superior or inferior races or of the 'supremacy of the white race', but insist on the necessity to preserve the Dutch social body from foreign infiltration. Moreover, they touch on the reasoning of 'welfare chauvinism' whereby the benefits of the welfare state go first of all and, in case of a shortage of resources, only to Dutch citizens. In their programmes, they stigmatize and emphasize the support and reception given to foreigners, implying that it drains resources to the detriment of poorer Dutch people (Van Holstein and Mudde 1992: 20–1).

In short, the basic traits of the CD world-view are opposition to a multicultural society, populist anti-party sentiment, fighting crime, stringent controls on immigration, and a generous welfare system (for the indigenous population only) coupled with free market incentives (Mudde 1998: 218–19).

The CP'86 is more radical and expresses a strong hostility to multiculturalism. Ethnocentrism and xenophobia are associated with an organic conception of the state, and whoever interferes with its healthy functioning must be expelled or eliminated. The means of accomplishing this aim are the standard ones: far more severe legislation, a much tougher penal code including harsher punishments, and considerably fewer restrictions on the police.

DE-PILLARIZATION AND IMMIGRATION

A long term precondition for the development of new parties, and therefore for the extreme right, might well be the demise of the iron segmentation of Dutch society, the end of the 'pillarization' along socialist, liberal, and religious lines (Lijphart 1975). This process, already underway from the 1960s, accelerated sharply in the 1980s, fostering higher electoral volatility (Irwin and Dittrich 1984; Daalder 1987, 1989; Mair 1994; Koole 1999). A large number of voters, liberated from traditional political loyalties, were attracted by new political parties, first of the left (PRP, PPS, D66, and then the Groen link) and later of the right (CP and CD). The presence of more floating voters, due to the crumbling of the *verzuiling* (pillars), was only a precondition. Further elements were needed to foster the rise of the extreme right. Two of these were particularly effective: (a) the emergence and salience of new issues, and (b) the radicalization in political discourse and system polarization which occurred at the same time as both parties took off. The former is the more relevant and needs to be discussed at length.

A very sensitive new theme that arrived on the Dutch political agenda was immigration. The presence of immigrants from Dutch ex-colonies of the Pacific and the Caribbean is not a recent phenomenon. The first influx occurred in the early-1970s, related to the strong demand for unskilled labour. By the end of the 1980s the number of immigrants from Suriname exceeded 200,000 and those from the Dutch Antilles numbered almost 50,000 (Husbands 1992a: 96–7). More recently a specific Turkish and Moroccan presence had come to be added to these ethnic groups. By the early 1990s, non-EU immigrants and asylum-seekers were estimated to constitute 3.9 per cent of the population (Koopmans 1996).

The Low Countries boast a tradition of hospitality similar to that of the Scandinavian countries, and numerous plans have been launched to integrate the newcomers, such as the right to vote at local level since 1986. This widespread image of the Low Countries is somewhat at odds with a series of empirical data on ethnic prejudice and xenophobia. A survey carried out between 1986 and 1987 revealed 'an uncaring or strongly hostile attitude' towards foreigners: 50 per cent agreed with the hypothesis (overtly supported by the CD) to financially support the return of immigrants to their home countries, and 60 per cent did not see any benefit in their presence in Holland (Husbands 1992*a*: 98, see also Scheepers, Felling, and Peters 1991: 302–6). Other research on attitudes towards various ethnic groups taken from samples of students showed that, even in the absence of negative evaluations against different ethnic groups, the students set up ethnic hierarchies: 80 per cent rank-ordered the various ethnic groups indicating first the Europeans, then the people from the Dutch ex-colonies, and, at the bottom, the new wave of immigrants from Mediterranean countries (Hagendoorn and Hraba 1989: 449–50). Further support for the existence of a latent hostile climate was offered by Dutch teenagers who expressed a dislike to having Turkish (35%) or Moroccan (14%) friends (Verkuyten 1992: 747).

Notwithstanding these data, only 7 per cent of the population in 1989 considered the presence of ethnic minorities as one of the major national problems (Scheepers, Schmeets, and Felling 1997: 146). This attitude changed abruptly in the following years. The percentage of those who would have liked to restrict immigrant rights *doubled* from 1988 to 1992 (Melich 1995: 18). Furthermore, in 1994, during the heyday of the CD (and CP'86), a Dutch election study showed that '40 per cent of the electorate was in favour of curtailing immigration of at least some categories of immigrants; and almost 10 per cent wanted to close the borders altogether to all categories of immigrants (Scheepers, Schmeets, and Felling 1997: 155). Moreover, 40 per cent questioned equal treatment for foreigners, 17 per cent asked for differential treatment in the labour market, and 21 per cent strongly opposed affirmative action in favour of immigrants (Scheepers, Schmeets, and Felling 1997: 155–6).

Apparently, ethnocentric reactions ware spreading, providing fertile ground for the potential development of extreme right parties. At first glance, the relationship between high immigration and votes for the extreme right seemed to be confirmed by the successes of the CD and the CP'86 in cities with a high percentage of foreigners like Amsterdam, The Hague, Rotterdam, and Utrecht (around 10%). More particularly, in some districts with a high density of immigrants, the two parties achieved 20 per cent of the vote in the March 1994 local elections and even reached 30 per cent in some Rotterdam inner boroughs. But the strength and unambiguous nature of the relationship between votes and the presence of foreigners has not been statistically established (Husbands 1992*b*). On the other hand, ecological analyses (Witte 1991) and surveys (van Holstein 1990) demonstrate that both the CP and CD are not only strong in areas of high immigration, but also in traditional socialist strongholds. The ability of the extreme right to make inroads in the socialist electorate rests on the feeling of misrepresentation experienced by this group. Especially among the lowest income and most marginal groups, the perception (although false) of foreigners receiving privileged treatment under

TABLE 9.3. *Political attitudes of CD voters compared to a national sample (1993)*
(% of respondents who agree with the item)

Item	CD voters	Other voters
We should allow people from developing countries to enter our own country	11	31
Development aid should be stopped	30	6
All unemployed foreigners should be sent back to their own country	72	32
Unemployed Dutchmen should take over the jobs of foreigners, who should then be sent to their own country	52	24
Capital punishment should be restored for serious crimes	72	36
No trust in the major traditional parties	30	12

Source: Adapted from Mudde and Van Holsteyn (1998: 157).

the welfare system has provoked resentment in the socialist constituency, manifesting itself in votes for the extreme right (Van Holstein 1990: 161; Husbands 1992a: 117). Significantly, the electorate of the CD and the CP'86 comprises a consistent quota of working class and low-income people (Voerman and Lucardie 1992; Lucardie 1998: 120; Tillie and Fennema 1998: 240).

If we link these insights to the analysis of the world-view of extreme right voters (Table 9.3), we see that such views are consistent with the programmes and images that both CD and CP/CP'86 (especially the former) present. A recent study on the voter attitudes of these parties demonstrated that: (a) the CD is unambiguously perceived and located on the extreme right; (b) it is preferred by those who place themselves on the extreme right; (c) respondents who score high on the ethnocentric scale prefer right-wing parties (especially CD and VVD, and to a lesser extent CDA). '*After all the general determinants of parties are accounted for, ethnocentric-right voters still have a higher preference for the extreme right (and only the extreme right)*' (Tillie and Fennema 1998: 239). In other words, ethnocentrism appears to have acquired the status of a reliable predictor of party preference in the Netherlands. Within this framework, the CD is perceived as the party that better fits the voters' ethnocentric attitudes, not only because of its programme but also because of its right-extreme location on the political spectrum. In fact, 'the more ethnocentric a voter, the more he or she prefers a right-wing party' (Tillie and Fennema 1998: 240).

Furthermore, the conjunction between nationalistic sentiments and feelings of powerlessness provide further fuel for extreme right votes. The more ethnic nationalist and isolated (those who perceive a subjective feeling of social marginality) people are, the more they vote extreme right (Tillie and Fennema 1998: 246).

The second element of explanation involves system evaluation and dynamics. Traditionally, confidence in the system has been comparatively quite high, *but in the early 1980s, coinciding with the first CD success*, trust in political institutions sharply declined (and then recovered) (Holmberg 1999: 107). In that period the Netherlands experienced a crisis of confidence in the system, which touched upon the 'political class' and traditional parties. The anti-establishment sentiments thus fostered were shared by 20 per cent of the population on the eve of the 1994 elections (Mudde and van Holsteyn 2000: 159–60). The presence of such a 'politically (very) cynical' constituency of the electorate might have provided the extreme right with potential for development. Furthermore, the collapse of the 'pillarization' of Dutch society has progressively freed more and more voters from previous alignments, increasing electoral volatility, which rose steeply again in the 1990s (Koole 1999), *coinciding with the second CD breakthrough.*

As far as the system dynamic is concerned, in the early 1980s the CP and the CD could have profited from a wave of radicalization and polarization induced by the main parties during the late 1960s and 1970s (Tromp 1989; Wolinetz 1993; ten Napel 1998: esp. 176). The VVD in particular occupied a rather extreme position on the political spectrum and had quite a conservative political agenda (Van Schuur 1984; Pennings 1995: 11). This positioning of the VVD in the early 1980s could have paved the way for the CD's more radical stances, thus favouring its first rise. But later on, in front of the second wave of right-extremism in the mid-1990s, the adoption of a tough position on the immigration issue and the articulation of gradually increasing anti-welfare, anti-tax sentiments by the VVD itself undermined the position of CD (Lucardie 1998; Tillie and Fennema 1998). Therefore, 'pragmatic voters who wished to cast an anti-immigrants vote may in such case decide to vote for the larger mainstream party (such as the VVD) than for the the more radical "outcasts" ' (van der Brug, Fennema, and Tillie 2000: 95) such as the CD. Therefore the CD should rely only on their own 'true believers'. In the Netherlands two different dynamics were at work. In the 1980s the radicalization on the right by the established moderate parties paved the way for the first appearence of the extreme right, as was the case in France in the same period. In the 1990s, a different dynamic took hold. The VVD's quite conservative standpoint limited the comeback of the extreme right.

To conclude, notwithstanding the existence of a growing ethnocentrism in the population, the extreme right parties did not take hold, except for some fleeting appearances. While the Dutch tolerant tradition (Daalder 1989) seems to be more a myth than a dam to the extreme right (Lucardie 1998: 122), it would probably be more fruitful to explain present extreme right irrelevance by concentrating instead on the effective liberal–conservative statements and policies on tax and immigration by the VVD, the still high system confidence, and the CD and CP/CP'86 internal frailties. On the other hand, probably in no other country has the counter-mobilization against the extreme right proved so vigorous as in the Netherlands, both on the streets (including with many violent events) and inside the institutions. Finally, the organizational weakness and lack of leadership in both the CD and the CP/CP'86 proved enough to inhibit organizational expansion after the 1984 and 1994 breakthroughs.

10

Great Britain: A Case of Failure

The extreme right in Great Britain has never experienced success. Fascist leanings in Britain were easily kept under control both in the 1930s, when an avowedly fascist party was formed, and in the post-war years, when right-extremists tried in vain to acquire political relevance.

OSWALD MOSLEY AND THE BRITISH UNION OF FASCISTS

The first appearance of a movement with distinct fascist tendencies was that of the British Fascists (BF) in the 1920s. The party was founded in 1923 by a fervent admirer of Mussolini, but it was more its organizational style (paramilitary structure, blue shirt uniform) that it had in common with Italian fascism than its ideology, which instead evoked British 'Die-hard conservatism' (Thurlow 1998: 33–37). Apparently, this movement did not progress beyond verbal agitation, unsupported by any effective action or by a sizeable organization, and its political impact was negligible (Cross 1961; Benewick 1972). Similarly marginal was Arnold Leese's Imperial Fascist League which was 'more truly fascist than the the BF' (Eatwell 1997: 126) and furiously anti-Semitic (Thurlow 1998: 47–51). While more recent sources question the irrelevance of the British Fascists (Lunn 1990), the true expression of British fascism lies in Oswald Mosley's British Union of Fascists (BUF) (Lewis 1987; Thurlow 1987, 1998).

Mosley, in keeping with his aristocratic origins, entered politics through the Tory party and became a member of Parliament in 1918. In 1924, he abandoned the Conservative benches and joined the Labour party. In 1929, he was part of the MacDonald government where he proposed an economic policy inspired by Keynes' theory. Notwithstanding Mosley's commitment, the Labour government did not approve his economic plan (*The Memorandum*) and, subsequently, the Labour party conference too rejected his proposals, although only by a few votes. After this defeat, and faced with increasing hostility from the party, Mosley left Labour. In 1931, along with one Conservative and five Labour MPs, he founded the New Party, forerunner of the subsequent British Union of Fascists.

The proposals for economic recovery highlighted in Mosley's *Memorandum* when he was in government are at the core of the New Party: cooperation amongst the classes, state planning, and national unity. Mosley distanced himself both from the Conservatives, because of their acceptance of an uncontrolled free market and their distrust of the masses, and from Labour, because of its conception of class struggle and its feeble national spirit. Despite the initial leftward leaning of the New Party, Mosley wanted to occupy a centre position in the political space which would be perceived as putting the interests of the nation above all partisan difference and vested interests. In reality, since it advocated an economic policy based on planning and corporatist mechanisms such as cooperation between capital and labour, it was, by definition, leaning toward the fascist 'synthesis'.

The brief parabola of the New Party was put aside in just over one year, when sharply increasing hostility from Labour provided Mosley with the opportunity to create a paramilitary formation (NUPA, abbreviation of New Party) to 'defend' its own initiatives from the aggressions of Labour activists. While the 'defensive' thesis seems to be supported by recent researches (Cullen 1993: 247), the establishment of the NUPA constituted a decisive step towards the acceptance of latent fascism, a term which both surfaced in the leader's writings from time to time and was increasingly used in relation to Mosley's movement by its adversaries. In fact, the party moved towards a 'Tory socialism', that is to say the synthesis of the Right and Left cemented by nationalism, and an appeal to the masses (both typical of fascist ideology). The old Labour members abandoned the New Party, and in so doing facilitated its transformation into the British Union of Fascists (BUF).

Mosley founded the BUF in 1932 after a meeting with Mussolini in Rome. The BUF, as its leader repeatedly underlined, distinguished itself from the established political parties both in its ideology and in its organization (paramilitary structure, black shirts, the *Führerprinzip*). Initially, the Conservatives attempted to bring Mosley back into the mainstream of parliamentary democracy, employing his movement as a Tory militant arm (Lewis 1987: 66). Moreover, at local level, cooperation between the Conservative Party and the BUF (in a similar vein to connections with the British Fascists a decade earlier) was not infrequent (Lunn 1996: 170ff). However, the Tories soon gave up in face of its increasing anti-parliamentarism and anti-Semitism, and because of its violent actions. The BUF's symbolism, clearly derived from the continent, as well as its 'modernity' and populist appeal, made it increasingly more extraneous to the Conservatives, mainly because all of this was just not 'British' (Lewis 1987: 147). For the Conservatives, this simply left no room for manoeuvre. The outbreak of WWII heralded the end of the BUF. Despite its overt declarations of national loyalty, the prospect of a feared German invasion led to Mosley and another 750 party members being interned for reasons of state security in May 1940. The BUF was then dissolved by government decree (Thurlow 1987: 198, 210).

The BUF did not represent a danger to British democracy: 'it was merely a minor irritant for the government' (Thurlow 1998: 87). At its peak after the Olympia meeting in 1934, when the party was sponsored by the *Daily Mail*, its organized strength reached around 50,000 members; but in few months it fell quite abruptly to some 5000, due to public awareness of its anti-Semitic stance and violent actions. It then recovered, having a membership of around 20,000 members at the end of the decade (Webber 1984: 577; Griffin 1996b: 154; Thurlow 1998: 91ff). Even the high profile rallies and paramilitary marches never gained a massive audience: on the other hand, they did provoke fierce reactions from civil rights associations and leftist organizations, especially from the communists. Finally, the BUF performed poorly in the electoral arena too. In 1937, the party participated in elections for the first time. It fielded candidates in three wards in the election for the London County Council, respectively obtaining 23, 19, and 14 per cent of the vote, and it contested eight seats in five London boroughs in the following city council election, coming second in six (Thurlow 1998: 85). Whilst these results were not negligible, outside London the BUF 'performed disastrously' (Thurlow 1998: 85). In addition, in the first few months after the declaration of war, the BUF contested three parliamentary by-elections, arguing for a 'vote for peace' and against the Labour–Conservative pact, but it was a miscalculation: the results were derisory (Lewis 1987: 70–1).

THE EXTREME RIGHT IN THE POST-WAR PERIOD AND THE BIRTH OF THE NATIONAL FRONT

The post-war British extreme right resumed its appearance with Mosley founding the Union Movement in 1948. This movement displayed some characteristics common to the BUF, but diverged both on ideological and organizational levels. On the ideological level, a limitation on State intervention in the economy, a shifting from integral corporativism to socio-economic cooperation, a recognition, *obtorto collo*, of the principles on democracy, and a substitution of British nationalism with a pan-European one on the basis of new fierce anti-communism, were postulated. Organizationally, fascist symbolism and the militia structure were abolished.

The success of the mid-1930s proved unrecoverable: the Union Movement had less than 1500 members (Lewis 1987: 241) and no longer involved people in classic direct 'actions' such as marches in districts with a high density of immigrants and Jews, like London's East End, gathering together in pubs, or clashes with anti-fascist demonstrators. The electoral results produced a series of total defeats, even when Mosley finally decided to stand in the elections himself, for the first time. In the 1959 general election in London's district of North Kensington, Mosley polled a derisory 8.1 per cent of the vote (Eatwell 1992b: 176). The result was drastically inferior to what he had expected, since the year before that particular district was affected by serious racial incidents, and Mosley, despite his intellectual opposition to biological racism, had unscrupulously given his assent to racist speculations, directing hostility toward the new influx of almost one million immigrants from the Commonwealth. On the other hand, Mosley himself combined the anti-immigrant appeal with socially orientated provisions and pledges for 'European Socialism', thus making his supposedly 'racist' voters quite puzzled (Thurlow 1998: 216–7). The Union Movement just about survived this defeat up until 1966, when a further fiasco (again Mosley's), in the Shoreditch and Finsbury constituency by-elections (4.6%), led to the UM break-up.

The British extreme right of the 1950s and the 1960s was not confined to Mosley's movement. In 1954 A. K. Chesterton, an ex-leader of the BUF, founded the League of Empire Loyalists (LEL), a reactionary, anti-Semitic, and imperialistic movement. This movement, which never exceeded 3000 members and rapidly faded, gave rise however to a new generation of extreme right leaders, such as Martin Webster, John Tyndall, and Colin Jordan. Many protagonists of extreme right movements up until the 1980s came from the defunct LEL.

Jordan in fact left and founded the White Defence League in 1958, as did Tyndall who formed the National Labour Party in 1957. These two groups merged in 1960 giving life to the short-lived British National Party (BNP), which aimed at securing Britain from the Communist threat, from the control of Jewish international finance, and from racial contamination, by creating a 'Popular racial-nationalist State'. The new formation split again in 1962 when Tyndall and Jordan left, arguing for a truly neo-Nazi 'Strasserist' policy, and founded the National Socialist Movement (NSM). This movement attracted a certain amount of attention for its brutal anti-immigrant activities, which led to clashes with anti-fascist organizations and the imprisonment of some NSM militants, including Jordan himself.

The concern amongst the public, created by such a tiny sect, was testimony to the existence of a growing but still underground 'immigration issue', but neither the BNP nor the NSM were able to exploit it. The BNP presented a handful of candidates in the 1964 general elections, scoring as high as 9 per cent where the party leader stood as a candidate, but then dissolved. The NSM was torn apart by personal conflicts between Jordan and Tyndall, most probably over the disputed love affair with the heiress of the famous French *couturier*, Dior, and, also, over the emphasis placed on British nationalism rather than on Nazi revivalism. As a result, Tyndall and Webster left and founded the imperial-nostalgic Greater Britain Movement.

None of these groups made any impact on British politics. Even the concern created in public opinion by the race riots in Nottingham and London's Notting Hill in 1958 (Layton-Henry 1992: 40, 73ff) did not favour the extreme right's development. The NSM, and other extremist fringes that had become quite vociferous and active in race-sensitive areas, remained squeezed between a double action. On the one hand, the antiracist mobilization met with success: for example, the Jewish Defence Committees collected almost half a million signatures for a petition calling for legislation against racial incitement (Kushnick 1988: 88). On the other hand, the Consertives took a clear stand in the immigration issue. Since the 1961 party conference, in fact, the Tory leadership decided to back local party resolutions and actions on immigration control, and the Conservative government introduced the somewhat restrictive Commonwealth Immigration Act in 1962 (Karapin 1999: 429). Similarly, at the 1964 general election, local Tory candidates played the racist card in immigrant sensitive districts. The victory by the Conservative Peter Griffith in Smethwick over the incumbent Labour spokesperson for immigration Gordon Walkers suggested that anti-immigration stances were electorally rewarding. Actually, the Smethwick outcome proved to be an exception rather than the rule. On one side, the Tory candidates who had played the racist card 'had electoral payoffs in only a handful of places in 1964' (Karapin 1999: 422) and, on the other, the immigrant issue was far removed from the electorate's concerns (Butler and King 1965: 128–9).

The politicization of that issue and the apparently tough attitude by the Conservatives, while not particularly rewarding for the Tory party in electoral terms, nevertheless inhibited any penetration by the extreme right. Moreover, the bipartisan consensus on the immigration question since the mid-to-late 1960s de-emphasized its salience. Even the significant and much publicized speech made by Enoch Powell in 1968 on the dangers—'the rivers of blood'—of an uncontrolled coloured immigration did not alter the low profile and bipartisan policy on the issue. Not by chance, Powell was forced to resign from the Tory shadow cabinet after his speech, despite the wide acceptance and support he had received from public opinion (Eatwell 1992*b*: 181; Norton 1996). In sum, the internal quarrels and the (apparently tough) positions taken by the Conservatives on the immigration issue in the early 1960s gave the extreme right a marginal status (Eatwell 1998*a*: 144).

A further attempt to gather the remnants of the British extreme right was made in 1967 by the formation of the National Front (NF). This new organization, initially led by the Tyndall and Webster duo, was the most successful extreme right party in post-war Britain. After an initial period of irrelevance, the NF attracted a following both in terms of activists and of votes, reaching its peak in the late 1970s. The party did not offer any new ideological–political discourse as it fused—with varying degrees of success—the various tendencies of British right extremism, from neo-Nazism to Mosleyite corporatism.

The first noticeable if uninspiring electoral result came in the 1970 general election, when the ten National Front candidates got, on average, 3.6 per cent of the vote (with a maximum of 5.6%). A few years later, the NF in the 1973 by-election in West Bromwich polled 16.4 per cent, the best result ever achieved by an extreme right party in a British general election (Taylor 1993: 177). In this period, the organizational strength of the party touched its zenith by recruiting 14,000 members, two-thirds of whom joined in 1973 (Eatwell 1992*b*: 178; Taylor 1993: 180). This sudden influx of members was mainly composed of ex-Tory and Monday club members, the so-called 'populists' (Thurlow 1998: 253ff). This group of discontented Tories was unhappy with the 'wet' policy of the Heath government,

TABLE 10.1. *Vote for the NF and BNP in parliamentary and European elections*

	BNP			NF		
Year	Vote nationwide (%)	No. of constituencies contested	Vote in the constituencies contested (%)	Vote nationwide (%)	No. of constituencies contested	Vote in the constituencies contested (%)
1970				0.04	10	3.6
1974 Feb.				0.25	54	3.3
1974 Oct.				0.40	90	3.1
1979				0.63	303	1.4
1983	0.05	54	0.6	0.09	60	1.1
1987	0.01	2	0.5			
1992	0.02	13	1.2	0.01	14	0.7
1997	0.12	56	1.4	0.01	6	1.2
1999E	1.00					

Source: Eatwell (2000); Caramani (2000).

especially on the immigration issue. In particular, the 'liberal' management of the Ugandan–Asian crisis—the 50,000 people of Asian origin expelled by that country and accepted in Britain by the Conservative Heath government in 1972—and the rejection of a 'Powellite' anti-immigration motion at the 1972 annual party conference, had irritated the most right-wing constituency within the Tories (Layton-Henry 1992: 86–7). The former Tories that entered the National Front at the time argued for a less proto-fascist and a more 'racial-populist' appeal, which might be attractive for those inner-cities densely populated with immigrants. This attempt to modify the party image did not improve the electoral appeal of the party. In the general elections of February and October 1974 it averaged around 3 per cent of the votes cast in the constituencies it contested.

This modest outcome was somewhat offset by the party's capacity to present a higher number of candidates (from 10 in 1970 to 90 in October 1974) and by the number of constituencies where they obtained up to 10 per cent of the vote (Eatwell 1992b: 178). Nonetheless, the disappointing results inspired a takeover of the party leadership by the ex-conservative 'populists' who installed John Read as head of the party in 1975. However, the new leadership soon proved unable to cope with a boycott by the original group led by Tyndall. Because of the latter's control over the organization, he was able to force the 'populists' into splitting away. Despite the exit of the more moderate wing, the NF achieved positive outcomes in the 1976 local elections where it polled 8.9 per cent—in the wards contested—with a 16.6 per cent peak in Leicester, where it came within 62 votes of electing a councillor (Husbands 1994: 568). In the following year, the NF totalled almost 250,000 votes in local elections, 119,000 of which were obtained in the elections for the Greater London council (Husbands 1988: 67). They constituted 5.3 per cent of the total vote in London, where the NF presented candidates in 91 out of the 92 wards. This placed the party on the verge of making an electoral breakthrough, giving it access to a position among the mainstream parties. In order to fulfil this ambition the National Front presented its own candidates in almost half the constituencies (303 out of 635) in the general election of 1979—an inconceivable organizational effort until a few years before.

The party expectations were justified by the importance of the immigration issue and the growing acceptance of the party itself by a proportion of the electorate. In a national survey, 21 per cent of citizens declared that 'it is a good thing that a party such the NF exists' (Harrop, England, and Husbands 1980: 281); and, even more, the Conservative party leader, Margeret Thatcher, endorsing the 'validity' of NF voters' concerns, made unheard of statements about the risk of Britain being 'swamped' by inflows of immigrants (Layton-Henry 1992: 184ff); finally, public opinion acknowledged the salience of the immigration issue, as 21 per cent of respondents in an opinion poll taken in February 1978 (just after Thatcher's interview) mentioned it as one of the two most urgent national problems. All this notwithstanding, the electoral outcome was dismal: the NF vote dropped to 1.4 per cent—less than half of that achieved in the previous election—and its best result did not exceed 7.6 per cent (Eatwell 1992*b*: 178). In reality, the Conservative initiative to halt the NF's surge had proved effective.

Hence the party did not break into the party system. But throughout the 1970s the NF were a thorn in the side of British politics. The attention devoted to this party by the mass media and scholars bore witness to the concern expressed over the emergence of a potential new political force (Husbands 1988: 67). This might be viewed as excessive concern, perhaps, since the NF did not obtain a single parliamentary seat—not even coming close. The 1973 by-election (16.4%) was its best result. Only in the local elections did the NF perform better, although, ironically, the only two town councillors elected—in Blackburn (Lancashire) in May 1976—belonged to a tiny splinter faction of the NF which had left the party the year before that election (Walker 1977: 198; Eatwell 1990: 226). However, while the electoral outcomes were modest, they were incomparably higher than those scored previously by all other extreme right movements, the BUF included.

The 1979 electoral debacle inevitably brought about tensions and divisions. The cleavage, which placed the moderate wing, led by Martin Webster, and the radical Nazi faction of the Chairman, John Tyndall, in opposition to each other, forced the latter to exit. The party did not profit from this supposed de-radicalization because a new up-coming generation of militants brought about a novel, even more radical alignment. This group introduced the Evolian reference to the 'political soldiers', a handful of 'selected' men who testify by their own lifestyles their radical opposition to the system and to modernity itself. This 'esoteric appeal' (Eatwell 1997: 342) contributed to a further fiasco in the 1983 general election where the party's 60 candidates polled only 1.1 per cent of the vote on average. Afterwards a new leadership represented by Griffin and Pierce took hold of the party, expelling Webster himself. However, even the new group followed the classical quarrelsome routine with personal splits and charges of infiltration and betrayal.

The struggles among the internal factions reached the point that, in 1989, two groups claimed the title of National Front. The first one, under the control of Griffin and Holland, dissolved in 1990. The second, known also as the National Front Support Group (or Flag Group, from the name of the magazine), finally inherited the 'trademark' of the organization. After failing to merge with the British National Party because of quarrels over Tyndall's chairmanship (yet again), its 14 candidates in the 1992 general election polled the worst results in the history of the NF: 0.7 per cent on average (Eatwell 1992*b*: 179–80). Apparently, the radicalism of this residual fringe had the counter-effect of alienating a potential reservoir of supporters. The crisis of the National Front, confronted by the even more violent radicalism of groups such as Combat 18 and by the highly publicized and somewhat successful competing party, Tyndall's BNP, led a group of few hundred former members to leave the organization on the point of collapse. They set up the National Democrats (ND) (or National Democratic Party) in 1995. In the 1997 general election, the ND fielded 21 candidates who polled an average vote of 1.2 per cent (one get 11.4%) (Eatwell 1998*a*: 145), while a mere 6 NF candidates gathered 1 per cent on average (Whine 1998: 301).

THE IDEOLOGY OF THE NF

National Front ideology was moulded according to different leaderships and strategies. At its birth the NF was characterized by a nationalistic (otherwise defined as 'populist') (Thurlow 1987, 1998) racism and strong anti-Semitism, mainly due to Arnold Leese (Lewis 1987: 260), combined with the socio-economic views of the pre-war Mosleyite tradition. NF racism was typically argued on genetic/biological grounds: (1) physical and behavioural differences have genetic origins; (2) genetic differences are at the basis of racial differentiation; (3) races and nations can be ranked along a hierarchical grading system because of different abilities in various fields; (4) the superior races are caught in a trap in their (rightful) position of domination over the inferior races; (5) the most insidious threat comes from the Jews who, on account of their control over financial resources in the international markets and their support for free immigration, liberalism, communism, and leftist tendencies (all Jewish characteristics), wish 'to destroy the national spirit and British virtues.' The supremacy of the white race and particularly 'northern Aryanism' (occasionally the term 'Anglo-Saxonism' also appears) are the foremost important values to defend in order to recover the imperial role that British history (or, rather, 'tradition') implies (Taylor 1993).

During the 1970s, the fascist heritage was officially discarded, precisely to attract discontented conservatives. Anti-Semitism was toned down and supplanted by hostility towards coloured immigration. The new target of the NF's verbal and physical violence became the immigrants. In that period, thanks to economic corporativism and the hierarchical-organicistic conception of the state, the National Front could be defined as a traditional, neo-fascist extreme right party.

In the 1980s, after the expulsion of the former leaders (Tyndall and Webster) and the emergence of a 'third generation' of right-extremists (Griffin and Pierce first, and then Griffin and Holland), these stances were abandoned by the NF, though they were kept alive by Tyndall's British National Party (BNP). The ideological references of the National Front from the mid-1980s deviated from the previous ones on many points. The NF leant more and more towards anti-capitalism, to the point of sustaining the miners in their long 1984–5 strike; it emphasized a return to nature (a naturalist-ecologist feature of the tradition), condemning the city as a place of physical and moral depravation; it opposed nuclear energy, both for civilian and military purposes; and it advocated an exit from NATO. In some respects, the NF was influenced by the Italian radical right whose members were refugees in England, particularly those of the terrorist group 'Third Position', and it inserted into its ideology the elaboration of thinkers such as the socially-minded Nazi, Otto Strasser, and the traditionalist anti-modernist, Julius Evola (Husbands 1988: 72; Thurlow 1998: 262–7). This line, explicitly stated in the NF party manifesto, meaningfully entitled 'The Third Way', was especially sustained by Griffin, while Pierce, a former ally of Griffin in the struggle against the old guard, rejected it. In 1987 the ideological split and personal bickering produced the two above-mentioned groups, which disputed the copyright of the National Front 'trademark'. Pierce's group was more visible and active; it maintained a Strasserian line inspired by left anti-capitalism, but also advocated a policy (and supported actions) against immigrants, with the usual assertions of Jewish conspiracies (Veugelers 1992: 22). Griffin followed a more esoteric path along Evola's idea of the 'political soldier'—the brave man who proclaims his purity and his extraneousness to the corrupt rotten modern world by committing 'exemplary acts', and by keeping himself prepared for the final combat (Eatwell 1996a: 99–117). The virtual disappearance of the NF in the 1990s somehow reflected this radical, anti-modern, and mystical ideology.

THE NEWCOMER: THE BNP

The political heir to the 1970s NF is the BNP (which adopted the same name of the party established in 1960 which collapsed in 1967). The BNP's founder, John Tyndall, long-lasting leader of the NF, advocated continuity of his former party (Copsey 1996: 120). Nationalistic racism and the destiny of Great Britain were its cardinal points. Its policy proposals concerned forced repatriation of immigrants, tough measures for criminals, drastic cuts to the welfare system, the death penalty for terrorists, and legal prohibition of abortion and of homosexual conduct. While the BNP ideology displayed a marked continuity with the National front stances of the late 1970s, it did attempt to present itself as more 'democratic'. For example, it abandoned the Führerprinzip and introduced internal rules more in tune with democratic standards (Copsey 1996: 121). This change did not however increase the party's recruitment.

In the 1983 general election the BNP stood in 53 seats in order to benefit from five minutes of national broadcasting, allowed to all parties which presented more than 50 candidates. Notwithstanding this new advantage, the party's results were poor, 1.3 per cent on average. Apparently, this modest performance did not harm the party because the leadership's main goal was to develop the organization and promote a militant campaign on its own issues at the local level, rather than to participate in the election. But the party did not achieve satisfactory results in terms of membership recruitment and militancy. While the self-destructive dynamic of the National Front had left it virtually alone to represent the British extreme right, the BNP's membership deteriorated to slightly over 1000 and its press did not enjoy a circulation of over 500 regular subscribers (Copsey 1996: 124). The organizational frailty—the party never had more than 2000 members (Husbands 1994: 575) or 3000 members (Eatwell 1998*a*: 146) even in its heyday in the mid-1990s—was confirmed by the decision to withdraw from the 1987 general election (only two candidates ran, collecting 553 votes).

In 1990, there were signs of an upturn. In a local election in the London borough of Tower Hamlets the BNP candidate polled more than 9 per cent in two wards (Husbands 1994: 570ff) (which represented a dramatic increase compared to the 1.9 per cent polled two years before in the same area). While the 1992 general election was hardly a successful outcome for the party—1.0 per cent on average in the 13 contested constituencies (Husbands 1994: 570)—a significant leap forward occurred in October 1992 with 20 per cent gained in a local by-election, again in Tower Hamlets. The breakthrough finally came the following year when the BNP candidate attracted 34 per cent of the vote in the Millwall district of London's Isle of Dogs and got elected. The party's 'Rights for Whites' campaign, which was later adopted as a national party slogan, aptly reflects BNP racial populist, covert fascist nostalgia, especially concerning authoritarian corporatism (which is further complemented by ideology).

The success proved quite ephemeral. The 'anti-fascist' mobilization, counter-initiatives by the major parties, a persistent proto-fascist party agenda, and lack of leadership, inhibited any positive follow-ups. Nonetheless the BNP dramatically increased its share of votes in the 1994 local elections: their 29 candidates, the majority of which stood in the London area, polled 8.4 per cent on average (Copsey 1996: 134), while 5 of them passed 20 per cent, and a remarkable 33 per cent was obtained in Newham. However, despite the fact that the BNP incumbent in Millwall gathered 1713 votes—an increase of 561—with an unprecedented district turnout of 67%, he was not re-elected. This defeat, far beyond the other positive outcomes, deeply influenced the party's mood: a feeling of failure spread amongst the rank and file leaving room for the appeal of more radical groups such as Combat 18. The 1.4 per cent of votes gained in the 1997 general election (the mean of 55 candidates) confirmed the marginal status of the party. Not even access to the national media—two of them censored some racist passages—favoured the BNP (Eatwell 1998*b*: 14–20). At any rate, the party still persists. It collected more than 100,000 votes in the 1999 European elections, with a significant increase in outer-East London. For the first time in the post-war period an extreme right party reached 1.0 per cent of the votes *nationally*, in a nationwide election—albeit with a very low turnout. Compared with the previous national outcomes, *all below 0.1 both for NF and the BNP*, the result is a resounding one.

A MALE, WORKING-CLASS, AND MARGINAL
SELF-EMPLOYED ELECTORATE

The electoral analyses of the extreme right vote do not support any direct correla-tion between concentration of immigrants and the success of the NF. While the first studies seemed to establish a direct relationship between immigration and extreme right voting, (Fielding 1981: 31–2) more accurate analyses have repudiated such a relationship (Taylor 1979; 1993: 81; Husbands 1988). The NF polled well in areas *bordering* high-density immigrant neighbourhoods; undefined notions of threat, of fear of invasion, of transgressing the borders of one's 'safe area', apparently pro-duce a defensive reaction which favours a rise in extreme right support (Husbands 1983). Moreover, it has been highlighted that the urban environments conducive to NF support are either those where rapid economic expansion has come to a halt or areas which are in the process of de-industrializing (Husbands 1983).

The social profile of the NF's electorate and its activists is similarly controver-sial. The hypothesis suggested by Paul Whiteley (1979), that the NF attracted votes from the authoritarian 'working class', is challenged by Christopher Husbands, who found a working-class presence only among the most militant party supporters, while the more moderate ones belonged to the 'marginal self-employed' (Husbands 1983: 136ff).

On the other hand, the recent BNP breakthrough in areas of East London, the his-torical bastion of the extreme right, seems to reinforce the hypothesis that attributes the best preconditions for extreme right development to territorial isolation and marginality. As Husbands (1994: 576) has summarized: 'the (meagre) quality of life of inner-city ethnic minorities, especially in parts of London, has been and remains the real effect of the BNP'. The 'Rights for Whites' campaign in fact proved quite appealing to those who felt a 'sharp loss of community' (Eatwell 1998a: 149).

This picture is consistent with the extreme right internal debate on which social constituency to address. The project of gaining consensus among the workers (patronized above all by Webster in the 1970s NF) has been the target of fierce internal disputes by those who aimed instead at the dissatisfied conservative middle class. The latter approach, which implied softening the party's political agenda, did not last for long. The flirtation with the 'populist' ex-Conservatives in 1974–6, when the 1974 double Conservative defeat brought fresh troops from disappointed Tories into the party, ended in under two years.

In conclusion, according to Husbands (1994), the extreme right voter 'probably maintains the social and demographic characteristics of the preceding decade', that is male, working-class, and marginal self-employed.

THE HANDICAPS OF THE BRITISH EXTREME RIGHT

The question as to why Britain has never experienced fascism, not even in the form of a potentially dangerous movement, leads to two different strands of explanation. One refers to what historians call 'national character' and political scientists call 'political culture': the leaning towards gradualism and the inheritance of a culture of rights, the deeply rooted liberal-democratic institutions, and the bargaining, pragmatic attitudes. All these aspects, related to a civic culture nurtured by a long-standing practice of the rule of law, are at the basis of the 'culturalist' interpretation of the weakness of fascism in Britain (for a critique of such an interpretation see Lunn 1996). The other strand, which also includes elements of the first, has been best illustrated by Roger Griffin and Roger Eatwell. Griffin has recently emphasized the role of 'structural factors', which inhibited a fascist takeover in the inter-wars years (Griffin 1995, 1996b: 153ff): the management of the economic crisis (in an early industrialized country); the solidity of the traditional right; the constitutional tradition; the reinstatement and reinforcement of national pride thanks to victory in the First World War; and the virtual non-existence of a Bolshevik threat. If one relates all these elements to the characteristics of the fascist political protagonists (from the British Fascists up to the NF), with special reference to their 'quixotism' and lack of leadership, the destiny of British fascism continues to be one of irrelevance.

Most of the these arguments also go to explain the post-war failure of the extreme right (Eatwell 1998a,b, 2000). More specifically, the first explanation concerns the connection of the British extreme right with either Italian or German historical Fascism. While the BUF, and especially Mosley himself, were unquestionably tied to the tradition of Italian fascism (the corporatist socio-economic synthesis), the NF and the BNP were more closely linked to the Nazi tradition, though with different accents according to different leaderships. However, all the analysts (with only one exception) define the NF, and later the BNP, as a neo-fascist party along Nazi lines. This proto-Nazi mould, however much hidden, has raised an insurmountable barrier for many right-wing Conservatives.

The second reason for both the NF's and the BNP's limited success concerns their leaders' lack of ability, none of whom are even comparable to Mosley or, nowadays, to Le Pen or Haider, and their destructive and ceaseless factionalism.

Thirdly, the strategy of the Conservative Party when faced with a potential competitor has played an important role. In the first few years, Conservative policy, to a certain extent, favoured the rise of the National Front. For instance, the radical marginalization of Enoch Powell (member of the Conservative shadow cabinet) after his famous 1968 speech on 'the rivers of blood', and the liberal politics of the Conservative government under Heath, especially in light of the entry of 50,000 Asian refugees expelled by Uganda in 1972, provided good opportunities for NF anti-immigration propaganda. In fact, between 1972 and 1977 the NF attracted its largest following. In addition, a large section of public opinion firmly supported (around 75% of those interviewed) Powell's concerns (Eatwell 1992b: 181); and in the 1970s around a quarter of the electorate agreed with forced repatriation of immigrants (Särlvik and Crewe 1983: 231, 243). Later on, Margaret Thatcher radically modified Tory policies on this issue (Layton-Henry 1992; Karapin 1999). Even before becoming premier, Margaret Thatcher, in a famous

1978 interview, expressed the necessity of facing the problem of immigration so as to avoid being 'swamped' by an alien culture, and made references to the understandable concerns of those who had voted for the NF. Thatcher argued that the concern over immigration was a real problem that affected a certain part of the population and the Conservatives had to solve it. The most severe proposals on the problem of immigration (adopted in the following years with the 1981 Nationality Act) and the 1986 restrictions on entry for new Commonwealth citizens, plus a covertly xenophobic sentiment fed by think-tanks and groups referring to the 'The Salisbury Review', undermined the NF. The same strategy seems to have been in practice vis-à-vis the BNP resurgence in the mid-1990s after its 'success' in London's Millwall district: de-emphasis of the race relations problem via minimizing official declarations, and concern for the recovery of consensus in the local areas affected by the extreme right's rise.

Fourthly, the NF and BNP have been vigorously confronted by the mobilization of anti-racist movements which have always contested their provocative actions: the counter-mobilization of immigrant communities and liberal public opinion has held the party under constant observation.

Finally, an institutional feature such as the majoritarian first-past-the-post electoral system, penalizing the growth of new and extreme parties, plays a crucial role. It might well not be a coincidence that the highest national percentage of votes ever gained by the extreme right (in this case the BNP) occurred at the last European election where, for the first time, a (type of) proportional system was introduced.

For all these reasons—the identification with foreign ideologies, the low profile of the party leaders and inner factionalism, the anti-racist counter-mobilization, the skilful containment operated by the Conservatives by raising and then suffocating the immigration issue, and the majoritarian electoral system, plus the cultural features of the British system—the extreme right never acquired a relevant status in Great Britain.

The right-extremist parties never benefited from full political legitimacy (Eatwell 1998a); they were never perceived—not even after the famous 1978 Thatcher interview—as 'normal' political actors. Indulgence in street violence, overt racist and anti-Semitic statements, and generalized nostalgia for all sorts of fascist tendencies, marginalized the NF at the time and the BNP nowadays. Not even the salience of the immigration issue (albeit not as acute as in other countries) and the severity of racial violence (in this case higher than in other countries) (Koopman 1996: 189–91), that might have offered propitious conditions for an extreme right breakthrough, seemed enough to overcome the above-mentioned cultural, political, and institutional obstacles. And, finally, their attachment to the traditional fascist mould, contrary to the most successful extreme right parties in Europe, signalled the 'end game' (Griffin 2000) for these parties.

11

The Mediterranean Countries: Too Late for Nostalgia, Too Early for Post-material Protest

In the three Mediterranean countries where democratic systems have only been established in recent times, namely Spain, Portugal, and Greece, the extreme right has not developed. These countries became democratic after having been ruled by right-authoritarian regimes for many decades: Portugal and Spain uninterruptedly since the 1930s, and Greece from 1967 to 1974, but with a 'low intensity' democratic regime in the post-war years until 1967. In the mid-1970s all three abandoned their fascist-like regimes (Gunther, Diamandouros, and Puhle 1995; Linz and Stepan 1996; Morlino 1998; Diamandouros and Gunther 2001). Notwithstanding, or because of, this heritage, no sizeable extreme right party has ever emerged.

SPAIN

The transition to democracy in Spain 'left behind' the main components of the extreme right, Franco's nostalgics and the phalangists (Payne 1987).

First, the nostalgic milieu, in the immediate aftermath of Franco's death, was confident that there would be some continuity with the past regime guaranteed by the Army and by the new King, Juan Carlos, who, according to Franco's own designation, was to be his successor. This conviction was coupled with the extraneousness to organizational practices, inherited by the de-mobilizing style of the dictatorship that never favoured the development of organized forms of political support for the regime itself (Payne 1987; Rodriguez 1994, 1997). This deprived the Francoists of viable organizational tools at the moment of the Caudillo's death. Second, some sectors of the old regime had already been working cautiously towards the opening up and modernization of both society and the political system for many years. Therefore, the 'continuistas' sank into isolation even in their own milieu. Finally, contrary to the wishes of the Francoist supporters, the change of regime took the path of a rapid and smooth transition to full democracy (Maravall 1981; Cotarelo 1992). Neither the King nor the Army attempted to arrest or delay the process. The Army was largely restricted by its confidence in a conservative and traditionalist role for the King who, on the contrary, fuelled the democratization process (Aguero 1995: 127–30).

The successful '*ruptura pactada*'—the consensual breaking up of the old regime—left the nostalgic Francoists in despair. The absence of any radicalization in the years of the transition meant that the possibility of explicit and tough confrontation was in reality quite remote. The mood in civil society was totally opposed to any attempt at radicalizing the political conflict, given the risk of reviving the civil war strife. That spectre was too appalling to run even the minor risk of being caught up in that particular spiral again (Linz and Montero 1986; Morlino and Montero 1995). In addition, Spanish society had been changing quite rapidly in the late 1960s and early 1970s towards modernization in the economy and in the areas of social relations, customs, and traditions. The process of secularization, in particular, had weakened the attractiveness of Catholic traditionalism. The heirs of Franco could no longer avail themselves of the ideological strongholds of the old regime. Hence the traditional themes of socio-economic corporatism, economic conservatism, isolationism, exaltation of the *hispanidad*, and religious tradition, plus the revival of the evils of the civil war, could in no way be invoked by the extreme right to play a role. And, furthermore, the traditional institutions which should have been more in line with Francoism— Army, King, and Church—were, for one reason or another, outside their reach (Rodríguez 1991, 1994; Casals 1998*a,b*, 2001).

For all these reasons, the first elections of 1977 found the nostalgic Francoists organizationally unprepared and politically displaced. The most relevant movements that contested the 1977 election reflected the different streams of the Franco regime: the Falange Espanola de la JONS (Spanish Phalanx of the Committees for National Syndacalist Offence), the Falange Espanola de la JONS autentica (i.e. the non-Francoist branch of the historical Phalanx), the Frente National Espanol (Spanish National Front), and Fuerza Nueva (New Force). Collectively they did not gather 1.0 per cent of the votes. This debacle, in addition to the above mentioned reasons, reflected also the impossibility of gathering in a single list the different traditions of the former Francoist supporters during the regime.

The party that has best represented the extreme right in democratic Spain is Fuerza Nueva. It was nurtured during Franco's regime. Its premises were already established in 1966 by a Franco's Minister, Blas Piñar, who took the opportunity offered by a religious meeting to gather together a group of 'renovators' (Rodríguez 1991: 266ff). Actually, this group, which named itself Fuerza Nueva after the magazine it edited, pointed to a *spiritual* renewal along the lines of Catholic traditionalism and against secularizing tendencies, rather than to socio-economic modernization. An extremely close involvement with religious fundamentalism remained a characteristic element of Fuerza Nueva, even in the post-1976 democratic regime, to the point where its leader, Blas Pinar, opposed the new constitution on the basis of 'a natural or revealed divine right' (Rodríguez 1991: 269).

Fuerza Nueva was founded as a genuine political party in 1976. In its first congress, held in December 1976, it overtly manifested its affective, ideological, and political ties with Franco's regime. The final declaration depicted the party as 'a vanguard of the Organic State and of the National Revolution' (Rodríguez 1994: 204). Well beyond its ambitions, Fuerza Nueva remained absolutely marginal in the electoral arena. The alliance with the Falange Espanola de la JONS (in 16 provinces) in the first election of 1977 under the name of Alianza Nacional 18 de Julio (National Alliance of the 18th July—the day of the 1936 coup led by Francisco Franco) was a fiasco: 0.35 per cent of the vote. Slightly better was the result of a renewed electoral coalition for the 1979 election where some nostalgic groups gathered in the Union nacional (National Union). In this venture the coalition got 2.1 per cent and the Fuerza Neuva leader Blas Piñar was elected (the first and only right wing extremist to enter the *Cortes*). This (relative) success allowed a certain organizational development, the creation of the somewhat paramilitary youth movement (Fuerza Joven) being the most important outcome, and more intense mobilization, especially in (frequently violent) street actions (Jabardo 1996; Casals 1998*b*).

Notwithstanding Piñar's election and the party's higher visibility, Fuerza Nueva could not avail itself of favourable assets. First, loyalty to the *Generalissimo* and to traditionalist Catholicism, the two main traits of the party, were not matched by widespread popular sentiment. Second, the attempt to represent a larger, nostalgic, and moderate constituency conflicted with the patently anti-system features of the party. Third, the very successful transition to democracy had dissipated fears of instability and tensions which could have revived nostalgia for the 'old order'. And finally, it had to face competition from another political party, Alianza Popular (AP) (Popular Alliance), also quite nostalgic, but which had nevertheless accepted the new democratic framework.

Beyond electoral competition, Fuerza Nueva pursued another strategy. Since it had failed to gain votes from the anti-system opposition it tried to activate the nostalgic sectors of the Army. Actually, it did not pursue this strategy to the ultimate end, since it was still in a marginal position at the time of Lieutenant Tejero's coup in February 1982. Moreover, Blas Piñar distanced himself from that action, attempting to present himself as a more responsible political figure; but in so doing, he lost the support of Fuerza Nueva's radical anti-system constituency (Casals 1998*a*). This position generated the disaster of the 1982 election (0.4%) and the subsequent dissolution of the party. Piñar left and founded a cultural institution (CESPE) in order to prepare for a political comeback. In fact, inspired by Le Pen's success in France, in 1987 he founded a new party, named Frente Nacional (National Front) (Casals 1998*b*: 60–1). Yet even this further attempt did not achieve any positive result. In the 1987 European elections it collected 0.6 per cent of the votes (Casals 2001) (Table 11.1).

In the mid-to-late 1980s, four main factors inhibited the development of any extreme right movement as well as the success of Piñar's Frente Nacional: the persistent and resolute opposition to the restoration of a nostalgic-authoritarian regime by the overwhelming majority of the electorate (Linz *et al.* 1981; Linz and Montero 1986; Mòran and Benedicto 1995); the appearance of flamboyant populist figures

TABLE 11.1. *Vote for the extreme right in Spain in parliamentary and European elections*

1977	0.8
1979	2.3
1982	0.7
1986	0.2
1987E	0.8
1989E	0.5
1989	0.1
1993	0.1
1994E	0.2
1996	0.1
1999E	0.2

Notes: All extreme right parties together, excluding José Ruiz Mateos party.

Source: Casals (2001).

such as José Ruiz Mateos and, later, Jesus Gil y Gil who attracted discontented voters (the former got 3.8% in the 1989 European election); the relative impact of the political *desencanto* and of the neo-conservative agenda; the competition provided by the quite rightist, albeit democratic, Alianza Popular.

Actually the AP, in the first decade of post-Francoism, was quite close to the extreme right. While its later development completely dispels any allegiance to the extreme right, the distinction was not so clear in the early years. The survey analyses by Montero (1986, 1987) and Lopez-Nieto (1988) provide in fact a rather different picture with respect to its later evolution. The AP was founded at the end of 1976 from a loosely connected federation of circles, groups, and notables led by former Franco ministers (Lopez-Nieto 1988, 1998). This group of 'liberal' Francoists had the self-declared intention of assuring a smooth and *continuista* transition and, consequently, aimed at occupying a centre-right position in the political arena. Their high expectations in the 1977 election were frustrated—they got 8.4 per cent, as opposed to around 50 per cent which they had anticipated—because the electorate had a perception quite different from the party's own self-image. Contrary to the aim of the leadership, 'AP was perceived as a party located in between the right and the extreme right, naturally aligned with the ideological references to Francoism, and therefore, of dubious democratic legitimacy' (Montero 1987: 10). The presence of well-known former—albeit 'liberal'—Francoist politicians in the AP national and local lists gave the party a 'reactionary and/or authoritarian connotation' (Montero 1987: 10). The survey data demonstrate quite clearly that in 1977/78 the AP was considered by 69 per cent of the electorate a 'Francoist' party and by 47 per cent a 'non-democratic' party (Montero 1987: 11). As the overwhelming majority of the AP voters expressed positive or very positive views about the former dictatorship, and half of them declared themselves ideologically linked to Francoism (Montero 1987: 12), it is not surprising that the party was located by the electorate at 7.9 point in a 1–10 left–right scale (Montero 1987: 32). In short, the party image in 1977 was basically a 'Francoist' one (Montero 1987: 29). This nostalgic characterization, notwithstanding the ideological and strategic revision fostered by the 1979 Third Congress and the consequent party personnel renewal, lasted for many years. In 1985, the AP was still perceived as an 'authoritarian' party by 65 per cent of the electorate rather than a 'democratic' party (21%) and *only half of its voters preferred a democratic system to an authoritarian one* (Montero 1987: 29).

All these data would qualify the AP as a 'traditional' extreme right party but, in reality, this is not the case. The self-declared intentions of the leadership to abandon any authoritarian legacy, especially after 1979, is the crucial element in excluding the AP from the extreme right. Even if its supporters were very nostalgic and even extremist, the party's official ideology did not follow the same path, rather the contrary. Since the party's self-portrayal can be considered far more important than the attitudes of its voters when evaluating party ideology in the light of a contradiction, then the former should prevail in assessing party identity. This is the main reason why the AP, unquestionably after 1979, should not be included in the extreme right family.

Having dispensed with the AP, the Spanish extreme right remains largely irrelevant. It neither found favourable conditions in the aftermath of the democratic transition nor after its settlement. In the first phase, the efficient, smooth, and consensual transition to democracy; the inability of the old political elites to enforce polarization by pursuing radical anti-system politics; the competition over the same constituency by a very conservative but semi-loyal party (AP) in the first years of the democratic regime; the lack of appeal of over-radical messages, highly reinforced by the failure of the February 1982 coup; the disproportional effects of the PR electoral system; all these elements inhibited the extreme right's development. Later on, further elements such as the persistent political depolarization and the relatively high level of system support (Morlino and Montero 1995), the emergence of populist figures who catalyzed physiological discontent, and, above all, the enduring nostalgic references of the right-extremist milieu themselves, confirmed the extreme right's irrelevance.

Even the newly born Democracia National (National Democracy), which partly embodies the intellectual elaboration of the *Nouvelle Droite* and which advocates a national identity against Maastricht and regional autonomy (seemingly without any xenophobic suggestions), has not attracted any support as such (0.04% in the 1999 European election). The very recent attention given to the immigration question could feasibly support the rise of an extremist force, but up until now the Spanish extreme right is still trapped by its inability to 'accommodate the right extremist "traditional" values with the "post-industrial" values, that is to say the legacy of Franco with the modernity of Le Pen' (Casals 1998*b*: 89).

GREECE

The evolution of Greek democracy displays some similarities to the Spanish experience, even if the 'outcome was more controlled because part of the state (the hierarchical military) overthrew the regime and transferred power immediately to a conservative but democratic leader' (Linz, Stepan, and Gunther 1995: 111). The establishment of the democratic regime after the fall of the colonels' regime (1967–74) carried on a profound renewal of some of the traditional features of the Greek political system. In particular it implied the disappearance of the traditional military interventionist attitude, the removal of the very conservative monarchy, and the detachment of a sizeable part of the traditional right from authoritarianism because of its non-involvement with the colonels' regime (Diamandouros 1986, 1998). The right-wing forces which managed the transition realized they had to break with any ties from the past. As the old, prestigious conservative leader Constantine Karamanlis, back from exile to lead the transition and then the first democratic prime minister, assessed, 'a new political climate that could . . . lead away from the mentality and the habits of the past' (quoted in Pappas 2001: 240) had to be introduced in the country. The consequent strategy enforced by Karamanlis' party, Nea Demokratia (ND) (New Democracy), was a move to the centre and a distancing not only from the vituperated colonels' regime but also from the quasi-authoritarian pre-colonels' regime (Pappas 1998). Given this strategy, which proved very successful as ND got an absolute majority at the first democratic election in 1974, the authoritarian constituency had no chance other than to appeal to the usual right-extremist and neo-fascist issues of the Communist threat and of the defence of tradition. Actually, this radicalization was not rewarded by the electorate.

Already in the first elections in November 1974, an extreme right formation was in contention, the Ethniki Demokratiki Enosis (National Democratic Union) (EDE). This party voiced demands for amnesty and rehabilitation of the military junta's members, playing on anti-Communist feelings. It collected 1.1 per cent of the votes and no seats. The fiasco led to the party's rapid dissolution. Its legacy was picked up by the Ethniki Paretoxi (EP) National Alignment which downplayed references to the authoritarian regime and adopted the classical inventory of pre-1967 Greek authoritarian conservatism (Dimitras 1992). This party profited from the leadership of a well-known personality, Stephanos Stephanopoulos, former prime minister in the early 1960s and long time arch-rival of Karamanlis. Due to its less aggressive profile it attracted more rightist supporters from the dominant conservative party 'dissatisfied with ND's reformist policies' (Pappas 2001: 242), and it scored 6.8 per cent of the vote winning 5 seats in 1977. ND was affected by this potential competitor on its right and shifted rightward (Sefariades 1986); in so doing it gained the allegiance of the EP's members of parliament provoking the collapse of that political force (Table 11.2).

TABLE 11.2. *Vote for the Greek extreme right in parliamentary and European elections*

1974	EDE	1.1
1977	EP	6.8
1981	KP	1.4
1981E	KP	2.0
	ENEK	0.9
1984E	EPEN	2.3
	KP	0.2
	ENEK	0.03
1985	EPEN	0.6
1989 June	EPEN	0.3
1989E	EPEN	1.2
	ENEK	0.2
1990	EPEN	0.1
1993	EK–EPEN	0.1
1994E	EPEN	0.8

List of abbreviations
EDE = Ethniki Demokratiki Enosis (National Democratic Union); EP = Ethniki Parataxis (National Alignment); KP = Komma Proodeftikon (Progressive Party); EPEN = Ethniki Politiki Enosis (National Political Union); ENEK = Enomeno Ethniko Kinema (United National Movement); EK = Ethniko Komma (National Party).

Source: Kapetanyannis (1995); Grunberg, Perrineau, and Ysmal (2000).

While the EDE and the EP were quite in tune with the pre-colonels authoritarian tradition, more truly right-extremist formations emerged in 1979: the Enomeno Ethniko Kinema (ENEK) (United National Movement), a national-socialist movement which did not last for long after having polled 0.9 per cent in the 1981 European elections; and the Komma Proodeftikon (KP) (Party of Progress) which had more success (Kapetanyannis 1995). In the 1981 European elections, the KP polled 2.0 per cent electing a representative to the Strasbourg assembly, while in the simultaneously held national election, it did not win any seats scoring only 1.4 per cent. Absence from the national parliament proved an impossible obstacle to overcome. Even the KP dissolved and the extreme right found a new interpreter in the Ethniki Politiki Enosis (EPEN) (National Political Union).

The party contested the 1984 European elections on the basis of the traditional nostalgic repertoire beginning with amnesty for junta leaders, and this produced a positive outcome—2.3 per cent and one MEP (Papadoupolos 1988). Thanks to this success the EPEN became 'the' representative of the Greek extreme right: its entry into the Euro-right group in the European Parliament, and the media exposure acquired by then, gave it political relevance. Nea Demokratia, a few years after the EP attack, now had to face a further potential competitor on its right and was again encouraged to radicalize its discourse to stop the EPEN rise (Sefariades 1986: 436).

But the EPEN performance at the 1984 European elections was to prove an isolated incident. The EPEN did not succeed in electing any further representatives to the Greek or European parliaments. It polled around 1 per cent of the vote in all the following elections until the final fiasco in the 1994 European elections (0.8%).

The extreme right however made other attempts in the 1990s with the emergence of parties such as the Ethniko Komma (EK) (National Party). This party, abandoning any neo-fascist or pro-colonel tendencies, pursued a populist appeal following the new right-extremist European parties. It combined anti-tax and direct 'people' democracy appeals with the growing nationalistic sentiment, especially directed against Macedonians and Turks (Dimitras 1992). The high level of xenophobia affecting Greek society is in fact primarily concerned with the populations on its borders rather than with third-world immigrants. However, not even with xenophobic sentiments being quite diffuse did the EK made a breakthrough, as it never obtained more than 1 per cent of the vote.

In conclusion, the reasons for the failure of the Greek extreme right could be summarized as: the unappealing nostalgic references to the authoritarian regime of the colonels (Morlino and Montero 1995), which was an integral component of almost all the numerous expressions of right extremism with the exception (partially) of the KP and of the EK; the lack of leadership, again with the exception of the KP; the very conservative positions of New Democracy, receptive to any change springing up on its right; the populist, charismatic figures of the major parties leaders; and the high barrier to entry into parliament despite a proportional electoral system (Diamandouros 1998).

PORTUGAL

The Portuguese case differs slightly from the other two. The transition to democracy (Maxwell 1995) has been in fact more traumatic and troublesome. The 'revolution of carnations' fostered by the Army captains against the right-authoritarian regime in April 1974 inaugurated a period of military rule with a strong left-extremist leaning. Even after the first parliamentary elections in 1975, the liberal-democratic institutions were not solidly established. There was mass mobilization promoted by the revolutionary military committee, the Movimento das Forças Armadas (Armed Force Movement), and by the very militant radical left-wing—including the pro-Moscow Communist party—in order to enforce a social revolution. The opposition by the two strongest political parties, the socialists and liberal-conservatives, and by the more moderate sectors of the Army, prevented anti-democratic development. The failure of General Antonio Spinola's leftist coup in November 1975 demonstrated the recovery of the pro-democratic forces. Therefore, from the end of 1975 a process of more peaceful and legal transition was implemented (Linz, Stepan, and Gunther 1995).

Within this context, nostalgics for the Salazar regime had few opportunities to play a role. In particular, the process of purging (the *saneamento*), which involved some 20,000 people by the end of 1975, deprived the nostalgic constituency of its backbone. Even if they were soon reintegrated after 1976 (Costa Pinto 1995*b*: 118), few of them moved back into party politics, building up instead a network of cultural and editorial activities which blossomed especially in the mid-late 1980s. The only openly nostalgic organization was founded in 1977 by a veteran of the colonial wars, the general Kaùlza de Arriaga, the Movimento Independete para a Reconstruçao Nacional (MIRN) (Independent Movement for National Reconstruction). Notwithstanding a certain moderation of tone and the alliance with the Partido da Democracia Crista (PDC) (Party of Christian Democracy), the result in the 1980 election was a modest 0.4 per cent. This failure was followed by the dissolution of the MIRN; and with it the end of any attempt to revive the old regime (Table 11.3).

The only party of the extreme right which has contested elections since 1976 (at the time of the first election in 1975 it was not yet legalized) is the PDC, a Catholic-traditionalist party hostile to the principles of liberty and equality on the basis of an anti-modern traditionalist approach. Up to the 1980s, it had never succeeded in gaining more than 1.0 per cent of the vote and it was no longer able to contest elections after the 1989 European election (Gallangher 1992).

No other movement, neither the ephemeral Força Nacional-Nova Monarquia (FN-NM) (National Force-New Monarchy), Portuguese forerunner of the French *Nouvelle Droite*, nor the most radical Movimiento de Acçao Nacional (MAN) (Movement of National Action) has succeeded in becoming politically effective.

Similarly to the Spanish and the Greek ND, a non-extremist right-wing party monopolized the most rightward members of electorate. The CDS has been considered 'the rightmost party of the Portuguese system' (Nogueira Pinto 1989: 204) of the 1980s. Its spatial location on the left–right continuum was in fact quite skewed toward the right extremeness, as 36 per cent of its supporters located themselves

TABLE 11.3. *Vote for the PDC*
in parliamentary and
European elections

1976	0.5
1979	1.1
1980*	0.4
1983	0.7
1985	0.7
1987	0.6
1987E	0.7
1989E	0.7

* Together with the MIRN.

Source: Costa Pinto (1995: 121); Grunberg, Perrineau, and Ysmal (2000).

in the two more extreme cases of the continuum (Bacalhau 1989: 253). The CDS gathered some notables and followers of the old regime and—together with the PPD/PDS—acted as an umbrella for the nostalgic constituency. But parties did not however indulge in compliance with the past and even if they opposed the 1976 constitution, they nonetheless declared their loyalty to it once it was approved (Magone 1999: 244). The flattery over the extreme right constituency by the CDS, plus the virtual absence of nostalgia for Salazar's regime and the limited diffusion of system discontent and anti-political sentiments (Linz, Stepan, and Gunther 1995: 108–9), deprived the Portuguese extreme right of any chance.

CONCLUSION

The late democratized Mediterranean countries are now devoid of any perceptible extreme right presence. The legacy of the authoritarian regimes have had a counter-effect on the development of nostalgic political organizations. The nostalgic con-stituencies were absorbed by the—fairly right-wing but *pro-system*—conservative parties in the initial phases of the new regimes. Moreover, the consensual process of transition avoided violent and traumatic purges (with the, rather limited, excep-tion of Portugal). The legitimacy rapidly gained by the democratic institutions and by political parties proved stable enough to encompass the wave of *desencanto* which affected the three countries, particularly in the mid-1990s when disaffection with the political system broke out; moreover, the entry into the European Union has provided a solid linkage with democratic institutions and practices.

More generally, the process of socio-economic modernization:

contributed to the gradual ascendancy—and in the case of Spain and Portugal, the eventual dominance—of a universe of values, attitudes, behavioural practices, and "cogn-itive maps" reflecting open-ended and positive-sum conceptions of the world and of social change. These conceptions, in turn, sustain a culture geared toward arrangements and solutions to social and political problems that are inclusionary rather than exclusionary; toward moderate and conciliatory politics and, more generally, toward the logic of dialogue and compromise in the daily practices, tactics and strategies of both individual and collective actors. (Diamandouros 1997: 8)

These cultural changes have removed the foundations of right-extremist values, and in particular have distanced the mass public from its traditional authoritarian and neo-fascist heritage. In addition, the extreme right failed to provide adequate organizational and political articulation for the populist anti-system protest which emerged during the mid-1980s. As a consequence, it was unsuccessful in attract-ing a sizeable audience in these recently democratized countries.

12

Extreme Right Parties: The By-product of a 'Silent Counter-revolution'?

The extreme right does not appear to be a temporary phenomenon. In the last two decades of the twentieth century it has increased in size quite dramatically with the creation of brand new parties, the sudden and steep rise of formerly minuscule and marginal organizations, and the radicalization of former 'moderate-conservative' parties. The electoral trend since the 1980s is quite clear (Table 12.1).

Taking the results of the elections which each party actually contested, and excluding the countries where the extreme right was irrelevant and fleeting, between the 1980–9 and the 1990–9, the extreme right parties went from 4.75 per cent of votes cast to 9.73 per cent, with a mean increase of +4.98 per cent (see Table 12.2). The most relevant increase took place in Austria where the FPÖ, which is now the strongest party of this political family, obtained a mean of 21.79 per cent in the 1990s. In second place comes Italy (if the Northern League is included) with 20.90 per cent. Then France, Belgium, Norway, Switzerland (and Italy without the League) range around 10 per cent. Sweden, Germany, and the Netherlands are lowest, no longer having any parliamentary representation.

The dispersion of extreme right parties all over Europe is one of the most striking features of the present 'wave' of right extremism, compared to its concentration in Italy and, partly, Germany in previous decades. In addition, the extreme parties have reached the threshold of governmental power. The first took place when the MSI/AN entered the short-lived Berlusconi government in 1994; the second by the FPÖ participation in the Schüssel government in February 2000. Moreover, the support of the Danish and Norwegian Progress Parties have, on several occasions, been accepted by the mainstream parties in national and local governments; and the French Front National managed to form coalitions (albeit with limited success) at a local level.

An 'extreme right' political family, defined along the ideological core of its components, clearly exists. But its identity is no longer provided by its allegiance to fascism, as was the case until the 1980s. This is the residual domain of a limited number of tiny parties. The overwhelming majority of the extreme right family members does not share, and even rejects quite strongly, any reference to fascism. Nevertheless, their ideological core, whilst not articulated or sophisticated, presents a series of elements that depicts a right extremist ideology or, better, 'mentality'.

Table 12.1. *Electoral results of the extreme right parties 1980–99*

	80	81	82	83	84	84E	85	86	87	88	89	89E	90	91	92	93	94	94E	95	96	97	98	99	99E
Austria																								
FPÖ				5.0				9.7					16.6				22.5		21.9	27.6E			26.9	23.4
Belgium																								
UDRT		2.7					1.1																	
FNb									0.1					1.0				2.9	2.3				1.5	1.5
VIB		1.1				1.3	1.4		1.9			4.1		6.6				7.8	7.8				9.9	9.4
Denmark																								
FRPd		8.9			3.6	3.5			4.8	9.0		5.3	6.4				6.4	2.9				2.4		0.7
DFP																						7.4		5.8
France																								
FN		0.2				11.1		9.8		9.6		11.8				12.7		10.6			15.3			5.7
MN																								3.3
Great Britain																								
NF				0.09											0.01						0.01			
BNP				0.05					0.01						0.02						0.12			1.0
Greece																								
EPEN		1.4				2.3							0.1											
KP		1.9E				0.2	0.6				0.3J	1.2						0.8						
ENEK		0.9E										0.2						0.1						
Italy																								
MSI/AN				6.8		6.5			5.9			5.5			5.4		13.5	12.5		15.7				10.3
LN												1.8			8.6		8.4	6.6		10.1				4.5
MS-FT																				0.9				1.6

Germany									
NPD	0.2	0.2	0.8	0.6				0.3	0.4
REP	0.1				7.1	2.1	3.9	1.8	1.7
DVU						1.6		1.2	
Netherlands									
CP + CP86	0.4		2.5	0.4	– 0.9		1.9		
CD	0.8	0.1		0.1	0.8		0.4 2.5	1.0	
Portugal									
PDC	0.4	0.7	0.7	0.6 0.7E	0.7			0.6	
Norway									
FRPn	4.5		3.7		13.0	6.3		15.3	
Spain									
FN and others	0.7	0.7		0.2 0.8E	0.1 0.5	0.1	0.2	0.1	0.2
Sweden									
NyD	0.2			6.7			1.2	0.2	

Table 12.2. *Electoral trend of extreme right parties by country (1980–99)*

	1980–89	1990–99	1980–99	Diff. 1980–99/1990–99
Austria	7.36	21.79	17.10	+14.61
Belgium	2.76	9.73	6.40	+6.97
Denmark	6.57	7.53	6.98	+0.96
France	6.53	13.60	9.36	+7.07
Germany	0.33	2.53	1.43	+2.20
Italy*	6.53	11.50	9.46	+5.15
The Netherlands	0.80	1.80	1.18	+1.00
Norway	7.06	10.80	8.56	+2.74
Switzerland	5.05	8.36	7.04	+3.31
Mean	4.75	9.73	7.50	+4.98

Notes: Included only those countries where an extreme right party gained a seat in a regional parliamentary or European elections more than once.
* Calculated excluding the Northern League; when the Northern League is included the mean is 20.90; in the decade 1990–99.

Further to any precise assessment of their ideological characteristics, these parties could be described generically as anti-system parties (Capoccia 2002) as they have all displayed a similar pattern of undermining system legitimacy (Minkenberg 1998*b*: 2). The repeated homage paid to the democratic rules by these parties should be carefully scrutinised as it usually has the scope to avoid stigmatization from other political actors and from the public at large, as democracy is almost universally accepted as 'ideal type' of regime. This attitude prevents the anti-system parties from being marginalized or even banned whilst allowing them to exploit the rules of the game to their own advantage, especially in the institutional arenas. Vladimir Ilijc Lenin skilfully demonstrated how to proceed down the institutional road by bearing in mind, and implementing, radically alternative goals. And others followed suit. At any rate, the anti-egalitarianism, anti-pluralism, and anti-parliamentarism which emerges from the parties' manifestos and their leaders' statements, either in their 'esoteric or exoteric' form (Eatwell 1992*b*, 1996*a*), is the lowest common denominator of the non-fascist extreme right parties.

The extreme right family consists of two types of party: the 'traditional' one, closely linked to the fascist tradition; and the newly emerged 'post-industrial' one which denies any overt reference to fascism, displaying instead a set of beliefs, values, and attitudes nurtured by novel issues and the needs of a post-industrial society. The first type is increasingly residual. The distancing of the AN from its fascist origins and the decline and even disappearance of the other parties, especially in the Mediterranean countries, leave only the NPD the MS-FT and the BNP to represent this tendency (with the DVU and VlB being on the margin). The second type comprises the vast majority of extreme right parties. What are the conditions for the latter type's development?

VALUE CHANGES IN WESTERN SOCIETIES: THE 'SILENT COUNTER-REVOLUTION'

The post-industrial development of Western societies enforced the decline of economic-related cleavages and the rise of non-material conflicts. This epochal change produced a new *value-based* axis of conflict centred on 'quality of life' issues rather than acquisitive ones. The youth revolution of the 1960s represented the first manifestation of a value system that emphasized self-affirmation, individualized lifestyles, democratic participation, equality, and informal interpersonal relationships. Its critical thrust was against 'fundamental aspects of modern life' (Brand 1990: 28) and set the basis for overcoming the standard belief in liberal-democracy and/or social democracy. However, *the same process of class and value de-alignment provoked by post-industrialism has produced different and even opposite concerns*. While on one side the post-material agenda and its political by-products—the left-libertarian and green parties—expressed the drive for *self-affirmation*, on the other, a different set of post-industrial outcomes such as the weakening of state—and national—authority in the domestic and international arena, the erosion of traditional social bonds, the perceived collapse of conventional moral standards and sexual mores, and the waning of an ordered, hierarchical, homogeneous, and safe society fuelled the need for *self-defence and self-reassurance*.

The above mentioned factor plus the decline in national identity via the supranational institutions' growing role and globalization, determined the spread of uncertainty and displacement, thus creating demands for identity and reassurance. These new demands reflected 'non-material' concerns, similarly to the demands arising from the left-libertarian agenda (Ignazi 1992, 1997*a,b*; Minkenberg 1992, 1998*a;* Betz 1993, 1994; Kitschelt 1995, 1997; Ivaldi 1998*b*). The need for being taken care of, being part of an aggregate, and being provided with an identity have fermented in Western countries for quite some time with no political interpretation. They had remained 'silent' because of a lack of interpreters, contrary to what happened on the left side. They have propelled a form of 'silent counter-revolution' in attitudes.

The rapid diffusion of the neo-conservative mood was the first sign of the existence of unaccounted demands for a different—rightward—value set. However, the ideological turn of the conventional 'moderate', centre-right parties towards neo-conservatism could not follow some of its premises to their ultimate end due to the risk of modifying their own ideological core. Even the neo-conservative agenda therefore did not, *and could not*, offer a fully satisfactory answer to the demands arising from that 'displaced' electoral constituency. Over and above the interplay between political supply and demand (highlighted particularly by Kitschelt (1995) and Veugelers (1999)), the conservatives could not push the new issues which had been brought to the political fore too far because of intrinsic political–ideological barriers. Newly established or revived parties could therefore respond better than traditional ones to original issues. Only more radical parties could fully voice sentiments which reflected the demands for identity (hence nationalism), for homogeneity (hence xenophobia), and for order, hierarchy, and strong leadership (hence authoritarianism). Finally, only non-established parties could attack the democratic representative systems by undermining their legitimacy, fully displaying all the populist rhetorical weapons (Mény and Surel 2000).

The process which led to the post-industrial society weakened the status of that section of the population (mainly self-employed and manual workers) affected by the process itself. In particular, the loss of social bonds and the feeling of distance and isolation vis-à-vis the institutions and representative mechanisms heightened sentiments of displacement and alienation and, potentially, of resentment (Betz 1993). These sentiments were transferred politically into the issues of tough law and order, national identity and pride, traditional moral standards, and state enforcement, all of which reflect the need for recasting a symbolic belonging: in other words, an identity for self-defence against the outer, threatening world. These strains—rather than articulated demands—were not represented until the traditional cleavages had partly lost their relevance in favour of a 'new axis of conflict', and until a new ideological discourse (neo-conservatism) had surfaced to voice them.

According to a recent empirical test, 'the new right is more responsive to contemporary politics than to the past. The data confirms the hypothesis of a "silent counter-revolution" and not of a resurgence of the older nostalgic fascist tradition. The electoral performances of left-libertarian and contemporary right-wing extremist parties have a lot more to do with one another. . . . Contemporary right-wing extremism and left-libertarianism go together and both appear to be the outgrowth of the current post-industrial circumstances in Western Europe' (Weinberg, Eubank, and Wilcox 1995: 8).

In short, the same process which fostered the leftward post-material value set mobilized the rightward 'non-material' value set (Kaymak and Mayer 1995: 25). Where the crisis of conventional moral standards, to take one issue, was greeted as liberation by the leftward offspring of post-industrialism, the same issue was viewed as a highly regrettable, negative occurrence by its right-wing counterpart.

The underground change in value priority, which we have labelled a 'silent counter-revolution', found its effective and authentic interpreters only when new political entrepreneurs in tune with these non-material rightward demands emerged by exploiting a favourable structure of opportunities (Veugelers 1999, 2000). The conditions that allowed the 'silent counter-revolution' to be transferred into the political/partisan arena matured around Europe more or less during the same period, with the exception of the Scandinavian countries. They comprise a long set of interwoven factors such as:

- radicalization of the political discourse;
- party system polarization;

- the breakthrough and politicization of new issues;
- the inability of traditional parties to respond to the new issues;
- the low institutional thresholds for entry into the representative arenas (especially the national one);
- the growing crisis of system legitimacy/confidence;
- the growing dissatisfaction towards corporatist state management and clientelistic practices (including political corruption).

The above-mentioned cultural, societal, and political conditions represent one side of the coin. The other one is provided by the existence of 'partisan' conditions in the extreme right domain to meet the demands (as acutely underlined by Veugelers 1999: 47ff). In order for an unaccounted constituency to be represented in the political arena, a set of minimal conditions has to be present: the existence or building up of organizational and symbolic networks to embed the potential electoral constituency by providing it with a strong sense of belonging; an appealing, charismatic, and uncontested leadership which could prevent and control internal factionalism and attract the attention of the media; a strategic flexibility in order to exploit whatever favourable circumstances might arise. All the successful parties of the extreme right have displayed these characteristics. The strong and creditable leadership, coupled with the highest adaptability to strategic needs, are the partisan tools for the success of Le Pen's FN and Haider's FPÖ, or Bossi's League and Dewinter's VlB, or Glistrup's FRPd and Hagen's FRPn.

In the summing up of our interpretative schema, the chain of reasoning is as follows. Post-industrial development enforced a change in value priority and belief systems and loosened the linkages between organized interests and political parties. This development had a two step impact on party systems. The first produced a radicalization of political discourse and a polarization of the party system, while the second produced a partisan/electoral de-alignment: such radicalization and polarization enlarged the political space and created room for new and more radical right-wing parties; de-alignment contributed to creating an unbounded and novel electoral constituency open to new electoral/partisan offers. These two processes, the former at the individual level, the latter at the systemic, set the conditions for a party breakthrough into the system. Where radicalization and polarization increased due to a move to the right of the mainstream societal mood—the neo-conservative moment—new right-wing parties were able to emerge. The radicalization was not only a consequence of the diffusion of the neo-conservative agenda, but was due also to the eruption and politicization of new issues such as immigration, national identity, and security, initially brought into the political arena by the traditional conservative parties. However, these latter parties did not provide satisfactory answers for that electoral constituency, which, while limited in its size, was particularly concerned by such issues. At least in Great Britain, France, and Germany—with different time spans—these issues were at first dealt with, somewhat superficially and instrumentally, by the mainstream conservatives and then abandoned whenever they regained power (see Shain 1988; Layton-Henry 1992; Trandhardt 1995; Perrineau 1997; Minkenberg 1998a; Eatwell 1998b; Karapin 1999; Veugelers 2000). However, the 'legitimization' offered by these issues which had previously been excluded from mainstream political discourse, and their own (novel) salience, especially for a well-defined constituency, represented a splendid opportunity for more radical, right-extremist parties to come forth.

The conservative parties had played the role of '*apprentis sorcier*' by attempting to manage very sensitive and borderline issues. They did not realize that once the ethnic-based themes had entered the political arena with all their related issues of nationalism, egalitarianism, identity, and security, a process of radicalization was the inevitable consequence. And as almost all European countries were already experiencing a rightward turn in the 1980s (Klingemann 1995; Knutsen 1998)—according to some (Kim and Fording 2000) since the early-mid 1970s—the new rightist issues found fertile soil in which to grow. The point is that this move of the conservatives back and forth toward more radical stances in the late 1970s–early 1980s, and their subsequent return to more centre-located and moderate stances once they recaptured governmental positions, left the way open to more radical (right-wing) proposals, voiced by new or reframed political actors. In contrast to what is argued by some authors—Kitschelt (1995), for example (see *infra*)—what really counts is the oscillation by the conservative parties, first radicalizing then de-radicalizing, rather than the de-radicalizing movement alone.

The societal post-industrial transformation fostered a loosening of traditional linkages, higher electoral volatility, and new value-sets, partly leftward and partly rightward. This process produced a change in party systems towards (rightward) ideological radicalization and system polarization, where new sensitive (right-wing) issues entered the political arena. Their mismanagement by the conservative parties favoured the entry into the system of new (right-wing) parties. The demand for representation by a constituency mobilized by a specific set of right-extremist values and issues was already there: the new extreme right parties shaped their offer to meet that demand.

The general framework of interpretation of the extreme right rise needs however a further element of explanation. The extreme right parties are in fact the by-product of another general trend: the mounting crisis of confidence in the democratic and representative institutions because of their inefficacy and inability to implement adequate policies, and because of being perceived as distant and uncaring towards ordinary citizens. All the comparative researches (see, in particular, Gabriel 1996; Fennema and Pollman 1998; Ivaldi 1998b; Knigge 1998; van der Brug, Fennema, and Tillie 2000; Gibson and Swenson 1999.) have demonstrated that beyond immigration there is an anti-establishment, anti-partisan, and even anti-system attitude which mobilizes citizens in favour of extreme right parties. And, in many cases, as it will be argued *infra*, it is the most powerful drive.

OVERVIEW OF THE FACTORS FOR SUCCESS

Within this general framework of affirmation and consolidation, of the extreme right parties, some factors have played a greater role than others in the various countries. In this section the 'breakthrough-factors' are dealt with, in order to assess their country-specific presence and relevance.

Institutional Setting

As with every new/minor party, extreme right parties need low institutional/electoral thresholds to enter the political arena. The thresholds are low when the electoral system is proportional, the requirements to participate (financial deposits, signatures, etc.) are minimal, and when the first electoral contest is run in a 'second order election'. These factors were all present for seven cases (FN, FNb, VlB, REP, CP/CP'86, CD, EPEN) and partially for three more (MSI, FPÖ, FRPn).

Institutional factors played a very important role in the rise of the French Front National. The FN made its first 'public' appearance in a by-election in 1983 (run in one of the very few party strongholds). Secondly, it made an impressive breakthrough in the *European* election of 1984 (from 0.2 to 11.1 per cent) held with a proportional system. Thirdly, it profited from the change in the electoral system in the subsequent parliamentary election of 1986, exceptionally held with a PR system, which allowed the FN to enter Parliament and, consequently, to somewhat institutionalize itself.

A similar set of second-order elections characterized the German Republikaner rise. They broke into the national German political scene in 1989, first in a regional election (Berlin) and then at the subsequent European election. However, this success was anticipated by their far from negligible score in the *Land* election of Bavaria in 1986 (3.0%). The same pattern involves the other German right extremist parties: in short, local elections have always provided an opportunity to keep them alive thanks to some good, although sporadic, results.

The Dutch right extremist CD made a comeback in the early 1990s in the local elections of 1990/91 and of 1994: those performances propelled the party to its best ever success in the 1994 parliamentary election.

The Belgian Vlaams Blok exploited the European election of 1989 to acquire the status of a relevant party, and later on its performance in the local election in Antwerp consolidated its position.

Even three minor parties such as the Belgian FNb, the Dutch CP, and the short-lived Greek EPEN experienced their moment of glory in European elections, of 1984 for the latter two and 1994 for the former, where they unexpectedly had an MEP elected.

The three more established parties—MSI, FRPn, and FPÖ—also fit the same pattern to a certain degree. In the case of the MSI, the local election of 1993 set the conditions for its success in the general election the year after. The same goes for the recent recovery of the Norwegian Progress party, which performed quite well in the local election of 1995 prior to its best ever result in the parliamentary election of 1997. Finally, Haider's FPÖ could follow the post-1986 radicalizing pattern thanks to the immediate, very positive outcome in the election in the *Land* of Carinthia, where the party took charge of the local government (chaired by Haider himself) for the first time in post-war Austria. With the relevant exception of the Danish FRPd, almost all the successful extreme right parties have profited from favourable institutional/electoral settings. The *a contrario* evidence is provided by the British NF and BNP which, amongst other, crucial, weaknesses, were certainly penalized by the majority electoral system and the jugulatory requirements for contesting. Also Greece, Spain, and Germany have a high threshold of representation on account of their peculiar proportional systems. The four per cent barrier in Sweden had only been surmounted once. In Portugal, Finland, and Ireland no particular institutional handicaps exist, and therefore the failure of the extreme right parties can be said to be linked to other factors.

Both the institutional framework and the type and sequence of contested elections have played a role in the appearance and/or consolidation of extreme right parties. A less narrative and more formalized test of this hypothesis carried out by Jackman and Volpert (1996: esp. 515–6) reaches the same conclusion: a low electoral threshold, in a multiparty system, positively affects the extreme right parties' performance.

De-alignment

The account of the societal evolution towards post-industrialism highlighted in the previous paragraph should be accompanied by an analysis of the *political* effects of such a transformation. In other terms, we should focus upon the process of de-alignment implied by structural societal change. The hypothesis is that an ongoing process of de-alignment, in terms of higher voter volatility and decline of previous party identification and party loyalty, should have created a propitious context—that is, availability of non-identified voters—for the development of new parties including therefore the extreme right parties (especially where the de-alignment affected social bonds).

According to Gallagher *et al.* (1995), the mean volatility in West European countries decreased in the 1980s compared to the 1970s: 8.0 against 8.2. However, this mean reflects only part of the reality. In fact, there are only four countries which show a decrease in volatility in the 1980s (Denmark, the Netherlands, Norway, and Great Britain), while seven countries display an increase and one remains constant. Three out of the four countries which exhibit a decrease in volatility (excluding therefore Great Britain) experienced a high level of party system fragmentation in the 1970s; and two of them (Denmark and Norway) saw the (earlier) birth of an extreme right wing party in that decade. Therefore, the relationship between increasing volatility and the ascendancy of an extreme right party appears confirmed—the only exception being the Netherlands. This relationship has strengthened in the 1990s: almost all the countries have experienced higher volatility with a consequent increase in right extremist scores. In short, electoral de-alignment appears to be conducive to the development of political formations on the extreme right side as well. Moreover, the country by country analysis discussed in the previous chapters leads us to assess that the extreme right breakthrough occurs when volatility sharply increases. That was the case for the elections in Denmark and Norway in 1973, the Netherlands in 1984 and 1994, France in 1984 and 86, Belgium and Sweden in 1991, and Italy in 1992 and 1994. Germany, on the other hand, is an exception in this respect.

A similar trend affects party identification and party recruitment. The data shows that the pattern of the eighties (Katz and Mair 1994; Mair 1997) has become a steep decline in the nineties. Falls in party membership have been recorded in all the established democracies (Mair and van Biezen 2001), the same being true in the case of the level and intensity of party identification (Dalton 1996; Norris 1999).

In conclusion, the electoral and partisan indicators of de-alignment highlight a pattern of higher availability of voters open to new political offers.

Ideological Radicalization, Party System Polarization, and the Politicization of New Issues

The party system could be described as a rather oligopolistic market where a few actors control their respective shares of consumers/voters. All parties occupy a precise location in the political space. In addition to controlling their 'own' electorate, they attempt to conquer some part of the bordering electorate by small programmatic shifts (Shepsle and Cohen 1990: 39–40). The only way to break into such market is to introduce a brand new product: in other terms, only if a party offers a new set of issues and images to the public can it strengthen its position in the party system. This Downsian approach leads us to test whether, in countries where new parties emerged, the established parties had previously moved along the left–right continuum, leaving 'open' some segment of that continuum. As long as voters feel they are underrepresented, a political entrepreneur might try to fill such a 'vacuum'. This is precisely the approach followed by Herbert Kitschelt when he states that '*[t]he convergence of SD [social democratic] and MC [moderate conservative] parties together with an extended period of government participation by the moderate conservatives thus creates the electoral opening for the authoritarian Right that induces voters to abandon their loyalty to established conservative parties*' (1995: 17). This hypothesis fits in with the spatial theory very neatly, namely the shift to the centre of the conservative parties may have left room for a new political actor on their right. If in fact this were the case, the moderate parties should have moved to the centre *before* the growth of the extreme right parties; and this 'prior' move should have produced a reduction of the polarization (the distance between the most rightist and leftist parties in the system). Did this actually happen at the moment of the extreme right parties' rise?

Our tentative answer states that the process had two distinct steps. First, *the 'mainstream right (moderate-conservative) parties' moved to the right before the extreme right parties rise* (generally speaking around the late 1970s and early 1980s) due to the influence of the neo-conservative mood (see Girvin 1988 for a comparative overview); and second, *only when the conservative parties regained a more centrist position did the extreme right parties ascend*. The test for this schema is provided by the 'timing' of radicalization and polarization—or policy competitiveness and ideological opposition, according to the Bartolini and Mair (1990) terminology—and the rise of the extreme right parties.

The distance between parties (see Hazan 1997: 43 for a detailed empirical account) or party families on the basis of their ideological programme profile, grew overall in the 1980s: 'the positive impact on the level of polarization is due to the centrifugal pattern exhibited largely by moderate parties' (Hazan 1997: 47). Analysing the party manifestos, the range between the most distant political families (communists and conservatives) grew in the 1980s, compared to the 1970s, from 2.30 to 2.86 (Klingemann 1995: 190). The larger gap between political families is attributable to the rightward move of the conservative parties rather than any leftward move of the socialists or communists. In fact, 'there was an average trend towards the right in the party systems in Western Europe from 1982 to 1993' (Knudsen 1998: 86). Each political family shifted to the right, and the conservatives' move was the largest of all political families (Kim and Fording 2000). In other terms, *the conservatives went right and their shift was momentous*.

This rightward move by the conservatives (Wilson 1997; Raniolo 2000) is inconsistent with a centre-ward and more moderate positioning argued by Kitschelt. Actually, the accepted wisdom is that whenever the conservative parties returned to government in the 1980s (in Great Britain in 1979, in Germany in 1982, in France in 1986, in The Netherlands in 1982), they de-radicalized their stances, especially on the salient issues of immigration, national identity, and security. But the crucial point is whether they actually radicalized their discourse *prior* to the extreme right parties entering the system.

The study on party manifestos by Bartolini and Mair (1990), while based on the economic divide only, confirms the pattern of an increasing distance *before* the extreme right parties' breakthrough. The radicalization in the 1965–75 decade, preceding the FRPd and FRPn rise in Denmark and Norway, was higher than in the following decade. In Belgium and France the 1976–85 decade was the most polarized period, occurring precisely before the VlB and FN took off. In four cases, our hypothesis of a previous radicalization is confirmed by Bartolini and Mair analysis. On the other hand, the data on Germany and Austria does not offer any real clue. The country-specific studies (see Minkenberg 1998*a*, 1999, 2000*a* for Germany; Luther 1998: 127–8 for Austria) do confirm, however, this radicalization trend before the rise of the Republikaner and the other extreme right parties in Germany, and before the transformation and success of Haider's FPÖ in Austria. Italy is a deviant case because, contrary to most European countries, neo-conservatism had no impact at all in Italy in the 1980s and, instead, radicalization declined in that decade (while polarization remained fairly constant over-time (Pappalardo 1996; Ignazi 1999)). The MSI/AN success is not linked to this schema.

The Bartolini and Mair (1990) study of party system radicalization is based on the parties' standings on economic issues; but the set of issues introduced in the political arena by neo-conservatism did not exclusively concern 'economic' or 'material' interests. On the contrary, national identity, moral traditionalism on sex and family roles, statecraftism, (as well as individual entrepreneuriality and anti-welfare stances) were the issues that had been introduced and 'legitimized' by the 'mainstream right parties' during their neo-conservative mood. Had these further issues been taken into account, the ideological radicalization would feasibly have been even higher.

The legitimization, though transient, offered by the mainstream right parties to a set of borderline 'non-material' issues on the neo-conservative agenda brought out the existence of an underrepresented constituency of voters who had been particularly concerned for quite some time by these unaddressed issues. The survey data offered by the French polling institutes, for example, demonstrates quite clearly that French people had been concerned for many years about these questions. Support for the death penalty, the feeling of insecurity, anti-immigrant sentiment, decline in national pride, and a gloomy perception of personal and systemic future were already there from the early 1970s (Ignazi 1989*b*: 71–2; Perrineau 1997: 156–79; Schweisguth 1998: 24, 31). One can argue therefore that the sudden breakthrough of the Front National is linked to the unresponsiveness of traditional political parties to issues particularly salient for a well-defined constituency. Even if French society has progressively moved away from the neo-conservative agenda and its more radical accents (Grunberg and Schweisguth 1997; Schweisguth 1998), nevertheless, when the FN ascended in the early 1980s, those attitudes were widespread and, above all, perceived as being of the utmost importance to this constituency. The sharpening of the discourse of the established *droite* in the early 1980s after becoming the opposition for the first time (Ysmal 1984; Taguieff 1985*a*,*b*), and the right-wing shift in the self-location of the mainstream conservative parties' cadres (Brechon, Derville, and Lecomte 1986: 131) and electorate, all document the high level of polarization just before the 1984 Front National breakthrough. Accordingly, 'the FN benefitted from a general rightward movement of the French electorate in the years of its take-off (1984–6)' (Veugelers 1997: 40).

In Germany, concern for the unresolved question of national unification and compliance with the past, along with the advocacy of traditional conservative (and also authoritarian) themes, had been a lasting feature in German society: again in 1980 the SINUS study revealed the presence of 5 million potential right extremists. The '*bürgerblock*' *and* the moderate strategy implemented by Konrad Adenauer in the fifties and later followed by his successors (Stöss 1991) was the key in keeping out right-extremists. When the CDU went into opposition in the 1970s, it moved rightward, increasing system radicalization and polarization (Klingemann and Volkens 1992: 199). The 'turn'—*Die Wende*—promised by Helmut Kohl prior to his party's comeback to power (and the consequent regaining of a centrist position) fostered a radicalizing right-wing discourse. The *Historikerstreit* and the politicization of the national question along *völkish* lines were by-products of a shift to the right by the mainstream party that proceded the rise of the extreme right (Minkenberg 1999: 14).

In Austria, the dynamic has been different, since no 'new' party emerged on the right extreme, while an established party (the FPÖ) moved to the extreme right itself. Therefore, the major Conservative Party (the ÖVP) did not move to the right under the neo-conservative wave. The polarizing dynamic was provided by the attack on the 'red-black' duopoly and consociational practices by the newcomers on the left (the Greens) and, above all, by the radicalized FPÖ. The political agenda since the mid-1980s has been filled with 'new and in part very divisive issues' so that 'the nature of the political discourse in the electoral and parliamentary arenas has again became much more polarized' (Luther 1998: 130; see also Müller and Jenny 2000). However, in this case the representation of long-unaccounted feelings of public dissatisfaction (concentrated on the *Proporz* and party penetration into society) was provided by a party already in existence, whose move to the right coincides therefore with higher system polarization. The FPÖ in fact moved within the left–right spectrum from 7.25 in 1985 to 8.27 in 1991 (Campbell 1992: 169) or from 7.1 in 1982 to 8.6 in 1993 (Knutsen 1998: 78).

In Belgium, the rightward turn of the Liberal party (of both linguistic wings) in the early 1980s (Pennings 1995: 11) is not strictly linked to the development of the extreme right, especially in Flanders. What is more important is the location occupied by the Volksunie, the competing regionalist party of the Vlaams Blok. Actually, the Volksunie moved to the right in the mid-1980s in an attempt to stop the VlB rise, but this strategy failed as the latter profited from the radicalization of the regional issue to introduce its xenophobic and authoritarian agenda (de Winter and Dumont 1999: 203).

In the Netherlands, the distance between parties greatly increased from the late 1960s, reaching a peak in the early 1980s, particularly because of the Liberal party's move towards the right (Tromp 1989: 96; Pennings 1995: 11). Actually the VVD had begun to voice some radical issues which enflamed the Dutch political discourse when it was in opposition (1981–2 and 1989–94). In the mid-1990s, precisely at the moment when the VVD made a comeback to power after a period in opposition, the Dutch extreme right obtained its best score, thanks especially to the politicization of the immigration issue (Tillie and Fennema 1998).

In Great Britain, on the other hand, the radicalization promoted by the Conservative party in the wake of the 1979 elections over the question of immigration and crime was quite effective in marginalizing the National Front. The famous Birmingham 'Barrier of Steel' speech by Margaret Thatcher in April 1979, among others, politicized the issues primarily dealt with by the NF (Layton-Henry 1992). This strategy succeeded, thanks also to the working of the institutional barrier (the single ballot majoritarian electoral system), whereby the National Front made an unprecedented but unsuccessful effort to acquire relevant status by contesting half of the seats in the 1979 election. However, as soon as the Tories got back into power, they immediately softened on the immigration issue (Karapin 1999).

A somewhat different trend appears to have been at work in Norway and Denmark. The introduction of a non-politicized issue such as income taxation by Glistrup and Lange in the early 1970s matched a long time present, albeit 'silent', dissatisfaction. Such an issue attacked the corporatist fabric of Denmark and Norway, breaking up a solid compromise between bourgeois and social democratic parties. The provocative Progress parties' manifestos brought new themes into the political arena which, unlike in other countries, the bourgeois parties had never dealt with. In fact, the Progress party profited from the dissatisfaction created by the bourgeois parties during previous governments. The centripetal strategy by the Labour and bourgeois parties in Norway (Miller and Listhaug 1990; Strøm and Leipart 1992: 105–6) and Denmark (Pedersen 1987; Gooskens 1993) produced a vacuum ready for a radical right-wing entrepreneur to fill. Actually, once the Progress parties had entered the parliamentary arena, a greater polarization occurred in both countries (Bille 1989: 52; Urwin 1997: 43). This pattern seems to have favoured the persistence of the Progress parties and their second take-off, especially in Norway since the mid-1990s. In Sweden, however, the same trend appears to have been at work: the turn to the right of the bourgeois coalition in the eighties (Knutsen 1998: 80; Arter 1999) might have paved the way for the flashing surge of the Ny Demokrati party.

Finally, in Italy's case, the pre-existing status of its polarized system, with an already present extreme right party, remained constant until the late 1980s–early 1990s, even if radicalization decreased considerably throughout the 1980s. The surge of the extreme right in the early-mid 1990s, including both the MSI/AN and the Northern League, *is totally unrelated* to the above-mentioned systemic dynamic; rather, it is related to the collapse of the previous party system which has 'liberated' an unprecedented amount of 'frozen' votes and rewarded the parties untouched by political corruption scandals.

In short, radicalization and polarization, together with the politicization of new, salient, and misconceived issues, seem to be at the heart of the dynamic that fostered the rise of extreme right parties. This occurred in France, Germany, the Netherlands, Belgium, Sweden, Austria, and with the exception of the conservative parties' radicalization, which occurred at a later time, in Denmark and Norway. Where radicalization and/or polarization decreased and no issue on the new right agenda was successfully politicized, such as in Italy, Spain, Portugal, Greece (Morlino and Montero 1995), and Great Britain, the 'old' extreme right parties declined to the point of disappearing or were forced to change in order to survive, as in the Italian case.

In a way, the above-mentioned systemic dynamic 'forced' political entrepreneurs to set up new, or radicalize pre-existing, parties offering a novel, radical agenda. Where this dynamic did not occur, the traditional neo-fascist parties were pushed either to marginality or radical renewal.

The Key to Success and Endurance: The System's Crisis of Confidence

A further syndrome of post-industrial societies which contribute to fully understand the rise of extreme right parties, as well as their consolidation, is the 'crisis of legitimacy' in Western societies.

The reason why we hypothesize a linkage between system confidence decline and extreme right performance is that the extreme right agenda is not limited to an exclusionist, nationalist, or xenophobic discourse. It also includes an opposition to the legitimizing bases of liberal-democratic systems, basically, individual freedom and individual representation through collective agencies (political parties), pluralism and managed conflict among individuals and groups, and equality of man (on the same vein see Backes 2001). The holistic and monistic political culture in which the extreme right parties are embedded produces hostility to immigrants, but this latter attitude is only the epiphenomenon of a more articulate set of beliefs. And it is precisely this set of beliefs that defines their anti-system political culture. Well beyond their official and programmatic declarations, which do not overtly stipulate any anti-democratic proposals, extreme right parties—with the partial exception of the Scandinavian Progress parties—display nonetheless an anti-system patterning. The case of the Republikaner, that modified its stance so as to satisfy the dictates of the Office for the Protection of the Constitution of the Ministry of the Interior, thus avoiding being banned, demonstrates that it would be quite naive to disregard the legal constrains in the 'appeasing' of official party manifestos.

Thus, if extreme right parties standing, it could be argued that their development is linked to a crisis of confidence in the democratic system itself: *when confidence declines, more opportunities spring up for these parties to prosper.*

The thesis of a crisis of legitimacy has circulated since the mid-1970s, when the Frankfurt School's criticism of capitalist and consumerist society and the pending fiscal crisis of the state merged together, putting on trial the essence and workings of the democratic system. Various research projects attempted to provide empirical grounding to that received wisdom. On the basis of extensive mass surveys, the level of citizen satisfaction for the democratic system has remained fairly constant over the post-war period as a whole. In fact, democracy per se, as an ideal political system, proved to be accepted by an overall majority across Western Europe (around 95%) (Fuchs, Guidorossi, and Svensson 1995: 349). However, satisfaction with *the workings of democracy* has a much lower percentage (57%), with high oscillation across time and country (Fuchs, Guidorossi, and Svensson 1995: 341). Also, the rating of political institutions presents a rather poor picture: 'less than half of the public in each nation expresses confidence in the national legislature, rating it eighth in the list of ten institutions' (Dalton 1996: 269). In short, while democracy as an ideal system, contrasted with authoritarianism or dictatorship, receives almost unanimous consent, the evaluation of political institutions and of system performance is more critical.

This overall, rather positive, picture darkens when attention is focussed upon the people located on the right-end side of the political continuum. In every country, with few exceptions (Denmark), those located at the extreme right are less supportive of democracy. The supporters and/or voters for extreme right parties are by far the most alienated vis-à-vis the democratic institutions and their functioning: *the constituency which feels alienated from the system is concentrated on the right pole and in extreme right parties.*

Between 1988 and 1994 extreme right supporters shared a strong anti-system attitude in Belgium, France, Germany, and Italy (Gabriel 1996: 354–5). The same is true for other countries (Fennema and Pollman 1998; Ivaldi 1998b. For single country assessment see Andersen and Bjorklund 1999: 209; Nielsen 1976: 149ff; Fuchs 1993: 262–3; Gooskens 1993: 17–18; Swyngedouw *et al.* 1999: 22; Ignazi 1996c; Brechon and Cautres 1998: 244–5; Luther 1999; Riedlesperger 1998; Stöss and Niedermayer 1998; Mayer 1999; Natale 1999; Stöss 1999; Tillie and Fennema 1999: 239). Given the over-representation of extreme right voters among those dissatisfied with the system, a relationship between decline in overall citizens' confidence and extreme right success could be envisaged.

The case of France illustrates the operation of such a relationship quite well. Confidence in the system and institutions (plus more general life-satisfaction) was at its lowest in 1984, precisely when the FN broke into the system (Mayer 1999: 213). In Germany, system support had declined before 1989, setting the conditions for Republikaner success. Unification then provided a sentiment of euphoria which depressed Republikaner support (Fuchs 1993). Not by chance the extreme right recovered when confidence fell again in 1992. And when the confidence trend went up again, it went into decline once again.

The same applies to Norway where confidence sharply declined in 1985–9 (Miller and Listahug 1993), in Austria after 1989 (Luther 1998), in Denmark in 1970, in Belgium throughout the 1990s and in, the Netherlands and Italy in the early 1990s.

A comparative and more formalized assessment of this relationship is provided by Pia Knigge's (1998) test on voting intentions for extreme right parties in Belgium, France, Italy, Denmark, Germany, and the Netherlands, and the public's dissatisfaction with the political regime in the ten years from 1984 to 1993. The empirical analysis yields evidence in support of *a positive and strong relationship between extreme right support and political dissatisfaction* (Knigge 1998: 271). This consideration is further validated by a twelve-country analysis which concludes that political dissatisfaction increases the likelihood of voting for extreme right parties. (Gibson and Swenson 1999.) In particular, as far as the 'master case' of France is concerned, Nonna Mayer, for example, has argued that 'the FN vote cannot be reduced to a racist or xenophobic vote, since it derives from a complex combination of motivations where criticism of the parties and the political system, has the same weight as the demand for the "national preference"' (Mayer 1999: 149).

Further to the evaluation of democracy's efficacy by the public at large it is appropriate to raise the question about attitudes concerning the 'linkage agents' of the democratic system, namely the political parties and politicians. Here the picture becomes quite gloomy. The 'increasing public scepticism of political elites appears to be a common development in many advanced industrial democracies' (Dalton 1996: 269). This anti-establishment mood is reinforced by a diffuse 'anti-party sentiment' (Poguntke and Scarrow 1996): 'there is a wide gap of confidence between the elites of the established parties and their electorate' (Deschouwer 1996: 276). This loss of trust affects the whole of Europe to varying degrees, (with the exception of the British Isles). In Germany, a new word has even been coined to express this sentiment—*Parteienverdrossenheit* (disaffection with party) (von Beyme 1996; Scarrow 1996: 309ff). In Belgium, the Netherlands, and Austria the consociational practices has come under attack, whilst in France the loss of confidence dates back to the early 1980s (see Mayer 1999; Cayrol 1994; Ignazi 1989). In Italy the absence of confidence in parties and politicians (and politics in general) represents an enduring element of national political culture (see Almond and Verba 1963 and, more recently, Morlino and Tarchi 1996).The emergence of extreme right parties in Scandinavia (1973 in Denmark and Norway, 1991 in Sweden) has been related to 'the fact that the electorate in those countries was influenced by feelings of distrust towards politicians' (Gooskens 1993: 17; see also Andersen and Bjorklund, 1999).

This creeping and widespread sentiment needed political entrepreneurs in order for it to be represented. Once more, as in the case of the new right agenda, the extreme right parties were, and are, better placed for expressing anti-party sentiment. Extreme right parties are anti-party because in their genetic code one finds the ideal of 'harmonious unity' and the fear of division: the national or local or ethnic community is to be preserved against any sort of division. Pluralism is extraneous to extreme right political culture. Unity, strength, harmony, nation, state, ethnos, Volk are recurring references. The individual never attains his own specificity: individual self-affirmation pertains to liberalism and therefore is totally alien to the political culture of extreme right parties. They seek a national or sub-national identity and cannot conceive of a community where people are not 'similar' to one another, because difference would entail division. And since division under the species of pluralism is the essence of liberal-democracy, their search for unity and identity leads them into conflict with the principles of the democratic system. This search does not emanate from 'fascist' inspiration: it is the by-product of a (widely shared) world-view where society must be an harmonious community. What otherwise is the rationale for xeno-phobic messages? No one supports biological racism any longer (with very few exceptions). The answer lies in the adherence to a monistic world-view, to anti-pluralism. And what therefore are the obvious targets of anti-pluralism? Political parties at the political level, and foreigners at the societal level.

The distrust vis-à-vis politicians and parties (both 'established' parties and the party per se) in fact permeates the political discourse of extreme right parties. Politicians and parties are the target of the populist messages of the extreme right. The French Front National leader, Jean-Marie Le Pen, used to address the four established French parties as the 'gang of four', emphasizing the extraneousness of the FN to that 'club'. The same goes for all the other leaders of extreme parties, from Haider to Dillen and Dewinter, from Bossi to Karlsson, from Glistrup and Kjaeresgaard to Lange and Hagen, from Ferret to Janmaat, from Almirante and the early Fini to Shönhuber and Frey. The attitudes of the various extreme right par-ties' voters are in tune with such feelings. As many as 58 per cent of FN voters, against a national mean of 36 per cent, think that politicians do not care for the average person (Perrineau 1997: 116–8). FPÖ voters pointed out that the most important motive for supporting Haider's party was precisely the extraneousness of the FPÖ to 'the other parties' scandals and privileges'. The Glistrup party 'tried to undermine the legitimacy of the regime of the old parties' (Bille 1989: 49) by voicing anti-political feelings, as did its Norwegian sister-party. In Belgium and the Netherlands, anti-party statements flowed from the party programmes of the Vlaams Blok and of the CD and CP/CP'86 (Witte 1991; Swyngedouw 1995; Mudde 1996*b*, 1998; Swyngedouw and Ivaldi 1999). In Italy, the AN and Lega voters are the most cynical (Cova 1999: 308–13), and the same goes for the German right extremists (Falter 1994: 119–25): in the general election of 1998, 56 per cent of the Republikaner vote was motivated to support the party by political dissatisfaction (Stöss and Niedermayer 1998).

The evidence *supra* outlined supports the relationship between diffusion of an anti-party sentiment and the growth of the extreme right.

THE EXTREME RIGHT AT THE TURN OF THE CENTURY:
PROLETARIZATION AND (UNEVEN) RADICALIZATION

The 1980s represent a watershed in the history of the post-war extreme right. Prior to then, the extreme right was represented basically by the Italian MSI, the only party which had gained parliamentary representation with sizeable percentages (around 5%) since 1948. Other parties had made some fleeting appearances, but neither won parliamentary seats at national level nor lasted for long. The German nationalist-nostalgic parties in the 1949 election and the Austrian VdU are partial exceptions. The Danish and the Norwegian Progress parties, on the other hand, made their breakthrough earlier than the others, in the mid-1970s, and might be considered forerunners of the extreme right (and, in the same period, the National Action and the Republicans in Switzerland might be viewed in the same way).

In the mid-1980s, the political landscape of the right wing changed. The French FN emerged from a 'decade of darkness and sarcasm', as Le Pen declared after the 1984 European elections, and became a relevant actor in the French party system. In a few years, newly born parties such as the Belgian FN and the German Republikaner, or pre-existing ones such as the Belgian Vlaams Blok, the Dutch CD, and, above all, the Austrian FPÖ, followed the French example. With national variations, they all represented hostility to the representative liberal-democratic institutions, both because of their malfunctioning and their intrinsic features. Consequently, the extreme right parties played upon advocacy of traditional and reframed right-extremist issues centred on ethnocentrism, authoritarianism, moral traditionalism, distrust towards the establishment, the traditional parties, and the politicians, and, albeit more implicitly, the representative democracy.

The ascendancy of the extreme right was linked to its capacity for mobilizing resources, in particular by gaining the support of citizens unsupportive of the system and alienated from politics, and by being attentive to non-politicized issues such as immigration, law and order enforcement, morality, and national identity. This allowed its political entrepreneurs to exploit a favourable structure of opportunities at the political level (system polarization and radicalization) and at the cultural level (the rise of a neo-conservative movement in the intellectual elite, with its impact on the masses' beliefs).

By the end of the twentieth century, except in Ireland, Great Britain, Sweden, Finland, and the Mediterranean countries, the extreme right have made inroads. Its strongholds, however, have definitely moved north. The transformation of the MSI/AN into something different, but predictably away from this political family, has reduced the relevance of the Italian parties (while a question mark still lies over the Lega Nord); and Spain, Portugal, and Greece remain absent from the extreme right landscape. Moreover, with the recent crisis of the French extreme right, even this remaining Mediterranean country is losing ground.

Austria's FPÖ now leads the group, followed by the Norwegian FRPn, the Vlaams Blok, the new Danish DFP: they represent the strongest expression of this political family by the turn of the century. All the other political formations (not considering the Swiss Democrats and the other Swiss right-extremists) survive. Some of them are active on a militant base (the German NPD or the British BNP), others attain partly notable performances in some 'second order' or local elections (the German DVU, and the Belgian FN, for example); others, such as the Dutch CD or the Swedish NyD, have almost dissolved.

At any rate, in the last twenty years neo-fascism has almost disappeared. With the exception of the BNP and the NPD, no other party could now be defined as a truly neo-fascist party. The diverging development of new 'post-industrial' parties and traditional neo-fascist parties is, in a sense, related to their different historical origins: the former are the offspring of the present—post-industrial—society, and they reflect demands and needs that diverge from those which nurtured the neo-fascist parties. The post-industrial extreme right parties are the by-product of a dissatisfaction for government policies on issues such as immigration and crime and, at a more profound level, of growing uneasiness in a plural, conflicting, multicultural, and globalizing society. They dream therefore of a monist, well-knit, and identity-providing (idealized) society.

In recent years, a twofold development can be identified. On the one hand, some parties (the Scandinavian Progress parties, the Italian AN, and, partly, the FPÖ) went down the path of 'moderation' and the search for an agreement with the conservative right. On the other, the majority of them have fostered a spiral of 'radicalization', leading to a sharper confrontation with the 'system' and offering themselves as the only and ultimate alternative 'for the sake of the country'. This divergent strategy has rewarded both groups and, at this time, it is difficult to assess which will prevail.

However, both the accommodating and confrontational parties share (the AN being a major exception) the same transformation in the socio-demographic profile of their supporters. The larger parties of the nineties—FN, FPÖ, VlB, Northern League, Progress parties, and their offspring—plus the German, Dutch, and British ones have all become 'workers parties'. In some cases, the quota of blue-collar and low-income people is even larger than in the socialist parties. The massive presence of working class people among the extreme right's electorate is the most novel aspect compared to the 1980s. The picture is completed by a young male over-representation (with the exception of the German Republikaner).

This socio-demographic profile reinforces the premise that extreme right parties are no longer the recipients of the protest votes from those moderate sectors (employees, professionals, middle-aged) radicalized by the dissatisfaction over the mainstream conservative parties and willing to 'send them a signal'. Instead, the present right-extremist voters represent a specific constituency mobilized by feelings of alienation towards the political system and of dissatisfaction towards the socio-economic dynamics of post-modernization and globalization, which they do not control and from which they feel excluded. This constituency is mainly composed of the weakest strata of the 'risk society'. Their feeling of powerlessness and marginality finds sympathy in the populist anti-establishment and anti-system appeals fostered by the extreme right parties.

The political-electoral development of this political family has improved during the last years of the twentieth century. The factors for its breakthrough in the 1980s have already been discussed. Its persistence and further development is basically related to the overall deepening of the 'crisis of confidence' in political institutions, including parties, politicians, and politics *tout court* (Dogan 1999; Norris 1999). Mistrust towards political institutions and their performance produces feelings of alienation and detachment, which leads either to the rejection of politics (abstensionism is the most direct manifestation) or to radical anti-system options, support for the extreme right being one of the outcomes. The latter is so attractive now because it displays the highest expression of extraneousness to the system and it offers 'a world apart' vis-à-vis the political mainstream. Even more appealing is the prospect of renewed integration in an ethnic-religiously homogeneous and holistic community—at national or subnational level—bound by strong and hierarchical social relationships within the boundaries of a *völkisch* community.

The post-industrial development of Western societies and their most recent supranational tendencies, both economically and politically, have displaced a growing constituency of people whose lack of confidence in the face of such development has been the reason for their embracing an anti-liberal (authoritarian), anti-pluralist (monistic), and anti-egalitarian (xenophobic) world-view. It is precisely this view that is offered by extreme right parties. Whether these parties will in effect de-emphasize their anti-systemness (as in the case of the Norwegian FRPn and the Italian AN) is the question for this century.

The attitude of mainstream parties is crucial to this outcome: until now it has been twofold either integrating—extreme right parties within the system, as in the case of Austria and Italy and, partly, of the Scandinavian countries, forcing them to fully accept the rules of the game; or keeping tight the '*cordon sanitarie*' of isolation, waiting for their collapse (as in the case of France, Germany, Belgium, and The Netherlands) or dramatic transformation along moderate lines.

Epilogue to the Paperback Edition

A quick glance at recent volumes of the major political science journals would give the impression that the most important political family in Europe, and also in the West, is the extreme right. The number of articles published thereon, and of panels organized, by the main political science association meetings surpasses all other party coverage. Not even the social-democratic parties benefit by such attention.

The abundance of information on the extreme right parties (Erp) invites an assessment of the literature and a proposal for some lines of research. This new *epilogue* to the paperback edition will focus on a certain number of questions that seem unanswered, or that have reached a debatable conclusion. Let us first briefly list the points which will be dealt with below.[1]

1. The first one—inevitably, and yet again—concerns the existence and boundaries of the 'political family' of the extreme right. Unfortunately many works on the radical/far/extreme right take for granted the existence of such a family without any account of its characteristics or specificity. This is even more astonishing since all these parties (actually, *their voters*) are frequently lumped together in the same database to be treated with powerful statistical tools. But the decision whether to include a party in the database or not inevitably affects the results. Therefore careful investigation and in-depth discussion as to the pertinence of a party to the extreme right political family should be a necessary starting point for any analysis. This is not an easy question, especially when one considers that Erp do not partake of a common supranational organization. They have no European-based network, no transnational federation, no EU parliamentary party group, and, *a fortiori*, no international (extra European) institutional linkages (Fieschi 2000). In sum, if Erp do not recognize themselves as members of the same family, the researcher should be quite attentive about loading those parties into the same basket.

   The only advance in recent times on this aspect comes with the proposal of a different paradigm—the introduction of the 'populist' category—rather than from any further more consistent criteria of classification. Many studies refer nowadays to radical or right-wing *populist* parties. In some works, this only implies a change of label for the Erp, though by climbing the 'ladder of abstraction', it does allow for the inclusion of further parties, as in the case of *Forza Italia*. In other works, instead, the reference to populism adds substance to the analysis. These works are enriched by details of the party configuration—style of leadership, for example—and by precise references to party discourse such

---

[1] In this new *epilogue* the Swiss case has not been considered, notwithstanding its importance, for homogenity with the main text.

as the direct appeal to the people bypassing representative democracy and the creation of an imaginary heartland; nostalgia for an idealized, harmonious past; and the creation of dichotomies for group identification and rejection (us/them. big business/small business, establishment/common man, natives/foreigners, etc.). After the seminal contributions by Taguieff (1984, 1985*a,b*), Taggart (1995, 1996), Betz (1993, 1994), and Pfhal-Traughber (1993, 1994), the recent studies by Mény and Surel (2000, 2002) have brilliantly outlined the populist presence, characteristics, and impact in present–day democracies. The populist category challenges that of the extreme right; but the latter is not yet devoid of all significance.

2. Another crucial question deals with the impact of the Erp on the political and party system. Since these parties have consolidated their presence in their respective party systems—the Scandinavian progress parties have already celebrated their thirtieth anniversary, and the MSI/AN, and FPÖ are long-sellers too—has their presence affected the system's political culture, level of polarization, and coalition behaviour? Is their presence a transient irritant for the political body, deemed to be absorbed by the moderate mainstream parties, or will they endure and entrench?

   Related to these questions are the inter-play between the moderate and the extreme right, and the internal (intra-party) and external (to the party system) impact of the Erp's access to the governmental area. All these issues have attracted some attention by scholars but more light still needs to be shed.

3. Quite surprisingly, the socio-demographic profile continues to draw researchers' attention. It might seem an old-fashioned topic since all major parties have diluted their '*classe guardée*', but in this context the question still holds a certain relevance. For three reasons. First, because the prevalence of blue collars, unemployed, and routine non-manual workers, rather than self-employed (the *petite bourgeoisie*), or white collars, or liberal professions, or managers, seems to add a novel socio-demographic profile to this political family. Second, because such a profile will reinforce the populist/anti-system character of these parties, since we know that anti-system sentiments are more widespread among the less privileged strata of society. Third, because such a low-income profile raises the problem of the relationship with other parties and the definition of their respective political space: in short, who will compete with the Erp for the support of the underprivileged constituency? Mainstream right-wing parties or leftist and socialist ones? No clear answer has yet been provided to these questions, and the Erp sociological profile—and its consequences—has itself not found unanimous consensus. In what follows we will try to provide our own interpretation.

4. One 'classical' topic in this domain concerns the motives for the Erp rise *and* endurance. The very large and rich production on the conditions for the Erp success has not yet produced any path-breaking innovative contributions. At the risk of being over-pretentious, my 1989 paper dealing with the causes behind the rise

of the French *Front National* gave quite an exhaustive inventory, later entirely or partially recapitulated by many others (without acknowledgement, in some cases). The inventory concerned institutional factors—such as proportional representation *and* the timing of *'sans-enjeu'*, or second order, elections—the process of radicalization and polarization in the party system especially by the mainstream right-wing parties, the politicization of new issues salient to a specific constituency and how they get wrapped in a new ideological frame, the crisis of confidence, plus the mass media coverage, and the presence of both an effective party organization and a high-profile, outspoken leader (Ignazi 1989). Nearly all these factors—to which, in my 1992 paper *'The Silent Counter-revolution'*, I later added the process of electoral and partisan de-alignment and the impact of post-industrialism, which were not taken into account in the earlier essay—are now present in any analysis of the emergent Erp.

More specifically, both supply and demand sides were already considered. The match between voter demand and Erp offer was already present in my analysis of the emerging *Front National*. The celebrated 'two-level analysis' advanced by Herbert Kitschelt (1995), whose work undoubtedly represents a remarkable piece of research, followed (while reframing) that track. Again, the most recent and authoritative single-author book on the topic, by Pippa Norris (2005), apart from a sophisticated empirical analysis and an in-depth discussion of the institutional constraints (pushed rather too far in its implications[2]), does not add any further element. Still worse, a recent paper (Rydgren 2005) announces nothing less than 'a new model' (*sic*) explaining the success of the Erp when, in reality, it repeats what had already been highlighted more than a decade earlier: as, for example, the distinction between old and new Erp, and the importance of the *Nouvelle Droite* in framing the Erp discourse.

In conclusion, one of the limits of the present literature on this point is the excessive emphasis on Erp voters, rather than either on Erp ideology, policies, strategies, and organizational resources, and on party system dynamics and the general ideological discourse.[3]

As for the endurance of the Erp, the field appears more promising and new hints and suggestions have been put forward, ranging from an application of the theory of spatial competition (e.g. Cole 2005) to the interplay between moderate and extreme parties (e.g. Bale 2003), from party organization and leadership resources (e.g. Coffé 2005; Luther 2003*b*, 2005) to its hegemony over the political discourse in the national polity (e.g. Minkenberg and Shain 2003; Betz 2004*a,b*).

---

[2] Elisabeth Carter (2002: 138) is right in assessing the lack of strict relationship between electoral rules and Erp performance: 'The share of the vote won by the right-wing extremist parties appears unrelated to the type of electoral system employed' (see also Carter 2004). But PR becomes is relevant for the party *breakthrough*. All the Erp had their first and foremost success at PR elections: CD, EPEN, FN made their first appearance on the national political stage at the 1984 European election; the same occurred for the Republikaner and the VlB at the 1989 European election and for the BNP at the 2004 European elections.

[3] The same Rydgren (2004), on the other hand, has carefully illustrated the relevance of the ideological framing of the extreme right discourse examining the case of the rise of the Danish Progress Party and of the Danish People's Party.

1. STILL AN EXTREME RIGHT?

Parties may be grouped into a political family according to various criteria. Mair and Mudde (1998) made a very useful summary of the state of the art, advocating a return to ideology as a way of grouping parties into a political family. Very few, however, have heeded their advice. The list of the properties which should characterize parties, and aggregate them in the same group, are rarely discussed at any length. The German tradition in the field has been particularly attentive to this point: the recent works by Backes and Jesse (2001), Minkenberg (1998, 2005*a,b*), and Stöss (1999), though dealing with a single country, provide clues to the definition and demarcation of the extreme right family. One of the most comprehensive efforts in this direction has been by Cas Mudde (2000) who proposed an elaborate set of properties by which to screen party ideology. This approach has been promisingly adopted in two different cases: in Italy (Tarchi 2003) and Israel (Pedahzur and Perlinger 2004). The added value of Mudde's work is not so much the identification and thorough discussion of the properties denoting the extreme right (nationalism, exclusionism, xenophobia, strong State, welfare chauvinism, traditional ethics, and revisionism) since these are not so different from those suggested by other researchers; rather, what is remarkable is his extensive testing of extremist properties, notably screening the 'internally-oriented party literature' (party papers, leaflets and other grey materials), rather than the 'externally-oriented party literature' (official party programmes) (Mudde 2000: 168). The focus on party propaganda beyond the official programme aims to highlight the extreme right parties' backstage or 'esoteric' face (Eatwell 1992a), which is crucial for any assessment of their 'disloyal, semi-loyal or loyal' (Linz 1978: 74ff) attitudes and behaviour. This procedure, which should be extended to every party for a better understanding, is crucial with 'extremist' parties, since it uncovers their deeply rooted—and probably disguised—attitudes and world views. The discarding of this aspect by many authors is quite puzzling, as is the suspicion of a non-objective use of this approach (see especially McGann and Kitschelt 2005: 154).

In the present book a three-fold passage has been suggested for assessing both the pertaining of a party to the 'extreme right family' and the internal differentiation of the family into two types. We should here distinguish the *logic* of the classification from the *typology* leading to the construction of two types of Erp (old/neo-fascist extreme right and new/post-material extreme right).

The *typology* question is nowadays deprived of much of its validity: the transformation of the major parties of the old/neo-fascist type—the Italian Msi—and the recent ideological revision of parties such as the BNP and the VlB have reduced membership of this type to fringe movements. Other typologies may better suit the variety of the extreme right family of the twenty-first century. For example, by combining ideology and socio-demographic structure, Kitschelt (1995) identified two types—new radical right and anti-statist populist—which nicely fit the present-day reality of the extreme right. With an ideological approach, starting from the 'basic tenets' of four streams of the right (liberal, nationalist, neo-conservative, and universalist), and speculating on Hannah Arendt's concept of 'ideological increase', Pourier (2001) underlined how the new right-wing parties implied an upgrading from one ideological configuration to another more intense one.

As for the *logic* of classification, this has been amply discussed in the field and often critically scrutinized. Many criticisms seem to originate from a misunderstanding (among the most recent McGann and Kitschelt 2005; Norris 2005; Betz 2004*a*). I will thus try to make myself clearer. The point of departure is, once more, the 'nominalistic' *querelle*: how to define the parties under consideration. Extreme right, radical right, far right, and right-wing populist are the most common labels. Note that the term 'fascism' has disappeared. Among those who are newcomers to this field of research this absence goes unnoticed; but for those who initiated their work almost 20 years ago, the absence of the term 'fascism' from the analyses of the extreme right signifies an important step in the recognition of the birth and establishment of a 'new' political family, which has very little, or even nothing, to share with the fascist tradition.

At the beginning of the nineties a path-breaking (if I may say so) ECPR workshop at Bochum, organized by Colette Ysmal and myself, brought together a group of scholars studying the extreme right. One important outcome of that workshop was the shared view that we were confronted by a new phenomenon and that the old categories deriving from the study of fascism were no longer applicable. Hence new criteria and frameworks of analysis were needed in order to understand the emerging phenomenon.

In particular, the 'master case' of the French Front National, and the attention it attracted from the political science community (think of the seminal *Le Front National à decouvert* (1989) edited by two prominent scholars in the field such as Pascal Perrineau and Nonna Mayer), plus the sudden 1989 emergence of the Republikaner in Germany and the resilience of the Progress Parties in Scandinavia, offered the cues for examining these parties as 'new' phenomena. After the discarding of the fascist or neo-fascist label—only applied to those residual cases that deserved it (the Italian MSI until the mid-1980s, the British NF, the Spanish Fuerza Nueva, the pre-1990s German NPD, and, with caution, the Belgian VlB)—the question of a novel, comprehensive label remained.

Paul Hainsworth, in his book significantly called *The Extreme Right in Europe and the USA*, published in 1992, eschewed the usefulness of the terms fascism or neo-fascism. In his *Introduction* (1992: 5) he clearly stated that 'these terms could be misleading and unhelpful' and that 'it would be erroneous and reductionist to stereotype the post-war extreme right as simply parodies of earlier fascist movements'. The term extreme right, however, did not get universal acceptance and was—and still is—challenged by labels such as far right (but only in the English-speaking world, since in the other languages this has no meaning), radical right, and, more recently, populist right. The 'battle of words' is not yet settled.

At any rate, this book has clearly opted for the term 'extreme right', even though it should be acknowledged that the rival term 'populist right' (comprising its variants: neo-populist right, radical-right populism, national populism, etc.) has many merits and might prove even more useful in the future. One of most frequent charges against the label 'extreme right' arises from a misunderstanding as to the *supposedly* inescapable relationship between extremism and violence: if a party is extreme, it is also *necessarily* violent (for a critique on this point see Mudde 2000: 179 and Backes 2001: 21ff). This interpretation has noble origins: Aristotle's degeneration of the pure form of government (democracy–demagogy, aristocracy–oligarchy, monarchy–tyranny); the loss of the *juste milieu* entails the degeneration of the original forms. The larger the move from the median position, the more aggressive and violent politics become. Fascism, in all its incarnations, used violence as a normal tool of political action, and post-war neo-fascism was alleged to be adopting the same violent means. The fact that fascism was considered right-extremist, meant that the extreme right was violent too: extremism and violence have been thus far strictly linked. But this overlapping/coincidence loses cogency when neo-fascism and extreme right are disentangled. Hence, two questions arise. First, what is and what do we mean by *extreme*? And second, what is and what do we mean by *extreme right*?

The best approximation to a clear-cut comprehensive definition comes from the German tradition, nicely summarized and reframed by Uwe Backes (2001), among others. Following this interpretation, extreme is 'something' (a party, an individual, an idea, an ideology, a policy, etc.) which amply distances itself from the centre, from the mainstream; and the connotation of 'right' is provided by the location in the political spectrum *and* by the attitudes, world views, beliefs, ideas which challenge the fundamental values, principles, and rules of the liberal-democratic thinking and regimes.

Given such a framework, how can we empirically assess the *extremeness* property and the (related) *right* property? In two ways.

First, by measuring the location in the political spectrum: as the extremeness is provided by the distance from the centre, the location in the Left–Right spectrum offers the best indicator for assessing individual and party positions. Once more: extremeness does not entail any 'violent' characteristics; it just shows that a party, for example, is located close to the end of the continuum (it goes without saying that the Left–Right divide remains highly useful and relevant, and Ch. 1 of this book offers some evidence on this point). Therefore, once we have established that a party occupies the rightmost position, it is entitled to be labelled an 'extreme right party'. But the location in the political spectrum is 'blind': it does not clarify the content(s) of that extremeness. A party could be located at the extreme but fully conforming to the rules, principles, and traditions of the regime. One case in point was the Italian Radical Party in the 1970s and the 1980s, whose location at the extreme left went together with a (radically) libertarian and non-violent agenda.

To avoid the blindness of the survey respondents' location in the Left–Right continuum, a second way should be pursued: the evaluation of the party's political discourse or 'ideology'. The party position in the political space, and its deviation from the mainstream, is therefore (much better) assessed by the party's 'ideological' output. Moving into the realm of political ideas, the most radical deviation from the political mean in present-day democracy consists in rejection of the principles of equality and of pluralism. When this aspect is ascertainable in the party's ideology, the party should be considered an *extreme right party*.

But the ideological features represent only one side of the anti-system property. The other side is represented by a relational element, which is how parties interact with each other and which entails assessing their respective distance and their mutual hostility. A party sent back to a corner, marginalized by all the others, and treated as a 'pariah' is clearly not considered a legitimate partner by mainstream politics. Such a party will pursue a policy of outbidding and of delegitimizing messages in order either to modify the mainstream parties' approach toward the party itself, or to shake and alter the system, typically through a polarizing dynamic.

In this sense, keeping in mind these two aspects as aptly emphasized by Capoccia (2002) in his reconsideration of Sartori's seminal conceptualization (1976), the parties analysed in this book actually did endanger—*at a certain phase of their life, at least*—the legitimacy of the system in which they operate by displaying an incompatible ideology and/or by undermining its logic and functioning. In order to cross the line and enter the 'space of acceptability' (Smith 1987), their political discourse and their distance from the neighbouring parties needs to change dramatically. This has been the case of Alleanza Nazionale and of the Norwegian Progress Party, but probably not as far as the Danish People's Party and the FPÖ are concerned (as argued by Heinisch (2003: 98); *contra* Luther (2000) and McGann and Kitschelt (2005)).

Instead, there is no doubt that the *Front National*, to take one case, pursues a delegimating action against the democratic representative government by denouncing its inability to consider the real needs of the people and by advocating radical change to overcome these defects. The *Front National* does not promote violent action neither does it advocate the elimination of political pluralism, but it denounces the danger and damage produced by pluralism and openness. On the one hand, it operates to delegitimate the system, and on the other it proposes a homogeneous and closed system. Whilst many—especially French—scholars share this interpretation, Minkenberg and Schain (2003: 169) by contrast consider that 'the FN is not anti-system as far as the *political* aspect of the values are concerned. Values such as equality and tolerance are not essential ingredients of the current political order in France'. These two authors tend to relativize values such as equality and tolerance that, in my view, are cornerstones of the liberal-democracy.

The entire FN ideological compound—as discussed below—runs counter to the foundations, not merely the working, of the system.

Apart from the specific case of the FN, Hans-Georg Betz (2003: 89, emphasis added) has underlined the distinction between rules of the game and values: '(t)he threat *is not that the radical right might undermine the democratic rules of the game*. Rather it stems from the fact that the radical right promotes values that are fundamentally opposed to the values that form the basis of post-war liberal democracies in Western Europe and elsewhere. The danger is that the growing appeal of radical right–wing policies and ideas will lead to a further erosion of openness, solidarity and historical sensitivity while encouraging prejudice, intolerance, self-righteousness and blatant egoism.' Actually, while we agree on the danger, we diverge on the effect of such danger. Since Betz does not see a direct attack on the rules of the game, he also underestimates the *indirect* effect of promoting 'radical right-wing policies and ideas' on the working and legitimacy itself of the system. In my view, on the contrary, the anti-system property of the extreme right party lies *precisely* in its undermining activity against the principles of the system. Betz himself, together with Johnson, seems to come close to my interpretation when he later writes that 'the radical right (. . .) still promotes an aggressive discourse *that directly aims at weakening and undermining the values and institutional arrangements and procedures central to liberal democracy* and replacing them with a fundamentally different system'—that is, an 'ethnocratic regime' (Betz and Johnson 2004: 312, emphasis added).

A further, widespread misunderstanding of the anti-system concept regards the acceptance of the rules of the game by the Erp. It is frequently argued that if a party stands for election it cannot be anti-system, and even more so if it enters government. These two criticisms do not hold. The first argument is challenged by the practice of revolutionary parties which 'exploited' the opportunities offered by the democratic systems to achieve their aims: some adjusted to the system like the socialists, others not, like the fascists and the bolsheviks. The second argument is similarly challenged by the participation of the communist parties in government immediately after World War II. Their anti-system connotation *at the time*, both in the West and in the East, is unquestionable. Therefore participation in government coalition is not an ultimate indicator of accommodation with the system, as the events in Central-East Europe in the late 1940s dramatically demonstrated. The heuristic validity of the concept of anti–system is not contradicted by these two arguments.

In short, all parties which are at the extreme edge of the political system and which display an anti-system pattern are anti-system: the fact that they declare they accept the democratic system and the rules of the game, while puzzling, is not enough to move them to another category. To ascertain their anti-systemness thus calls for careful evaluation of the party's ideology/political discourse/political culture and any reference it may have to a peculiar 'style of thought'. Unfortunately, an uneasiness with, or underrating of, the history of ideas pervades much of the literature on the extreme right. On the other hand, Minkenberg and Schain (2003: 162–3) offer a nice example of an appropriate framing of Erp ideology. They argue that, at the core of the radical right-wing political ideology,

'is a myth of homogeneous nation, a romantic and populist ultra-nationalism which is detected against the concept of liberal and pluralistic democracy and its underlying principles of individualism and universalism. The nationalistic myth is characterized by an idea of nation and national belonging by radicalizing ethnic, religious, cultural, and political criteria of inclusion/exclusion and to condense the idea of nation into an image of extreme collective homogeneity'.[4]

On the same track, Roger Griffin (2000: 174, emphasis added) has brilliantly summarized the Erp ideology, suggesting that

'their axiomatic rejection of multi-culturalism, their longing for 'purity', their nostalgia for a mythical world of racial homogeneity and clearly demarcated boundaries of cultural differentiation, their celebration of the ties of blood and history over reason and a common humanity, their rejection of ius soli for ius sanguinis, their solvent-like abuse of history, represent a reformist version of the same basic myth [represented by fascism]. *It is one which poses a more serious threat to liberal democracy than fascism because it is able to disguise itself*'.

These quotations are intended to make clear that the ideology behind the Erp is distinct from, and antithetical to, the pluralist, liberal-democratic mould of contemporary democracies, and such ideology is also *threatening*.

If one keeps in mind these suggestions, the ideological origin of the Erp policies becomes clearer. Let us take the case of the anti-immigration policy.

Such a policy does not *per se* qualify a party as an extreme right one. The question is, what world view does this policy come from? For example, in the case of the British Conservative party of the late 1970s, the famous Margaret Thatcher declaration of Britain 'swamped' by immigrants did not originate in a closed, authoritarian, xenophobic world view: it represented a tactical and demagogic move to steal the issue of immigration from the hands of the National Front and thus marginalize it. Instead, the NF, and later BNP, anti-immigration positions mirror the idea of a hierarchy of races and cultures, imbued with white suprematism. Their approach derives from an anti-egalitarian and anti-democratic tradition of thought, incompatible with the conservative tradition because the *conception of man* is radically different. This example stresses the need for a broader ideological framework in interpreting a party's political discourse; in particular, one should carefully ascertain the presence of non-liberal, non-pluralist and non-egalitarian traditions of thought.

Some works on contemporary right extremism argue that the Erp do not embrace an anti-democratic ideology. Unfortunately, in many cases this is the result of a superficial and naïve reading of those parties' positions. For example,

---

[4] On this point see also Minkenberg (2005a: 54).

very few speculate on the reasons why these extreme right parties are anti-immigrant: in other words, why do they want to limit/marginalize/send back/exclude immigrants? Because they want to defend a native constituency in the labour market in face of growing competition—from immigrants—over scanty resources (interest xenophobia)? Or because they 'play the racist card', stressing the differences among men or races—usually through the mediation of the *Nouvelle Droite* theorization of the '*droit à la différence*'—in order to defend the purity of the community from alien presences (identity xenophobia) (see Taguieff 1986*b*, 2004 and Wieworka 1993 for the general framework, and Gibson and Swenson 2005 for a recent empirical application of this distinction)? In short, does rejection of the 'other' stem from rational-economic considerations or from emotional-cultural ones? Pym Fortuyn in his tragic dandyism played more on the former argument rather than the latter (van Holsteyn and Irwin 2003). His exclusionary logic was not absolute or definite: given different conditions (more space and resources, to put it bluntly) there would have been no reason for not accepting alien presences. On the contrary, proper exclusionary thinking wants to ban from the community whoever presents different traits.

The building up of a close and harmonious community represents an underlying pattern common to all right-wing 'styles of thought' (Eatwell 1989). It was at the heart of Carl Schmitt's authoritative speculation which intellectually nurtured Nazism, as well as of Charles Maurras writings, advocating purification of French society from the '*métèques*' (Jews, anarchists, free-masons and socialists) which polluted the nation; while Giovanni Gentile, 'the' ideologue of Fascism, in turn emphasized the holistic role of the State: 'nothing out of the State, everything in the State'. Even though in many cases (but not all, as in the case of the French *Front National*) the leaders of the contemporary Erp are unconscious of the intellectual excogitations which inspire their ideas, nonetheless their agenda is imbued with an anti-liberal, anti–plural, and anti-egalitarian styles of thought. And even if a party rejects and denies any relationship with those traditions of thought, an attentive and trained eye will recognize where the sources of its discourse lie. The French *Nouvelle Droite* and its national variants offered attractive and articulated tools to frame a political discourse which was 'modern' and in tune with the democratic system, *and*, at the same time, anti-liberal and anti-egalitarian. The *droit à la différence* has in fact become the standard reference when arguing for rejection of foreign people. When the Erp invoke the expulsion of immigrants, this is not because they rate the immigrants 'inferior' but because there are 'different': thus, everybody to their own place. The party's programmes and the leaders' declarations by almost all the Erp use these rhetorical weapons so that they cannot be charged with overt, old-style biological racism; they are 'only' in line with 'differential racism'.

This example touches on a central issue of the Erp. It might seem enough to argue their irreconcilability with the democratic system. But there is more in their discourse. When they argue against the working of democracy, do they express that betrayed passion for real and authentic democracy which Meny and Surel (2000) referred to as the misconceived face of populism, or do they insist on delegitimating the basis of the representative democratic system in favour of a different, plebiscitarian-ethnocratic, one? When Le Pen declares that in France 'we live under a totalitarian yoke with a democratic mask' which 'even disguised in smooth and often anonymous way is notwithstanding terribly oppressive' and that the 'national way is the only solution against the socialist or free-market false solutions' (Le Pen 2005), is he only being hypercritical of the way democracy works, which is perfectly legitimate and does not display any anti-system predisposition? or is he demolishing the foundations of the democratic-representative pluralist system in favour of another one, under his own, pure, national yoke? This question, which might be replicated for all the Erp, has no clear-cut answer: some scholars claim that even if these arguments are 'dangerous and threatening', they do not lead to labelling these parties as anti-system; others, including myself, maintain a different answer.

Finally, anti-systemness carries a more articulated and multifaceted connotation rather than a mere anti-immigration stance. Most of the studies categorize the extreme right parties as anti-immigrant or, even more restrictively, anti-asylum seeker, reducing to one issue a complex of attitudes, beliefs and world views. This *reductio ad unum* is inadequate because these parties are not at all single-issue parties (see Mudde 2000; Eatwell 2003; Betz 2004*a*). Just as we cannot define the socialist parties as only 'welfarist' or the liberal ones as simply 'pro free-enterprise', though these issues are central to their discourse and agenda, in the same vein it is inappropriate to reduce the extreme right parties to their most publicized issue.

2. ERP SPATIAL AND IDEOLOGICAL LOCATION AND THEIR RELATIONSHIP WITH THE MAINSTREAM RIGHT PARTIES

Hard-line and accommodating Erp

Undoubtedly all the Erp are still located far to the right of any other party. An inventory of all the data on party location along the Left–Right continuum provides evidence *ad abundantiam*. Some exception to this comes from the Manifesto Research Project (MRP) where the coding of certain issues has produced bizarre results: see for example the rather central location of the Msi in the Italian political spectrum because of the 'social concerns' in its programme (Pelizzo 2003) or, more recently, of the *Vlaams Blok* too (Pennings and Keman 2003: 61). The experts and the mass public's location of parties, by contrast, is very consistent with an extreme location of all these parties (see Lubbers 2001: 29–31 for the experts, and Oscarsson 2005 for the mass public).

TABLE 1. *ERP Location on the Left (0)–Right (10) continuum (2000, 1993)*

Country	Party	2000	1993	2000/1993
A	FPÖ	8.50	8.48	+0.02
Bfl	VlB	9.30	9.71	−0.41
Bwl	FN	9.50	—	—
DK	DFP	8.65	—	—
DK	FRPd	8.73	9.03	−0.30
F	FN	9.50	10.00	−0.50
D	REP	8.70	9.22	−0.52
D	NPD	—	—	—
D	DVU	9.39	—	—
UK	BNP	9.48	—	—
I	LEGA	7.55	7.22	+0.33
I	AN	8.17	9.25	−1.08
I	MS–FT	9.66	—	—
NL	CD	8.97	9.44	−0.47
N	FRPn	8.14	9.09	−0.95

Source: 2000 data: see Lubbers (2001).
          1993 data: see Huber and Inglehart (1995).

Placing such data in their time series will allow us to check whether the Erp have shifted towards the centre or gone even further rightward, and whether the mainstream right-wing parties have moved to the right or not, in relation to any Erp shift or not. According to the most recent expert survey carried out in 2000 (Lubbers 2001), only two Erp had radicalized vis-à-vis the 1993 survey (Huber and Inglehart 1995)—FPÖ in Austria and, more consistently, the Lega in Italy—while all the others had deradicalized, sometimes dramatically (Table 1). The only puzzling datum concerns AN which, contrary to other evaluations (see below), has been considered as moving to the right.

If we then compare the movements of the mainstream parties in the two surveys, no clear trend appears. The ÖVP in Austria, the CVP in Belgium-Flandres, the Venstre in Denmark, Forza Italia—compared to the DC or even the PLI—in Italy, all went to the right, while the CSU in Germany and the RPR in France had only a slight rightward shift. The Liberals in Belgium-Wallonia, the Tories in Great Britain, the CDA and the VVD in the Netherlands, the Høyre in Norway shifted to the centre (Table 2). These data lead to the conclusion that, in countries where Erp were non-existent or fringe phenomena in the year 2000 (with the exception of Norway), the mainstream parties moved towards the centre; in all the other cases they moved towards the right, trying to occupy the political space conquered by the Erp and *possibly* steal their fire. It should be noticed that the most limited shift to the right by mainstream parties occurred in two countries with different conditions: in Germany where the electoral score of an Erp is marginal, and in France where, on the contrary, it is considerable. A plausible explanation might

TABLE 2. *Location in the left (0)-right (10) continuum of the mainstream and the extreme right parties (1993, 2000)*

Country	Party		2000		1993	
	Mainstream right	Extreme right	M-R	E-R	M-R	E-R
A	ÖVP	FPÖ	6.25	8.50	5.83	8.48
Bfl	CDA	VlB	5.78	9.30	5.56	9.71
Bfl	VLD	VlB	6.76	9.30	6.88[1]	9.71
Bw	PSC	FNb	5.66	9.50	5.23	–
Bw	PRL	FNb	6.61	9.50	6.99	–
DK	KF	DFP	7.20	8.65	–	–
DK	KF	FRPd	7.20	8.73	7.56	9.03
DK	V	DFP	7.70	8.65	–	–
DK	V	FRPd	7.70	8.73	7.29	9.03
F	UDF	FN	6.43	9.50	6.30	10.00
F	RPR	FN	7.50	9.50	7.64	10.00
D	CDU	REP	6.36	8.70	6.02	9.22
D	CSU	REP	7.13	8.70	7.00	9.22
UK	CON	BNP	7.07	9.48	7.46	—
I	FI	LEGA	6.65	7.55	–	–
I	FI	AN	6.65	8.17	–	–
I	DC	LEGA	–	–	5.92	7.22
I	PLI	AN/MSI	–	–	6.99	9.25
NL	VVD	CD	6.71	8.97	6.89	9.44
N	H	FRPn	7.41	8.14	7.78	9.06

Sources: 2000 data: see Lubbers (2001).
  1993 data: see Huber and Inglehart (1995).

Notes: [1]Estimates provided by Knutsen (1998: 90).

The table include those extreme right parties which where actually surveyed in the 1993 and 2000 surveys. As for Italy, the mainstream parties changed since the DC and PLI disappeared and FI emerged.

point to the presence of a tight *cordon sanitarie* which somehow exonerates the mainstream parties from following the Erp in their domain. (But other explanations might be fruitful too: for example, a shift to the right already experienced by mainstream parties in previous years, which inhibits any further shift in the same direction (see Minkenberg 2001).)

The move along the continuum, however, might be a blind indicator (not considering the MRG data), useful for comparative and statistical analysis but poor in terms of actual content (party policies, programmes, and discourse). Hence, both levels should be integrated: *measurement of the location in the political space and argumentative analysis of the party's strategy and ideology.*

On the latter point, accurate and comprehensive comparative analyses encompassing all the Erp are quite limited. To the best of my knowledge, Hans-George Betz, thanks to his unusual language skills, has provided the most encompassing account of party programmes and leaders' statements from original sources

(Betz 2004*a,b*; Betz and Johnson 2004). Beyond Betz's contribution, single country studies or limited comparisons offer the only material for investigating this point.

For the purpose of this analysis, the Erp could be divided into two groups according to their respective degree of proximity to the governmental area. In the first group are those Erp which are more distant from the mainstream parties and government. The second group is made up of those parties which have entered government or willingly supported it. The rationale for this division posits a linkage between exclusion and party attitude, behaviour and influence. The hypothesis says that the first group has maintained its anti-system profile and had no impact on the public sphere and the mainstream parties, while the second group has either accommodated to mainstream values *or* played a role in the political discourse and policy agenda.

In the first group we find the French FN, the Belgian VlB, and a series of rather marginal parties such as the British BNP, the Belgian FN, the Italian MS-FT and Alternativa Sociale (Social Alternative), and the three German parties REP, DVU, and NPD.

The most consistent is the Front National. Since its strategic change in 1990 at its VIII Congress, reinforced at the X Congress in 1997, it has decided to challenge all the established parties and to present itself as the sole alternative advocating a 'system alternative'. No alliance with the mainstream right has been kept up: the party opted for a confrontational attitude *à tous azimut*. The FN appeal is still deeply nationalistic, exalting the sense of belonging and unity of the French people in juxtaposition to foreigners and supranational powers (such as the EU). The famous slogan *Les français d'abord* (French first)—that travelled around all the other European Erp—sums up this position well. The defence of French interests implies the defence, above all, of the common people, and even more of those '*en bas*', the powerless and humble, yet honest and hardworking, caring for their families and their country but mistreated by the establishment. In sum, traditional values, nationalism, xenophobia, authoritarianism, and social concern, as against a market dominated by multi/supranational interests, continue to characterize the FN line (see the 2002 programme of the party (FN 2002), and Ysmal 2000). The party does not accommodate to the system. Its location in the French political space is still considerably detached from all other parties (Chiche *et al.* 2000, and for recent mapping see Laver, Benoit and Sauger, 2006: fig. 1 and 2).

Similarly, the Vlaams Blok has long maintained its very radical stance, lumping together, if not fusing, issues of national independence argued along ethnocentric and even racist lines, with an authoritarian agenda and a 'corporatist' socio-economic programme (Mudde 2000; Swyngendouw and Ivaldi 2001, De Winter 2005).The recent, forced transformation of the party into Vlaams Belang (Flemish Interest), due to the disbanding of the Vlaams Blok by a Belgian Court of Cassation ruling on November 2004 for infringement of the law against racism, has brought some changes in its political discourse too. The party statute and its declarations of principle had been somewhat amended on the eve of the Court decision to meet the expected requirements. Apparently the VlB went along with a 'slight softening of xenophobia' and adopted a 'neo-liberal economic model' tempered by 'reference to the principle of solidarity'(Erk 2005: 495). These transformations, however, have been explicitly soft-pedalled by party leader Filip Dewinter (still a prominent figure even though Frank Vanhecke is now president of the Vlaams Belang) since he declared in an interview that such changes did not affect the content but were merely tactical (Erk 2005: 498).

The other minor or even fringe 'pariah' parties—the British BNP, the Belgian FN, the Italian MS-FT and Alternativa Sociale (Social Alternative), and the three German REP, DVU, and NPD—all maintain their anti-system profile, though some have attempted a cosmetic change in style and language.

According to Zimmermann (2003: 245) the right-wing extremist parties in Germany have undergone an '(often tactical) moderation'. The Republikaner, in particular, have since the mid-1990s pursued a strategy of deradicalization, if only to avoid intervention by the Office for the Protection of the Constitution (Stöss 1999) A comparison between the first party manifesto of 1986 and that of 1994, prepared after a warning from the Office for the Protection of the Constitution, shows a clear moderation (Cole 2005). More recently, Republikaner local councillors offered their support to CDU and even SPD legislative initiatives (Minkenberg 2001: 7). These sporadic attempts, however, have neither rewarded the party, which reached the nadir of its electoral fortunes in the Bundestag elections of 2005, nor led to any dramatic modification of its agenda.

The NPD have followed a different path, keeping tightly to its radical stances at the cost of being banned. That risk was actually avoided when some *agents provocateurs* from the national security services were discovered to have infiltrated the party's rank and file. The party tried some embellishment of its Nazi hankerings, concentrating rather on nationalistic–ethnocentric and workerist–welfarist issues (Minkenberg 2005a: 68); but no significant change in its references, agenda, or strategy is perceptible. Its anti-system opposition is consistent with its partly imposed, partly self-imposed isolation.

In short, then, in the 2005 general elections the German Erp confirmed their status as a minority; although the Npd increased from 0.8 per cent to 1.6 per cent, the Republikaner remained stuck at 0.6 per cent. However, as Minkeberg underlines, the local outburst of consent, as for the NPD in the Land election in Saxony (9.2% of the votes) in 2004, and the persistence and militancy at the level of social movements and a subculture milieu (Minkenberg 2002), leave the door open to future developments.

In the Italian party system two fringe parties have emerged in recent years. One is the MS-FT, a splinter of AN. After the unaccountably positive results at the 1996 general elections, the MS-FT was torn apart by in-fighting and bickering which reduced it to fringe status, even though, again very surprisingly, it was able to send one MEP to Strasbourg at the 2004 European election (0.7%). Although the founder of the party, Pino Rauti, former secretary of the MSI in 1990–91, was expelled by his own party in 2004, the MS-FT keeps to its original ideological mould of 'left-wing fascism' (anti-capitalist, anti-American, European-nationalist, welfarist), while it has embraced a more radical attitude on the immigration issue (Tassinari 2001; Tarchi 2005: 46). For this peculiar blend of policies the MS-FT is sometimes bizarrely located to the left of AN (see for example Oscarsson 2005).

The other, very recent, newcomer to the Italian extreme right is Alternativa Sociale (Social Alternative). It was founded by Mussolini's grand-daughter, Alessandra Mussolini, in 2004 after her exit from AN because of 'outrageous [critical] comments on the nature of fascism' made by the party leader Gianfranco Fini. Alternativa Sociale collects a series of radical fringe groups. It merges neo-fascist, Evolian-traditionalist, third-wayist, and ethnocentrist stances, with some 'post-material' concerns, especially on women's rights, promoted by Alessandra Mussolini herself, and even on immigration (Tarchi 2005: 46–7). Alternativa Sociale won 1.6 per cent at the 2004 European elections and sent one MEP to Strasbourg but failed to get a single regional councillor elected at the regional elections in 2005 (the best result being 1.9% in Latium).

The BNP, after having been a bastion of the old/traditional extreme right along neo-Nazi lines and Evolian-traditionalist thinking, has been undergoing some shifts from its historic identity to the point of relaxing its demand for the repatriation of all immigrants. The positive performance at the polls in the 2004 European election (4.9%: the best ever result for the extreme right in Great Britain) and the expulsion/marginalization of some old figures such as Tyndall have reinforced this accommodating strategy. The outcome at the 2005 general elections, however, did not reward the party so much as it gained only 0.7 per cent of votes nationally (4.2% in the 119 constituencies where it fielded candidates).

All these parties, whether large—FN and VIB—or minor—MS-FT, AS, BNP, REP, DVU, NPD, FNb—have maintained their anti-system profile: they still keep themselves distant from the mainstream parties and, except for some superficial smoothening of language and style, as in the case of the VIB and the BNP, they exhibit either an anti-plural and anti-egalitarian ideology or a delegitimizing discourse. Their extreme location in the political space is consistent with their ideology. Both Italian extreme right parties, however, have recently been approached by Forza Italia in an attempt to build up an electoral agreement for the 2006 general elections.

The second group of parties to analyse are those that recently set foot in the sphere of acceptability. Erp have entered government in Italy (in 1994 and from 2001 to December 2005), in Austria (from 2000 to December 2005), in the Netherlands (actually for 87 days only in 2002), while in Switzerland the SVP has always formed part of the government. In Denmark (from 2001 to December 2005), and Norway (from 2001 to the November 2005 general elections), they backed the government without entering it. In another section we will examine the interrelationship between the Erp and the mainstream parties and their respective influence as far as agenda-setting and policy-setting are concerned. In this part, we will concentrate on signs of evolution of party ideology and discourse in connection with their entry into government.

The Netherlands is a special case due to the very recent formation (and probable dissolution) of the List Pim Fortuyn (LPF). The LPF entered government immediately after it was created. It is therefore impossible to assess any relationship between a move by the party on the Left–Right continuum and its entry into the government.

As for its ideology, apart from getting the label of 'populist' which attached to Pim Fortuyn (among others, see Pennings and Keman 2003: 63–4), on the basis of his writings and of LPF parliamentary activity, the party has been seen as characterized by a 'liberalism of fear with a militant and radical type of civic nationalism' (Akkerrman 2005: 351). In other words, the party presents a 'substantial overlap with liberal and nationalist principles' (ibidem: 350) because the kind of nationalism it advocates is not founded on ethnic homogeneity but rather on a civic basis: immigrants are targeted not so as to defend the purity of the Dutch nation but for their unwillingness to accept the principles of Dutch society. On the economic side, the party programme has combined tax-cuts and deregulation with income redistribution and opposition to privatization (Pellikaan, van der Meer, de Lange 2003: 41–2). But, as stated by van Holsteyn and Irwin (2003: 53), the key issue of the 2002 elections was not the economy but identity.

However, despite all the peculiarities of this 'flash party' and difficulty in classifying it, the mass public clearly located it at the extreme right of the Left–Right continuum: 8.56 points on the 0–10 point scale (van Holsteyn, Irwin and den Ridder 2003: 77ff). When it comes to the conservative—progressive scale, the LPF position changes according to the different issues: the voters are anti-immigrant and tough on law and order but also pro-euthanasia, anti-nuke and social-minded (ibidem: 82–4).

The death of Fortuyn and the meteoric fortune of the party, entrapped in a series of in-fights up to the clash between the parliamentary party and the party headquarters in the fall of 2004 and the ensuing appeal to the court for legal use of the brand name, further complicate the assessment of any clear pattern in party discourse. Lastly, no evidence of change could be gleaned from its 87 days of government participation.

In Italy, the AN entry to power in 2001 is apparently unrelated to any move along the Left–Right continuum: opinion poll data show that in 1999 (Oscarsson 2005) and 2001 (Ignazi 2005*a*) AN is still perceived at the right-most position. However, in terms of policy and ideology the party has unquestionably moved: the extent of this shift is widely discussed. The thorough investigation of party programmes by Tarchi (2003, 2005) leads to the conclusion that there has been a significant, while still patchy and faltering, step out of the reach of right-wing extremism (see also Ignazi 2004*a,b*, 2005*a*). Analysing the same party programmes, but through different lenses (those provided by the MRG scheme), Cole reached a similar conclusion: already by 1996 the MSI/AN had 'become more moderate over time' (Cole 2005: 221). In effect, even at first sight, the language and the references of the party documents—and also the 'back-stage' materials—highlight its distance from the other ERP. AN now perceives itself—and is perceived by the other Italian parties— as a mainstream right-wing party, fully legitimate as a governmental partner and more moderate than the Lega Nord and even Forza Italia in some circumstances (Ignazi 2005*b*). Only one example to support this assumption: in the Fall of 2003 the uncontested party leader, Fini, proposed extending the right to vote to legal immigrants in local elections: a blasphemy for any Erp party! Not even Hagen or Kjaersgaard have ever envisaged such a proposal. Moreover, an opinion poll carried out a few days after Fini's declaration showed that the party rank-and-file were also in tune with the leader (Ignazi 2004*a*)—as were the members *interviewed in 2001*, well before Fini's statement, on the right to vote for immigrants in local elections (see Ignazi and Bardi 2006).

AN's unquestionable deradicalization, initiated well before its 2001 entry into government, contrasts with the rather extreme location still attributed to the party. The puzzle might be attributed to the endurance of political images and perceptions which need time to change (see Laver, Benoit and Sauger 2006).

An even more problematic puzzle concerns the other Italian party often included in the extreme right, the Lega Nord. The Lega used to be assigned a centre-right location in the Left–Right continuum. However, contrary to what is stated in Ch.3, nowadays this party has reached the land of right-extremism. (Biorcio 2003, Ignazi 2004*b*) In the late 1990s, the Lega abandoned the federalist approach and a central positioning—as pointed out by its programme's spatial location in 1996 (Cole 2005: 220–1)—and embraced the strategy of secession of Padania (the regions around the Po valley) from Italy. This strategy has 'in itself' an anti-system connotation as it implies the break-up of the political community. Moreover, such a strategy entailed framing a novel 'Padanian' identity, the creation of a new motherland. The building up of this ethnic commonality entailed in turn an exclusionary logic, much harder than the previous approach, since the aliens were no longer Italian southerners but foreign immigrants. More specifically, the demonising propaganda on immigrants on the same track as other Erp, the prohibition against allowing Muslim immigrants a place of prayer in the cities governed by the Lega, the protest marches against immigrants (to the point of conducting pigs to a field where a mosque was supposed to be built near Milan), and the proposal to greet boats crowded with immigrants approaching Italian shores with gunfire are some examples of the Lega's xenophobic drive (Biorcio 2003). If one adds the conspiracy-theory world view, an anti-EU and anti-globalization position, an anti-establishment attitude, a populist argumentative style and the development of a paramilitary organization (the Green Shirts), the pieces of the puzzle design an extreme right party. In short, its presence in government since 2001 has not altered its stances.

As in the case of AN, so in the case of the Lega Nord the location on the political spectrum is not consistent with its profile since it is generally located rather close to the centre in spite of its extremist agenda. At present, and since the beginning of the 2000s, the position between the two parties has had to be reversed (a cursory reading of the respective party dailies, *La Padania* and *Il Secolo d'Italia*, would lead to the same conclusion).

In short, An has profited by its participation in government among other things to (continue to) deradicalize, while the Lega has not been affected by its participation and has kept—or even reinforced—its radical stances.

In Austria, the entry into government of the FPÖ was not related to any *previous* significant change either in its spatial location or in its ideology and policy. When it won the 1999 elections, the party was still totally steeped in its traditional anti-system political culture. Its location was even further to the right than in 1993. But as it moved on in government it had to review 'themes, tone, style and targets' (Luther 2003*a*: 201; see also Müller and Fallend 2004: 819). Actually, the policy of the new government 'd(id) not bear the mark of right-wing extremism' partly because the FPÖ longed for 'a growing willingness to send a signal of "respectability" and "moderation"' (Luther 2003*b*). Few FPÖ legislative initiatives had a radical tone. (Luther 2003*a*). However 'business as usual' (Müller and Jenny 2004) in the parliamentary arena was constantly endangered by Haider's free-riding incursions in the public arena. Even before his resignation from the government coalition committee in February 2002, Haider had embraced his old politics of 'attack not accommodation' (Luther 2003b: 197), criticizing the government and even his party fellows, and inflaming the political debate with his provocative declarations—such as the proposal of one year of imprisonment for the crime of 'national denigration' (Leconte 2005: 47)—and spectacular exploits—such as the visits to Saddam Hussein in 2002.The disintegration of the FPÖ before and after the 2002 elections plummeted it to the same level as 1986 at the European elections of 2004. With the abandoning of the more moderate and well-reputed former ministers Rita Riess-Passer and Karl-Heiz Grasser, the rump party has entirely recaptured its anti-system flavour. However, a further Haider comeback provoked further division in the party. This time Haider criticized the 'extremism' of the party but, much to his surprise, he did not convince either the leadership or the activists. He, therefore, left the FPÖ and founded a new party in April 2005, the Bundis Zukunnft Österreich (BZÖ) (Alliance for Renewal) (Luther 2005). Thus, the former FPÖ, while still in government, plays the role of the hardliner, whereas the BZÖ presents itself as a more moderate and responsible force. These events once more prove the devasting force of a charismatic leader such as Jörg Haider whose repeated irruptions into party life had finally led to divisions, splits, and then marginalization.

In Denmark, while the old Progress Party (FRPd) was definitely traumatized by the final come back of Mogens Glistrup which cost the party exclusion from Parliament in the 2001 general elections, the Danish People's Party (DFP) got its best electoral outcome with 12.0 per cent of the vote. Thanks to the rightward shift by the Danish party system in those elections, the DFP was officially involved in negotiations for the programme by the new Liberal-Conservative government which could since then count on constant and loyal DFP parliamentary support. Pia Kjaersgaard's party left aside its old anti-tax rhetoric (but not its anti-establishment tirades) and concentrated its politics on anti-immigration regulations and pro-welfare provisions (Bjørklund and Goul Andersen 2002). Adopting this two-fold line, on the one hand it reconciled itself with the basic principles and tradition of the Danish welfare state (abandoning thus far that anti-system trait), but, on the other, it reinforced its ethnopluralist approach. Even if the DFP is one of those Erp that have been seen as moving towards the centre of the political spectrum, it has maintained a hard line on immigration (Rydgren 2004)—though combined with a pro-welfare position.

In Norway, since the general election of 2001 and the formation of a minority bourgeois government, the Progress Party has lost its status as a pariah party. First, its electoral performance put the FRPn in third position in the Norwegian party system, and then, it obtained recognition as a reliable coalition partner by the government since it negotiated its support in Parliament with the moderate parties. On the other hand, the party 'owned' two salient issues: immigration and welfare provision, especially care of the elderly. The first issue had lost its relevance in the 2001 electoral campaign and only four per cent of the electorate—compared to 20 per cent in 1997—rated it very important. However, after 9/11 (the elections were held on September 10!) the issue came back with a vengeance and the party successfully drove the government to adopt restrictive regulations on the matter. At the same time, precisely to avoid any stigmatization or charges of racism and lack of 'human value', the 2001 party programme acknowledged 'respect for the individual character of every human being' and condemned 'different treatment of human beings based upon their race, gender, religion or ethnic origin' (quoted in Heidar 2002). On the economic side, the party has since played down the issue of tax reduction, emphasizing the need to increase welfare policies, while maintaining its traditional approach of welfare chauvinism: more welfare spending, but only for the natives. This welfarist tendency, in line with its enlarging proletarian constituency, goes hand in hand with the demand for tax cuts. In so arguing, the party tries to combine its old, but more and more toned down, anti-tax stance with a highly vocal demand for increasing public spending. This combination would be a typical over-promising proposition in every country except Norway where the revenues from North Sea oil could afford it (Bjørklund and Saglie 2004). The outstanding success in the 2005 elections, where it reached second position with 22.1 per cent of the votes, proves that the FRPn profited from this balancing.

The Progress Party had long yearned for final recognition as a 'normal' party and it self-depicted already in its 2001 programme as 'a liberal party building on the Norwegian constitution, Norwegian and Western traditions and the cultural heritage based on a "Christian view of life"' (Heidar 2002). On the basis of these changes, assessed by the tough interventions of the leadership against some racist temptations still circulating in the party, the FRPn should by now be considered

out of the extreme right family. Its political influence however has not matched
the expectations raised by the 2005 elections since the government swang left,
thus reducing the FRPn relevance.

The division of the Erp into two groups on the basis of their respective proximity
to government makes it clear that the first group, composed of those parties excluded
from the *'jardin des délices'* of power, keeps its property of anti-systemness more or
less intact, whereas the second group has a more diversified pattern: from a decisive
incentive to deradicalize to the point of quitting the realm of right extremism by AN,
the FRPn, and probably the DFP, to the short-lived and dramatically failed attempt
to follow the same path by the FPÖ, as well as to continuity in radical stances
through double talk and populist rhetoric by the Lega.

In conclusion, the party location in the Left–Right continuum is still consistent
with the ideology, policies, and strategies of the first group of 'pariah' parties, but
not of the second grouping of governmental parties; in this latter group, stability
in the extreme location of Erp is less consistent—for most of them—with their
discourse. Given this divergent path, it is necessary to shed more light on the relationship between the Erp and the other parties and the party system in general.

Erp and the mainstream right parties: hegemonizing or hegemonized?

The electoral and political successes of the Erp focused researchers' attention on
the influence of the extreme right discourse and agenda on mainstream right-wing
parties and the mass public in general. In this book and in earlier works the 'legitimizing' and whitewashing of the Erp discourse by the mainstream parties has been
considered one of the routes for the Erp inroads into the system. This interpretation is shared, with some variants, by many country-specific studies (see Ch.12 for
the references) and is still considered one of the crucial explanations for the rise of
the Erp. Actually, the mainstream parties played the role of the *apprentis sorcier*:
they legitimize a discourse and an agenda which was in the hands of the extreme
right; and the latter were in fact the authentic interpreters of such unacknowledged
issues. They had long been 'censured by the conspiracy of silence' of the establishment when they had tried to bring to the fore the question of national identity
and of physical and social security. Thus, *they* were the real carriers of those issues,
and the electorate identified them in this way. A recent comparative analysis of
party programmes endorses this thesis, arguing that the Erp 'successfully compete
with other national parties because the established parties have largely ignored
(. . .) the new right dimension of party competition' (Cole 2005: 223).

Speculating on the interplay between mainstream right parties and 'far' right
on the basis of the parties' policies rather than the voters' opinions, Tim Bale
(2003) has pointed out that the centre-right '(o)ver time, but especially recently,
(. . .) has helped to prime (and therefore increase the salience of) the far
right agenda—most notably, though not exclusively, on immigration, crime and

welfare abuse—thus rendering it both more respectable and more than a vote winner' (2003: 69).

This is exactly the dynamic highlighted in this book, albeit in a different context. My concern pointed to the rightward movement of the mainstream right *prior* to the Erp breakthrough rather than to their 'acceptability' in recent times. But the logic of the interplay is the same: once the mainstream parties radicalize, they pave the way to *either* the emergence *or* the acceptability of the Erp. This interpretation challenges another stream of analysis originally and brilliantly articulated by Herbert Kitschelt—re-stated in a recent paper by McGann and Kitschelt (2005)—and then followed by others, which argues that it was actually the centripetal move of the mainstream right that favoured the rise of the Erp.

In this section, we will examine this issue once again through a would-be accurate reading of the literature. Differently put, the relevant questions are the following: did the Erp discourse affect the mainstream parties, and—if so—did it occur *before or after* the parties' entry into, or support for, governments?

In the case of France, there is a shared consensus among French scholars on the marginalization of '*lepenisme*' from the public sphere. The FN's ethnocentric and authoritarian agenda distinguishes and separates it from all the other parties (Ivaldi and Bréchon 2000; Mayer 2002; Grunberg and Schweisguth 2003; *contra* Andersen and Evans 2003). The public at large has become more attentive to the issues of immigration and security since the FN politicized them, but it has not espoused the FN discourse. The *frontiste* value system has remained neatly isolated, not shared by the moderate right. At the level of voters' attitudes, 'the rejection of universalistic values' by the extreme right voters is incomparable higher than among moderate right voters (Grunberg and Schweisguth 2003: 351). In fact, 42 per cent of voters with a high level of both xenophobia and authoritarianism, are willing to vote for the FN, compared to 28 per cent preferring the mainstream right; on the other hand, only 1 per cent of those who display low xenophobia and high or low authoritarianism vote Front National (ibidem: 351). The cleavage between the two electorates deepens further when 'economic liberalism' is added (ibidem: 357): a further confirmation of the hostility to free-market policy by *lepeniste* supporters. In short, there is an '*irréductible différence*' between the moderate right and the extreme right political cultures (Ysmal 2000). Again, the mass mobilization against the candidature of Jean-Marie Le Pen after his victory in the first ballot of the 2002 presidential elections highlighted very vividly the widespread 'refusal' of the Front National and its leader by large sections of public opinion.

As for their programme and policies, neither the UMP nor, *a fortiori*, the UDF, have shifted to the right by courting the FN. The resilience of the Front National, election after election, has forced all the other parties to deal with the issues owned by it but, unlike what was suggested by Minkenberg and Schain (2003: 178ff), the FN did not affect the agenda of the *droite modérée*. The risk of a breach in the *cordon sanitaire* was overcome after the RPR and UDF's disastrous 1998 regional elections when the moderate party national leaderships intervened to stop all agreement with the FN over the election of the president in four regions to the point even of expelling the proponents of such an agreement. After the 2002 presidential election, the dividing line with the FN has become even sharper. Competition between former President Jacques Chirac and Jean-Marie Le Pen at the second ballot has itself favoured further distancing of the mainstream right from the FN. Not by chance, the crucial issue of security during the presidential electoral campaign of 2002 was dealt with in a very different way by Chirac and Le Pen (Perrineau 2003: 214). On the other hand, the UMP leader Nicolas Sarkozy has recently initiated his long presidential campaign by placing himself quite to the right, emphasizing law and order enforcement and tough regulation of immigration (demonstrated during the fall 2005 revolt of the *banlieues*) precisely to steal votes from the FN but also to differentiate himself from other potential Gaullist competitors and from the President of the Republic himself. However, even Sarkozy proves very hostile to the FN and Le Pen personally: the row he had with Le Pen in a TV debate on the immigration question, where the UMP leader vindicated his own foreign, Hungarian, origins, provides a remarkable example. The FN has not made a breakthrough either in mass public attitudes, where authoritarian feelings are still quite limited and neatly separated, or in the mainstream parties, where the 'Republican values' still mould people's references and policies.

Apparently, the Vlaams Blok did manage to push the mainstream parties to endorse its agenda on crucial issues, such as the splitting of the bilingual Brussels region into two homogenous linguistic districts or on Flemish autonomy and law and order. The party 'made a serious difference in many policy cases' (De Winter 2005: 113) to the point where 'while Vlaams Belang takes the extremist edge off some of its policies, mainstream Flemish parties are increasingly adopting elements of the party's discourse' (Erk 2005: 500). Essentially, the Vlaams Blok was able to engrain a radicalization drive in Flemish political discourse by imposing its own radical positions on the agenda. The outstanding recent performance by the party at the Flemish regional elections in June 2004 launched the party into first position with 24.2 per cent of the votes. This result created a divergent reaction: a sort of defeatist atmosphere in the Flemish parties leading sooner or later to lifting the *cordon sanitarie* (Hossay 2002: 184; De Winter 2005), or a hard-line reaction, which involved even Prince Philippe, especially supported by the French-speaking community.

The meteoric appearance of the LPF and its impact have been carefully scrutinized. One current of interpretation points out that the Netherlands have not been immune from extreme right framing of the political discourse. Cuperus stresses the 'decline of political correctness *in the 1980s* as to the multicultural society' (Cuperus 2005: 159 emphasis added) and Bale (2003: 78) signals that the VVD had in the past picked up CD anti-immigrant outbursts targeting immigrants as scroungers and potential criminals. Similarly, Pennings and Keman (2003: 57–9) state that the public shifted towards conservatism following 1989 and towards the right after 1998 and the VVD was the party which moved the furthest rightwards.

However, analysing survey data on the 2002 and 2003 elections, neither the electorate nor the moderate parties show any sign of a dramatic shift to the right (van Holsteyn, Irwin, and der Ridder 2003: 71–5). The sudden emergence of the LPF is thus not linked to short-term changes. However, a constituency of voters attentive to anti-establishment and anti-immigration sentiments had been there, maybe for a while, and it only needed an opportunity to express its voice (ibidem: 75) Exactly what happened in the case of the FN. Apparently, the LPF provided the opportunity for the mainstream parties to sharpen their agenda, especially on immigration; in this way the mainstream parties matched demands which had been latent in the electorate for many years. But the electorate was not moved in the short run by the LFP discourse: *it had shifted earlier*. And the mainstream parties 'profited' by the volcanic intrusion of the LPF to advance policies in tune with its party agenda, especially on immigration. The LPF affected the mainstream parties' agenda mainly because they were already inclined to move in that direction and they were waiting for the right moment to do so.

The BNP continues to be kept in a corner. Its discourse has not been taken up consistently by the Conservatives (Eatwell 2004). During the 2004 European election campaign, Tory leader Michael Howard defined the BNP as 'a bunch of thugs dressed up in a political party'. Moreover the BNP has had to face continuous surveillance by the police and judiciary indictments by the courts for stirring up racial hatred. Not even the July 2005, bombing in London seems to have opened the route for the party: in autumn 2005 its publication *Voice of Freedom* was seized owing to its content. On the other hand, the immigration issue, sub species of the asylum-seeker debate, has been mounting in Great Britain. But even during the general election campaign of 2005 it was not consistently politicized by the Conservatives: as *The Guardian* (9 May 2005) wrote: 'Mr Howard, who focused strongly on immigration in the early part of his campaign, abandoned plans to return to the charged issue in the final days because he wanted to present an upbeat message of what he would do as prime minister'. Howard's move is highly expressive of the attitude of British Conservatives on this issue (even though it may have cost the loss of some MPs) and towards the BNP.

In Austria the FPÖ has played a 'bridging function' (Heinisch 2003: 103) by introducing into mainstream politics its own themes and making them acceptable by the ÖVP which would appear to have moved far to the right since 1994 (ibidem :125). This function has been eased by two features. First, the widespread consensus among the electorate on the issues owned by the FPÖ—anti-establishment, anti-Proporz, anti-corruption, and anti-immigration (Müller and Jenny 2003): in no other country has an Erp been able to capture for so many years the attention of such a large constituency of voters. Second, the non-marginalization of the FPÖ in the political system since it had been a partner in central government with the SPÖ in 1983–86—albeit with a radically different (truly liberal) leadership and agenda—and in the Land governments, even leading some of them as in Haider's home pastures of Carinthia. After the FPÖ joined the central government its agenda was basically taken up and some ÖVP members of the Schüssel government expressed even more radical positions than the FPÖ itself (Luther 2003b: 151). This implies that the entry into government was 'prepared' by reception of the FPÖ discourse among the public and in the mainstream party. (Bale 2003: 76–7) We can thus agree with Minkenberg (2001: 13–14) when he writes that 'even when still in opposition, the FPÖ managed to shape part of Austrian policy-making in typical right-wing issues; (. . .) some of its elements were passed as law in the twentieth legislative period.'

The Danish moderate parties' acquaintance with the DFP after the 2001 elections was fostered by an electoral campaign largely centred around the question of rules restricting immigration as advocated by Kjaersgaard's party. An inevitable occurrence since the elections took place two months after September 11. Even though this theme had acquired centrality in the political debate, and the mainstream right parties, even including the Social Democrats, seemed inclined to follow the line dictated by the DFP, nevertheless public opinion was not affected by any such climate: on the contrary, it displayed a more tolerant attitude to the point where Bjørklund and Goul Andersen (2002: 131) could conclude that 'an open discussion of the problems of immigration does not necessarily mobilize intolerance'. The success of the Social Liberals in the 2005 elections with a campaign against the tightening-up policies of the government on immigration (Petersen 2005: 1105) seems to confirm this interpretation. However, such a 'positive reaction' by the public opinion, which Bjørklund and Goul Andersen refer to, might be endangered in the long run by a discourse centred on the idea of ethnic differentiation which could lead to stigmatization, discrimination, and even harassing of immigrants. At any rate, by 2002 the DFP had gained 'a decisive influence on general economic and social policy '(Bille 2003: 933). In particular it imposed its own agenda on immigration 'tightening the rules of immigration and family reunion, and abolition of the Board of Ethnic Equality' (Bjørklund and Goul Andersen 2002: 132). In sum, the DFP has affected the political discourse and the policy of the mainstream parties; it has been able to impose its ethnopluralist and narrow views on the other right-wing parties, thereby pushing them further to the right.

After the 2001 Norwegian general elections, the FRPn was in a position to get the government to discuss and basically accept its 54 conditions for supporting it (Heidar 2002). Its influence was propelled by the events of September 11 which had raised the immigration issue again. This subject actually had a very low rating in voters' priorities during the electoral campaign. Moreover, at that time, the party was still considered a pariah by the other parties: before the elections the members and the middle-level elites of all parties considered the Progress Party the most remote party (with the exception of the conservatives who rated Labour more beyond the pale than the FRPn).

The centrality acquired by the immigration issue after the election put the FRPn in the position to exploit its own ownership on the issue. The government followed most of the Progress party suggestions on immigration. But the FRPn had long laid a claim to other issues which were to become even more salient during the legislature: as well as tax-cuts—whose relevance had become minor—the other issue emphasized by the party concerned welfare provisions, especially for the elderly. Thanks to the credibility of the party on these issues the FRPn was able to dictate the agenda to the government parties. The Progress Party success in the 2003 local elections (Bjørklund and Saglie 2004) and the outstanding performance in the 2005 general election when it gained second position in the *Storting* demonstrate the 'dramatic' inroads made by this former pariah party into the Norwegian party system. Clearly, the FRPn has affected the agenda but at the same time offered enough evidence of accommodation in its turn to the principles and rules of the system. After the formation of the centre-left goverment following the November 2005 elections, the FRPn lost hold on government policies but it may continue to affect the mainstream right and its electorate, as the post-election surveys show.

The Italian case is the most complicated one—and not by chance the least studied and the worst interpreted in the literature, mainly because of the language barrier and the consequent inability to draw on adequate sources (the most notable exception in terms of comparative analysis is that provided by Betz 2003, 2004*a,b*). The list of misreadings and misinterpretations would be too long. Only one aspect merits some attention because it comes from a recent and highly scholarly book on the topic (Norris 2005). In that work the Italian 'radical right parties'—AN, Lega Nord, and MS-FT—are pooled together in the same dataset—*collected in 2002*— as if they were all the same. This procedure is even more astonishing since the criteria of inclusion are provided not only by the party location on the Left–Right continuum, but the party position on the immigration issue (ibidem: 47)—thereby ignoring that AN has for some time now not been at all comparable to other extreme right, or even mainstream, right-wing parties, on this issue.Mixing up these very different parties dramatically distorts the analysis of the 'radical right voter'.

One apparently paradoxical feature of Italian politics lies precisely in the respective roles played by the centre-right parties. Within the Italian governing coalition, *An has played a moderating function vis-à-vis* the Lega Nord and also components of Forza Italia itself. The search for full legitimacy by a party heir to the neo-fascist tradition has forced its leadership to tone down any authoritarian or repressive drive. As far as immigration is concerned (Veugelers and Chiarini 2002), the issue owner is not AN but rather the Lega Nord (Biorcio 2003; Ignazi 2005*a,b*). The AN and Lega Nord leaders co-signed a new immigration law which was certainly tougher than the previous one (Colombo and Sciortino 2003), but the hardliner was the Lega which later also tried, unsuccessfully, to stop the legalization of illegal immigrants. In an attempt to distance An from xenophobic messages, as already mentioned, in autumn 2003 party leader Gianfranco Fini called for immigrants to be given the right to vote in local elections. It was a very clear message to differentiate AN from the Lega, which in fact mobilized against it. With the passing of time—apart from further thorough attempts to cleanse the party of fascist nostalgia—Fini has stepped up number and tone of his moderate statements. The most provocative ones concerned acceptance of some form of same-sex legal union and support for liberalization of medical-assisted fertilization, even against the other partners in the coalition and a large part of his own party (and also the Church). These limited examples highlight the paradox of the Italian context where the *former* 'most right-extremist' party outstripped in moderation the other *former* mainstream right-wing parties, the Lega Nord and, sometimes, Forza Italia too. In short, then, the AN entry into government did not produce any radicalizing impact on the other parties, but rather the reverse (Ignazi 2005*b*).

The Lega, on the other hand, has played a major role in bringing extremist, anti-plural and anti-egalitarian stances into the public sphere. Bossi's agenda has often been willingly followed by Prime Minister Berlusconi and by a large part of Forza Italia. Almost all the proposals put forward by the Lega on its sensitive points—immigration, security, devolution, economic protectionism, anti-EU,—have been adopted by the government, or have deeply affected its behaviour. Thus, the Lega has had an extraordinarily high influence on the government and contributed so far to shifting it to the right, thanks to the intimate though disguised consent of the prime minister himself.

To conclude, in this section we have examined (1) the spatial location of mainstream and extremist parties, (2) the eventual Erp change of discourse or policy in the last few years, especially in relationship to their closeness to government, and (3) the Erp impact on mainstream right-wing discourse and policy. The basic outcomes of this analysis, based on as exhaustive an analysis as possible of the relevant literature and of the most recent available data, are the following.

First, in terms of spatial location on the Left–Right continuum:

(1) the general rightward swing by mainstream right parties in the decade that preceded the rise of Erp, described in Ch.12, has continued in recent times. *In the year 2000, the mainstream right parties were generally more to the right than in the year 1993,* with the exception of the Norwegian Høyre—where a sizable Erp exists—and the British Conservatives and Dutch VVD and CDA—where, at the time, only fringe parties existed (see Table 2);

(2) *by the year 2000 (as against 1993) all the Erp had further radicalized* with the exception of the quite marginal Republikaner, and the two large and influential Progress parties in Norway and Denmark (even in comparison to the splinter-group DFP) (see Table 1);

(3) *by the year 2000 (as against 1993), all party systems, with the exception of Flanders, had decreased their polarization,* assessed by the distance between the most rightward and the most leftward parties; this occurred not only as a consequence of the shift to the centre by the Erp, but also because the extreme leftist parties did not shift any further to the left but rather moved to the centre (see Table 3).

TABLE 3. *Polarization (distance between the right-most and the left-most party) (2000, 1993)*

Country	Party	2000	1993
A	FPÖ/GRÜNE	6.00	6.41
Bfl	VlB/AGALEV	6.65	6.30[1]
Bw	FN/ECOLO	7.42	—
DK	FRPd/EL	7.70	7.92
F[2]	FN/PCF	8.00	8.61
D	REP/PDS	7.76	8.76
UK[3]	BNP/CON	5.50	—
I	LEGA/PRC	6.84	—
I	AN/PRC	7.46	9.25
I	MS-FT/PRC	8.95	—
NL	CD/SP	7.54	—
NL	CD/GL	6.61	8.57
N	FRPn/RDV	6.14	
N	FRPn/SV	5.97	7.37

Notes: [1] Estimates provided by Knutsen (1998: 90).
[2] The Trotzskists are not considered even if in 2000 they were more to the left because they did not exist in 1993.
[3] The Green are not considered even if in 2000 they were more to the left because they did not exist in 1993.

Source: 2000 data: see Lubbers (2001).
1993 data: see Huber and Inglehart (1995).

Second, in terms of discourse and policy:

(1) the parties out of reach of government did not change their ideological pro-file (and we argue that the parties kept their profile independently of any chance of entering government); this concerns large (FN and VLB) and small (BNP, FNb, MS-FT, AS, REP, NPD, DVU) parties;

(2) parties gaining direct or indirect access to the governmental area displayed two different patterns: *prior* to entry into government, two, and probably three, parties were already involved in a process of deradicalization (FRPn, AN and, more dubiously, FRPd) while the other two had not *previously* altered their discourse (FPÖ and Lega); moreover, once within reach of government, the first three parties stepped up their accommodating attitude and behaviour and the FPÖ attempted to follow the path of deradicalization with uneven results and a dramatic *finale*; only the Lega Nord stuck to its previous, rather extremist, positions.

Third, in terms of the interplay between moderate and extreme right–wing parties:

(1) in the Netherlands, in Norway, in Denmark, in Austria and, to a lesser extent, in Belgium, Erp agenda-setting had a direct impact on the mainstream right;

(2) in France, and also in Germany, the *cordon sanitaire* against the Erp was so rigid that despite some verbal concessions to extreme right discourse, this did not entail any acceptance of these parties; more specifically, in France the outstanding Le Pen performance at the 2002 presidential election had a negative effect on the FN capacity to influence the *droite*, which intransigently keeps out of any contact with the party while stealing some messages from it; while in Germany the electoral irrelevance of the Erp inevitably toned down their influence on the mainstream right parties;

(3) in Italy, the Lega Nord did shift the government to the right, while, paradoxically, AN had a rather moderating effect on the government on the whole.

3. WHO VOTES FOR THE EXTREME RIGHT PARTIES?

Research on the Erp social profile has taken a bizarre route. A number of studies seem to revive a determinist—neo-Marxist or sociology-biased—approach. Kitschelt (1995), McGann and Kitschelt (2005), in particular, but also Norris (2005), are the most authoritative representatives of this approach: they identify and classify the Erp partly on the basis of their social profile and infer their policy, their strategy, and even their discourse from their social composition. McGann and Kitschelt (2005: 149) have in fact restated 'Kitschelt's (1995) concept of a "new radical-right" 'party [that] is based *as much on the party's constituency* as on its ideological appeal' (emphasis added). Actually, I tend to share the warning of van der Brug and Fennema when they write that 'if a relationship exists between the social characteristics of voters and their electoral choices, this does not allow valid conclusions about the motives of voters' (2003: 58). That is, workers may not vote for pro-labour parties, and managers or entrepreneurs may not choose pro-market ones. This is quite banal, but it should be reiterated when the social profile of voters is taken too far as a criterion of identification, performance and agenda-setting of parties, and especially of Erp.

It has in fact been amply demonstrated that the socio-demographic characteristics have no *direct* role in determining the choice of the Erp. Apart from all the evidence from country-specific studies, a recent comparative empirical analysis concludes that

'the key determinants of far right support [lie] not in the demographic or socio-economic characteristics of voters but rather in political attitude. *Regardless of respondent's gender, education or standing in the labour market, anti immigration sentiment and political disaffection drive support to the extreme right'* (Kesseler and Freeman 2005: 283; emphasis added).

Since the socio-demographic structure does not represent the key to understanding pro-Erp voting behaviour, an analysis emphasizing the (deterministic) linkage between social class and vote, or social class and political attitudes, risks landing up in a *cul de sac.*

Keeping in mind the 'sociological bias' in party research rejected by Panebianco (1988), who sees the party claim to being 'the' representative of a social class as quite unacceptable, *mutatis mutandis* we cannot accept that a class should (any longer) have a pre-determined ideological and political orientation. It is thus quite hard to accept a statement such as 'the small business owners (. . .) are economically liberal' (McGann and Kitschelt 2005: 150) with reference to the FPÖ. From one point of view, one could argue that this is no longer true: the small business owners might nowadays, in the global economy, be more protectionist rather than free market, especially in a stagnating economic cycle. On the other hand, it is highly questionable whether such a constituency could cause the Erp to adopt a pro-market agenda: all the Erp, starting from the *Front National*, as demonstrated *ad abundantiam* by Perrineau (1997, 2003, 2005), Ysmal (2000) Mayer (2002, 2003, 2005), Evans and Ivaldi (2005), Laver, Benoit, and Sauger (2006), have first and foremost stressed in their programmes and propaganda the defence, or even the expansion, of the welfare provisions. The success of most of these parties has been precisely linked to this welfarist profile, not to the neo-liberal approach: besides the FN, this is certainly the case with anti-tax parties such as the FRPn and the DFP, (which have centred their last electoral campaigns on care of the elderly), the Vlaams Blok, and also, to a lesser extent, the Lega Nord, AN and the FPÖ. Why did Haider, despite the disaster to his party at a federal level, keep all his votes in Carinthia (42.1%) in the 2004 Land elections? Is this linked to the amazingly generous welfare system offered to his Carinthian citizens? (Luther 2000, 2003*a,b*). It is highly probable. By the way, back in 1996, the FPÖ party manifesto suggested that the party would retain a policy such as *concern for the welfare state and unemployment* (Cole 2005: 217–19).

One further consequence of the emphasis on Erp voters' socio-demographic distribution is the crucial importance that is attributed to the economic dimension (welfare vs. market) in the parties' programmes and the voters' priorities. That the facts deny the relevance of this relationship is abundantly clear. The most recent and convincing support is provided by Elisabeth Ivarsflaten at the end of a very accurate comparison of FN and DFP voters' profiles: she writes that 'issues crosscutting the economic dimension explain more of the sociodemographic structure of the populist right vote than issues along the economic dimension' and, moreover, that voters are 'prepared to discount [centrist economic preferences] and vote for the issues they do agree on—immigration, law and order, the European Union and government corruption' (2005: 482). This analysis reinforces the interpretation—stressed in Ch. 12 of this book—that Erp voters never indicate any economic policy or proposal as their prime motives for voting for such parties. Moreover, *Erp are never 'valued' for their ability to intervene in economic matters*: voters rate these parties competent and effective on their primary topics—immigration, corruption, law and order (and also national identity and defence of the common man)—but not on the economy (see also Müller and Jenny 2004). Erp voters do not care so much—and often, not at all—about the parties' proposals on economic matters because their issue priorities are different and because they consider the Erp the most effective in dealing with their most cherished non-economic issues. The Erp issue ownership on immigration, law and order, and anti-establishment/corruption qualifies them as the first choice for those who prioritize such themes. It is quite odd to assert that 'economic liberalism was the strongest predictor of whether someone voted FPÖ in 1989' (McGann and Kitschelt 2005: 151) when the economy issue was not even mentioned in the first four motives for voting FPÖ, according to the Fessel GfK (1999) series of electoral surveys. Moreover, in the French Presidential elections of 2002, the two issues which ranked as the highest concern for Le Pen voters—security and unemployment—had clearly always been 'owned' by the FN. The fact that, for the first time, one of these issues—security—was also salient for the electorate at large helps explain the FN success: the difference in the level of priority between the Le Pen and the general electorate was—exceptionally, given the peculiar climate in that period—limited to eight points out of a 0–100 scale on security, whereas immigration had the (traditionally) huge difference of 45 points (Mayer 2002: 507). This example—which could be transferred to all the other parties—proves that Erp voters have a clear hierarchy in mind, in some way related to a precise world view. As many researchers have argued—particular attention to this aspect has been devoted by van der Brug, Fennema, and Tillie (2000), van der Brug and Fennema (2003) and Bergh (2004)—Erp voters are not merely protest voters, because they know what they want, and they have an ideological core (though it may only be revealed as the faintest of watermarks).

In the search for the socio-demographic profile we should finally remember that the Erp are no longer a new entry in their respective party systems. They are by now consolidated and, therefore, in the last 20 years or so, they may have experienced different phases depending on changes either in their own internal environment (cohesion and stability of the dominant coalition, agenda, and strategy) or in the external environment (institutional, social, and political context). A change in strategy in order to occupy a different space in the system may lead to emphasising different themes and constituencies: launching the 'conquest of power' strategy also meant that from the 1990s on the *Front National* has challenged the moderate right parties as well as the leftist ones by appealing to the underprivileged components of society, discarding the Thatcherite neo-liberal flavour of the mid-1980s, in favour of a more social minded policy. Again, the Lega Nord experienced a u-turn moving from secular, neo-liberal, federalist, pro-EU and mildly anti-(Italian)immigrant positions to clerical, welfarist, secessionist, anti-EU and xenophobic ones, and its social constituency varied considerably over time, in accordance with the different political-strategic lines laid down by the party leadership. Thus, it is difficult to assess a *linear evolution common to all parties over the last two decades*, concerning their discourse, policy, location, and strategy, and also concerning their socio-demographic constituencies.

Unfortunately, it is quite common to disregard the changes over time and space (an appropriate warning on this point comes from Evans (2005), Ivarsflaten (2005: 469–70), Carter (2004: 93), and Lubbers and Scheepers (2001)). The present research mainstream leads rather to pooling survey data from different elections, in many countries, for all the Erp, and then producing a series of generalizations on *the* Erp voter in general. The most problematic aspect of this procedure—besides the frequent absence of any discussion of case selection—is that it neglects the time dimension. No one would accept an analysis on the 'European socialist voter' that first mixed up the data—Old Labour voters (say 1983) with New Labour voters (say 2001), the pre- and post-Mitterrand PS voters, Lafontaine-led mixed with Schroeder-led SPD voters—and then, after sophisticated statistical data treatment, offered a generalization on the factors behind 'the socialist party vote'. This kind of analysis would be rejected by the scholars' community. Similar accuracy is needed for the Erp political family. Outcomes are very different if one groups together late 1980s AND late 1990s FN, or 1980s MSI AND 2000s AN, and so on. Or, even worse, if one include AN, MS-FT and Lega Nord in the same category, simply because they are all Italian! In short, most of the generalizations on the Erp voter's socio-demographic structure reach misleading conclusions through failing to distinguish time and cases. A step in the right direction has been taken by Evans (2005) when he divides a (still overstretched time-wise) set of parties into 'Scandinavian' and 'continental' and looks for a time-point which could highlight a change of trend. Similarly, while debatable in other respects, Kitschelt (1995) built his typology precisely to assess different trends and characteristics within the Erp family.

Despite this plea for careful consideration of the differences among Erp, if a commonality exists in the early 2000s it regards their social profile. Considering the larger and more established Erp—FN, FPÖ, VLB, FRPn, FRPd/DFP, Lega Nord—but also the fringe BNP and NPD, their share of poorly educated, low income, and especially blue collar voters has increased dramatically. The empirical evidence from the single country studies presented in the previous chapters illustrates a large quota of underprivileged citizens among the Erp electorate.

The same picture emerges when we analyse data from the 2003 European Social Survey (Minkenberg and Perrineau 2005: 86–7) (Table 4): even though the social class classification is somewhat large, the Erp voters are overrepresented in the *workers and 'employés'* with the plausible exceptions of Italy (the Lega Nord and MS-FT).

It is not without meaning that a party such as the Italian Alleanza Nazionale—appropriately not included in the Minkenberg and Perrineau (2005) study—should display a completely different socio-demographic profile and, in particular, be underrepresented in the working class (Ignazi 2004a). This profile might be assumed as a *further* indicator of the divergent path undertaken by the party for the past decade: here again the party is not leading back to its previous political family.

TABLE 4. *Percentage of workers and routine employee in the ERP electorates and difference from the mean (2003)*

Country	%	Difference
D	76	+16
B	78	+19
DK	75	+18
F	76	+25
I	69	+1
N	81	+19
NL	67	+13

Source: European Social Survey data (2003) in Minkenberg and Perrineau (2005: 87).

Many analysts have related the proletarization of the social bases of the Erp to the 'modernization loser' theory. In particular, Betz and Johnson recently asserted that the Erp

'have been increasingly successful in appealing to those groups that have felt most threatened both by the loss of their relatively privileged position (e.g. skilled unionised blue-collar workers from the dominant ethnic social group) and by the rejection of those political parties that once defended their interests and espoused their cause' (Betz and Johnson 2004: 324).

Actually, there is some truth in this, even though the argument should not be pushed too far, nor suggest a mechanical relationship. The warning made by Norris that 'we should look sceptically upon the idea that radical right parties are purely a phenomenon of the resentment among the new social cleavage of low skilled and low qualified workers in inner-city areas' (2005: 147) is correct. However, the theory of resentment by the modernization losers cannot be challenged on the basis of the existence of a cross-class electoral alliance between petite bourgeoisie and blue collars as advanced by the same author (Norris 2005: 139).This for a series of reasons. First, because, contrary to what Norris states (2005: 271), the largest share of Erp voters is among the blue collars and routine non-manual workers, and *not* among the petite bourgeoisie. Second, because the overrepresentation of these two social groups is largest among blue collars. Third, because the workerist–welfarist appeal overwhelms the neo-liberal one. And finally, because the Erp do indeed appeal 'across all social sectors equally'. Actually, the Erp speak to the entire 'nation' and to 'the people' precisely because they have an encompassing 'national' message, not limited to a particular constituency. And if one constituency is flattered, that is the 'common man', the 'honest and hard-working producer', underprivileged and mistreated by the establishment. A simple reading of the press and the speeches of *all the Erp* provides enough evidence of the nationwide/nationalistic and cross-class appeal. This cross—or, better, 'beyond'—class message is consistent with their ideology: the unity of the nation, conceived in organicist and ethnocentrist terms, represents 'the' highest value for the Erp, and the class differences are disturbances to be bypassed. The absence of references to the nation as an organic body by some parties such as the FRPn and the AN and, with some qualifications, by the DFP and the LPF, qualifies these parties for a different position *vis-à-vis* the other Erp, that is, on the outer edge of the political family, or even outside it.

To sum up, the electoral fortunes of the Erp in the 1990s are strictly linked to their process of proletarization; the more the relative quota of blue collars increased in their electorate, the more votes the party gained. The increasing per centage of workers in the FPÖ in the years up to its best electoral performance in 1999 provides a perfect illustration of this dynamic (see table 6.5 in Ch. 6). The same is true *for* all the major Erp: the FN, the FRPn, the FRPd, the DFP, the VlB and also the Lega display this trend.

It is also true, that the Erp have also progressed because they are able to keep the support of the petite bourgeoisie. But it is the relative importance of the two social groups that reveals the 'new' centrality of blue collars in extreme right-wing social stratification (Evans 2005:76–7). The FPÖ collapse in the 2002 election provides evidence *a contrario* of our thesis. The party's electoral reversal is in fact linked to the haemorrhage of blue collars much more than white collars: while the latter halved, from 22 per cent to 11 per cent, the former plunged from 47 per cent to 16 per cent (Fallend 2004: 117). This means that the major contribution to the defeat was provided by the massive defection of the blue collars. Appropriately, Luther points out that, once in power, the FPÖ debated whether the party should keep or deemphasize the reference to blue collars, where FPÖ penetration had probably reached a ceiling or rather address white collars and the self-employed (Luther 2003a: 200–1).

To conclude this overview on the research into the socio-demographic structure of the Erp voter, one might dwell on a quite bizarre point made in the recent, and relevant, book by Pippa Norris (2005). This work repeatedly stresses a sort of continuity between contemporary extreme right and interwar fascism on the basis of a similar socio-demographic profile: as the author says, 'the continued attraction of the petite bourgeoisie to the contemporary radical right, for example, indicates that there are deeper roots which also characterized interwar fascism' (Norris 2005: 139). As, according to Norris, the petite bourgeoisie was crucial to the fortunes of interwar fascism (ibidem: 130), 'if there is some continuity in the social basis of contemporary politics, then the theory predicts that electoral support for radical right parties will be concentrated most strongly among the petite bourgeoisie' (ibidem: 130). Actually this assumption runs up against two insurmountable obstacles. On the one hand, the importance and size of the petite bourgeoisie is limited in contemporary Erp, as we have demonstrated above. Rather, what characterizes contemporary Erp is *both* their penetration among the working class and other low income strata, where they have in some cases supplanted the socialist parties as 'the' worker parties, *and* the (novelty of the) enduring alliance between small business and the proletariat (Evans 2005). On the other hand, more recent research on interwar fascism illustrates that, contrary to old, rather stereotyped, interpretations, the bulk of (Italian) fascist support came from 'landless wage labourers' rather than urban bourgeoisie, as Spencer Wellhofer (2003: 101) has brilliantly demonstrated in his path-breaking and landmark analysis of Italian fascism. Hence the assumption of some line of continuity between interwar fascism and present-day extreme right on the basis of a similar socio-demographic structure is contradicted by the empirical analyses on both sides; and, moreover, it is contradicted by Norris herself when she argues against (her own) deterministic approach in stating that 'political attitudes predicted support for the radical right far more strongly than social characteristics' (2005: 209).

4. THE ERP RISE: NOT ONLY IMMIGRATION

Many contributions purporting to explain the rise of the Erp have somewhat minimized the crisis of confidence and the dealignment at a *system level*, as well as the social and political alienation coupled with resentment against the political system, the parties, the establishment, and so on, at an *individual level*. In spite of this quite complex and articulated set of conditions (highlighted in Ch. 12), most studies have focused their attention on the immigration issue alone, to the point of labelling parties as 'anti-immigrant'. However, there is ample consensus—even among those who define the Erp as 'anti-immigrant parties' (see van der Brug and Fennema 2003)—that immigration is not the only, or even the most important, issue for Erp voters, or for the Erp themselves as far as their agenda and their ideology are concerned (see Lubbers 2001; van der Brug and Fennema 2003; van Holsteyn and Irwin 2003; Mayer 2003; Betz and Johnson 2004: 317; Evans 2005; Luther 2005; Minkenberg 2005*a*,*b*).

Concentrating on the immigrant question raises many problems. In the first instance, there is widespread confusion as to who exactly are immigrants: asylum-seekers, as the British tend to emphasize, or job-securing immigrants, or second generation citizens but of foreign origin. Second, the statistics on immigrant/foreign people are at best patchy and, above all, inevitably do not take into account the large number of illegal immigrants; this failing is particularly unfortunate since illegal immigrants are the more frequently responsible for illegal operations which creates high concern in some sectors of the population. Hence, ecological analyses computing the number of (registered) immigrants are likely to be founded on a quicksand of unreliable data. Norris (2005) provides indirect confirmation of such difficulties. After making a proper distinction among refugee asylum-seekers, resident non-citizens and residents born overseas, and after having recognized the unreliability of available statistics (2005: 173) she decides to adopt data from survey estimates for the last two categories (2005: 174). Third, the *direct* effect of the number of immigrants in determining Erp fortunes has not yet been assessed as the change in the unit of analysis gives different and even contradictory results, leading to the formulation of various theories such as the proximity-experiential factor and the '*effet halo*'. Last but not least, the immigration issue *per se* has rarely been the most powerful predictor of the Erp vote.

This final point deserves more attention. As Nonna Mayer, among others, has very well demonstrated, in order to 'develop' an anti-immigrant attitude—even if one is in competition with immigrants in the job market—an ethnocentric world view needs to be developed (1999: 149). In other words, one is anti-immigrant because one has a set of attitudes which lead to hierarchizing the people/races, rejecting others, seeking homogeneity and harmony, refusing pluralism, and emphasizing the nation. *The anti-immigration attitude is part of a more complex syndrome.*

Thus, the most powerful drive to voting for the Erp lies beyond the twin themes of immigration and security. Disaffection and distrust towards the political figures and institutions, amounting to alienation and cynicism towards politics as such, explain better than any other causes. The more one is alienated and cynical, the more likely one will support an Erp. And in the balance between these 'political' factors and the 'social' ones (immigration and security), the former prevail *in all countries*. For example, attentive analysis of such a dramatic and flashy phenomenon as the List Pim Fortuyn shows that 'political cynicism has more discriminating power than the immigration issue' (van der Zwan 2004: 82) And the same occurred in the case of all the other parties, from the Front National to the FPÖ, from the Lega Nord to the Vlaams Blok, from the German right extremist parties to the Scandinavian Progress parties. The reason to vote for extreme right parties is bound up with the citizens' relationship with politics: their detachment and rejection drive them to look for a radical alternative which might answer their queries, provide a harbour, and soothe their resentment.

To sum up, the conditions for the rise of the Erp reside in the societal and political transformations which favoured the birth of new parties within the party systems, and more specifically, in the matching of voters' unmet demands and the party's right-wing offer. In particular, the feelings of political un-representativeness, social alienation, and economic uncertainty have been transplanted onto a demand for security, authority, and identity. This multifaceted demand have been aptly matched by the Erp precisely because their genetic code expresses the ideal of unity and harmony, stability and hierarchy and a return to an idealized past (even on the economic side): what prevails is 'a desire to return to a *status quo ante* perceived as superior to the current state of affairs' (Evans 2005: 77). The myth of a golden age, with its corollary of a compound and homogeneous community, is at the heart of the Erp discourse. And its powerful drive lies in just such a subliminal message.

The nostalgia for a confident, reassuring and gentle past is masterfully illustrated by this passage of Raoul Girandet in his *Mythes et Mithologies Politiques*: '*rêve de limpidité, de communion, d'effusion et d'harmonie, le mythe de l'Age d'or se révèle encore rêve de permanence. Sa diffusion, sa puissance d'attraction demeurent inséparables de la vision—très profondément, très intimement vécue, toujours intensément présente à travers la pluralité de ses expressions*—d'un temps figé, solidifié, cristallisé . . . Le monde de l'Age d'or est celui des horologes arrêtées' (1986: 128–9 emphasis added).

5. CONCLUSIONS. WHERE ARE THE EXTREME RIGHT PARTIES GOING?

The present fate of the Erp is unclear. Some have abandoned the political family—as defined in this book; others are on the verge of doing so. Still others are still firmly entrenched in the family.

Alleanza nazionale is by now out of the realm of right-extremism. Some fascist nostalgia is still harboured by the rank-and-file but it refers more to personal–psychological motives than to ideological and political alignments. The party is still torn by contradictory references as Tarchi (2003, 2005) has dutifully demonstrated, but it no longer displays any common alignment with the political agenda of the other Erp. Alleanza nazionale represents an intriguing case of evolution from die-hard neo-fascism to post-fascism and finally even away from extremism. In a few years, the MSI leadership exploited the unique window of opportunity opened up by the earthquake which devastated the Italian party system to abandon its backward image. The success encountered by this transition has encouraged the leadership to proceed along that path, albeit in a slow, contradictory, and often underground fashion. The entry into the centre-right Berlusconi-led government in 2001 and, more recently, access to the Ministry of Foreign Affairs by Party Leader Gianfranco Fini (plus the attaining of a sizeable share of votes, between 10 and 13 per cent in the 2004 European and 2005 regional elections) testify to the achievement of full legitimacy.

AN's entry into government in 2001 might be fruitfully contrasted with the FPÖ entry in 2000. The two events have had an amazingly different evaluation by the international community and produced different feedbacks in the parties themselves. The FPÖ success shook Europe as a whole, leading to the declaration by 14 EU heads of government and the establishment of the 'comité des sages' to control government democratic accountability; AN entry went unnoticed (unlike what happened in 1994 when it participated in the short-lived first Berlusconi government). However, the divergent reactions were also motivated by the different size in parliament and in the government coalition: the FPÖ got the same votes and seats as the ÖVP, while AN got one-third of the votes and half the seats of the major party in the coalition (Forza Italia). Finally, the governmental experience brought self-destruction to the FPÖ and consolidation to AN. The FPÖ failed to hold out either against the external pressure on the leadership, leading to Haider's still inexplicable resignation and extrusion from party life until his disastrous comeback, or against ÖVP competition which led to a split in the party. AN, on the contrary, maintained its internal cohesion, absorbing deeply provocative modernizing and liberalizing overtures by the party leader, centring on the right to vote for immigrants, the definition of fascism as 'absolute evil', and support for medical-assisted fertilization in the 2005 referendum on that issue.

The Scandinavian parties too are on the way out. The Norwegian FRPn has moved broadly outside the right-extremist ideological and policy domain. Its 2001 Manifesto, implemented by a series of consistent acts to stop xenophobic drives, its recent declarations of full endorsement for liberal and pluralist democracy and its rejection of any truck with the right extremist milieu, candidates this party as a member of the mainstream right rather than of the extreme right. The Danish DFP has taken a similar path but at a slower and more uncertain pace. It is highly probable that it will confirm this trend, thus getting out of the extreme right political family. On the other hand, governing parties such as the Lega Nord and the FPÖ are somewhere on the edge because the balance between radicalization and accommodation is uncertain, and probably unclear to the parties themselves. The other parties are still entrenched in the extreme right domain.

For twenty years the Erp have represented a new phenomenon. They rose because they expressed unmet demands. These demands may become more salient and thus bring further benefit to them. But these parties have probably reached the ceiling of their electoral expansion. The moderate right has adopted various strategies to counter their rise from flattering and stealing some issues to ignoring and demonizing them. It is still too early to assess the validity of these strategies. In the past, the courting of extreme right issues by the mainstream right proved disastrous and indeed paved the way for the Erp rise, with the exception of Great Britain, where Mrs. Thatcher's strategy of attention toward the *National Front* themes succeeded thanks to the plurality electoral system. In more recent times, the issue-priming of the Erp has only been effectively challenged by the mainstream parties in Austria and partially in the Netherlands, thanks to a shift to the right by these parties. In other countries, the mainstream parties' movement to the right, as in Belgium, for example, failed to stop Erp growth.

Actually, the dynamics of Erp and moderate parties could hide a more significant connection, between Erp and socialist parties. This aspect, highlighted by some authors in relation to the French and the Norwegian cases (Perrineau, Mayer, and Evans), is based on Erp penetration into the lower strata. The so-called '*ouvrière-lepénisme*' in the French context indicates the FN attraction felt by the working class which was previously monopolized by the socialist and communist parties. If these trends continue, in the near future the Erp might compete on the electoral market more with the socialists than the moderate right, even though the ideological divide is much larger.

In sum, the Erp have performed a '*tribunicienne*' (Lavau 1981) function in the main. Their populist appeal has affected the political discourse in many countries; the principles of individual rights, pluralism, and equality have been, and still are, under attack, albeit indirectly, in a covert and disguised way. Although with few exceptions these parties have not gained—or maintained for long—a primary role, their influence on mass beliefs and attitudes has apparently gone well beyond their electoral scores.

References to the Epilogue

Akkerman, T. (2005). 'Anti-Immigration Parties and the Defence of Liberal Values: The Exceptional Case of the List Pim Fortuyn'. *Journal of Political Ideologies*, 10: 337–54.

Andersen, R. and Evans, J. A. J. (2003). 'Values, Cleavages and Party Choice in France, 1988–1995'. *French Politics* 1: 83–114.

Bale, T. (2003). 'Cinderella and Her Ugly Sisters: The Mainstream and Extreme Right in Europe's Bipolarising Party Systems'. *West European Politics*, 26: 67–90.

Bergh, J. (2004). 'Protest Voting in Austria, Denmark, and Norway'. *Scandinavian Political Studies*, 27: 367–89.

Betz, H. G. (2003) 'The Growing Threat of the Radical Right', in Merkl, P. H. and Weinberg, L. (eds.), *Right-Wing Extremism in the Twenty-First Century*. London: Frank Cass, 74–93.

—— (2004a). *Exclusionary Populism in Western Europe in the 1990s and Beyond*. UNIRID Programme Paper Number 9, presented at the 2001 Conference on Racism and Public Policy.

—— (2004b). *La droite populiste en Europe. Extrême et Démocrate?* Paris: Autrement.

—— and Johnson, C. (2004). 'Against the Current-Stemming the Tide: The Nostalgic Ideology of the Contemporary Radical Populist Right'. *Journal of Political Ideologies*, 9: 311–27.

Bille, L. (2003). 'Denmark'. *European Journal of Political Research*. 42: 931–4.

Biorcio, R. (2003). 'Italian Populism: From Protest to Governing Party', paper presented at the ECPR Conference, Marburg 18–21 September.

Bjørklund, T. and Goul Andersen, J. (2002). 'Anti-Immigration Parties in Denmark and Norway: The Progress Paries and the Danish People's Party', in Schain, M., Zolberg, A. and Hossay P. (eds.), *Shadows over Europe: The Development and Impact of the Extreme Right in Western Europe*. New York: Palgrave Macmillan, 107–36.

—— and Saglie, J. (2004). 'The Norwegian Progress Party: Building Bridges across Old Cleavages', paper presented at the 12th *Nasjonal fagkonferanse i statsvitenskap*. Tromso, 7–9 January.

Budge, I. (2001). *Mapping Political Preferences. Estimates for Parties, Electors and Governments 1945–1998*. Oxford: Oxford University Press.

Carter, E. (2002). 'Proportional Representation and the Fortunes of Right-Wing Extremist Parties'. *West European Politics*, 25: 125–46.

—— (2004). 'Does PR Promote Political Extremism? Evidence from the West European Parties of the Extreme Right'. *Representation*, 40: 82–100.

Chiche, J., Le Roux, B., Perrienau, P. and Rouanet, H. (2000). 'L' Espace Politique des Electeurs Français à la fin des années 1990'. *Revue Française de Science Politique*, 50: 463–88.

Coffe, H. (2005). 'Do Individual Factors Explain the Different Success of the Two Belgian Extreme Right Parties?' *Acta Politica*, 40: 74–93.

Cole, A. (2005). 'Old Right or New Right? The Ideological Positioning of Parties of the Far Right'. *European Journal of Political Research*, 44: 203–30.

Colombo, A. and Sciortino, G. (2003). 'La Legge Bossi-Fini: Estremismi Gridati, Moderazioni Implicite e Frutti Avvelenati', in Blondel, J. and Segatti, P. (a cura di) *Politica in Italia 2003*, Bologna: il Mulino, 195–216.

Cuperus, R. (2005). 'Roots of European Populism. The Case of Pim Fortuyn's Populist Revolt in the Netherlands', in Casals, X. (ed.), *Political Survival on the Extreme Right. European Movements between the Inherited Past and the Need to Adapt to the Future*, Barcelona: ICPS, 147–68.

De Winter, L. (2005). 'The Vlaams Blok: the Electorally Best Performing Right-extremist Party in Western Europe', in Casals, X. (ed.), *Political Survival on the Extreme Right. European Movements Between the Inherited Past and the Need to Adapt to the Future*. Barcelona: ICPS, 93–126.

Eatwell, R. (2003). 'Ten Theories of the Radical Right', in Merkl, P. H. and Weinberg, L. (eds.), *Right-Wing Extremism in the Twenty-First Century*. London: Frank Cass, 47–73.

—— (2004). 'The Extreme Right in Britain: The Long Road to "Modernization",' in Eatwell, R. and Mudde, C. (eds.), *Western Democracies and the New Extreme Right Challenge*. London: Routledge, 62–79.

Erk, J. (2005). 'From Vlaams Blok to Vlaams Belang: The Belgian Far-Right Renames Itself'. *West European Politics*, 28: 493–502.

Evans, J. A. J. (2005). 'The Dynamics of Social Change in Radical Right-wing Populist Party Support'. *Comparative European Politics*, 2005: 76–101.

—— and Ivaldi, G. (2005). 'An Extremist Autarky: The Systemic Separation of the French Extreme Right'. *South European Society and Politics*, 10: 351–66.

Fallend, F. (2004). 'Are Right-Wing Populism and Government Participation Incompatible? The Case of the Freedom Party of Austria'. *Representation*. 40: 115–30.

Fieschi, C. (2000). 'European Institutions: The Far Right and Illiberal Politics in a Liberal Context'. *Parliamentary Affairs*, 53: 517–31.

Front National (2002). *Le programme du Front National*. Paris: Edition du Front National.

Gibson, R. and Swenson T. C. (2005). ' "Its Nothing Personal but . . .": Individual versus Contextual Determinants of Support for Anti-Immigrant Parties in Western Europe', paper presented at the Annual Meeting of the American Political Science Association, 31 August–4 September, 2005. Washington DC.

Girardet, R. (1986). *Mythes et Mythologies Politiques*. Paris: Seuil.

Grunberg, G. and Schweisguth, E. (2003). 'La tripartition de l'espace politique' in Perrineau, P. and Ysmal, C. (dir.) *Le Vote de tous les Refus*. Paris: Presses de Sciences Po, 341–62.

Hainsworth, P. (1992). 'Introduction. The Cutting Edge: The Extreme Right in Post-War Western Europe and the USA,' in Hainsworth, P. (ed.) *The Extreme Right in Post-War Western Europe and the USA*. London:Pinter, 1–28.

Heinisch, R. (2003). 'Success in Opposition–Failure in Government: Explaining the Perfomance of Right-wing Populist Parties in Public Office'. *West European Politics*, 26: 91–130.

Heidar, K. (2002). 'Changing Patterns of Party Competition in Norway: The Role of the Progress Party', mimeo.

Hossay, P. (2002). 'Why Flanders?' in Schain, M., Zolberg, A. and Hossay P. (eds.), *Shadows over Europe: The Development and Impact of the Extreme Right in Western Europe*. New York: Palgrave Macmillan, 159–86.

—— (2004b). 'Changing the Guard on the Italian Extreme Right'. *Representation*, 40: 146–56.

Ignazi, P. (2004a) 'Strappi a destra. Le trasformazioni di Alleanza Nazionale'. *il Mulino*, 53: 67–76.

—— (2005*a*). 'Legitimation and Evolution on the Italian Right Wing: Social and Ideological Repositioning of Alleanza Nazionale and the Lega Nord'. *South European Society and Politics*, 10: 333–49.

—— (2005*b*). 'Gli anni Settanta e la memoria monca'. *il Mulino*. 54: 385–94.

—— and Bardi, L. (2006). 'Attivi ma Frustrati: Gli Iscirtti di Alleanza Nazionale'. *Polis*, 20: 31–58.

Ivaldi, G. and Bréchon, P. (2000). 'Le Rapport à l'Autre: Une Culture Xénophobe?' in Bréchon, P., Laurent, A. and Perrineau, P. (dir.), *Les Cultures Politiques des Français*. Paris: Presses de Sciences Po, 275–304.

Ivarslaflaten, E. (2005). 'The Vulnerable Populist Right Parties: No Economic Realignment Fuelling their Electoral Success'. *European Journal of Political Research*, 44: 465–92.

Kessler, A. E. and Freeman, G. P. (2005). 'Support for Extreme Right-Wing Parties in Western Europe: Individual Attributes, Political Attitudes, and National Context'. *Comparative European Politics*, 3: 261–88.

Lavau, G. (1981). *À quoi Sert le Parti Communiste?* Paris: Fayard.

Laver, M., Benoit, K. and Sauger, N. (forth.). 'Policy Competition in the 2002 French Legislative and Presidential Elections'. *European Journal of Political Research*. 45: 669–99.

Le Pen, J. M. (2005). 'Introduction' in *Programme du Front National*. www.frontnational.com.

Leconte, C. (2005). *L'Europe face au défi populiste*. Paris: Puf.

Lubbers, M. (2001). *Exclusionistic Electorates. Extreme-Right Voting in Western Europe*. Nijmengen: ICS-Dissertation.

——, Gijsberts, M., and Scheepers, P. (2002). 'Extreme Right-Wing Voting in Western Europe'. *European Journal of Political Research*, 41: 345–78.

Luther, K. R. (2003*a*). 'The FPÖ: From Populist Protest to Incumbency', in Merkl, P. H. and Weinberg, L. (eds.), *Right-Wing Extremism in the Twenty-First Century*. London: Frank Cass, 191–219.

—— (2003*b*). 'The Self-Destruction of a Right-Wing Populist Party? The Austrian Parliamentary Election of 2002'. *West European Politics*, 26: 136–52.

—— (2005). 'Die Freiheitliche Partei Österreichs (FPÖ) und das Bündnis Zukunft Österreichs (BZÖ)'. Keele European Parties Research Unit, Working Paper 22.

Mayer, N. (2002). 'Les Hauts et les Bas du Vote Le Pen 2002'. *Revue Française de Science Politique*, 52: 505–20.

McGann, A. J. and Kitschelt, H. (2005). 'The Radical Right in the Alps: Evolution of Support for the Swiss SVP and Austrian FPÖ.' *Party Politics*, 11: 147–71.

Meny, Y. and Surel, Y. (eds.) (2002). *Democracies and the Populist Challenge*. Houndsmill: Palgrave Macmillan.

Minkenberg, M. (2001). 'The Radical Right in Public Office: Agenda Setting and Policy Effects'. *West European Politics*, 24: 1–21

—— (2002). 'The New Radical Right in the Political Process: Interaction Effects in France and Germany', in Schain, M., Zolberg, A. and Hossay, P. (eds.), *Shadows over Europe: The Development and Impact of the Extreme Right in Western Europe*. New York: Palgrave Macmillan, 245–68.

—— (2003). 'The West European Radical Right as a Collective Actor: Modeling the Impact of Cultural and Structural Variables on Party Formation and Movement Mobilization'. *Comparative European Politics*, 1: 149–70.

Minkenberg, M. (2005*a*). 'From Party to Movement? The German Radical Right in Transition'. in Casals, X. (ed.), *Political Survival on the Extreme Right. European Movements Between the Inherited Past and the Need to Adapt to the Future.* Barcelona: ICPS, 51–70.

—— (2005*b*). *Demokratie und Desintegration: Der politkwissenschaftliche Forschungsstand zu Rechtsradikalismus, Fremdenfeindlichkteit und Gewalt.* Berlin: pro-business Verlag.

—— and Perrineau, P. (2005). 'La Droite Radicale. Divisions et Contrastes', in Perrineau, P. (dir.) *Le Vote Européen 2004–2005*, Paris: Presses de Sciences Po, 77–103.

—— and Schain, M. (2003). 'The Front National in Context: French and European Dimension', in Merkl, P. H. and Weinberg, L. (eds.), *Right-Wing Extremism in the Twenty-First Century.* London: Frank Cass, 161–90.

Müller, W. and Fallend. F. (2004). 'Changing Patterns of Party Competition in Austria: From Mumtipolar to Bipolr System'. *West European Politics*, 27: 801–35.

—— and Jenny, M. (2004). ' "Business as Usual" mit getauschten Rollen oder Konflikt–statt Konsensdemokratie? Parlamentarische Beziehungen unter der ÖVP-FPÖ-Koalition'. *Österreichische Zeitschrift fur Politikwissenschaft,* 33: 309–26.

Norris, P. (2005). *Radical Right. Voters and Parties in the Electoral Market.* Cambridge: Cambridge University Press.

Oscarsson, H. (2005). 'Mapping the European Political Space', in Rommele, A. and Schmitt, H. (eds.), *The Electoral Connection.* London: Routledge.

Panebianco, A. (1988). *Political Parties: Organization and Power.* Cambridge: Cambridge University Press.

Pedahzur, A. and Perliger, A. (2004). 'An Alternative Approach for Defining the Boundaries of 'Party Families': Examples from the Israeli Extreme Right-Wing Party Scene'. *Australian Journal of Political Science*, 39: 285–305.

Pelizzo, R. (2003). 'Party Positions or Party Direction? An Analysis of Party Manifesto Data'. *West European Politics*, 26: 67–89.

Pellikaan, H., van der Meer, T. and de Lange, S. (2003). 'The Road from a Depoliticized to a Centrifugal Democracy'. *Acta Politica*, 38: 120–49.

Pennings, P. and Keman, H. (2003). 'The Dutch Parliamentary Elections in 2002 and 2003: The Rise and Decline of the Fortuyn Movement'. *Acta Politica*, 38: 51–68.

Perrineau, P. (2003). 'La surprise lepéniste et sa suite législative' in Perrineau, P. and Ysmal, C. (dir.), *Le Vote de tous les Refus.* Paris: Presses de Sciences Po, 199–222.

Petersen, K. (2005). 'The 2005 Danish General Election: A Phase of Consolidation'. *West European Politics,* 28: 1101–8.

Pourier, P. (2001). La Disparité Idéologique des Nouvelles Droites Occidentales', in Perrineau, P. (dir.), *Les Croisés de la Société Fermée.* La Tour d'Aigues: Éditions de l'Aube, 31–49.

Rydgren, J. (2004). 'Explaining the Emergence of Radical Right-Wing Populist Parties: The Case of Denmark'. *West European Politics*, 27: 474–502.

—— (2005). 'Is Extreme Right-Wing Populism Contagious? Explaining the Emergence of a New Party Family'. *European Journal of Political Research*, 44: 413–37.

Swyngedouw, M. and Ivaldi, G. (2001). 'The Extreme Right Utopia in Belgium and France. The Ideology of the Belgian *Vlaams Blok* and of the French *Front National*'. *West European Politics*, 24: 1–22.

Taggart, P. (2004). 'Populism and Representative Politics in Contemporary Europe'. *Journal of Political Ideologies*, 9: 269–88.

Taguieff, P. A. (2004). *L'Illusion Populiste*. Paris: Universalis.

Tarchi, M. (2003). 'The Political Culture of the Alleanza Nazionale: An Analysis of the Party's Programmatic Documents (1995–2002)'. *Journal of Modern Italian Sudies* 8: 135–81.

—— (2005). 'The Far Right Italian Style', in Casals, X. (ed.), *Political Survival on the Extreme Right. European Movements Between the Inherited Past and the Need to Adapt to the Future*. Barcelona: ICPS, 35–50.

Tassinari, U. M. (2001). *Fascisteria*. Roma: Castelvecchi.

Van der Brug, W. (2004). Voting for the LPF: Some Clarifications. *Acta Politica*, 39: 84–91.

—— and Fennema, M. (2003). 'Protest or Mainstream? How the European Anti-Immigrant Parties Developed into Two Separate Groups by 1999.' *European Journal of Political Research*. 42: 55–76.

Van der Zwan, A. (2004). 'How the LPF Fuellend Discontent: A Comment'. *Acta Politica*. 39: 79–83.

Van Holsteyn, J. J. M., and Irwin, G. A. (2003). 'Never a Dull Moment: Pim Fortuyn and the Dutch Parliamentary Election of 2002'. *West European Politics*. 26: 41–66.

—— Irwin, G. A., and den Ridder, J. M. (2003). 'In the Eye of the Beholder: The Perception of the List Pim Fortuyn and the Parliamentary Elections of May 2002'. *Acta Politica*, 38: 69–87.

Veugelers, J. W. P. and Chiarini, P. (2002). 'The Far Right in France and Italy: Nativist Politics and Anti-Fascism', in Schain, M., Zolberg, A. and Hossay, P. (eds.), *Shadows over Europe: The Development and Impact of the Extreme Right in Western Europe*. New York: Palgrave Macmillan, 83–103.

Wellhofer, S. E. (2003). 'Democracy and Fascism: Class, Civil Society and Rational Choice in Italy'. *American Political Science Review*, 97: 91–106.

Wieworka, M. (1993). *L'Espace du Racisme*. Paris: Seuil.

Ysmal, C. (2000). 'Face à l'Extrême Droite, la Droite Existe-t-elle?' in Bréchon, P., Laurent, A., and Perrineau, P. (dir.), *Les Cultures Politiques des Français*. Paris: Presses de Sciences Po, 139–64.

References

Aardal, B. (1998). 'One for the record—the 1997 Storting Election'. *Scandinavian Political Studies*, 21: 367–81.

—— and Valen, H. (1997). 'The Storting Elections of 1989 and 1993 Norwegian Politics in Perspective', in Strøm, K. and Svasand, L. (eds.), *Challanges to Political Parties. The case of Norway*. Ann Arbor: University of Michigan Press, 61–76.

Abacus (1999). *L'Italia al microscopio*, Milano: Feltrinelli.

Abedi, A. (2002). 'Challenges to Established Parties: The Effects of Party System Features on the Electoral Fortunes of Anti-political-establishment Parties'. *European Journal of Political Research*, 41: 551–83.

Abramowicz, M., and Haelsterman, W. (1998). 'Belgique', in Camus, Y. (dir.), *Les Extrémismes en Europe*. La Tour d'Aigues: Editon de l'Aube, 84–111.

Adorno, T. W., Fraenkel-Brunswick, E., Levinson, D. J., and Sanford, R. N. (1950). *The Authoritarian Personality*. New York: Harper and Row.

Aguero, F. (1995). *Militares, Civiles y Democracia. La España post-franquista en prospectiva comparada*. Madrid: Alianza Editorial.

Alapuro, R. (1980). 'Mass Support for Fascism in Finland', in S. U. Larsen *et al.* (eds.), *Who Were the Fascists*. Bergen: Universitetsforlaget, 678–86.

Algazy, J. (1986). *La tentation néo-fasciste en France 1944–1965*. Paris: Fayard.

Almond, G., and Verba, S. (1963). *The Civic Culture*. Princeton: Princeton University Press.

Anderlini, F., and Leonardi, R. (1991). 'Introduzione', in F. Anderlini, e R. Leonardi (a cura di), *Politica in Italia edizione 91*. Bologna: Il Mulino, 266–9.

Andersen, J. G. (1992). 'Denmark. The Progress Party: Populist Neoliberalism and Welfare State Chauvinism', in Hainsworth, P. (ed.), *The Extreme Right in Postwar Europe and USA*. London: Francis Pinter, 193–205.

Andersen, J. G., and Bjørklund, T. (1990). 'Structural Changes and New Cleavages: the Progress Parties in Denmark and Norway', *Acta Sociologica*, 33: 195–217.

—— —— (1999). 'Anti-Immigration Parties in Denmark and Norway: The Progress Parties and the Danish People's Party', mimeo.

—— —— (2000). 'Radical Right-wing Populism in Scandinavia: From Tax Revolt to Neo-liberalisms and Xenophobia', in Hainsworth, P. (ed.), *The Politics of the Extreme Right. From the Margins to the Mainstream*. London and New York: Pinter, 193–223.

Antisemitism World Report 1993 (1993). London: Institute of Jewish Affairs.

Arter, D. (1992). 'Black Faces in the Blond Crowd: Populist Racism in Scandinavia'. *Parliamentary Affairs*, 45(3): 357–72.

—— (1999). *Scandinavian Politics Today*. Manchester: Manchester University Press.

Azema, J.-P. (1993). 'Vichy', in Winock, M. (dir.), *Histoire de l'extrême droite en France*. Paris: Seuil, 191–214.

—— and Wieviorka, O. (1999). *Vichy (1940–1944)*. Paris: Perrin.

Bacalhau, M. (1989). 'Mobilidade e Transferencia de voto atraves dos sondagens', in Coelho, M. B. (ed.), *Portugal. 0 Sistema Politico e Costitutional 1974–1987*, Lisboa: Istituto de Ciencas Socias de Universidade de Lisboa, 237–56.

Backes, U. (1990). 'The West German Republikaner: profile of a nationalist, populist party of protest'. *Patterns of Prejudice*, 24: 3–18.

Backes, U. (1997). 'Organisationen 1996', in Backes, U., and Jesse, E. (hrsg.), *Jahrbuch Extremismus & Demokratie*. Baden-Baden: Nomos, 133–42.

—— (2001). 'L'extrême droite: les multiples facettes d'une catégorie d'analyse', in Perrineau, P. (dir.), *Les croisés de la société fermée. L'Europe des extrêms droites*. La Tour d'Aigues: Editions de l'Aube, 13–30.

—— and Jesse, E. (1993). *Politischer Extremismus in der Bundesrepublik Deutschland*. Bonn: Bundeszentrale für politische Bildung.

—— and Moreau, P. (1993). *Die Extreme Rechte in Deutschland*. München: Akademischer Verlag.

—— and Moreau, P. (1994). *Die Extreme Rechte in Deutschland*. München: Akademischer Verlag, revised edition.

Bailer Galanda, B. *et al.* (1992). 'Politischer Extremismus (Rechtsextremismus)', in Dachs H. *et al.* (hrgs.), *Handbuch des politischen Systems Österreichs*. Wien: Manzsche Verlags-und Unversitätsbuchhandlung, 286 –95.

Balance, F. (1994). *De l'avant et l'aprés guerre. L'extrême droite en Belgique Francophone*. Bruxelles: de Boeck Wessmael.

Baldini, G., e Vignati, R. (1996). 'Dal MSI ad AN: una nuova cultura politica?'. *Polis*. 10: 81–101.

Bardi, L., e Pasquino, G. (1995). 'Politicizzati e alienati', in Parisi, A. and H. Schadee (a cura di), *Sulla soglia del cambiamento*. Bologna: Il Mulino, 17–41.

Bartolini, S. (2000). *The Political Mobilization of the European Left, 1860–1980*. Cambridge: Cambridge University Press.

—— and Mair, P. (1990). *Identity, Competition and Electoral Availability*. Cambridge: Cambridge University press.

Bauer, P., and Niedermayer, O. (1990). 'Extrem Rechtes Potential in den Ländern der Europäischen Gemeinschaft'. *Aus Politik und Zeitgeschichte*, B46–47: 15–26.

Bauman, Z. (1998). *Globalization: the human consequences*. New York: Columbia University press.

Beck, U. (1998 [1986]). *La società del rischio*. Roma: Carocci.

Bell. D. (ed.) (1955). *The New American Right*. New York: Criterion Books.

—— (ed.) (1963). *The Radical Right*. New York: Doubleday.

—— (1980). *The Winding Passage*. Cambridge, MA: ABT Books.

Benewick, R. (1972). *The Fascist Movement in Britain*. London: Allen Lane.

Berglund, S., and Lindstrom, U. (1979). *The Scandinavian Party System(s)*. Lund: Studentlitteratur.

Bergmann, W. (1997). 'Antisemitism and Xenophobia in Germany since Unification', in Kürthen, H., Bergmann, W., and Erb, R. (eds.), *Antisemitism and Xenophobia in Germany after Unification*. Oxford: Oxford University Press, 21–38.

—— and Erb, R. (1991). *Antisemitismus in der Bundesrepublik Deutschland*. Opladen: Westdeutscher Verlag.

Bergstrom, H. (1991). 'Sweden's Politics and Party System at the Crossroads'. *West European Politics*, 14: 8–30.

Betz, H.-G. (1990*a*). 'Post-Modern Anti-Modernism: The West German Republikaner'. *Politics and Society in Germany, Austria and Switzerland*, 2: 1–22.

—— (1990*b*). 'Politics of Resentment. Right-Wing Radicalism in West Germany'. *Comparative Politics*, 23: 45–60.

—— (1993). 'The New Politics of Resentment. Radical Right Wing Parties in Western Europe'. *Comparative Politics*, 16: 413–27.

Betz, H.-G. (1994). *Radical Right-Wing Populism in Western Europe*. New York: St. Martin's Press.

—— (1998*a*). 'Against Rome: The Lega Nord', in Betz, H.-G., and Immerfall, S. (eds.), *The New Politics of the Right. Neo-Populist Parties and Movements in Established Democracies*, New York: St. Martin's Press, 59–76.

—— (1998*b*). 'Rechtspopulismus: Ein internationaler Trend?'. *Aus Politik und Zeitgeschichte*, B-9–10: 3–12.

—— and Immerfall, S. (eds.) (1998*a*). *The New Politics of the Right. Neo-Populist Parties and Movements in Established Democracies*, New York: St. Martin's Press.

—— and —— (1998*b*). 'Introduction', in Betz, H.-G., and Immerfall, S. (eds.), *The New Politics of the Right. Neo-Populist Parties and Movements in Established Democracies*. New York: St. Martin's Press, 1–10.

Beyme von, K. (1996). 'Party Leadership and Change in Party Systems: Towards a Postmodern Party-State?'. *Government and Opposition*, 31: 135–59.

—— (1988). 'Right-wing extremism in post-war Europe'. *West European Politics*, 11: 1–18.

Bille, L. (1989). 'Denmark: The Oscillating Party System'. *West European Politics*, 12: 42–58.

—— (1992). 'Denmark', in Katz, R., and Mair, P. (eds.), *Party Organizations in Western Democracies 1960–1980: A Data Handbook*. London: Sage, 199–271.

—— (1999). 'Auf und ab. Wahlresultate und Reaktionen der Sozialdemokratischen und der Liberalen Partei Dänemark', in Mair, P., Müller, W., and F. Plasser (hrsg.), *Parteien auf komplexen Wählermärkten: Reaktionsstrategien politischer Parteien in Westeuropa*. Wien: Sigmun-Verl, 353–90.

Billiet, J., and de Witte, H. (1995). 'Attitudinal Dispositions to Vote for a "New" Extreme Right-wing Party: The case of the "Vlaams Blok" '. *European Journal of Political Research*, 27: 181–202.

—— Beerten, R., and Swyngedouw, M. (1996). 'De houding van de kiezer tegenover politiek fatsoen'. *ISPO Bulletin*, 26.

—— and Swyngendouw, M. (1999). 'Les caracteristiques culturelles des électorats en Flandre', in Frognier, A.-P., and Aish, A.-M. (dir.), *Des élections en tromp-l'oeil*. Paris-Bruxelles: DeBoeck & Larcier, 161–84.

Biorcio, R. (1991). 'La Lega come attore politico: dal federalismo al populismo regionalista', in Mannheimer, R. *et al.*, *La Lega Lombarda*. Milano: Feltrinelli, 34 –82.

—— (1997). *La Padania promessa*. Milano: Il Saggiatore.

—— (1999). 'Gli italiani e gli immigrati extracomunitari: l'immaginario e la realtà', in Abacus, *L'Italia al microscopio*. Milano: Feltrinelli, 53–84.

Birembaum, G. (1992). *Le Front National en politique*. Paris: Balland.

Bjørklund, T. (1988). 'The 1987 Norwegian Local Elections: A Protest Election with a Swing to the Right'. *Scandinavian Political Studies*, 11: 211–34.

Blinkhorn, M. (1990). 'Introduction: Allies, rivals or antagonists? Fascists and conservatives in modern Europe', in Blinkhorn, M. (ed.), *Fascists and Conservatives*. London: Unwin Hyman.

Bobbio, N. (1999). *Destra e sinistra*. Milano: Donzelli.

Bonifazi, C. (1998). *L'immigrazione straniera in Italia*. Bologna: Il Mulino.

Borre, O. (1974). 'Denmark's Protest Election of December 1973'. *Scandinavian Political Studies*, 9: 197–203.

Botz, G. (1980). 'Varieties of Fascism in Austria. Introduction', in Larsen, S. U. *et al.* (eds.), *Who Were the Fascists*. Bergen: Universitetsforlaget, 192–201.

Boy, D. and Mayer, N. (1997). 'Les formes de la participation', in Boy, D. and Mayer, N. (dir.), *L'electeur a ses raisons*. Paris: Presses de Sciences Po, 25–65.

Brand, K. W. (1990). 'Cyclical Aspects of New Social Movements: Waves of Cultural Criticism and Mobilization Cycles of New Middle-class Radicalism', in Dalton, R., and Kuechler, M. (eds.), *Challenging the Political Order*. Cambridge: Polity Press, 23–42.

Brechon, P., Derville, J., and Lecomte, P. (1986). *Les cadres du RPR*. Grenoble: Cahiers du CERAT.

—— (1993). *La France aux urnes*. Paris: La documentation Française.

—— and Cautres, B. (1998). 'La cuisante défaite de la droite moderé', in Perrineau, P., et Ysmal, C. (dir.), *Le vote surprise*. Paris: Presses de Sciences Po, 225–51.

Brees, G. (1992). *L'Affront National. Le nouveau visage de l'extrême droite en Belgique*. Bruxelles: EPO.

Breuer, S. (1995 [1993]). *La rivoluzione conservatrice. Il pensiero di destra nella Germania di Weimar*. Roma: Donzelli.

Brewaeys, P., Dahaut, V., and Tolbiac, A. (1992). 'L'extrême droite francophone face aux élections', *Courrier hebdomadaire du CRISP*, 1350.

Brosius, H.-B. and Esser, F. (1996). 'Massenmedien und fremdenfeindliche Gewalt'. *Politische Vierteljahresscrhift*, 27: 204–18.

Brunet, J.-P. (1983). 'Un fascisme français:le Parti populaire français de Doriot (1936–1939)', *Revue française de Science Politique*, 33: 256–80.

—— (1986). *Jacques Doriot*. Paris: Balland.

Budge, I. (1999). 'Expert judgments of party policy positions: Uses and limitations in political research'. *European Journal of Political Research*, 37: 103–13.

——, Robertson, D., and Hearl (eds.) (1987). *Ideology, Strategy and Party Change: Spatial Analyses of Post-War Election Programmes in 19 Democracies*. Cambridge: Cambridge University Press.

Bundesminister des Inneren (2000). www.verfassungsschutz.de

Bürklin, W. (1991). 'Changing Political and Social Attitudes in the Uniting Germany', *Politics and Society in Germany, Austria, and Switzerland*. 4: 20–33.

Burrin, P. (1986). *La dérive fasciste. Deat, Doriot, Bergery, 1933–1945*. Paris: Seuil.

—— (2000). *Fascisme, nazisme, autoritarisme*. Paris: Seuil.

Butler, D. and King, D. (1965). *The General Election of 1964*. Basingstoke: Macmillan.

—— and Stoke, R. (1969). *Political Change in Britain*. New York: St. Martin's Press.

Campbell, D. (1992). 'Die Dynamik der politischen Links-rechts-Schwingungen in Österreich'. *Österreichische Zeitschrift für Politiwikssenschaft*, 21: 165–79.

Camus, J.-Y. (1989). 'Origine et Formation du Front Nationale', in Mayer, N., and Perrineau, P. (dir.), *Le Front National à Decouvert*. Paris: Presses de la Fondation Nationale des Sciences Politiques, 17–36.

—— (2001). 'La structure du «champ national» en France: la périphérie militante et organisationelle du Front National et du Mouvement National Républicain', in Perrineau, P. (dir.), *Les croisés de la société fermée. L'Europe des extrême droites*. La Tour d'Aigues: Editions de l'Aube, 199–223.

Capoccia, G. (2002). 'Anti-System Parties: A Conceptual Reassessment', *Journal of Theoretical Politics*. 14: 9–35.

Caramani, D. (2000). *Elections in Western Europe since 1815*. London and New York: Macmillan-Grove.

Casals, X. (1995). *Neonazis en España*. Barcelona: Grijalbo.

—— (1998a). *La tentación neofascista en Espana*. Barcelona: Plaza & Janés.

—— (1998b). *El Fascismo: Entre el legado de Franco y la modernidad de Le Pen (1975–1997)*. Barcelona: Ediciones Destino.

—— (2001). 'National-populisme en Espagne: les raisons d'une absence', in Perrineau, P. (dir.), *Les croisés de la société fermée. L'Europe des extrême droites*. La Tour d'Aigues: Editions de l'Aube, 323–38.

Cayrol, R. (1994). *Le grand malentendu. Les Français et la politique*. Paris: Seuil.

Chiarini, R. (1995). *Destra italiana*. Venezia: Marsilio.

—— (1999). 'La lunga marcia della destra italiana. L'integrazione passiva di Alleanza Nazionale'. *Nuova Storia Contemporanea*, 3: 79–102.

—— (2001). 'L'integrazione passiva', in Chiarini, R. and Maraffi, M. (a cura di) *La destra allo specchio. La cultura politica di Allenza Nazionale*. Venezia: Marsilio, 13–42.

Chiroux, R. (1974). *L'extrême droite sous la V° Republique*. Paris: LGDJ.

Cofrancesco, D. (1986). 'Fascismo: Destra o Sinistra?', in Bracher, K. D. and Valiani, L. (a cura di), *Fascismo e Nazionalsocialismo*. Bologna: Il Mulino, 55–140.

Conway, M. (1996). 'The Extreme Right in Inter-War Francophone Belgium: Explanation of a Failure'. *European History Quarterly*, 26: 267–92.

Copsey, N. (1996). 'Contemporary fascism in local arena: The British national party and the "Rights for Whites"', in Cronin, M. (ed.), *The Failure of British Fascism*. Basingstoke: Macmillan, 118–40.

Corbetta, P. (1993). 'La Lega e lo sfaldamento del sistema', *Polis*. 8: 229–52.

Corbetta, P., Parisi, A., and Schadee, H. M. A. (1988). *Elezioni in Italia. Struttura e tipologia delle consultazioni politiche*. Bologna: Il Mulino.

Costa Pinto, A. (1995). 'The radical right in contemporary Portugal', in Cheles, L., Ferguson, R., and Vaughan, M. (eds.), *The Radical Right In Western and Eastern Europe*. Harlow: Longaman, 108–28.

Cotarelo, R. (ed.) (1992). *Transición politica y consolidación democratica*. Madrid: CIS.

—— and Lopez Nieto, L. (1988). 'Spanish Conservatism, 1976–1987', *West European Politics*, 11: 80–95.

Cova, A. (1999). 'Opinioni, atteggiamenti, valori: un'analisi dei dati di trend', in Abacus, *L'Italia al microscopio*. Milano: Feltrinelli, 293–324.

Cross, C. (1961). *The Fascists in Britain*. London: Barrie and Rockliff.

Crapez, M. (1998). 'De quand date le clivage gauche/droite en France?'. *Revue Française de Science Politique*, 48: 42–75.

Cullen, S. M. (1993). 'Political Violence: The Case of the British Union of Fascists'. *Journal of Contemporary History*, 28: 245–67.

Daalder, H. (1966). 'The Netherlands: Opposition in a Segemented Society', in Dahl R. A. (ed.), *Political Opposition in Western Democracies*. New Haven: Yale University Press, 188–236.

—— (1987). 'The Dutch Party System: From Segmentation to Polarization—And then?', Daalder (ed.), *Party Systems in Denmark, Austria, Switzerland, the Netherlands and Belgium*. London: Pinter, 193–284.

—— (1989). 'The Mould of Dutch Politics'. *West European Politics*, 12: 1–20.

Dalton, R. (1996). *Citizen Politics* (2nd ed.). Chatam: Chatam House.

—— (1999). 'Political Support in Advanced Industrial Democracies', in Norris, P. (ed.), *Critical Citizens*. Oxford: Oxford University Press.

Damgaard, E., and Svensson, P. (1989). 'Who Governs? Parties and Policies in Denmark'. *European Journal of Political Research*, 17: 731–45.

de Benoist, A. (1983). *Le idee a posto*. Napoli: Akropolis.

—— (1992). 'Risposte ad Alain Caillé'. *Diorama*, 154: 37–48.

De Felice, R. (1969). *Le interpretazioni del Fascismo*. Bari: Laterza.

—— (1975). *Intervista sul Fascismo*. Bari: Laterza.

—— (1981). *Mussolini il Duce*. Vol. II. *Lo Stato totalitario 1936–1940*. Torino: Einaudi.

De Napoli, D. (1980). *Il movimento monarchico*. Napoli: Loffredo.

de Winter, L. (1996). 'Party Encroachment on the Executive and the Legislative Branch in the Belgian Polity'. *Res Publica*, 38: 325–52.

De Winter, L. and Dumont, P. (1999). 'Belgium: Party System(s) on the Eve of Disintegration?', in Broughton, D. and Donovan, M. (eds), *Changing Party Systems in Western Europe*. London and New York: Pinter, 183–206.

Della Porta, D., and Rossi, M. (1986). *Cifre Crudeli*. Bologna: Materiali dell'Istituto Carlo Cattaneo.

Delwit, P. (1998). 'Qui vote pour le Front national en Belgique', in Delwit, P. *et al.*, *L'extrême droite en France et en Belgique*. Bruxelles: Editions Complexe, 167–80.

—— and De Waele, J.-M. (1997). 'Origines, évolutions et devenir des partis politiques en Belgique', in Delwit, P., and De Waele, J.-M. (dir.), *Les partis politiques en Belgique*. Bruxelles: Editions de l'Université de Bruxelles, 7–24.

—— and De Waele, J.-M. (1999). 'Partis et systèmes de partis en Belgique: 1830–1998', in Delwit, P. *et al.* (dir.), *Gouverner la Belgique. Clivages et compromis dans une société complexe*. Paris: Puf, 113–54.

Delwit, P. *et al.* (dir.) (1999). *Gouverner la Belgique. Clivages et compromis dans une société complexe*. Paris: Puf.

Deschouwer, K. (1994). 'The Decline of Consocialism and the Reluctant Adaptation of the Belgian Mass Parties', in Katz, R., and Mair, P. (eds.), *How Parties Organize*. London: Sage, 80–108.

—— (1996). 'Political parties and democracy: a mutual murder?'. *European Journal of Political Research*, 29: 263–78.

—— (1999). 'In der Falle gefangen. Belgiens Parteien und ihre Reaktionen auf abnehmende Wählerloyalitäten', in Mair, P., Müller, W., and Plasser, F. (hrsg.), *Parteien auf komplexen Wählermärkten: Reaktionsstrategien politischer Parteien in Westeuropa*. Wien: Sigmun-Verl, 285–313.

Devigne, R. (1993). *Recasting Conservatism. Oakeshott, Strauss and the Response to Postmodernism*. New Haven and London: Yale University Press.

Dewachter, W. (1987). 'Changes in the Particratie: the Belgian Party System from 1944 to 1986', in Daalder H. (ed.), *Party Systems in Denmark, Austria, Switzerland, The Netherlands and Belgium*, London: Pinter, 285–364.

Diamandouros, N. (1986). 'Regime Change and the Prospect for Democracy in Greece, 1974–1983', in O'Donnell, G., Schmitter, P., and Whitehead, L. (eds), *Transition from Authoritarian Rule. Prospect for Democracy. Baltimore and London*, Johns Hopkins University Press, 138–65.

Diamandouros, N. (1997). 'Southern Europe: A Third Wave Success Story', in Diamond, L. et al. (eds), *Consolidating the Third Wave Democratization. Regional Challenges.* Baltimore and London: Johns Hopkins University Press, 3–25.

—— (1998). 'The Political System in Post-Authoritarian Greece (1974–1996): Outline and Interpretations', in Ignazi, P., and Ysmal, C. (eds.), *The Organization of Political Parties in Southern Europe.* Westport: Praeger, 181–201.

—— and Gunther, R. (2001). *Parties, Politics, and Democracy in the New Southern Europa.* Baltimore and London: Johns Hopkins University Press.

Diamanti, I. (1993). *La Lega.* Milano: Donzelli.

—— (1994). 'La Lega', in Diamanti, I. and Mannheimer, R. (a cura di), *Da Milano a Roma. Guida all'Italia elettorale del 1994.* Roma: Donzelli, 53–62.

—— (1997a). 'La Ligue du Nord, toujours plus', in Diamanti, I. and Lazar, M. (dir.), *Politique à l'Italienne.* Paris: Puf, 151–67.

—— (1997b). 'L'identità cattolica e comportamento di voto', in Corbetta, P., and Parisi, A. (a cura di), *A domanda risponde: il cambiamento del voto degli italiani nelle elezioni del 1994 e del 1996.* Bologna: Il Mulino, 317–36.

Dimitras, P. E. (1992). 'Greece: The Virtual Absence of an Extreme Right', in Hainsworth, P. (ed.), *The Extreme Right in Europe and the United States.* New York: St. Martin's Press, 246–68.

Dogan, M. (1999). 'Deficit de confiance dans les démocracties avancées. Une analyse comparative', Paper presented at the VI Congress of the Association Française de Science Politique, Rennes, 28 September–1 October 1999.

Downs, A. (1957). *An Economic Theory of Democracy.* New York: Harper and Row.

Druwe, U. and Mantino, S. (1996). 'Rechtsextremismus. Methodologische Bemerkung zu einem politikwissenschaftlichen Begriff'. *Politische Vierteljahresschrift*, 27: 66–80.

Duhamel, O., and Jaffré, J. (1993). 'Abécédaire de the opinion', in Sofres, *L'état de l'opinion 1993.* Paris: Gallimard, 213–42.

Dumont, L. (1991 [1996]). *Homo Hierarchicus. Il sistema delle caste e le sue implicazioni.* Milano: Adelphi.

—— (1993 [1983]). *Saggi sull'individualismo.* Milano: Adelphi.

Duprat, F. (1972). *Les mouvements d'extrême droite en France depuis 1944.* Paris: Albatros.

Durkheim, E., and Mauss, M. (1951 [1901–02]). *L'origine dei poteri magici.* Torino: Einaudi.

Duverger, M. (1951). *Les partis politiques.* Paris: A. Colin.

Eatwell, R. (1989). 'The Nature of the Right, 2: The Right as a Variety of "Styles of Thought"', in Eatwell, R., and O'Sullivan, N. (eds.), *The Nature of the Right. European and American Politics and Political Thought Since 1789.* London: Pinter, 62–76.

—— (1990). 'Fascism in Post-War Britain', in Kushner, T., and Lunn, K. (eds.), *Traditions of Intolerance.* Manchester: Manchester University Press, 218–38.

—— (1992a). 'Towards a New Model of Generic Fascism'. *Journal of Theoretical Politics*, 4: 161–94.

—— (1992b). 'Why Has the Extreme Right Failed in Britain?', in P. Hainsworth (ed.), *The Extreme Right Europe and the USA.* London: Pinter, 175–92.

—— (1996a). 'The Esoteric Ideology of National Front in the 1980s', in Cronin, M. (ed.). *The Failure of British Fascism.* Basingstoke: Macmillan, 99–117.

—— (1996b). 'On Defining the "Fascist Minimum": The Centrality of Ideology'. *Journal of Political Ideology*, 1: 303–19.

Eatwell, R. (1997). *Fascism: A History*. New York: Penguin Books.

—— (1998*a*). 'Britain, The BNP and the problem of legitimacy', in Betz, H.-G., and Immerfall, S. (eds.), *The New Politics of the Right. Neo-Populist Parties and Movements in Established Democracies*. New York: St. Martin's Press, 143–55.

—— (1998*b*). 'The Dynamics of Right-wing Electoral Brekthrough'. *Patterns of Prejudice*, 32: 3–31.

—— (2000). 'The Extreme Right and British Exceptionalism: The Primacy of Politics', in Hainsworth, P. (ed.), *The Politics of the Extreme Right. From the Margins to the Mainstream*. London and New York: Pinter, 172–92.

Escobar, R. (1995). 'Simbolo, spazio, ordine', *Filosofia Politica*, 9: 409–24.

Etienne, J. M. (1968). *Le Mouvement rexiste jusqu'en 1940*. Paris: Presses de la FNSP.

Evans, J. (1998). *Electoral deviancy as normality: modelling left-right voter defection to the extreme right in France*. PhD Thesis: Florence, European University Institute.

Evans, J. (2001). 'Le bases sociales et psychologiques du passage gauche-extrême dorite. Exception française ou mutation européenne?', in P. Perrineau (dir.), *Les croisés de la société fermé*. La Tour d'Aigues: Editions de l'Aube, 73–102.

Evola, J. (1951). *Gli uomini e le rovine*. Roma: Volpe.

—— (1969 [1934]). *Rivolta contro il mondo moderno*. Roma: Edizioni mediterranee, revised edition.

—— (1973 [1961]). *Cavalcare la Tigre. Orientamenti esistenziali per un epoca della dissoluzione*. Milano: Scheiwiller, revised edition.

Falter, J. (1994). *Wer wält recht?*. München: C. H. Beck.

—— and Schumann, S. S. (1993). 'Nichtwahl und Protestwahl: Zwei Seiten einer Medaille'. *Aus Politik und Zeitgeschichte*, B11: 36–49.

Fennema, M. (1997). 'Some Conceptual Issues and Problems in the Comparison of Anti-immigrant Parties in Western Europe'. *Party Politics*, 4: 473–92.

—— and Pollman, C. (1998). 'Ideology of Anti-Immigrant Parties in the European Parliament'. *Acta Politica*, 33: 111–33

Ferraresi, F. (ed) (1984). *La destra radicale*, Milano: Feltrinelli.

—— (1988). 'The Radical Right in Postwar Italy'. *Politics and Society*, 16: 71–119.

—— (1995). *Minacce alla democrazia. La destra radicale e la strategia della tensione in Italia nel dopoguerra*. Milano: Feltrinelli.

Fessel-GfK (1999). *Exit Polls 1999*

Fielding, N. (1981). *The National Front*. London: Collins.

Fischer, J. (1996). *British Political Parties*. Hemel Hempstead: Prentice Hall.

Flanagan, S. C. (1987). 'Value Change in Industrial Society'. *American Political Science Review*, 81: 1303–19.

Franke, F. S. (1996). 'Ein ökonomisches Modell zur Erklärung der Wahlerfolge rechtsextremer Parteien', *Politische Vierteljahresscrhift*, 27: 81–94.

Freeden, M. (1996). *Ideologies and Political Theory. A Conceptual Approach*. Oxford: Clarendon Press.

Fuchs, D. (1993). 'Trends in Political Support', in Berg-Schlösser, D., and Rytlewski, R. (eds.), *Political Culture in Germany*, Basingstoke: Macmillan, 232–69.

—— (1999). 'The Democratic Culture of Unified Germany', in Norris P. (ed.), *Critical Citizens. Global Support for Democratic Governance*. Oxford: Oxford University Press, 123–55.

—— and Klingemann, H. D. (1990). 'The Left–Right Schema', in Jennings, M. K. *et al.*, *Continuities in Political Action*. Berlin-New York: de Gruyter, 203–34.

Fuchs, D., Guidorossi, G., and Svensson, P. (1995). 'Support for the Democratic System' in Klingemann, H.-D., and Fuchs, D. (eds.), *Citizens and the State*. Oxford: Oxford University Press, 323–53.

Gabriel, O. (1996). 'Rechtsextreme Einstellungen in Europa: Struktur, Entwicklung und Verhaltens-implicationen', *Politische Vierteljahresschrift*, 27: 344–60.

Gächter, A. (1992). 'Refugees in Austria—An Overview'. *Politics and Society in Germany, Austria and Switzerland*, 4: 59–69.

Galeotti, A. E. (1984). 'L'opposizione destra-sinistra. Riflessioni analitiche', in F. Ferraresi (a cura di), *La Destra radicale*, Milano: Garzanti, 253–75.

Gallagher, T. (1992). 'Portugal: The Marginalization of the Extreme Right', in Hainsworth, P. (ed.), *The Extreme Right in Europe and the United States*. New York: St. Martin's Press, 232–45.

Gallangher, M., Laver, M., and Mair, P. (1995). *Representative Government in Modern Europe*. New York: McGraw-Hill, revised edition.

Galli, C. (1981). 'Introduzione', in Galli, C. (a cura di), *I controrivoluzionari*. Bologna: Il Mulino, 7–56.

Gamble, A. (1988). *The Free Economy and the Strong State*. Basingstoke: Macmillan.

Gardberg, A. (1993). *Against the Stranger, the Gangster and the Establishment*. Helsinki: Swedish School of Social Sciences.

Gasperoni, G. (1995). 'Dimensioni della fluidità elettorale', in Parisi, A., and Schadee, H. (a cura di), *Sulla soglia del cambiamento*. Bologna: Il Mulino, 321–55.

Gauchet, M. (1994 [1992]). *Storia di una dicotomia. La destra e la sinistra*. Milano: Anabasi.

Geingembre, G. (1989). *La Contre-Revolution ou l'histoire désespérante*. Paris: Imago.

Gentile, E. (1995). *La via italiana al totalitarismo. Partito e Stato nel regime fascista*. Roma: Carocci.

—— (1996). *Le origini dell'ideologia fascista (1918–1925)*. Bologna: Il Mulino.

Gentile, G. (1925). *Che cosa è il fascismo*. Firenze: Vallecchi.

Gibson, R., and Swenson, T. (1999). 'The Politicization of Anti-Immigrant Attitudes in Western Europe: Examining the Mobilization of Prejudice Among the Supporters of Extreme Right-Wing Parties in EU Member States, 1988 and 1994'. Paper presented at the 95th Annual Meeting of the American Political Science Association. Boston, MA.

Giddens, A. (1994). *Beyond Left and Right*. Cambridge: Polity Press.

Gijsels, H. (1992). *Het Vlaams Blok*. Leuven: Uitgevij Kritak.

Gijsels, H. et al. (1988). *Les barbares. Les immigrés et le racismes dans the politique belge*. Bruxelles: Epo/Halt/Celsius.

Gilljam, M., and Oscarsson, H. (1996). 'Mapping the Nordic Party Space', *Scandinavian Political Studies*, 19: 25–43.

Girardet, R. (1955). 'Notes sur l'esprit d'un fascisme français, 1934–1940'. *Revue Française de Science Politique*, 5: 529–46.

Girvin, B. (1988a). 'Introduction: Varieties of Conservatism', in Girvin, B. (ed.), *The Transformation of Contemporary Conservatism*. London: Sage, 1–12.

—— (1988b). *The Transformation of Contemporary Conservatism*. London: Sage.

Gooskens, M. P. J. (1993). *How extreme are the extreme right parties in Scandinavia?*. MA Thesis, Leiden: University of Leiden.

Govaert, S. (1992). 'Le Vlaams Blok et ses dissidences', *Courrier hebdomadaire du CRISP*, 1365.

Grande, E. (1988). 'Neoconservatism without Neoconservatives? The Renaissance and Transformation of Contemporary German Conservatism', in Girvin, B. (ed.), *The Transformation of Contemporary Conserevatism*. London: Sage, 55–77.

Griffin, R. (1993). *The Nature of Fascism. The Future of Radical Politics*. London, New York: Routledge.

—— (1995). *General Introduction* in Griffin, R (ed.), 'Fascism. A Reader'. Oxford: Oxford University Press, 3–17.

—— (1996a). 'The "Post-Fascism" of Alleanza Nazionale: A Case Study in Ideological Morphology'. *Journal of Political Ideologies*, 1: 123–45.

—— (1996b). 'British Fascism: the Ugly Duckling', in Cronin, M. (ed.), *The Failure of British Fascism*. Basingstoke: Macmillan, 141–65.

—— (1998). 'Introduction', in Griffin, R. (ed.), *International Fascism. Theories, Causes and the New Consensus*. London: Arnold, 1–20.

—— (2000) 'Interregnum or endgame? The radical right in the "post-fascist" era' in *Journal of Political Ideologies* 5: 163–178.

Grunberg, G., and Schweisguth, E. (1997). 'Recomposition ideologique', in Mayer, N., and Boy, D. (dir.), *L'electeur a ses raisons*. Paris: Presses de Sciences Po.

Gunther, R., Diamandouros, N. P., and Puhle, H.-J. (eds.) (1995). *The Politics of Democratic Consolidation. Southern Europe in Comparative Perspective*. Baltimore and London: The Johns Hopkins University Press.

Hagendoorn, L., and Hraba, J. (1989). 'Foreign, different, deviant, exclusive and working class: anchors to an ethnic hierarchy in the Netherlands', *Ethnic and Racial Studies*, 12: 441–68.

Hagtvet, B. (1980). 'On the Fringe: Swedish Fascism 1920–1945', in Larsen S. U. *et al.* (eds.), *Who Were the Fascists*. Bergen: Universitetsforlaget, 715–42.

Hainsworth, P. (2000). 'Introduction: The Extreme Right', in Hainsworth, P. (ed.), *The Politics of the Extreme Right. From the Margins to the Mainstream*. London and New York: Pinter, 1–17.

Hammar, T. (1991), 'Cradle of Freedom on Earth: Refugee Immigration and Ethnic Pluralism'. *West European Politics*, 14: 182–97.

Harmel, R., and Svasand, L. (1989). 'From Protest to Party: Progress on the Right in Denmark and Norway', paper presented at the 85th APSA Annual Meeting, Atlanta.

—— and Janda, K. (1994). 'An Integrated Theory of Party Goals and Party Change'. *Journal of Theoretical Politics*, 6: 259–88.

—— and Gibson, R. (1995). 'Right-Libertarian Parties and the "New Values": A Re-Examination'. *Scandinavian Political Studies*, 18: 97–118.

Harrop, M., England, J., and Husbands, C. T. (1980). 'The Bases of National Front Support'. *Political Studies*, 28: 271–83.

Hazan, R. (1997). *Centre parties: Polarization and Competition in European Parliamentary Democracies*. London and New York: Continuum.

Heidar, K. (1989). 'Norway. Levels of Party Competition and System Change'. *West European Politics*, 12: 143–56.

—— (2001). 'Changing Patterns of Party Competition in Norway: The Role of the Progress Party'. Paper presented at the Conference "New Parties in Government". Brussels: Vrije Universiteit Brussels.

Hermes, G., and Knudsen, K. (1992). 'Norwegian Attitudes towards New Immigrants'. *Acta Sociologica*, 35: 123–39.

Hertz, R. (1994 [1928]). *La preminenza della destra*. Torino: Einaudi.

Himmelstein, J. L. (1990.). *To the Right. The Transformation of American Conservatism*. Berkeley: University of California Press.

Hoffman, S. (1976). *Sur la France*. Paris: Seuil.

Hoffman, S. *et al.* (1956). *Le mouvement Poujade*. Paris: Colin.

Hoffmann-Lange, U. (1996). 'Das rechte Einstellungspotential in der deutschen Jugend'. *Politische Vierteljahresscrhift*, 27: 121–137.

Hofstedter, R. (1967). *The Paranoid Style in American Politics*. New York: Vintage Books, revised edition.

Holmberg, S. (1999). 'Down and Down We Go: Political Trust In Sweden', in Norris P. (ed.), *Critical Citizens*. Oxford: Oxford University Press.

Holmes, S. (1993). *The Anatomy of Antiliberalism*. Cambridge and London: Harvard University Press.

Huber, J. D. (1989). 'Values and Partisanship in Left–Right Orientations: Measuring Ideology'. *European Journal of Political Research*, 17: 599–621.

—— and Inglehart, R. (1995). 'Expert Interpretations of Party Space and Party Locations in 42 Societies'. *Party Politics*, 1: 73–111.

Huntington, S. P. (1957). 'Conservatism as an Ideology', *American Political Science Review*, 51: 454–73.

Husbands, C. T. (1981). 'Contemporary Right-Wing Extremism in Western European Democracies: A Review Article'. *European Journal of Political Research*, 9: 75–100.

—— (1983). *Racial Exclusionism the City*. London: Allen and Unwin.

—— (1988). 'Extreme Right-Wing Politics in Great Britain: the Recent Marginalization of the National Front'. *West European Politics*, 11: 65–79.

—— (1992*a*). 'The Netherlands: Irritants on the Body Politic', in Hainsworth P. (ed.), *The Extreme Right in Europe and the USA*. London: Pinter, 95–125.

—— (1992*b*). 'Phoenix from the Ashes? The Recovery of the Centrumpartij 86 and the Centrumdemocraten, 1989–1991'. *Jaarboeck 1991 DNPP*, 84–102.

—— (1992*c*). 'Belgium: Flemish Legion on the March', in Hainsworth P. (ed.), *The Extreme Right in Europe and the USA*. London: Pinter, 126–50.

—— (1994). 'Following the "Continental Model"?: Implications of the Recent Electoral Performance of the British National Party'. *New Community*, 20: 563–79.

Ignazi, P. (1989). 'Un nouvel acteur politique', in Mayer, N. and Perrineau, P. (dir.), *Le Front national à decouvert*. Paris: Presses de la FNSP, 63–80.

—— (1992). 'The Silent Counter-revolution. Hypotheses on the Emergence of Extreme Right Parties in Europe'. *European Journal of Political Research*, 22: 3–34.

—— (1993). 'The Changing Profile of the Italian Social Movement', in Merkl, P. H., and Weinberg, L. (eds.), *Encounters with the Contemporary Radical Right*. Boulder: Westview Press, 75–92.

—— (1994). *Postfascisti? La trasformazione del Movimento Sociale in Alleanza Nazionale*. Bologna: Il Mulino.

—— (1996*a*). 'From Neo-Fascists to Post-Fascists? The transformation of the MSI into AN'. *West European Politics*, 19: 693–714.

Ignazi, P. (1996*b*). 'Antipartitismo, antimmigrazione e fascismo: nuovi e vecchi nodi della politica italiana'. *Political Trend*, 12: 23–9.

—— (1996*c*). 'The Intellectual Basis of Right-wing Anti-partytism', *European Journal of Political Research*, 29: 279–96.

—— (1998*a* revised edition [1989]). *Il Polo Escluso. Profilo storico del Movimento Sociale Italiano*. Bologna: Il Mulino

—— (1998*b*). 'MSI/AN: A Mass Party with the Temptation of the Führerprinzip', in Ignazi, P., and Ysmal, C. (eds.), *The Organization of Political Parties in Southern Europe*. Westport: Praeger, 157–77.

—— (1998*c*). 'Gianfranco Fini è in fuga ma il suo plotone arranca', *il Mulino*, 47: 233–40.

—— (1999). 'I partiti e la politica (1963–1992)', in Sabbatucci, G., e Vidotto, V. (a cura di), *Storia d'Italia*, Vol. VII. Bari-Roma: Laterza, 102–232

—— and Perrineau, P. (2000). 'L'extrême droite en Europe: marginalité du néo-fascisme et dynamique de l'extrême droite post-industrielle', in Grunberg, G., Perrineau, P., and Ysmal, C. (dir.), *Le vote des Quinze. Les élections européennes du 13 juin 1999*. Paris: Presses de Sciences Po, 223–42.

—— and Ysmal, C. (1992). 'New and Old Right-wing Parties. The French Front National and the Italian Movimento Sociale'. *European Journal of Political Research*, 22: 101–21.

Imbriani, A. M. (1996). *Vento del sud*. Bologna: Il Mulino.

Inglehart, R. (1977). *The Silent Revolution*. Princeton: Princeton University Press.

—— (1990). *Culture Shift*. Princeton: Princeton University Press.

Irwin, G., and Dittrich, K. (1984). 'And the Walls Came Tumbling Down: Party Dealignment in the Netherlands', in Dalton, R. J., Beck, P. A., and Flanagan, S. C. (eds.), *Electoral Change in Advanced Industrial Democracies: Realignment or Dealignment?*. Princeton: Princeton University Press, 267–97.

Ivaldi, G. (1998*a*). 'The Front National. The Making of an Authoritrian Party', in Ignazi, P., and Ysmal, C. (eds.), *The Organization of political parties in Southern Europe*. Westport: Praeger, 43–69.

—— (1998*b*). 'L'extrême droite ou la crise des systèmes des partis'. *Revue Internationale de Politique Comparée*, 6: 201–46.

—— (2001). 'L'analyse comparée des soutiens électoraux du national-populisme en Europe occidentale. Apports et limites des grands programmes d'enquêtes transnationales (1990–1998)', in Perrineau, P. (dir.), *Les croisés de la société fermée. L'Europe des extrêmes droites*. La Tour d'Aigues: Editions de l'Aube, 53–71.

—— and Bréchon, P. (2000). 'Le rapport à l'autre: une culture xonophobe?', in Bréchon, P., Laurent, A., and Perrineau, P. (dir.), *Les cultures politiques des français*. Paris: Presses des Science Po, 275–304.

Jabardo, R. (1996). 'La extrema derecha española, 1976–1996: estrategias de movilizacion y estructura de la oportunidad politica', *Sistema*, 135: 105–22.

Jackman, R. W. and Volpert, K. (1996). 'Conditions Favouring Parties of the Extreme Right in Western Europe'. *British Journal of Political Science*, 26: 515–16.

Jaschke, H. G. (1993 [1990]). *Die Republikaner. Profile einer Rechtsaußen-Partei*. Bonn: Dietz.

—— (1999). 'Die Rechtsextremen Parteien nach der Bundestagswahl 1998: Stehen sie sich selbst im Wege?', in O. Niedermayer (hrsg.), *Die Parteien nach der Bundestagswahl 1998*. Leverkusen: Leske-Budrich, 141–57.

Kalliala, M. (1999). 'Traditions of the Radical Right in the Finnish Political Culture', in Pekonen, K. (ed.), *The New Radical Right in Finland*. s.l.: the Finnish Political Science Association, 61–83.

Kapetanyannis, V. (1995). 'Neo-Fascism in Modern Greece', in Cheles, L. Ferguson, R., and Vaughan, M. (eds.), *The Radical Right in Western and Eastern Europe*. Harlow: Longman, 129–44.

Karapin, R. (1998) 'Explaining the Far-Right Electoral Success in Germany. The Politicization of Immigration-Related Issues'. *German Politics and Society*, 48: 24–61.

—— (1999). 'The Politics of Immigration Control in Britain and Germany'. *Comparative Politics*, 31: 423–44.

Katz, R. and Mair, P. (eds.) (1994). *How Parties Organize*. London: Sage.

Katzestein, P. J. (1977). 'The Last Old Nation. Austrian National Consciousness since 1945'. *Comparative Politics*, 9: 147–72.

Kaymak, E. and Mayer, L. C. (1995). 'Populism and the Rise of the New Right in Industrial Democracies'. Paper presented at the APSA Annual Meeting, Chicago.

Kim, H. and Fording, R. (2000). 'Voter Ideology in Western Democracies'. *European Journal of Political Research*, 27: 73–97.

Kirchheimer, O. (1966). 'The Vanishing Opposition', in Dahl, R. (ed.), *Political Opposition in Western Democracies*. New Haven and London: Yale University Press, 237–59.

Kitschelt, H. (1997). 'European Party Systems: Continuity and Change', in Rhodes, M. Heywood, P., and Wright V. (eds.), *Developments in West European Politics*. Basingstoke: Macmillan, 131–50.

Kitschelt, H. (in collaboration with McGann, A. J.) (1995). *The Radical Right in Western Europe. A Comparative Analysis*. Ann Arbor: The University of Michigan Press.

Klein, M. and Falter, J. (1996). 'Die dritte Welle rechtsextremer Wahlerfolge in der Bundesrepublik Deutschland'. *Politische Vierteljahresscrhift*, 27: 288–312.

Klingemann, H.-D. (1995). 'Party Positions and Voter Orientations', in Klingemann, H.-D., and Fuchs, D. (eds.) (1995). *Citizens and the State*. Oxford: Oxford University Press, 183–205.

Knapp, A. (1999). 'Frankreich; Die 'Vierebande' und die extreme rechte. Verurteilung und Komplizenschaft', in P. Mair, W. Müller, and F. Plasser (hrsg.), *Parteien auf komplexen Wählermärkten: Reaktionsstrategien politischer Parteien in Westeuropa*. Wien: Sigmun-Verl, 155–99.

Knigge, P. (1998). 'The Ecological Correlates of Right-wing Extremism in Western Europe'. *European Journal of Political Research*, 34: 249–79.

Knight, K. (1985). 'Ideology in the 1980 Election'. *American Political Science Review*, 47: 828–53.

Knutsen, O. (1995). 'Value Orientation, Political Conflict and Left–right Identification: A Comparative Study'. *European Journal of Political Research*, 28: 63–93.

Knutsen, O. (1998). 'Expert Judgments of the Left-Right Location of political party. A Comparative Longitudinal Study'. *West European Politics*, 21: 63–94.

Kolckey, J. M. (1983). *The New Right 1960–1968*. Washington: University Press of America.

Kolinski, E. (1992). 'A Future for Right Extremism in Germany?', in Hainsworth, P. (ed.), *The Extreme Right in Europe and the USA*. London: Pinter, 61–94.

Koole, R. (1999). 'Die Antwort der niederländischen Parteien auf die wahlpolitischen Herausforderungen', in Mair, P., Müller, W., and Plasser, F. (Hrsg.). Wien: Signum, 315–352.

Koopmans, R. (1996). 'Explaining the Rise of Racist and Extreme Right Violence in Western Europe: Grievances or Opportunities?'. *European Journal of Political Research*, 30: 185–213.

Küchler, M. (1994). 'Germans and "Others": Racism, Xenophobia or "Legitimate conservatism"', *German Politics*, 3: 47–74.

—— (1996). 'Xenophobie in internationale Vergleich', *Politische Vierteljahresscrhift*, 27: 248–62.

Kulinski, J. H., Luskin, R. C., and Bolland, J. (1991). 'Where is the Schema? Going Beyond the 's' Word in Political Psychology'. *American Political Science Review*, 85: 1341–55.

Kurthen, H., Bergmann, W., and Erb, R. (1998). *Introduction: Challanges to German Democracy*, in Kurthen, H., Bergmann, W., and Erb, R. (eds.), 'Antisemitism and Xenophobia in Germany after Unification'. Oxford: Oxford University Press, 1–8.

Kushnick, L. (1998). *Race, Class, and Struggle*. London and New York: Rivers Oram Press.

Lafferty, W. (1989). 'The Political Transformation of a Social Democratic State: As the World Moves in, Norway Moves Right'. *West European Politics*, 11: 79–100.

Laponce, A. (1981). *Left and Right. The Topography of Political Perception*, Toronto: University of Toronto Press.

Larsen, S. U. (1980). 'The Social Foundation of Norwegian Fascism 1933–1945: An Analysis of Membership Data', in Larsen S. U. *et al.* (eds.), *Who Were the Fascists*. Bergen: Universitetsforlaget, 595–620.

Laurent, A. and Perrineau, P. (1999). 'L'extrême droite éclatéee'. *Revue Française de Science Politique*, 49: 633–42.

Lavau, G. (1969). 'Le parti communiste dans le système politique français', in AA. VV. *Le communisme en France*, Paris: Fondation Nationale des Sciences Politiques/A. Colin, 7–81.

Layton-Henry, Z. (1992). *The Politics of Immigration*. Oxford: Blackwell.

Lewis, D. S. (1987). *Illusions of Grandeur. Mosley, Fascism and British Society, 1931–1981*. Manchester: Manchester University Press.

Lijphart, A. (1975) *The Politics of Accommodation. Pluralism and Democracy in the Netherlands*. Berkeley: University of California Press.

Linz, J. (1978). *The Breakdown of Democratic Regimes. Crises, Breakdown and Reequilibrium*. Baltimore and London: Johns Hopkins University Press.

—— and Montero, J. R. (1986). *Crisis y cambio: Electores y partidos en los años ochanta*. Madrid: CIS.

—— and Stepan, A. (1996). *Problems of Democratic Transition and consolidation. Southern Europe, South America and Post-Communist Europe*. Baltimore-London: Johns Hopkins University Press.

—— —— and Gunther, R. (1995) 'Democratic Transition and Consolidation in Southern Europe in Comparative Perspective' in Gunther, R., Diamandouros, N. P., and Puhle, H.-J. (eds.), *The Politics of Democratic Consolidation. Southern Europe in Comparative Perspective*. Baltimore and London: The Johns Hopkins University Press, 77–123.

Linz, J. *et al.* (1981). *Informe sociologico sobre el cambio politico en España*. Madrid: Euramerica.

Lipset, S. M., and Raab, E. (1978). *The Politics of Unreason. Right Wing Extremism in America 1790–1977*, 2nd edn. Chicago: University of Chicago Press.

Listhaug, O. (1997). 'The decline of class voting', in Strøm, K., and Svasand, L. (eds.), *Challanges to Political Parties. The Case of Norway*. Ann Arbor: University of Michigan Press, 77–90.

—— and Wiberg, M. (1995). 'Confidence in Political and Private Institutions', in Klingemann, H.-D., and Fuchs, D. (eds.), *Citizens and the State*. Oxford: Oxford University Press, 298–322.

—— Macdonald, S. E., and Rabinowitz, G. (1990). 'A Comparative Spatial Analysis of European Party Systems'. *Scandinavian Political Studies*, 13: 227–54.

Loch, D. (2001). 'La droite radicale en Allemagne: un cas particulier?', in Perrineau, P. (dir.), *Les croisés de la société fermée. L'Europe des extrêmes droites*. La Tour d'Aigues: Editions de l'Aube, 303–22.

Lodge, M. *et al*. (1991). 'Where is the Schema? Critiques'. *American Political Science Review*, 85: 1357–81.

Lööw, H. (1995). 'Racist Violence and Criminal Behaviour in Sweden; Myths and Reality', in Bjørgo, T. (ed.), *Terror from the Extreme Right*. London: Frank Cass, 119–60.

Lopez-Nieto, L. (1988). *Alianza Popular: Estructura y evolucion electoral de un partido conservator (1976–1982)*. Madrid: CIS.

—— (1998). 'The Organizational Dynamics of AP/PP', in Ignazi, P., and Ysmal, C. (eds.), *The Organization of Political Parties in Southern Europe*. Westport: Praeger, 254–69.

Lubbers, M. and Scheepers, P. (2000). 'Individual and Contextual Characteristics of the German Extreme Right Vote in the 1990s. A Test of Complementary Theories'. *European Journal of Political Research*, 38: 63–94.

—— —— (2001). 'Explaining the Trend of Extreme Right Popularity in Germany 1989–1998'. *European Sociological Review*, 17: 431–49.

Lucardie, P. (1998). 'The Netherlands: The Extremist Center Parties', in Betz, H.-G., and Immerfall, S. (eds.), *The New Politics of the Right. Neo-Populist Parties and Movements in Established Democracies*. New York: St. Martin's Press, 112–24.

Lukes, S. (1992). 'What is Left?'. *Times Literary Supplement*, 27 March 1992.

Lunn, K. (1990). 'The Ideology and Impact of the British Fascists in the 1920s', in Kushner, T. and Lunn, K. (eds.), *Traditions of Intolerance. Historical Perspectives on Fascism and Race Discourse in Britain*. Manchester and New York: Manchester University Press, 140–54.

—— (1996). 'British Fascism Revisisted: A Failure of Imagination', in Cronin, M. (ed.), *The Failure of British Fascism*. Basingstoke: Macmillan, 166–80.

Luther, K. R. (1988). 'The Freiheitliche Partei Osterreichs: Protest Party or Governing Party?', in Kirchner E. J. (ed.), *Liberal Parties in Western Europe*. Cambridge: Cambridge University Press, 213–51.

—— (1997). 'Die Freiheitlichen (F)', in Dachs H. *et al*. (hrsg), *Handbuch des politischen Systems Österreichs. Die Zweite Republik*. Wien: Manzsche Verlags-und Unversitätsbuchhandlung, 286–303.

—— (1999). 'Austria: From Moderate to Polarized Pluralism', in Broughton, D., and Donovan, M. (eds.), *Changing Party Systems in Western Europe*. London: Pinter, 118–42.

Luther, K. R. (2000). 'Austria: a democracy under threat from the Freedom Party?'. *Parliamentary Affairs*, 53: 426–42.

Luverà, B. (2001). *Il dottor H. Haider e la nuova destra europea*. Torino: Einaudi.

Magone, J. M. (1999). 'Portugal: Party System Installation and Consolidation', in Broughton, M., and Donovan, M. (eds.), *Changing Party Systems in Western Europe*. London and New York: Pinter, 232–55.

Maier, C. S. (1988). *The Unmasterable Past*. Cambridge: Harvard University Press.

Mair, P. (1994). 'The Correlates of Consensus Democracy and the Puzzle of Dutch Politics'. *West European Politics*, 17: 97–123.

—— (1997). *Party System Change. Approaches and Interpretations*. Oxford: Clarendon Press.

—— and Mudde, C. (1998). 'The Party Family and its Study'. *Annual Review of Political Science*, 1: 211–30.

—— and van Biezen, I. (2001). 'Party Membership in Twenty European Democracies, 1980–2000'. *Party Politics*, 7: 5–21.

Mannheim, K. (1989 [1925]). *Conservatorismo*. Bari: Laterza.

Mannheimer, R. (1993*a*). 'L'elettorato della Lega Nord', *Polis*, 8: 253–274.

—— (1993*b*). *The Electorate of the Lega Nord* in Pasquino, G., and McCarty, P. (eds.) 'The End of Post-war Politics. The Landmark 1992 Elections', Boulder, Co.: Westview Press, 85–107.

—— (1999). 'Un'analisi dei risultati delle europee '99', *Political Trend*, 41: 19–29.

Maor, M. (1990). 'The 1990 Danish Election: An Unecessary Contest?'. *West European Politics*, 12: 209–213.

Maravall, A. (1981). *La politica de la transición*. Madrid: Taurus.

Marino, L. (1978). *La filosofia della restaurazione*. Torino: Einaudi.

Martin, P. (1996). 'Le vote Le Pen: L'électorat du Front National'. *Notes de la Fondation Saint-Simon*.

Maxwell, K. (1995). *The Making of Portoguese Democracy*. Cambridge: Cambridge University Press.

Mayer, N. (1993). 'Le Front national', in Chagnollaud D. (dir.), *La vie politique en France*, Paris: Seuil.

—— (1999). *Ces Français qui votent FN*. Paris: Flammarion.

—— (2002) *Ces Français qui votent Le Pen*. Paris: Flammarion.

—— and Perrineau, P. (1993). 'La puissance et le rejets du lepénismes dans l'opinion', in Duhamel, O., and Jaffré, J. (dir.), *L'état de l'opinion 1993*. Paris: Seuil, 63–78.

—— and Rey, H. (1993). 'Avancée électorale, isolement politique du Front national', *Revue politique et parlamentaire*, 95: 42–48.

Meadely, M. (1990). 'Norway's 1989 Election: the Path to Polarized Pluralism'. *West European Politics*, 13: 287–292.

Melich, A. (1995). 'Comparing European Trend Survey. Data on Racism and Xenophobia', Paper presented at the ECPR Joint Sessions Bordeaux, 27 April–2 May.

Meny, Y., and Surel, Y. (2000). *Pour le peuple, par le peuple*. Paris: Fayard.

Merkl, P. H. (1992*a*). 'A New German Identity', in G. Smith *et al.* (eds.), *Developments in German Politics*. Durnham: Duke University Press, 327–48.

—— (1994). 'Are the Old Nazis Coming back?', in Merkl, P. H. (ed.), *The Federal Republic at Forty-five*. Basingstoke: Macmillan.

Merkl, P. H. (1997). 'Why are They so Strong Now? Comparative Reflections on the Revival of the Radical Right in Europe', in Merkl, P. H., and Weinberg, L. (eds.), *The Revival of Right-Wing Extremism in the Nineties*. London: Frank Cass, 17–46.

Miller, A. and Listhaug, O. (1990). 'Political Parties and Confidence in Government: A Comparison of Norway, Sweden and the United States'. *British Journal of Political Science*, 29: 357–386.

—— —— (1993). 'Ideology and Political Alienation'. *Scandinavian Political Studies*, 16: 167–92.

Milza, P. (1987). *Fascisme français.Passé et present*. Paris: Flammarion.

—— (1992). 'Le Front National: droite extrême . . . ou national populisme', in Sirenelli, F. (dir.), *Histoires des droites en France*. Tome I. Paris: Gallimard, 691–732.

—— (1994). 'Le Front National crée-t-il une culture politique?'. *Vingtième Siècle*, 44: 39–44.

Minkenberg, M., (1992). 'The New Right in Germany: The Transformation of Conservatism and the Extreme Right'. *European Journal of Political Research*, 22: 55–82.

—— (1993). *The New Right in Comparative Perspective. The USA and Germany*. Ithaca: Cornell Western Societies Papers, No. 32.

—— (1994). 'German Unification and the Continuity of Discontinuities: Cultural Change and the Far Right in East and West'. *German Politics*, 3: 169–92.

—— (1997). 'The New Right in France and Germany. Nouvelle Droite, Neue Rechte and the New Right Radical Parties', in Merkl, P. H., and Weinberg, L. (eds.), *The Revival of Right-wing Extremism in the Nineties*. London: Frank Cass, 65–89.

—— (1998a). *Die neue radikale Rechte im Vergleich. Usa, Frankreich, Deutschland*. Opladen-Wiesbaden: Westdeutscher Verlag.

—— (1998b). 'Context and Consequence: The Impact of the New Radical Right on the Political Process in France and Germany'. *German Politics and Society*, 16: 1–23.

—— (1999). 'The New Radical Right in the Political Process: Interaction Effects in France and Germany', unpublished paper.

—— (2000a). 'The Renewal of the Radical Right between Modernity and Anti-modernity'. *Government and Opposition*, 35: 170–88.

—— (2000b). 'Im Osten was Neues: Die radikale Rechte im Wahljahr 1998', in Pickel, G., Walz, D., and Brunner, W. (hrsg.). *Deutschland nach den Wahlen. Befunde zur Bundestagswahl 1998 und zur Zukunft des deutschen Parteiensystems*. Opladen: Leske + Budrich, 313–32.

—— and Inglehart, R. (1989). 'Neoconservatism and Value Change in the USA: Tendencies in the Mass Public of a Postindustrial Society', in Gibbins, J. (ed.). *Contemporary Political Culture. Politics in a Postmodern Age*. London: Sage. 81–109.

Mitten, R. (1994). 'Jörg Haider, the Anti-immigrant Petition and Immigration Policy in Austria'. *Patterns of Prejudice*, 28: 27–41.

Montero, J. R. (1986). 'El subtriunfo de la derecha:los apoyos electorales de AP-PDP', in Linz, J., and Montero, J. R. (eds.), *Crisis y Cambio: Electores y pardidos en la España de los ochenta*. Madrid: Centro de Estudios Costitucionales, 345–432.

—— (1987). 'Los Fracasos Politicos y Electorales de la Derecha Espanola: Alianza Popular, 1976–1986'. *Revista Espanola de Investigaciones Sociologicas*. 39: 7–43.

—— (1988). 'More Than Conservative, Less than Neoconservative: Alianza Popular in Spain', in Girvin, B. (ed.), *The Transformation of Contemporary Conservatism*. London: Sage, 145–63.

—— and Gunther, R. (1998). 'Electoral Volatility and Stability: A Comparative Analysis of the Social-Structural and (Two). Attitudinal Bases of Partisanship', Bologna: Istituto Cattaneo, unpublished paper.

Morán, M. L. and Benedicto, J. (1995). *La cultura politica de los Españoles*. Madrid: CIS.

Moreau, P. (1998). 'La Freiheitliche Partei Osterreich, parti national libéral ou pulsion austro-fasciste'. *Pouvoirs*, 87: 61–82.

Morlino, L. (1998). *Democracies between Consolidation and Crisis*. Oxford: Oxford University press.

—— and Montero, J. R. (1995). 'Legitimacy and Democracy in Southern Europe', in Gunther, R., Diamandouros, N. P., and Puhle, H.-J. (eds.), *The Politics of Democratic Consolidation. Southern Europe in Comparative Perspective*. Baltimore and London: The Johns Hopkins University Press, 231–60.

—— and Tarchi, M. (1996). 'The Dissatisfied Society: The Roots of Political Change in Italy'. *European Journal of Politcal Research*, 30: 41–63.

Mosse, G. (1975 [1974]). *La Nazionalizzazione delle Masse*. Bologna: Il Mulino.

MSI-DN (1994). *Pensiamo l'Italia [Tesi politiche per il XVII Congresso Nazionale del MSI-DN]*. Roma.

Mudde, C. (1995*a*). 'Right-wing Extremism Analyzed. A Comparative Analysis of the Ideologies of Three Alleged Right-wing Extremist Parties (NPD, NDP, CP'86)', *European Journal of Political Research*, 27: 203–24.

—— (1995*b*). 'One Against All, All Against One: A Portrait of the Vlaams Blok'. *Patterns of Prejudice*, 29: 5–28.

—— (1996). 'The War of Words: Defining the Extreme Right Party Family'. *West European Politics*, 19: 225–48.

—— (1998). *The extreme right party family. An ideological approach*. PhD Thesis. Leiden: Leiden University.

—— (2000). *The Ideology of the extreme right*. Manchester: Manchester University Press.

—— (2002). 'The Pink Populist: Pim Fortuyn for Beginners' in *e-Extreme*, vol.3, n.3.

—— and van Holsteyn, J. J. M. (1994). 'Over the Top: Dutch Right-Wing Extremist Parties in the Elections of 1994', *Politics*, 14: 127–34.

—— and van Holsteyn, J. M. M. (2000). 'The Netherlands: explaining the limited Success of the Extreme Right', in Hainsworth, P. (ed.), *The Politics of the Extreme Right. From the Margins to the Mainstream*. London and New York: Pinter, 144–70.

Mughan, A. (1992). 'Belgium', in Franklin, M. *et al.* (eds.). *Electoral Change*. Cambridge: Cambridge University Press, 83–100.

Müller, W. (1992). 'Austria', in Katz R., and Mair P. (eds.), *Party Organizations. A Data Handbook*. London: Sage, 21–120.

—— and Jenny, M. (2000). 'Abgeordnete, Parteien und Koalitionspolitik: Individuelle Präferenzen und politisches Handeln im Nationalrat'. *Österreichische Zeitschrift für Politiwikssenschaft*, 29: 137–56.

Müller, W., Plasser, F., and Ulram, P. (1999). 'Schwäche als Vorteil Stärke als Nachteil. Die Reaktion der Parteien auf den Rückgang der Wählerbidungen in Österreich', in Mair, P., Müller, W., and Plasser, F. (Hrsg.), *Parteien auf komplexen Wählermärkten: Reaktionsstrategien politischer Parteien in Westeuropa*. Wien: Sigmun-Verlag, 201–45.

Mussolini, B. (1932). 'Fascismo. Dottrina', in *Enciclopedia Italiana*, Vol. XIV, 847–51.

Natale, P. (1999). 'Gli italiani e il voto europeo: molte conferme, poche smentite'. *Rivista Italiana di Scienza Politica*, 29: 547–72.

Nielsen, H. J. (1976). 'The Uncivic Culture. Attitudes towards the Political System in Denmark and Vote for the Progress Party 1973–75', *Scandinavian Political Studies*, 11: 147–66.

Nielsen, H. J. (1998). 'The Danish election 1998'. *Scandinavian Political Studies*, 22: 67–81.

Noell-Neumann, E. (1994). 'Left and Right as Categories for Determining the Political Position of the Parties and the Population in Germany', paper presented at the Symposium on 'Political Parties: Changing Roles in Contemporary Democracies', Madrid, December 15–17, 1994.

Noguera Pinto, J. (1989). 'A Dereita e o 25 de Abril. Ideologia, Estrategia e Evolucào Politica', in Coelho (ed.), *Portugal. 0 Sistema Politico e Costitucional 1974–1987*. Lisboa: Istituto de Ciencias Sociais de Universidade de Lisboa, 193–213.

Norris, P. (ed.) (1999). *Critical Citizens*. Oxford: Oxford University Press.

Norton, P. (ed.) (1996). *The Conservative Party*. Hemel Hempstead: Prentice Hall.

—— and Aughey, A. (1981) *Conservatives and Conservatism*. London: Temple Smith.

Oakeshott, M. (1967). *Rationalism in Politics*. London: Methuen.

Offe, C. (1985). 'New Social Movements: Challanging the Boundaries of Institutional Politics'. *Social Research*, 52: 817–68.

Orlow, D. (1999). 'A Difficult Relationship of Unequal Relatives: The Dutch NSB and Nazi Germany, 1933–1940'. *European History Quarterly*, 29: 349–80.

O'Sullivan, N. (1989). 'The New Right: The Quest for a Civil Philosophy in Europe and America', in Eatwell, R., and O'Sullivan, N. (eds.), *The Nature of the Right. European and American Politics and Political Thought Since 1789*. London: Pinter, 167–91.

Papadopulos, Y. (1988). 'Parties, the State and Society in Greece: Continuity within Change'. *West European Politics*, 12: 55–71.

Pappalardo, A. (1996). 'Dal pluralismo polarizzato al pluralismo moderato. Il modello di Sartori e la crisi italiana'. *Rivista Italiana di Scienza Politica*, 26: 103–145.

Pappas, T. (2001) 'In Search of the Center: Conservative Parties, Electoral Competition, and Political Legitimacy in Southern Europe's New Democracies', in Diamandouros, N., and Gunther, R. (eds.). *Parties, Politics, and Democracy in the New Southern Europa*. Baltimore and London: Johns Hopkins University Press, 224–67.

Pauley, B. F. (1980). 'Nazis and Heimwehr Fascists: The Struggle for Supremacy in Austria, 1918–1938', in Larsen S. U. *et al.* (eds.), *Who Were the Fascists*. Bergen: Universitetsforlaget, 226–38.

Payne, S. G. (1980). 'The Concept of Fascism', in Larsen, S. U., Hagtvet, B., and Mykelbust, J. P. (eds.). *Who Were the Fascists*. Oslo: Universitetsforlaget, 14–25.

—— (1987). *The Franco Regime 1936–1975*. Madison: University of Wisconsin Press.

—— (1995). *History of Fascism 1914–1945*. Madison: University of Wisconsin Press.

Pedersen, M. (1982). 'Towards a New Typology of Party Life-Spans and Minor Parties'. *Scandinavian Political Studies*, 5: 1–16.

—— (1987). 'The Danish "Working Multiparty System": Breakdown or Adaptation', in Daalder H. (ed.), *Party Systems in Denmark, Austria, Switzerland, the Netherlands, Belgium*. London: Francis Pinter, 1–60.

—— (1988). 'The Defeat of All Parties: The Danish Folketing Election 1973', in Lawson K., and Merkl P. (eds.), *When Parties Fail*, Princeton: Princeton University Press, 257–81.

—— (1991). 'The Birth, Life and Death of Small Parties in Danish Politics', in Müller-Rommel, F., and Pridham, G. (eds.), *Small Parties in Western Europe*. London: Sage, 95–114.

Pekonen, K. (1999). 'Introduction to the Essays', in Pekonen, K. (ed.), *The New Radical Right in Finland*. s.l.: the Finnish Political Science Association, 9–26.

—— Heynyem, P., and Kalliala, M. (1999). 'The New Radical Right Taking Shape in Finland', in Pekonen, K. (ed.), *The New Radical Right in Finland*. s.l.: the Finnish Political Science Association, 31–61.

Pennings, P. (1995). 'Consociationalism and Party System Change. Towards a Comparative Operationalisation', Paper presented at the ECPR Joint Sessions Bordeaux, 27 April–2 May.

—— (1998). 'The Triad of Party System Change: Votes, Office and Policy', in Pennings, P., and Lane, J.-E. (eds.), *Comparing Party system Change*. New York: Routledge, 79–100.

Perlmutter, T. (1996). 'Immigration Politics Italian Style'. *South European Society and Politics*, 1: 229–52.

Perrineau, P. (1988). 'Front National: l' echo politique de l' 'anomie urbaine'. *Esprit*, 22–38.

—— (1993). 'Le Front National. La force solitaire' in Habert, P., Perrineau, P. and Ysmal, C. (dir.) *Le Vote Sanction*. Paris: Departement d'Etudes Politiques du Figaro/Fondation Nationale des Sciences Politiques 137–60.

—— (1995) 'La dynamique du vote Le Pen. Le poids du gaucho-lepénisme' in Perrineau, P. and Ysmal, C. (dir) *Le vote de crise*. Paris: Departement d'Etudes Politiques du Figaro/Fondation Nationale des Sciences Politiques, 249–61.

—— (1997). *Le Symptôme Le Pen*. Paris: Fayard.

—— (2002). 'Le vote d'extreme droite en France: Adhesion ou protestation?'. *Futuribles*: 5–20.

Pettersen, P. A. (1997). 'Parties, the Public, and Immigrants: Responses to New Political Issues', in Strøm, K., and Svasand, L. (eds.), *Challanges to Political Parties. The Case of Norway*. Ann Arbor: University of Michigan Press, 289–320.

Pfahl-Traughber, A. (1993). 'Rechtspopulistische Parteien in Westeuropa', in Jesse E. (hrg), *Politischer Extremismus in Deutschland und Europa*. München: Bayerische Landeszentrale für politische Bildungsarbeit, 39–56.

—— (1994). *Volkes Stimme? Rechtspopulismus in Europa*. Bonn: Dietz.

—— (1995). *Rechts Extremismus*. Bonn: Bouvier Verlag.

—— (1999). *Rechtsextremismus in der Bundesrepublik*. München: C. H. Beck.

Pierre, J. and Widefeldt, A. (1992). 'Sweden', in Katz, R., and Mair, P. (eds.), *Party Organizations in Western Democracies 1960–1980; A Data Handbook*. London: Sage, 781–835.

Plasser, F. and Ulram, P. (1992). *Ausländerangst als Parteien und medienpolitischen Problem*. Vienna: Fessel/Gfk-Institut.

—— —— and Grausgruber, A. (1987). 'Vom Ende der Lagerparteien. Perspektivenweschel in der österreichischen Parteien-und Wahlforschung', *Österreichische Zeitschrift für Politiwikssenschaft*, 16: 242–58.

Plasser, F., Ulram, P., and Grausgruber, A. (1992). 'The Decline of Lager Mentality' and the new Model of Electoral Competition in Austria' *West European Politics*, 15: 16–44.

Poguntke, T. and Scarrow, S. (eds.) (1996). 'The Politics of Anti-Party Sentiment'. *European Journal of Political Research*, (special issue No. 29).

Poulsen, H. (1987). 'The Nordic States', in D. Muehlberger (ed.), *The Social Basis of European Fascist Movements*. London: Croom Helm, 155–89.

Poulsen, H., and Djursaa, M. (1980). 'Social Basis of Nazism in Denmark: The DNSAP', in S. U. Larsen *et al.* (eds.), *Who Were the Fascists*. Bergen: Universitetsforlaget, 702–14.

Raniolo, F. (2000). *I partiti conservatori in Europa occidentale*. Bologna: Il Mulino.

Rattinger, H. (1993). 'Abkehr von den Parteien? Dimensionen der Parteiverdrossenheit', *Aus Politik und Zeitgeschichte.* B11: 24–35.

Rea, A. (1997). 'Le Front National: force électorale et faiblesse organisationelle', in Delwit, P., and De Waele, J. M. (dir.), *Les partis politiques en Beligique.* Bruxelles: Editions de l'Université de Bruxelles, 197–208.

Rémond, R. (1982). *Les droites en France.* Paris: Aubier.

Rey, H. (1996). *La peur de banlieus.* Paris: Presses de Sciences Po.

Riedlsperger, M. (1991). 'Austria: A Question of National Identity'. *Politics and Society in Germany, Austria and Switzerland,* 4: 48–71.

—— (1992). 'Heil Haider! The Revitalization of the Austrian Freedom Party since 1986'. *Politics and Society in Germany, Austria and Switzerland,* 4: 18–58.

—— (1998). 'The Freedom Party of Austria: From Protest to Radical Right Populism', in Betz, H.-G., and Immerfall, S. (eds.), *The New Politics of the Right.* New York: St. Martin's Press, 27–43

Roberts, G. K. (1992). 'Right-Wing Radicalism in the New Germany'. *Parliamentary Affairs,* 45: 327–44.

Rodríguez, J. L. (1991). 'Origen, Desarollo Y Disolucion de Fuerza Nueva'. *Revista de Estudios Politicos,* 73: 261–87.

—— (1994). *Reacionarios y golpistas. La extrema derecha en España: del tardofranquismo a la consolidacion de la democracia (1967–1982).* Madrid: CSIC.

—— (1997). *La extrema derecha española en el siglo XX.* Madrid: Alianza Editorial.

Rollat, A. (1985). *Les hommes de l'extrême droite.* Paris: Calmann-Levy.

Rossiter, C. (1955). *Conservatism in America.* New York: Knopf.

Rousso, H. (1992). *La syndrome de Vichy,* Paris: Seuil.

Roux, J. P. (1985). 'La revolte de Pierre Poujade', in AA. VV., *Etudes sur la France de 1939 à nos jours.* Paris: Seuil, 248–94.

Roy, J.-P. (1998). 'Le programme économique et social du Front National en France', in Delwit, P., De Waele, J.-M., and Rea, A. (dir.), *L'extrême droite en France et en Belgique.* Bruxelles: Editions Complexe, 85–100.

Saalfeld, T. (1993). 'The Politics of National-Populism: Ideology and Policies of the German Republikaner Party', *German Politics.* 2: 177–99.

Sainsbury, D. (1992). 'Swedish Election: Protest, Fragmentation, and the Shift to the Right'. *West European Politics,* 15: 160–66.

Sani, G., and Sartori, G. (1983). 'Polarization, Fragmentation and Competition in Western Democracies', in Daalder, H., and Mair, P. (eds.), *Western European Party Systems.* Beverly Hills: Sage, 307–41.

Särlvik, B., and Crewe, I. (1983). *Decade of Dealignment.* Cambridge: Cambridge University Press.

Sartori, G. (1976). *Parties and Party Systems.* Cambridge: Cambridge University Press.

—— (1982). *Teoria dei partiti e caso italiano.* Milano: Sugarco.

Sasso, G. (1998). *Le due Italie di Giovanni Gentile.* Bologna: Il Mulino.

Scarrow, S. (1996). 'Politicians Against Parties: Anti-party Arguments as Weapon for Change in Germany'. *European Journal for Political Research,* 29: 297–317.

Schain, M. (1988). 'Immigration and Changes in the French Party System'. *European Journal of Political Research,* 16: 597–621.

Scheepers, P., Felling, A., and Peters, J. (1991). 'Ethnocentrism in the Netherlands'. *Ethnic and Racial Studies,* 14: 280–308.

—— Schmeets, H., and Felling, A. (1997). 'Fortress Holland: Support for Ethnocentrist Policies among the 1994-electorate of the Netherlands'. *Ethnic and Racial Studies*, 20: 145–59.

Schepens, L. (1980). 'Fascists and Nationalists in Belgium, 1919–1940', in Larsen S. U., *et al.* (eds.), *Who Were the Fascists*. Bergen: Universitetsforlaget, 501–16.

Scheuch, E. K., and Klingemann, H. D. (1967). 'Theorie des Rechtsradikalismus in westlichen Industriegesellschaften'. *Hamburger Jahrbuch fur Wirtschafts—und Gesellschaftspolitik*, 12: 11–29.

Schleder, A. (1994). 'Die antipolitischen Stereotypen Jörg Haiders'. *Journal für Sozialforschung*, 35: 283–306.

—— (1996). 'Anti-Political-Establishment Parties'. *Party Politics*, 2: 291–312.

Schweisguth, E. (1998). 'France: le mythe du néoconservatisme'. *Futuribles*, 227: 21–34.

Scruton, R. (1980). *The Meaning of Conservatism*. Harmondsworth: Penguin Books.

Sefariades, S. (1986). 'Polarizzazione Partitica e Non-Proporzionalità Elettorale in Grecia'. *Rivista Italiana di Scienza Politica*, 16: 401–37.

Segatti, P. (1997). 'Un centro instabile eppure fermo. Mutamento e continuità nel movimento elettorale', in P. Corbetta, e A. Parisi (a cura di), *A domanda risponde. Il cambiamento di voto degli italiani nelle elezioni del 1994 e del 1996*. Bologna: Il Mulino, 215–60.

Seiler, D. L. (1980). *Partis et Familles Politiques*. Paris: PUF.

—— (1985). 'De la classification des partis politiques', *Res Publica*, 27: 59–86.

—— (1986). *De la Comparaison des Partis Politiques*. Paris: Economica.

Setta, S. (1975). *L'Uomo Qualunque 1944–1948*. Bari: Laterza.

Shain, M. (2001). 'L'impact du Front National sur le système politique français', in Perrineau, P. (dir.), *Les croisés de la société fermée. L'Europe des extrême droites*. La Tour d'Aigues: Editions de l'Aube, 287–302.

Shepsle, K. A., and Cohen, R. N. (1990). 'Multiparty Competition, Entry and Entry Deterrence in Spatial Models of Elections', in Enelow, J. M., and Hinich, M. J. (eds.), *Advances in the Spatial Theory of Voting*. Cambridge: Cambridge University Press, 12–45.

Siegfried, A. (1964 [1913]). *Tableau politique de la France de l'Ouest sous la III° republique*. Paris: Armand Colin.

Sirenelli, J.-F., and Vigne, E. (1992). 'Introduction générale. Des droites et du politique', in Sirenelli, J.-F. (dir.), *Histoire des droites en France*, 3 vol. Paris: Gallimard, 1, I–XLV.

Slama, A. G. (1986). 'Vichy était-il fasciste?', *Vingtième Siecle*, 11: 41–53.

Smith, G. (1987). 'Party and Protest: The two Faces of Opposition in Western Europe', in Kolinsky, E. (ed.), *Opposition in Western Europe*. London: Croom Helm, 55–76.

Sofres (1985). *Opinion publique 1985*. Paris: Gallimard.

—— (1990). *Opinion publique 1990*. Paris: Gallimard.

—— (1998). *Opinion publique 1998*. Paris: Gallimard.

Soucy, R. (1991). 'French Fascism and the Croix-de-feu: A dissenting interpretation'. *Journal of Contemporary History*, 26: 159–88.

Spruyt, M. (1997). 'Le Vlaams Blok', in Delwit, P., and De Waele, J.-M. (dir.), *Les partis politiques en Belgique*. Bruxelles: Editions de l'Université de Bruxelles, 209–18.

Steger, M. (1993). 'The New "Austria", the New "Europe" and the New "Nationalism"', paper pesented at the Annual Meeting of the American Political Science Association, Washington DC.

Steinfels, P. (1979). *The Neo-Conservatives*. New York: Simon and Schuster.

Sternhell, Z. (1976*a*). 'Anatomie d'un mouvement fasciste en France. Les Fascieau de George Valois'. *Revue française de Science Politique*, 26: 5–41.

—— (1976*b*). 'Fascist Ideology', in Laqueur, W. (ed.), *Fascism. A Reader's Guide*. Berkeley and Los Angeles: University of California Press, 315–77.

—— (1980). 'Strands of French Fascism', in Larsen S. U. *et al.* (eds.), *Who Were the Fascists*. Bergen: Universitetsforlaget, 479–500.

—— (1987). *Ni Droite ni Gauche. L'Ideologie Fasciste en France*, 2nd ed., Paris: Editions Complexe.

—— (with Sznajder, M. and Asheri, M.) (1989). *Naissance de l'Ideologie Fasciste*. Paris: Fayard.

—— (1994). *L'eternel retour*. Paris: Presses de la Fondation Nationale des Sciences Politiques.

—— (2000). 'Fascism: Reflections on the Fate of Ideas in the Twentieth Century History'. *Journal of Contemporary Ideologies*, 5: 139–62.

Stöss, R. (1991). *Politics against Democracy. Right-wing Extremism in West Germany*. New York-Oxford: Berg.

—— (1993*a*). *Rechtsextremismus in Berlin 1990*. Berliner Arbeitshefte und Berichte zur sozialwissenschaftlichen Forschung, No. 80.

—— (1993*b*). 'Rechtsextremismus und Wahlen in der Bundesrepublik', *Aus Politik und Zeitgeschichte*, B11: 50–61.

—— and Niedermayer, O. (1998). *Rechtsextremismus, politische Unzufriedenheit und das Wählerpotential rechtsextremer Parteien in der Bundesrepublik im Frühsommer 1998*, Arbeitspapiere des Otto-Stamme-Zentrums Nr. 1, Berlin: Freie Universität Berlin.

—— (1999). 'Rechtsextremismus und Wahlen 1998', in Meckenburg J. (hrg.), *Braune Gefahr. DVU, NPD, Rep, Geschichte und Zukunft*. Berlin: Elefanten Press, 146–76.

Strøm, K., and Leipart, J. (1989). 'Ideology Strategy and Party competition in Postwar Norway'. *European Journal of Political Research*, 17: 263–88.

—— (1993). 'Policy, Institutions and Coalition Avoidance: Norwegian Goverments, 1945–1990'. *American Political Science Review*, 87: 870–87.

—— and Svasand, L. (1997). 'Beyond the Nation-State: Foreign Policy Controversies', in Strøm, K., and Svasand, L. (eds.), *Challanges to Political Parties. The Case of Norway*. Ann Arbor: University of Michigan Press, 321–41.

Sundberg, J. (1999). 'The Enduring Scandinavian Party Systems', *Scandinavian Political Studies*, 22:

—— (1992). 'Norway', in Katz, R., and Mair, P. (eds.), *Party Organizations in Western Democracies 1960–1980: A Data Handbook*. London: Sage, 732–80.

Svasand, L. (1998). 'Scandinavian Right-Wing Radicalism', in Betz, H.-G., and Immerfall, S. (eds.), *The New Politics of the Right. Neo-Populist Parties and Movements in Established Democracies*. New York: St. Martin's Press, 77–93.

Svasand, L., Strøm, K., and Rasch, B. E. (1997). 'Change and Adaptation in Party Organization'. in Strøm, K., and Svasand, L. (eds.), *Challanges to Political Parties. The Case of Norway*. Ann Arbor: University of Michigan Press, 91–124.

Swyngedouw, M. (1995). 'Les nouveaux clivages dans la politique belgo-flamande'. *Revue Française de Science Politique*, 45: 775–90.

—— (1998*a*). 'L'ideologie du Vlaams Blok: l'offre identitaire', *Revue Internationale de Politique Comparée*, 5: 189–202.

—— (1998*b*). 'The Extreme Right in Belgium: of a Non Existent Front national and an omnipresent Vlaams Blok', in Betz, H.-G., and Immerfall, S. (eds.), *The New Politics of the Right. Neo-Populist Parties and Movements in Established Democracies*. New York: St. Martin's Press, 59–72.

—— (1998*c*). 'Anvers: une ville à la portée du Vlaams Blok?', in Delwit, P. *et al.*, *L'extrême droite en France et en Belgique*. Bruxelles: Editions Complexe, 291–315.

—— (2000). 'Explaining the relationship between Vlaams Blok and the city of Antwerp', in Hainsworth, P. (ed.), *The Politics of the Extreme Right. From the Margins to the Mainstream*. London and New York: Pinter, 121–43.

—— and Beerten, R. (1999). 'De Fragmentatie van Het kiezerskorps in Vlaanderen. Verschuivingen 1991–1995 en 1995–1999', *ISPO Bulletin*. 34.

—— ——, and Billiet, J. (1997). 'Les motivations électorales en Flandre', *Courrier hebdomadaire du Crisp*, 1557.

——, Beerten, R., and Kampen, J. (1999). 'De veranderingen in de samenstelling van de kiezerskorpsen 1995–1999', *ISPO Bulletin*, 35.

—— and Ivaldi, G. (1999). 'The extreme right Utopia in Belgium and France', *ISPO Bulletin*, 31.

Taggart, P. (1993). 'Muted Radicals: The Emerging "New Populism" in West European Party Systems', Paper prepared for the annual meeting of the American Political Science Association, Washington, D.C.

—— (1995). 'New Populist Parties in Western Europe'. *West European Politics*, 18: 34–51.

—— (1996). *The New Populism and the New Politics*. Basingstoke: Macmillan.

Taguieff, P.-A. (1983). 'La strategies culturelle de la Nouvelle Droite en France (1968–1983)', in Union des Ecrivans, *Vous avez dit fascisme?*. Paris: Arthaud/Montalba, 13–152.

—— (1984). 'La rétorique du national-populisme'. *Chaiers Bernard Lazare*, 19–38.

—— (1985*a*). 'Les Droites Radicales en France. Nationalisme révolutionnaire et National-libéralisme'. *Les Temps Modernes*, 41: 1780–1842.

—— (1985*b*). 'La démogagie à visage répubblicain'. *Revue Politique et Parliamentaire*, 87.

—— (1986*a*). 'La doctrine du national-populisme en France', *Etudes.*, 27–46.

—— (1986*b*). 'L'identité nationale saisie par la logique de racisation. Aspects, figures et problèmes de racisme differencialiste'. *Mots*, 12: 91–126.

—— (1988). *La force du préjugé*, Paris: La Decouverte.

—— (1994). *Sur la Nouvelle Droite. Jalons d'une analyse critique*. Paris: Descartes et Cie.

—— (1996). 'Le FN dans la durée', in Mayer, N., and Perrineau, P. (dir.), *Le Front national à decouvert*, 2nd edn., Paris: Presses de Sciences Po, 63–80.

—— (1997). 'Le populisme et la science politique. Du mirage conceptuel aux vrais problèmes'. *Vingtième Siècle*, 56: 4–33.

Tarchi, M. (1997). *Dal MSI ad AN*. Bologna: Il Mulino.

Tassani, G. (1986). *Vista da sinistra. Ricognizioni sulla Nuova destra*. Firenze: Arnaud.

Taylor, S. (1979). 'Coloured Population and Support for the National Front'. *British Journal of Political Science*, 9: 250–55.

Taylor, S. (1993). 'The Radical Right in Britain', in Merkl, P. H., and Weinberg, L. (eds.), *Encounters with the Contemporary Right*, Boulder: Westview Press, 165–84.

ten Napel, H.-M. (1998). 'The Netherlands: Resilience Amidst Change', in Broughton, D., and Donovan, M. (eds.), *Changing Party Systems in Western Europe*. London and New York: Pinter, 163–82.

Tettamanti, A. (1989). 'Il fenomeno storico del conservatorismo tedesco: interpretazioni e problemi'. *Filosofia Politica*, 3: 137–74.

Thomassen, J., and Schmitt, H. (1999). 'Issue Congruence', in Schmitt, H., and Thomassen, J. (eds.), *Political Representation and Legitimacy in the European Union*. Oxford: Oxford University Press, 186–208.

Thurlow, R. (1987). *Fascism in Britain. A History, 1918–1985*. Oxford: Blackwell.

Thurlow, R. (1998). *Fascism in Britain. From Oswald Mosley's Blackshirts to the National Front*. London and New York: I.B.Tauris Publishers.

Tillie, J. and Fennema, M. (1998). 'A Rational Choice for the Extreme Right'. *Acta Politica*, 33: 223–49.

Togeby, L. (1998). 'Prejudice and Tolerance in a Period of Increasing Ethnic Diversity and Growing Unemployment: Denmark since 1970'. *Ethnic and Racial Studies*, 21: 1137–54.

Trainhardt, D. (1995). 'The Political Use of Xenophobia in England, France and Germany', *Party Politics*, 1(3): 323–47.

Tromp, B. (1989). 'Party Strategies and System Change in the Netherlands'. *West European Politics*, 12: 82–97.

Ueltzhöffer, J. (1984). 'Zur Gesinnungslage der Nation. Die Sinus-Studie ber rechtsextremistische Einstellungen bei den Bundersbürgern', *Schriftenreihe der Bundeszentrale für politische Bildung*. Band 212 (Extremismus und Schule). Bonn, 80–94.

—— (1992). 'Rechtsextremismus', in Nohlen D. (hrg), *Lexikon der Politik*. München: Verlag C.H.Beck, Band 3, 382–87.

Ulram, P. (1997). 'Politische Kultur der Bevölkerung', in Dachs H. *et al.* (hrsg.), *Handbuch des Politischen Systems Österreichs. Die Zweite Republik*. Wien: Manzsche Verlags-und Universitätsbuchhandlung, 514–25.

Urwin, D. W. (1997). 'The Norwegian Party System from the 1880s to the 1990s', in Strøm, K., and Svasand, L. (eds.), *Challanges to Political Parties. The Case of Norway*. Ann Arbor: University of Michigan Press, 33–60.

Valen, H. (1990). 'The Storting Election of 1989. Polarization and Protest'. *Scandinavian Political Studies*, 13: 277–90.

Van der Brug, W., and van der Eijk, C. (1999). 'The Cognitive Basis of Voting', in Schmitt, H., and Thomassen J. (eds.), *Political Representation and Legitimacy in the European Union*. Oxford: Oxford University Press, 129–60.

Van der Brug, W., Fennema, M., and Tillie, J. (2000). 'Anti-immigrant Parties in Europe: Ideological or Protest Vote?'. *European Journal of Political Research*, 37: 77–102.

Van der Wusten, H. (1987). 'The Low Countries', in Mehlberger D. (ed.), *The Social Basis of Fascism*. London: Croom Helm, 213–41.

—— and Smit, R. (1980). 'Dynamics of the Dutch National Socialist Movement (the NSB): 1931–1935', in Larsen, S. U. *et al.* (eds.), *Who Were the Fascists*. Bergen: Universistetsforlaget, 524–41.

Van Deth, J., and Guers, P. (1989). 'Value Orientation, Left-Right Placement, and Voting'. *European Journal of Political Research*, 17: 17–34.

Van Donselaar, J. (1991). *Fout na de Oorlog. Fascistische en racistische organisaties in Nederland, 1950–1990*. Amsterdam: Uitgeverij Bert Bakker.

—— (1993). 'Post-war fascism in the Netherlands'. *Crime, Law and Social Change*, 19: 87–100.

Van Eesbeeck, (1985). *L'URDT. De la révolte antifiscale des indipendents au liberalisme anti-radical*. Bruxelles: ULB.

Van Holsteyn, J. (1990). 'En wij dan? De Kiezers van de Centrumdemocraten', *Socialisme en Democratie*, 6: 158–61.

—— and Mudde, C. (1992). 'Voorzichtig omspringen met begrip rechtextermisme'. *Namens*, 7: 19–23.

Van Schuur, H. (1984). *Structure in Political Beliefs*. Amsterdam: CT Press.

Ventrone, A. (1996). *La cittadinanza repubblicana*. Bologna: Il Mulino.

Verdlinden, P. (1991). 'Morphologies van extreem rechts binnen het Vlaams Nationalism', in de Schampheleire, H., and Thanassekos, Y. (eds.), *Extreem rechts in West-Europa/ L'extreme droite en Europe de the ouest*. Brussel: VUP Press, 235–46.

Verhoeyen, E. (1962). 'Nouvelles formes et tendances de l' extrême droite en Belgique', *Courrier Hebdomadaire du CRISP*, 140.

Verkuyten, M. (1992). 'Ethnic Group Preferences and the Evaluation of Ethnic Identity among Adolescents in the Netherlands'. *The Journal of Social Psychology*, 132: 741–51.

Verzichelli, L. (1995). 'I nuovi parlamentari', in P. Ignazi, e R. Katz (a cura di), *Politica in Italia edizione 95*. Bologna: Il Mulino, 139–60.

—— (1997). La classe politica della transizione, in D'Alimonte, R., and Bartolini, S. (a cura di), *Maggioritario per caso*. Bologna: Il Mulino, 309–50.

Veugelers, J. (1992). 'The Ideologies of the Right-wing Parties in Contemporary France and Britain', unpublished paper.

—— (1997). 'Social Cleavage and the Revival of Far-Right Parties: The Case of France's National Front'. *Acta Sociologica*, 40: 31–49.

—— (1999). 'A Challenge for Political Sociology: The Rise of Far-Right Parties in Contemporary Western Europe'. *Current Sociology*, 47: 78–105.

—— (2000). 'Right-Wing Extremism in Contemporary France: A "Silent Counter Revolution"?'. *The Sociological Quarterly*, 41: 19–40.

Vignati, R. (2001). 'La memoria del fascismo', in Chiarini, R., e Maraffi, M. (a cura di), *La destra allo specchio*. Venezia: Marsilio, 43–84.

Visser, R. (1992). 'Fascist Doctrine and the Cult of the Romanità'. *Journal of Contemporary History*, 27: 5–22.

Voerman, G. and Lucardie, P. (1992). 'The Extreme Right in the Netherlands: The Centrists and their Radical Rivals', *European Journal of Political Research*, 22: 35–44.

Walker, R. (1977). *The National Front*. London: Fontana.

Wallef, D. (1980). 'The Composition of Christus Rex', in Larsen S. U. *et al.* (eds.), *Who Were the Fascists*. Bergen: Universitetsforlaget, 517–23.

Wandrszuka, A. (1954). 'Österreichs politische Struktur. Die Entwicklung der Parteien und politischen Bewegung, in H. Benedikt (hrsg.), *Geschichte der Republik Österreich*, Vienna: Verlag für Geschichte und Politik, 289–485.

Webber, G. C. (1984). 'Patterns of membership and support for the British Union of Fascists'. *Journal of Contemporary History*, 19: 575–606.

Weil, F. D. (1997). 'Ethnic Intolerance, Extremism and Democratic Attitudes in Germany since Unification', in Kurthen, H., Bergmann, W., and Erb, R. (eds.), *Antisemitism and Xenophobia in Germany after Unification*. Oxford: Oxford University Press, 110–42.

Weinberg. L. (1993). 'Introduction', in Merkl, P. H., and Weinberg, L. (eds.), *Encounters with the Contemporary Radical Right*. Boulder: Westview Press, 1–15.

——, Eubank, L. E., and Wilcox, A. R. (1995). 'A Brief Analysis of the Extreme Right in Western Europe', mimeo.

Westlind, D. (1996). *The Politics of Popular Identity. Understanding Recent Populist Movements in Sweden and the United States*. Lund: Lund University Press.

Whine, M. (1998). 'Royaume Uni', in Camus, Y. (dir.), *Les Extrémismes en Europe*. La Tour d'Aigues: Editon de l'Aube, 299–314.

Whiteley, P. (1979). 'The National Front vote in the 1977 GLC elections: an aggregate data analysis'. *British Journal of Political Science*, 9: 370–80.

Widefeldt, A. (1992). 'The Swedish Parliamentary Election of 1991'. *Electoral Studies*, 11: 72–77.

—— (2000). 'Scandinavia: Mixed Success for the Populist Right'. *Parliamentary Affairs*. 53: 468–500.

Willetts, D. (1992). *Modern Conservatism*. London: Penguin.

Wilson, F. (1997). *The European Centre Party at the End of the Century*. London: St Martin's.

Winock, M. (1993). 'L'Action Français', in M. Winock (dir.), *Histoire de l'extrême droite en France*. Paris: Seuil, 125–56.

—— (1997). 'Populismes Français'. *Vingtième Siècle*, 56: 77–91.

Witte, R. B. J. (1991). 'De onbegrepen Verkiezingsuitslag voor extreem-rechts'. *Acta Politica*, 16: 449–70.

Wodack, R. (1990). 'The Waldheim Affair and Antisemitic Prejudice in Austrian Public Discourse'. *Patterns of Prejudice*, 24: 18–33.

Wolinetz, S. B. (1993). 'Reconstructing Dutch Social Democracy'. *West European Politics*, 16: 97–111.

Ysmal, C. (1984). 'Le RPR et l'UDF face au FN: concurrence et connivence'. *Revue Politique et Parlementaire*, 86: 6–20.

—— (1989). *Les partis politiques sous la Vème République*. Paris: Montchrestien.

—— (1991). 'Les habits nouveaux de l'extrême droite', in Sofres, *L'état de l'opinion publique 1991*. Paris: Gallimard.

—— (1992). 'La diversité des forces "anti-système"', in Habert, P., Perrineau, P., and Ysmal. C. (dir.), *Le vote éclaté*. Paris: Departement d'Etudes Politiques du Figaro et Presses de la FNSP, 187–208.

—— (2000). 'Face à l'extrême droite, la droite existe-t-elle?', in Bréchon, P., Laurent, A., and Perrineau, P. (dir.), *Les cultures politiques des français*. Paris: Presses des Sciences Po, 139–64.

Zariski, R. (1986). 'The Legitimacy of Opposition Parties in Democratic Political Systems: A New Use for an Old Concept'. *Western Political Quarterly*, 41: 29–47.

Zimmermann, E. and Saalfeld, T. (1993). 'The Three Waves of West German Right-Wing Extremism', in Merkl, P. H., and Weinberg, L. (eds.), *Encounters with the Contemporary Radical Right*. Boulder: Westview, 50–74.

Zucchinali, M. (1986). *A destra in Italia oggi*. Milano: Sugarco.

Zunino, P. G. (1985). *L'ideologia del fascismo*. Bologna: Il Mulino.

Index